INTERNATIONAL NUCLEAR PROLIFERATION

INTERNATIONAL NUCLEAR PROLIFERATION

Multilateral
Diplomacy and
Regional Aspects

Ashok Kapur

PRAEGER PUBLISHERS
Praeger Special Studies

New York   •   London   •   Sydney   •   Toronto

Library of Congress Cataloging in Publication Data

Kapur, Ashok.
    International nuclear proliferation.

    Bibliography: p.
    Includes index.

    1. Nuclear nonproliferation. 2. Under-
developed areas--Foreign relations. I. Title.
JX1974.73.K36   327'.174   78-19744
ISBN 0-03-046316-5

PRAEGER PUBLISHERS
PRAEGER SPECIAL STUDIES
383 Madison Avenue, New York, N.Y. 10017, U.S.A.

Published in the United States of America in 1979
by Praeger Publishers,
A Division of Holt, Rinehart and Winston, CBS, Inc.

9   038   987654321

PREFACE AND ACKNOWLEDGMENTS

Writing a book on an emotional subject like nuclear proliferation is not easy, and there are two ways to approach the subject.
The first, and probably the ideal, way would be to join a monastery
and to meditate about the subject before pronouncing upon it. Indeed, many scholars who speak about proliferation with religious
fervor might profit from a year of silence and quiet study.

The second way is the one I adopted because of the circumstances. A Canada Council research grant (1976-77) enabled me to
spend the summer and Christmas break of 1976 interviewing officials and experts in New York, Ottawa, and Washington, D.C. The
University of Waterloo granted me sabbatical leave (1977-78) and
that precious commodity—time—to research and travel. The
Canada Council offered a generous leave fellowship (with travel and
research support) that enabled me to travel to India, the Middle
East, Europe, and Asia. The University of Waterloo's Social
Sciences and Humanities Research Committee provided partial
support for travel to Vienna in the summer of 1978. The Strategic
and Defence Studies Centre at the Australian National University
offered travel support from Asia to Australia, utilizing funds from
the Ford Foundation arms control project. In addition I held visit-
ing appointments at the Institute of Commonwealth Studies, the
University of London (July-August 1977); the Center for International Security and Arms Control, the University of Pittsburgh
(September-October 1977); and the Strategic and Defence Studies
Centre, the Australian National University (February-April 1978).
Many thanks are due to J. I. Coffey, Peter Lyon, and R. J. O'Neill
for their encouragement and support, and to Professor Karl Kaiser
for the use of office space at his center in Bonn for two weeks in
June 1977. As much time during 1977-78 was spent in travel, it
was a great relief to have the hospitality of these institutions to
think and to write. Without their help the book would have taken
much longer to complete.

The book is based on confidential interviews in the following
Teheran research sites, in the order of my travel: New Delhi,
Teheran, Cairo, Bonn, Geneva, Berne, Vienna, London, New York,
Pittsburgh, Washington, D.C., Ottawa, Stockholm, Warsaw,
Moscow, Tokyo, Bombay, and Canberra. I was unable to visit
Pakistan because I was refused a visa. I would like to thank offi-
cials of the Polish Foreign Ministry for their hospitality during my
visit to Warsaw.

I did not have an opportunity to travel to South Africa but I was able to interview several senior South African officials. Overall, I interviewed about 200 officials including international officials. Most of the interviewees held the rank of counselor, ambassador, or senior scientific officer. There were exchanges of views with one prime minister and one senior political minister. In several instances I was able to have several interviews with the same sources. Each interview was conducted on the basis of an unstructured format to permit maximum exploration of the subject. In some cases the interviewees were invited to comment on the factual parts of select chapters and I am grateful for their cooperation. This was done with respect to chapters dealing with documentation that is still secret but has relevance for the study of multilateral post-NPT diplomacy.

A special word of thanks is due to several individuals. Arnold Kramish was a source of constant encouragement in my work. Peter Lyon read a section of the manuscript and offered useful comments. Chapter 9 was initially presented as a seminar paper at the Australian National University and I am grateful to the seminar participants for their comments. In Tokyo, Y. Kawashima, R. Imai, and several officials in the Japanese atomic energy industry offered useful insights, as did Professor Momoi of the National Defence College and J. Kishida of the Asahi Shimbun. The briefings I received in Tokyo and from several international officials in Europe and in New York (and elsewhere) were remarkably detailed; because of space limitations it is not possible to include all the available information in this book. It is regretted that I am not permitted to cite my sources and to offer the thanks that are due to these officials. I was received at the Institute for USA and Canada in Moscow and I take this opportunity to thank my several contacts in Moscow for their valuable help.

The book was drafted during the course of my travels and it is a pleasure for me to record the help I received from my secretaries. Joan Bauer and Linda Biscardo in Pittsburgh; Billie Darlrymple and the secretarial pool in Canberra; and Margot MacLeod, Lynn Karges, and Joan Boyer in Waterloo helped type different sections of the manuscript. Rienzi Crusz completed the task of index preparation, and T. J. Cheng was helpful as research assistant.

Some of my work pertaining to this study appeared in the Annals (March 1977), the World Today (August 1978), and the Bulletin of the Atomic Scientists (October 1978). I would like to thank the editors for allowing the use of these materials in revised and expanded form.

Finally, I thank my wife Deepika and my son Amit for suffering my long absences from home with much patience.

CONTENTS

LIST OF TABLES AND FIGURES

1

INTRODUCTION

Rethinking and renegotiating nonproliferation are related pillars of current arms control and disarmament negotiations. The starting point and the point of departure of the evolving exercise is the Nuclear Non-Proliferation Treaty (NPT). This treaty was negotiated in 1968, after protracted negotiations that originated with the Irish resolution in 1958.[1] The treaty came into force in 1970. (The annex to Chapter 1 lists the parties to the NPT and the states that are not parties to the treaty.)

The successful negotiation of the NPT and its acceptance by a majority of states generated optimism that the problem of nuclear proliferation (that is, the problem of further or "horizontal" proliferation rather than "vertical" proliferation by the existing nuclear weapon states) had been put to rest. The treaty was frankly viewed by all as discriminatory. This was justified, according to NPT parties, on the ground that the doctrine of national sovereignty ought to accept international constraints because of the dangers of nuclear proliferation to world order and stability. To them the willingness of many nonnuclear-weapon states (NNWS) voluntarily and contractually to renounce nuclear weapons or a nuclear explosives option signaled that a line had finally been drawn against more than five nuclear-weapon states (NWS). It signaled, as Hedley Bull noted,[2] that proliferation was not necessarily inevitable in the thinking of NPT parties.

It signaled also that a legal but discriminatory multilateral instrument was needed to secure nonproliferation. This regime was directed to a perceptual and a technological phenomenon. Because there was no technological distinction between a capacity to explode a peaceful nuclear device and the same capacity for a military device, the legal and psychological barriers were drawn against pro-

TABLE 1.1

Parties and Nonparties to NPT

98 states that are parties to NPT:		As of February 1976

Nuclear-weapon states:
  USSR
  United Kingdom
  United States

Nonnuclear-weapon states:

Afghanistan	Grenada	New Zealand
Australia	Guatemala	Nicaragua
Austria	Haiti	Nigeria
Bahamas	Holy See	Norway
Belgium	Honduras	Paraguay
Bolivia	Hungary	Peru
Botswana	Iceland	Philippines
Bulgaria	Iran	Poland
Burundi	Iraq	Republic of China[a]
Cambodia	Ireland	Republic of South Viet-Nam
Canada	Italy	Republic of Surinam[b]
Central African	Ivory Coast	Romania
Republic	Jamaica	Rwanda
Chad	Jordan	San Marino
Costa Rica	Kenya	Senegal
Cyprus	Korea, Republic of	Sierra Leone
Czechoslovakia	Laos	Somalia
Dahomey	Lebanon	Sudan
Denmark	Lesotho	Swaziland
Dominican Republic	Liberia	Sweden
Ecuador	Libyan Arab Republic	Syrian Arab Republic
El Salvador	Luxembourg	Thailand
Ethiopia	Madagascar	Togo
Fiji	Malaysia	Tonga
Finland	Maldives	Tunisia
Gabon	Mali	United Republic of
Gambia	Malta	Cameroon
German Democratic	Mauritius	Upper Volta
Republic	Mexico	Uruguay
Germany, Federal	Mongolia	Venezuela
Republic of	Morocco	Western Samoa
Ghana	Nepal	Yugoslavia
Greece	Netherlands	Zaire

States that are not parties to NPT:	As of February 1976

Nuclear-weapon states:[c]
  People's Republic of China
  France

2

Nonnuclear-weapon states:

Albania	Democratic Republic	Pakistan
Algeria	of Viet-Nam	Papua New Guinea
Argentina	Equatorial Guinea	Portugal
Bahrain	Guinea	Qatar
Bangladesh	Guinea-Bissau	São Tomé and Principe
Bhutan	Guyana	Saudi Arabia
Brazil	India	South Africa
Burma	Israel	Spain
Cape Verde	Liechtenstein	Uganda
Chile	Malawi	United Arab Emirates
Comoros	Mauritania	United Republic of
Congo	Monaco	Tanzania
Cuba	Mozambique	Zambia
Democratic People's	Niger	
Republic of Korea	Oman	

States that have signed NPT, but not yet ratified:

Barbados	Japan	Switzerland
Colombia	Kuwait	Trinidad and Tobago
Democratic Yemen	Panama[d]	Turkey
Egypt	Singapore	Yemen
Indonesia	Sri Lanka	

States outside NPT that have some, but not necessarily all, of their nuclear plants under safeguards:

Argentina	Indonesia	South Africa
Brazil	Israel	Spain
Chile	Japan	Switzerland
Colombia	Pakistan	Turkey
India	Portugal	

[a]An entry in this column does not imply the expression of any opinion whatsoever on the part of the Secretariat concerning the legal status of any country or territory or of its authorities, or concerning the delimination of its frontiers.

[b]By letter of November 29, 1975, the prime minister of the Republic of Surinam, which attained independence on November 25, 1975, informed the secretary general of the United Nations that his government "acknowledges that treaty rights and obligations of the Government of the Kingdom of the Netherlands in respect of Surinam were succeeded by the Republic of Surinam upon independence" and that it is "desired that it be presumed that each treaty has been legally succeeded to by the Republic of Surinam and that action be based upon this presumption until a decision is reached that it should be regarded as having lapsed."

[c]For purposes of the NPT, a nuclear-weapon state was defined as one that has manufactured and exploded a nuclear weapon or other nuclear explosive device prior to January 1, 1967.

[d]Panama has a comprehensive safeguards agreement with the IAEA because it has ratified the treaty setting up the Latin American nuclear free zone, which also requires such agreements.

Source: International Atomic Energy Agency, Vienna, March 1976.

liferation of nuclear weapons and nuclear explosives. The treaty prescribed against a narrow part of the nuclear problem, namely horizontal proliferation. It was not explicitly an instrument against vertical proliferation, although it asked the NWS to negotiate nuclear disarmament in good faith (Article VI). It was not necessarily against research and development that could lead to testing and development of nuclear weapons and explosives; untested possession of these was therefore permissible. It was not against possession of reprocessing plants and enrichment facilities. It permitted exports of these facilities by parties to the treaty to other parties, or by parties to the treaty to nonparties, provided the transfers were safeguarded.

The scope of safeguards was left open to negotiation. Article III of the NPT dealt with the safeguards obligations of nonnuclear weapon states party to the NPT. This article contains a major lacuna. There is no provision to safeguard nuclear technology transfers. Second, the status of heavy water (a crucial item in the Canada Deuterium-Uranium (CANDU) reactor system, and equipment to make heavy water is ambiguous in Article III. This article does not provide for control over heavy water plants. Third, the NPT left ambiguous the status of the International Atomic Energy Agency (IAEA) safeguard agreements (trilaterals) negotiated before 1968 by states who were not parties to the NPT. Lastly, the NPT did not address a set of questions about the overall and permanent utility of safeguards, given the uncertainties about the political and security motives of threshold states in the 1980s. For instance, some of the nuclear programs in India, Brazil, Israel, South Africa, South Korea, and Taiwan are under partial safeguards; some are fully safeguarded. Given the variations, how safe are the safeguards? In case of diversion of small amounts of fissionable materials, can safeguards provide warning in time for the so-called world community to act? Is it true that safeguards can at best only detect, or can they also prevent proliferation? Are there limits to the scope of safeguards, or must parties to the NPT (and nonparties who are under IAEA as distinct from NPT safeguards) accept the proposition that acceptance of the principle of safeguards means a need to constantly upgrade them (depending on technological developments) and to expand their scope; that is, safeguarding facilities, safeguarding the entire fuel cycle, requiring the supplier's prior consent for the end use of items supplied, and so on. Table 1.2 surveys the meanings and evolving scope of safeguards.

The NPT has succeeded in some ways and failed in some ways, and here lie the roots of the evolution of what is loosely called the NPT regime. The regime is an exercise in bringing technological developments, nuclear exports, strategic needs, and political compulsions all together under the rubric of an international nuclear order under complex conditions. India's peaceful test of May 1974 put the fear of proliferation back in the public's mind and on the policy agenda, thus eroding the smugness about the NPT as a barrier against further proliferation. India's test, therefore, signaled a failure of the perception that the NPT signaled the emergence of an international consensus against further proliferation.

The Indian government described its test as peaceful. The 1974 test was not the first of a series of tests because no test has taken place since 1974 even though India has the capacity to test more. India's behavior signaled an unwillingness to accept a contractual obligation as the basis of nonproliferation. But it expressed a willingness to behave, voluntarily and unilaterally, like a nonproliferator. The doctrine of accepting contractual obligations to prove its nuclear motives was rejected as a nonproliferation gesture by India. The doctrine of national sovereignty was reiterated by India's unwillingness to make unilateral concessions or to subject its future behavior to involuntary constraints. India's public positions revealed an unwillingness to commit itself in a discussion of its nuclear motives and its nuclear policies. In conversations with President Carter and Prime Minister Trudeau in 1977, the new government of Morarji Desai took a stand against nuclear proliferation, against nuclear weapons, against safeguarding of India's entire peaceful nuclear industry, against the NPT, against Indian export of sensitive nuclear technology, and against Indian participation in the Nuclear Suppliers Group. But such expressions were unilateral policy statements and not irrevocable commitments of future Indian generations.

India's behavior, despite its rejection of the NPT, reinforced the sense that proliferation was not necessarily inevitable. The NPT was clearly too rigid to cope with India's innovative behavior. India's repudiation of the NPT doctrine that nuclear explosives equaled a nuclear weapon status could not be fitted into the NPT regime. This repudiation has some theoretical and practical implications. India argues that what counts is the intention behind a nuclear test. On this basis, there is a difference between a peaceful and a military test. The problem with this argument is that it can be neither proved nor disproved. The ambiguity is troubling. For instance, the Agency for the Prohibition of Nuclear Weapons in Latin America (OPANOL) secretariat would have India sign Protocol II of the Tlatelolco Treaty of Latin America because of its nuclear weapon status.[3] But what exactly is the status of a one-time nuclear explosive power that is neither a nuclear weapon state (in terms of the NPT or in reality) nor a pure or virginal nonnuclear weapon state (in terms of the NPT provisions or in terms of reality)? How does one

TABLE 1.2

Typology of International Safeguards on Peaceful Nuclear Industry

Bilateral before IAEA	IAEA Safeguards	NPT Safeguards	Zangger Committee Discussions	New Policies Proposed
Examples of these are the India-Canada agreement of 1956, India-United States agreement of 1963, and so on.	This consists of the following: The first IAEA safeguards system is represented in INFCIRC/26, 1961. This was revised in 1964 as INFCIRC/26 and Add. 1. INFCIRC/66, date December 3, 1965; INFCIRC/66/Rev. 1 date September 12, 1967; INFCIRC/66/Rev. 2 date September 16, 1968, and GOV31621 date August 20, 1973. The last items represent the final IAEA safeguards system as of date of this writing. However, this is now considered inadequate and there is a proposal, still under consideration,[b] to apply safeguards to the granting of technical assistance also.	These safeguards were discussed in the Safeguards Committee (1970–71) and resulted in INFCIRC 153, accepted in 1971.	This was an informal group, that met to consider implementation of Article III (2) of the NPT; that is, to establish conditions for nuclear exports. It resulted in the development of the Trigger List (1974) as in INFCIRC/209.[a] Additional suppliers' guidelines were established in the London agreement in 1976.[c] The latter is commonly known as the Nuclear Suppliers Club or Group. The Zangger lists deal with the conditions of nuclear supplies; exports are permitted with appropriate safeguards. The London agreement also discusses nuclear supply conditions but there is a new orientation, namely to establish restraints in supply of sensitive nuclear material, equipment, and technology.	President Carter's April 1977 policy sought to restrain the national development of plutonium technology, particularly its export by West Europeans to Third World states and its national development by Third World states themselves. This policy has come under considerable criticism by Germany, France, and Japan but it paved the way for a two-year program to study alternative nuclear fuel cycle (the international fuel cycle evaluation program or INFCE).

^aThe Zangger list was less restrictive than the final Trigger lists, which emerged in 1976. These lists have no direct connection with the IAEA Safeguards. The IAEA cannot, strictly speaking, be guided by the Trigger lists because these lists have not been submitted to the board of governors for approval. Apparently, the nuclear suppliers involved in the Trigger lists did not feel confident in getting a majority in the IAEA and therefore chose to bypass the board on a matter of worldwide importance.

^bIn light of discussions in the Technical Assistance Committee in December 1976, the director general of the IAEA proposed to the board of governors in February 1977 that safeguards be applied in relation to the granting of technical assistance. In summary, the safeguards apply to any applications emerging from the transferred technology. It does not make the fellowship holder or the expert also safeguardable.

^cThe suppliers' guidelines go beyond the Zangger Memorandum of 1972. The public version of this Memorandum is known as INFCIRC/209, with various additions. The "209 system" was publicized in August 1974 with the publication of separate but identical letters sent by most but not all members of the Zangger Committee to the director general of the IAEA in August 1974 and thereafter. The suppliers' guidelines include the following: no nuclear explosions by a recipient; all sensitive technology is to be safeguarded for 20 years; the nuclear suppliers are to exercise restraint in export of sensitive technology; there are to be no deliveries of facilities that result in enrichment over 20 percent; the storage of fissile material is to be by mutual consent; prior consent is needed for retransfers. The relationship and the evolution in the supply regime from the Zangger Memorandum (1972) to the Trigger list (1974) and the Suppliers Agreement (1976) is discussed in Chapter 3.

Source: Compiled by the author.

conceptualize the existence of a state that has a demonstrated capacity to explode an atomic device, has an untested capacity to explode more devices, and is unwilling to accept a contractual obligation against nuclear weapons by signing the NPT or by accepting control over its entire nuclear industry? India's first test signals that the NPT is not a real barrier against proliferation. But on the other hand, India's refusal to test more, its refusal to make its first test as the first step to more tests, means that the original sense of the NPT that proliferation is not inevitable has been reiterated. As such, it might make sense to argue that India's first test and refusal over time to engage in more testing, taken together, signal restraint in behavior. After all, it is surely a sign of responsible behavior if a state can do something and demonstrates a capacity, and then proceeds not to engage in further demonstrations of the same or similar acts once the point has been made.

Yet, on the other hand, India's behavior does not signal a willingness to subordinate national sovereignty and national interests to the proof of an internationally visible and verifiable contractual obligation. All sovereignty arguments represent a legal defense of state interests. India's refusal to sign away its nuclear option, combined with its refusal to acknowledge the existence of this option, can mean one of the following: that India is masking its military intentions through peaceful claims; or that it is offering an ambiguous response to an ambiguous international situation, to guard against the possibility of isolation even though India's strategic environment presents the prospect of relative security at present. If it is the latter, the NPT is clearly unsuitable as an instrument to probe issues of political and strategic intelligence that the Indian case (and other similar but not identical cases) requires.

India's injury to the expectations about the NPT prior to 1974 and India's restraint since 1974 point to two conclusions. First, the NPT prescription that nuclear explosives equal nuclear weapons is technologically sound but politically and legally irrelevant. If a nuclear test is the great threshold that distinguishes between the proliferator and the nonproliferator, crossing the threshold implies necessarily, in the NPT logic, that the acquisition of nuclear weapons is the ultimate terminal condition of the process. Yet the preceding discussion suggests that the process after the first nuclear test can go in two diametrically opposite directions: toward nuclear weapons development; or toward continued research and development but with a continual decision against converting nuclear option into nuclear weapons, on the premise that there is mileage to be gained from the threatened conversion of the option and continual nonuse of the threat (that is, no implementation of the threat unless forced to do so by the other side). Here the strategy is to acquire the nuclear option and practice its nonuse, in contrast to the normal strategy of the NWS, which is to acquire nuclear weapons and then practice their nonuse. A common element of both strategies is that the burden of inducing restraint is on the opponent. The opponent is required to be constantly attentive to the security needs, political compulsions, and bureaucratic debates of the society practicing the nonuse of a nuclear option. The NPT is a failure because it has a conceptual mold that cannot appreciate the diplomacy of a nuclear option. Yet this may be the wave of the future in the Middle East, Latin America, South Africa, and Asia if current trends persist. That is, there is a slow trend toward normalization in interstate relations and a gradual devaluation of the prestige and influence of the superpowers. The economic and military security and self-confidence of the Third World societies accompanies the diffusion of power and influence in the world; this leads to new patterns of regional and international politics in the 1980s, if not earlier.

The second conclusion to be drawn from the Indian experience is that the source of restraint in the process of further horizontal proliferation lies in the security and political perceptions of the potential proliferator(s). The NPT can be bypassed by not signing it, as the case of a number of nonsignatories to the NPT suggests. It can be repudiated by withdrawing from it. Already some states, none of them significant as potential proliferators (for example, Yugoslavia and Rumania) have threatened to do so. Also possible is the violation of the NPT (that is, if a party to the treaty may secretly decide to prepare its option before legally withdrawing from the treaty). In other words, the contractual obligation inherent in signing the NPT is revocable but admittedly moral and other pressures exist in addition to the contractual obligation.

The essence of the NPT regime, however, is that it is a threat system against the deviant state. A state that rejects the NPT and also rejects nuclear weapons is a deviant, but the lack of flexibility in the NPT is a serious shortcoming in its utility as an instrument to discourage nonproliferation. In states where domestic perceptions and decisions are at present against nuclear weapons because of their declining military utility in the foreseeable future, the NPT exists as a convenient red flag to the bull in the bureaucratic debates. Politically necessary postures taken against the NPT are not necessarily meant to be postures toward nuclear weapons, but those postures can be viewed in such a way by the external audience of that state. Since the anti-NPT stance is usually more visible than the decisions against nuclear weapons, it is easy to minimize or underestimate the domestic sources of restraint. True, antiproliferation lobbies within a state can draw strength from the NPT. But, on the other hand, if the repudiation of the NPT enjoys wide societal support, if backtracking of the decision against the NPT is tantamount to political suicide, the constant waving of the NPT flag is a distraction rather than a contribution to the antinuclear weapon cause. As this author's study of the Indian nuclear case indicates,[4] political decisions do not necessarily follow the dictates of so-called technological determinism. A single test is not necessarily the first step toward further testing of nuclear weapons, and a single test has utility as a political signal rather than as an expression of interest in the military uses of atomic energy. In other words, there is a need to study the nuclear behavior of the potential proliferators in terms of their perceptions of and their decisions about their security and other needs. The perceptions and decisions should be the sources of evidence about national behavior.

This study deals with three different questions: What is the future of the NPT regime as it has evolved since the late 1960s? What is the future of nuclear proliferation as perceived by the potential proliferators? Finally, what is nuclear proliferation? Is the linkage between nuclear energy and nuclear proliferation such that unless societies adopt a no-growth stance, proliferation of nuclear capacities is unavoidable and the antiproliferation policy a lost cause?

The first question requires a survey of the developments, particularly since 1970, that constitute the NPT regime.* This regime consists of several components: the NPT; IAEA safeguards; IAEA/ NPT safeguards; and Zangger Group or Suppliers Group Agreement concerning conditions of supply. These components represent agreements that have been achieved. But these agreements are not thought to be comprehensive enough to meet the new concerns about nuclear proliferation. President Carter, therefore, announced on April 27, 1977 new policy guidelines urging restrictive U.S. nuclear export and incentives legislation,[5] and in response a dialogue about alternative nuclear fuel cycles was held in the London economic summit of May 1977.[6]

There is tension and polarization in European and Japanese views of the Carter initiatives. Also, an ongoing U.S. nuclear debate reveals a lack of identity among the views of the executive branch of the U.S. government, the congressional branch, and the nuclear industry. The ideological parameters and the evolving

---

*The select bibliography of this book identifies the general literature, but the evolution of post-NPT multilateral diplomacy is not systematically discussed in the literature. The literature is strong in advocacy rather than analysis.

mechanisms, and in some cases the contradictions between prescriptions and mechanisms, merit attention. Here the concern is
with a study of rethinking and renegotiation among parties to the
NPT, particularly among Western or westernized industrial or
postindustrial democracies. The issues that divide the West Europeans and Japan from the Carter perspectives are urgent, and,
given the spirit of compromise on all sides, they are negotiable.
Thus, the first task is to examine the general evolution of these issues and the underlying perceptions and decisions. The next task is
to assess the impact of the evolving debate on Third World societies.
Overall, does it indicate the emergence of a real, workable consensus on the appropriate approach and the means to carry it out?
What are the issues that divide these nations, and with what effects?
What lessons are to be learned about negotiations from a study of
the debates?

The second question, that of the future of proliferation as perceived by the potential proliferators, is rooted in three different
concerns. First, the behavior of potential proliferators in the
Third World is obviously affected, in many cases significantly, by
the United States-Europe-Japan safeguards. That situation is inescapable because societies seeking nuclear power development
have to negotiate against the ideological and political backdrop of
antiproliferation sentiment. A rather large number of such states
are worth studying: India, Pakistan, Iran, Egypt, Israel, South
Africa, Brazil, Argentina, South Korea, and Taiwan. Some of
these states accept the NPT but some do not. Both categories are
important, because among the NPT adherents are states with global
and regional ambitions, apart from those with genuine security concerns. Adherence to the NPT, therefore, is not irrevocable, as
noted earlier. The consensus among Western industrial societies
is based on the acceptance of the NPT, with its safeguards, but this
consensus does not necessarily restrict the development of sensitive
nuclear technology and alternative fuel cycles. West Europeans do
not repudiate a plutonium economy as does President Carter at
present. The international nuclear fuel cycle evaluation program
(INFCE), a study of the economics and technology of alternative nuclear fuel cycles, has drawn the major industrialized and industrializing nations into the dialogue. Carter would like to see a moratorium on further reprocessing and uranium enrichment in Europe
and an end to exports of the plants involved in these processes. The
Europeans have definitely committed themselves, because of their
urgent energy needs, to both reprocessing and uranium enrichment,
subject to satisfying environmental and safety conditions. Unless
Carter backs down, a consensus on the issue of reprocessing and
enrichment for domestic use may be hard to achieve. In addition,

the European decision not to export sensitive nuclear plants "at present" (made at the London economic summit in May 1977) may not be irrevocable. How does the consensus among the Western nuclear suppliers operate in inhibiting the development, with or without safeguards, of reprocessing and/or enrichment capacities, the former more than the latter?

A second factor is involved in how potential proliferators view proliferation. This study takes a skeptical view of the future of safeguards; that is, safeguards are not necessarily an insurance against proliferation of sensitive nuclear technology and materials. In a sense, safeguards provide a false sense of security. IAEA or NPT safeguards can provide a statistical account of diversion or loss of fissionable materials, but the real problem is to interpret the loss, assuming that the complete inventory of the safeguarded facility or nuclear industry was available before safeguards went into effect. The problem of diversion appears in one of two forms. So far, the principal focus has been against diversion of materials and equipment from peaceful to military purposes by the threshold states. The latest evidence, however, directs attention to diversion by a NWS party to the NPT to one of its allies. For instance, a CIA investigation reveals that up to 206 lbs. of enriched uranium has been diverted from a Pennsylvania plant to Israel.[7] This dimension of diversion is not stressed in the U.S. literature on arms control and proliferation, yet it is a dimension that indicates how bilateral relations dilute the actual commitment to nonproliferation without modifying the rhetoric. In a sense, therefore, safeguards are safe as long as the inspected state wishes them to be safe. At best, safeguards are just one barrier against proliferation. Safeguards implementation does not address the basic questions of the factors that push Third World states toward proliferation. If considerations of security or prestige induce a state to prepare for a nuclear option, the state's perceptions of its strategic environment, whether regional or international, will determine whether the moves made are peaceful or military. Studying the effects of regional and/or international disputes on the perceptions and decisions of nuclear policy makers is therefore important.

A third dimension of inquiry in the question of the perception of proliferation by potential proliferators is the investigation of the assumptions one makes about the conditions of stability and instability in international relations in the 1980s. Optimistic and pessimistic scenarios with supporting assumptions should be identified so that the assumptions can be assessed. At present, many North American views about European and Japanese behavior assume the continued existence of stable alliance relations, the existence of the superpower detente, domestic support in Europe and Japan for existing alliance ties, and a world order that in general follows the pattern of the 1960s and the 1970s. This study, however, wishes to explore the _new_ pattern of regional and international politics and to speculate about the prospects of gradual militarization and nucleari- zation of the international environment. The study examines the gradual diffusion of power and influence currently underway and its implications for some of the NPT parties, particularly Japan and West Germany.

The task here is to try to portray trends in optimistic and pessimistic settings without necessarily offering predictions about what is likely to happen. In the second and third dimensions of in- quiry mentioned above, the stress is on examining the perceptions of states other than the superpowers and the effects of these percep- tions on evolving negotiations. How do they view the prospects of stability and instability in international affairs? What are their de- cisions in response to their perceptions? What are the consequences of these decisions on their strategic neighbors? Studying regional interactions in the context of international developments is thus a central part of this study.

The third major question covered here—what is nuclear pro- liferation?—permeates the entire study. It is presented separately to highlight a point that is usually under-researched. The term pro- liferation has a large variety of meanings. The conventional mean- ing is that of the NPT: more nuclear explosions signal proliferation. President Carter, however, directs our attention to a new meaning: proliferation of reprocessing and enrichment plants signals prolifer- ation. Canadian experts differentiate between economical and un- economical reprocessing plants and imply that the latter signal pro- liferation prospects. India maintains that proliferation is an in- crease in the number of nuclear weapons states, rather than more peaceful nuclear explosions (PNEs). Chapter 2 identifies the differ- ent meanings of proliferation. This is done not with a view to reach- ing a consensus but to offer a perspective on how states go about negotiating something for which they do not even have an agreed definition—in other words, how states go about discussing the same problem from different perspectives.

The conventional approach in arms control and nonproliferation studies is to examine the technological capacities of potential pro- liferators and to infer intentions and decisions from the state of the nuclear program of the state concerned. An assumption of techno- logical determinism is inherent in this approach. Nuclear decision making is viewed as a phasal activity where step A is held to lead to Step B, and so on, until the bomb explodes or until an explosive capability is acquired—in tested or untested form. The problem with this approach to studying the technological ladder is that it tells us nothing about the decision process of the potential proliferator. It tells us nothing about the state's perceptions of the international, regional, and domestic environment. It says nothing about the interplay of domestic and international forces, the arguments for or against nuclear weapons, the arguments for or against civilian nuclear power, or the way other items compete in bureaucratic debates for a share of the national budget. The task of this study is to see how national perceptions of the environment shape the national decisions about nuclear power; to see if there are attitudes and policies in the thinking of states that differ from the conventional wisdom of the North American arms control literature; to see if the central scholarly and policy assumptions that permeate American thinking are shared by a bulk of humanity; to see if there are theoretical and practical alternatives to the sterility of some parts of the U.S. literature on arms control and disarmament. This study may not succeed in all its aims but it may lead to some new thinking about new and practical solutions to the problems of controlling the arms race and making interstate relations secure. Given that the superpower detente is a tenuous exercise—a view taken by the late Indian politician Krishna Menon in 1965,* and one that seems to make sense in the light of the Carter-Brezhnev controversy in 1977—negotiating arms control, disarmament, and nonproliferation cannot be separated from the central trends in contemporary world politics. Seen in this light, negotiating arms control and related political and cultural issues is very much a nontechnological rather than a technical exercise. Even the demand of some states that a particular exercise be treated as technical rather than political is itself political because it seeks to exclude the underlying political and philosophical differences that manifest themselves in decisions about nuclear technologies and nuclear commerce. For the purpose of this study, "politics" and "technology" are not separable tools of analysis; they are linked agents of change and negotiation.

Another objection to the conventional arms control literature is that it deals excessively with the Soviet-American problems, on the premise that this dyad is at the center of world politics. It is not this study's aim to detract from the importance of the Strategic Arms Limitations Talks (SALT) for superpowers' relations and for

---

*Cited in Ashok Kapur, India's Nuclear Option: Atomic Diplomacy and Decision Making (New York: Praeger, 1976), p. 51. According to the late Krishna Menon, the superpower detente "is of a limited character." This assessment was made in the mid-1960s.

contemporary world affairs. Indeed, a theme of the study is that SALT is not a strategic dialogue of interest to the superpowers only. George Quester, for instance, argues that SALT ought to be kept separate from the multilateral disarmament and nonproliferation machinery.[8] This advice carries some advantages. Insulating SALT from multilateral pressures is important so that there is no third party interference with the bilateral exercise. Here it is arguable that the exercise of SALT is complicated even in its bilateral form and that interference by a third party (or parties) will only make it even more complicated and difficult to negotiate. Also, keeping SALT bilateral establishes, in practice and through a tacit rule, that the Soviet-U.S.-PRC "triangle" in fact implies a distance between the PRC and the superpowers. This situation may be preferred by the PRC and by the superpowers for different reasons. Their military and technological policies and their ideological debates dictate such a distance because elite support for detente is an open question. Keeping SALT bilateral also insures secrecy; thus, the negotiator concerned with intelligence may wish to protect the exercise from multilateral scrutiny and pressures. Lastly, a secret SALT exercise can hide from the public view the importance of nuclear weapons and nuclear threats in the perceptions and behavior of the superpowers. Such hiding from third-party view could publicly imply that nuclear weapons and nuclear threats are devalued items in the behavior of the superpowers, even if privately the superpowers think highly of their nuclear diplomacy. In other words, it makes sense for the superpowers to convey the impression that SALT is not too central to world order problems and thereby to devalue the importance of superpowers' nuclear weapons. This stance has the added virtue of guarding against public exposure failures in reaching SALT agreements.

This study takes the view that the superpower arms control negotiations are central not only to the superpowers detente—a bilateral undertaking—but also to the slowing down of nascent arms races in regions bedeviled by regional and international conflicts. The effects of the detente and the SALT dialogue are felt directly in Western Europe and in the PRC, albeit differently. Movement in the SALT dialogue codifies the superpower relations and narrows the range of uncertainties in European international relations. It is one thing to view Eastern-Western European interactions between economic, political, and cultural spheres in the context of superpower cooperation, or to assess German and French Ostpolitik as an exercise in building political, economic, and cultural bridges between the West and the East in the context of growing interactions and interdependencies between Western Europe and North America. But it is quite another matter to view the continuation of European international relations without the supportive context of cooperative superpower relations.

In Central Asian international relations, however, the superpower detente in the West does not necessarily mean a detente in Sino-Soviet relations. The theory that peace and detente are indivisible is not necessarily true. If Peking's policies are still geared to the expectation of collusion between the superpowers (it is hard to tell whether this is still the PRC perception), evidence of movement toward U.S.-USSR detente and strategic arms agreement could imply Peking's isolation from the bilateral exercise. But on the other hand, the PRC's presence requires that the United States and the USSR keep levels of strategic arms high so that the gap between Soviet-American arms and PRC strategic arms remains intact. The role the PRC plays in the SALT exercise cannot be ignored. By taking the nuclear route, Peking has been able to raise the price for the SALT exercise, whether the superpowers admit it or not. Furthermore, in taking the nuclear route, Peking may also have gained some military security and international prestige. In other words, there is an advantage in being the third party in a two-party negotiation toward detente and arms control. There is an advantage in being present in the superpower context and yet being absent in the formal negotiating machinery. Either way, Peking wins. If the superpower detente process works, Peking's presence induces a level of strategic agreement by the superpowers that is costly to them. But, on the other hand, if the detente process begins to fail, the failure confirms Peking's analysis that contention is permanent and that it is necessary for the PRC to be ready for aggression. As long as the deterioration of the detente process does not lead to war, a no war-no peace situation is compatible with Peking's interests.

In short, superpower tension and the prospect of another cold war induces the West Europeans to strengthen their defense machinery. The extensive remarks by the French president recently[9] signal the new European concerns about President Carter's policy and its effect on the rules of the superpower game. The PRC's view that contention is permanent and collusion is temporary seems to be vindicated by the current trend in superpower relations. If contention is really permanent, if Kissinger's carefully built but delicate edifice of detente and arms control is eroded by President Carter, if the new orientation and process is toward confrontation rather than cooperation, the PRC's attentiveness to the strategic environment is likely to remain high. In this case, the failure of the SALT dialogue, or evidence of a protracted and inconclusive dialogue, introduces a fluidity to world politics. It opens up opportunities and possibilities for Moscow and Peking to take preliminary steps toward normalization of Sino-Soviet relations.

Conceptually, there are different ways to visualize how the superpower relations shape regional nuclear politics and are themselves influenced by regional nuclear politics. The literature on arms control and arms reduction* needs to cope with the emerging patterns of regional and international politics. There is no unified trend, but several contradictions and ambiguities indicate that the factors perceived by the major powers and regional states are likely to inhibit the achievement of formal arms control or arms reduction agreements. In view of the inhibitions against agreement, it is necessary to intensify the dialogue, to increase its scope by bringing in more countries, which will inject more diversity into the discussions. A demand to broaden the dialogue is the basis of ongoing discussions in the Nuclear Suppliers Group, in the Zangger Committee, and particularly in the program INFCE established after the London economic summit of seven Western leaders, including the United States, in May 1977. (This exercise is also inherent in President Carter's April 1977 policy statement but the evolution of the INFCE and Carter's thinking may not necessarily coincide in the next two years, during which time INFCE is expected to reach a conclusion.)

There are a number of ways in which superpower relations influence regional politics. These in turn affect nuclear proliferation and disarmament prospects. Conversely, there are a number of ways in which regional trends shape superpower relations and international developments in the nuclear and disarmament fields. Subsequent chapters examine these in detail. Here it is sufficient to provide an overview of the principal relations to be considered.

One important factor to examine is a superpower arms control agreement. The effects of such an agreement would vary depending, for example, on whether the agreement only regulates competition by superpowers, whether it codifies the rules of the game of continued conflict (that is, competition but no confrontation in world politics and regional politics), whether it does not involve arms

---

*This remark is meant to apply particularly to the work of Albert Wohlstetter and Theodore Taylor (outside the U.S. government) and Victor Gilinsky of the Nuclear Regulatory Commission (among others), U.S. Senators like Ribicoff, Percy, and Glenn, Congressman Zablocki, and former Congressional staffers like Paul Leventhal. These experts tend to think of antiproliferation in religious terms and fail to examine the nuclear factor in the context of specific domestic and international inducements and restraints for and against proliferation.

reduction, whether it strengthens the sense of bilateral exclusivity of the superpower relationship and thereby ratifies the notion of superpower preeminence, whether it lessens the chances of a nuclear war by design or by accident, and whether the thrust of an arms control agreement is to strengthen the barriers against outbreak of nuclear war (as distinct from nuclear threat making) or to limit the consequences of a nuclear war if one were to break out. Thus, depending on the terms of the agreement, there are a number of possible effects in regional international relations in different parts of the world.

Continued superpowers arms control (defined as the capping of the arms race through limitations on future quantitative and qualitative additions and improvements in deployed forces) can provide for gradual incremental change—or at least a continued dialogue toward change—in the structure of Western vis-à-vis East European military forces. Here the linkage between SALT and Mutual Balance force reduction (MBFR) is salient.[10]

But for the world community at large—in Asia, Latin America, Africa, and the Middle East—arms control and arms limitations are not the same things as arms reduction. Arms reduction is seen as something more than zero level arms but something significantly less than the existing high level of arms, which exceeds the minimum needed to act as a deterrent and protect national security. The advocacy of arms reduction is not an advocacy of zero level of arms (that is, of total disarmament), although zero level arms could be viewed as the aspiration of a few utopian dreamers. For the purpose of this study, therefore, disarmament involves arms reductions as the goal to work toward and arms limitation (that is, freezing existing levels of arms) as the medium to work through. There is a universal consensus that the process of achieving arms reduction should be balanced and should protect the security of all states concerned, or at least there is consensus that existing security should remain undiminished. A plea for arms reduction, therefore, is not a repudiation of military security or national security. It is a plea against unnecessary arms races as the basis of national security. It is a plea against greater reliance on military arms for security achievement and, conversely, a plea for gradual introduction of a lesser reliance on (or lower level of) arms for security. The Third World plea for arms reduction is therefore based on the perception that the existing nuclear weapon states have more arms than they need; that the trend is toward a quantitative and qualitative escalation of the arms race; that the trend ought to be reversed as an example to the rest of the world; that partial measures, expressed unilaterally or through bilateral or multilateral agreement (such as no first use of nuclear weapons in regions that have renounced nuclear weapons, NWS adherence to nuclear-weapons-free zones adopted through initiative of states within a region, such as Latin America, and so on) ought to be adopted by the NWS with a view to promoting the climate of arms reduction; that the NWS ought to devote more political will to negotiating vertical proliferation control and ought not to let their strategy against horizontal proliferation become one-sided; and generally, that the NWS, and particularly the nuclear superpowers, ought to demonstrate their real commitment, as distinct from talk, to move from arms control to arms limitation to arms reduction.

Generally speaking, Third World perspectives as expressed by India, Brazil, Argentina, Mexico, Egypt, and others involve the view that the public disarmament postures of the nuclear superpowers are two-faced and not to be trusted. The superpowers are unwilling to sacrifice any of their real interests, even limited ones. For example, they are unwilling to renounce their right to use nuclear weapons in areas of tension of the world, or to accept the notion of no first use of nuclear weapons. Such gestures are not offered by the superpowers because even though these are verbal and, hence, revocable, still they may be viewed as an erosion of their alliance commitments. Yet, on the other hand, other nations are urged by the superpowers to disarm or give up their options.

This study examines if and how, on a selective basis and given the pros and the cons, the goals of arms reduction and security of the parties concerned can be furthered by an implementation of various proposals. In examining the barriers to and the possibilities of implementing such proposals, it is worth recalling that any arms reduction or arms control proposal is merely the means to an end; namely, to further or to achieve <u>national security</u>. The study assumes that no state is going to accept an agreement if in its opinion there is a reasonable possibility that the agreement may affect its present or future national security. Third World perspectives, as Hedley Bull notes,[11] see superpower talk about "international security" as a cover in some ways for advancing their "national security." That is, international security talk is national security-centered and self-centered. It does not take into account the national security (and equally self-centered) interests of other participants in the arms control or arms limitation or arms reduction exercise. This study's task is to examine the negotiating process, that is, the capacity of states to negotiate in terms of the national security interests of the states concerned rather than in terms of the ambiguous notion of international security. Do Third World states perceive that there is an element of other-directedness in the behavior of the NWS that constitutes a basis for agreement or for consensus building? Does the style of presenting proposals (for example, how much consultation occurred before a proposal was sprung on an unsuspecting audience?) and the content of the proposal generate the sense that negotiations are moving forward? Are the nuclear weapon states, and particularly the nuclear superpowers,* aware that their legislative style and their style of thinking has an effect other than the one desired? How hard is it for the superpowers to backtrack once public positions have been taken? Generally, is there a case for more private diplomacy among a large group of states (for example, the INFCE dialogue, rather than the smaller suppliers' group meetings or the activities of the uranium cartel) supplemented by public announcements of consensus and/or significant areas of disagreement?

The foregoing discussion conveys optimism. It indicates that there is disappointment in the Third World about the progress by the NWS and particularly the nuclear superpowers toward arms reduction. There is, however, a hope or an expectation that the dialogue is not dead, but is still going on. This sentiment is accompanied by continuing and partly successful pressures from Third World countries and their disarmament allies in Europe to get the NWS to reconsider the disarmament prospects. The sentiment is based on the premise that a slowing down of the arms race between the superpowers could induce the governments of Third World nations also to reduce their enthusiasm for conventional and nuclear arms (or nuclear option) proliferation. Having said this, there is still a need to examine pessimistic scenarios and pessimistic outcomes.

The optimistic view is based on the idea that states actually go about successfully negotiating outcomes;[12] that is, an attempt is made to identify the outcomes that are desired and the means states adopt toward these ends. This approach assumes that states prefer agreement through negotiations. However, it is useful to alter this perspective considerably. The perspective of "negotiating desired outcomes" suggests that the principal audience for the foreign policy and military bureaucracy is the external one. It presupposes that a nation considers primarily external factors; one negotiates in terms

---

*The United States appears more willing than does the USSR to engage in an intellectual debate on nonproliferation and disarmament matters. Moscow's negotiating style is to stress the element of Soviet superpower status. In spite of this difference, the U.S. and Soviet styles have the same practical effect. Both superpowers in effect stonewall Third World interests and initiatives in the field of disarmament and nonproliferation.

of what the others are saying and doing—that is, one responds to outsiders; and given a will to negotiate, one seeks to bridge the differences between parties.

The pessimistic scenario, on the other hand, is more complicated than the foregoing, optimistic scenario. It does not reject the notion that there is an external audience. But instead of viewing "outcome" as a product of two (or more) outward-looking bureaucracies, one can feasibly and probably more realistically view the external "negotiating" setting as an internationally visible medium to maintain or redistribute the location of decision-making authority (with supporting budgetary measures) within the domestic bureaucracy. In this case, the domestic audience is the principal target of the external negotiations. A central purpose of bureaucratic behavior is to block the prospects of irrevocable change that might eliminate the usefulness of a particular bureaucratic organization. "Staying on the ground floor," whether or not one is thus able to negotiate international outcomes, is therefore an end in and of itself, although to some it may be a means to the end. Therefore, negotiating postures need to be examined in the context of bureaucratic interests as these differ from what are loosely described as national interests.

The implications of this phenomenon are startling. In Western democracies the news media are critical and innovative; leaks are a part of the political process. National security debates are truly public debates. A public debate is justifiable because it helps educate the public and keep it informed. It enables the public to participate in the policy making and, at times, policy-reversal processes. But at the same time a public debate helps identify and solidify the bureaucratic constituency and its societal allies in government, in private industry, among intellectuals and other opinion makers, and in the public at large at election time and through public opinion polls. A side effect of publicizing a national security debate is that once positions are taken by different players, to retain credibility it is often necessary to reiterate, indeed to reinforce, the positions. Thus compromise is made more difficult over a prolonged period of time. An old saying tells us that time is a great healer. One needs to explore whether this is necessarily so in highly complex emotive situations where positions are technical and political; where positions have been taken and repeated and vested interests have emerged among bureaucracies; where consensus making is supposedly an ongoing process rather than a terminal condition, but backtracking is difficult unless bureaucratic players are silenced, exiled, or replaced with new players with different interests. If a bureaucracy is politically conscious of what its head people have done, replacement of individuals does not necessarily guarantee the silencing of a particular viewpoint. The greater the opportunity to publicize competing bureaucratic view-points, the greater then is the opportunity to fight and shape intra-elite debates rather than to negotiate desired outcomes vis-à-vis external actors.

Furthermore, publication of diverse ideological and technical parameters of a debate usually slows the consensus-building pro-cess. This aspect cannot be ignored because consensus building is a valuable underpinning of democratic organizations. Alternatives have to be debated rather than merely decided by majority votes. Consensus building involves intrabureaucratic (interagency or inter-ministry) coordination in addition to coordination between legisla-tive and executive branches of government and finally between gov-ernment and public opinion.

The task of this study is to examine both perspectives—that is, how states go about negotiating desired outcomes, and how bureaucratic behavior in ideologically fragmented societies pre-cludes successful intergovernmental negotiations. On balance, the bias of the study (at the moment of writing this introduction) is toward the latter proposition. The absence of any significant post-1945 arms reduction agreement, conceivably because there is really no disarmament constituency in the world or among select influen-tial societies, demonstrates the point. The Soviet-U.S. bureau-cracies conceivably have arms control constituencies but it is un-clear if the commitment of these constituencies is to arms control (narrowly defined as war prevention or damage limitation if war occurs) or to broader and more provocative aims—namely, promot-ing détente to secure technological and commercial gains for the USSR; seeking liberalization of Soviet society—a gain for the United States; exacerbating the Sino-Soviet conflict; and so on.[13]

Overall, then, public posturing is a potential and a major barrier to multilateral and international negotiations.* It is true, for instance, that the international debate on nonproliferation dur-ing the mid-1960s led to the public emergence of an Indian nuclear option, whereas none had existed publicly before that time.[14] Simi-larly, the continued nonproliferation debate since 1970 (internation-ally and regionally), the continued disarmament debate, and the failure of the nuclear weapon states to disarm accounts for the edu-cation and emergence of bureaucratic and other intellectual con-stituencies within Third World societies. Among select Third World

---

*This is an argument against posturing, not against an open-minded public debate.

societies there has always been, since the 1950s, an attentive community in favor of disarmament. Today, however, the world has witnessed the emergence of bureaucratic communities dealing with civil uses of nuclear energy, potential military uses of nuclear energy, arms control implications of nuclear energy, international organizations and nuclear energy, environmental aspects of nuclear energy, safety aspects of nuclear energy, foreign policy and nuclear energy (that is, minimizing the danger of the pre-eminence of nuclear superpowers), and so on. The point is that the debates are becoming public, bureaucratic constituencies are emerging and growing strong, and Western-trained intellectuals are entering the policy ladders. An ironic but important side effect of training Third World students in the West, particularly in the United States and Canada, is that they are carriers of U.S. bureaucratic infighting techniques into the Third World. Consequently, the more prolonged the international debate, the greater the opportunity for bureaucratic debates in the Third World to flourish and to impinge on the policy consciousness in the developed societies. In other words, the ideological parameters are getting broadened across East-West (U.S./Soviet; U.S./West European) and North-South (U.S./Brazil; Canada/India; Australia/Japan) lines. These ideological differences are not manifested as abstract philosophical discussions. They are involved in the real world of negotiating nuclear supply agreements, where commercial, legal, and political considerations are linked and other nonnuclear issues can get linked. The picture is further complicated because the nuclear industry of many nuclear suppliers is essentially a national industry. There are no multinational nuclear corporations. A loss of reactor sales, for instance, cannot be compensated for by selling soap. Since the nuclear industry is truly national, the pressure for nuclear exports in the context of slow or lessening domestic demands means that either the national nuclear industry will starve for orders or the pressures for nuclear exports will complicate the nonproliferation agenda. The linkage then is not only between nuclear energy and proliferation. It is also between nuclear exports and proliferation. These linkages account for proliferation of nuclear option making or nuclear weapon capacities in the 1980s by a number of states such as India, Iran, Brazil, Taiwan, Pakistan, South Korea, and South Africa. (This list is not in any order of prediction as to when these states are likely to acquire a nuclear option.)

This study goes beyond these linkages to examine the perceptions of the potential proliferators, that is, states that are seen as proliferators by others and that may or may not view themselves as proliferators, now or in the foreseeable future. In this perspective, it is essential to cast the study of the bureaucratic and political

behavior of these potential proliferators in terms of their strategic
environment as they themselves perceive it; to identify the certain-
ties and uncertainties in the perceptions; to see if these states see
a linkage between a sense of relative security and nonproliferation
of nuclear weapons; to see if, in their perceptions, there is a mixture of a sense of security (to be discussed in subsequent chapters)
that at present warrants an assurance that nuclear weapons are not
needed and could in fact be counterproductive, and a concern about
possible contingencies in the 1980s if the pattern of world politics
changes as a consequence of shifts in Soviet-U.S. and Sino-Soviet
relations. In the latter case, changes in the world political situation
(the pattern of alignment) account for gradual militarization and
nuclearization of the global environment.

In the following pages, a number of optimistic and pessimistic
scenarios are sketched, not with a view to making predictions, but
with a view to exploring the underlying assumptions. The central
lesson to be drawn is that unless the superpowers establish by example that nuclear weapons are useless, or that they are becoming
less useful—explaining how it is one or the other—the potential proliferators cannot be expected to behave differently from how they now
do. This, of course, is not to suggest that Third World societies
will merely copy the NWS. They clearly will not. Each society
under consideration has its unique set of circumstances favoring or
inhibiting nuclear proliferation. The perceptions and bureaucratic
power plays vary from case to case, and one needs to guard against
excessive generalization. If the gap between India's test in 1974
and the PRC's in 1964 is meaningful, it suggests that proliferation already is slowing. The key variable to account for the slow movement toward proliferation is the sense of perceived security—as
seen by the potential proliferator rather than by an outsider. In this
respect, these states have not jumped into nuclear weapons by exploding devices on a crash basis even when they had a capacity to do
so. An unwillingness to rush into nuclear weapons is a sign of their
maturity and caution in decision making. In this respect, they have
chosen not to copy the existing proliferators. In addition to an emphasis on the perceived sense of security, conventional arms acquisition and economic development has contributed to a slowing of the
proliferation process in the Third World. However, as demands for
conventional arms and economic development are met, as atomic
energy constituencies emerge, and as evidence of persisting interest by the NWS in keeping their nuclear pre-eminence continues to
mount, the inhibitions against acquisition of explosives capabilities
are bound to lessen. In other words, the process is toward slow
and controlled proliferation of nuclear options in the 1980s without
a necessary commitment to expensive and militarily useless nuclear
weapons.

Generally speaking, an innovative element in the behavior of Third World countries is that they may, or are likely to, choose not to extend evidence of an explosives capacity, in tested or untested form, into weapons development and deployment. The Indian example is instructive in this regard. In some cases, the Israeli example may also be instructive if the society at issue has the reputation of proven technological prowess in the other areas of sophisticated arms. Therefore, one should look for significant differences in the pattern of decision making, when compared to the pattern for the NWS about nuclear power by Third World societies that are likely to emerge as the nuclear powers of the future. This observation assumes a steady, but not radical, deterioration of the international environment; namely, if the superpowers are unable to chart a steady course in international affairs, if they fail to build a record of successful negotiating behavior with lesser states, and if their threats continue to exceed their promises. How the superpowers cope with the decline of their power and influence in world politics in the coming decade, and whether their adversaries feel it necessary to inject the nuclear factor into their diplomacy and military planning to guard their interests—these are likely to be the two important elements in the forthcoming bureaucratic debates in the Third World and in select Western societies outside North America.

This is a study about perceptions and misperceptions. These concepts need explaining. Perceptions may be defined as one's view of the other side's expected behavior and its expected consequences. Included in the definition is one's self-image—what one is, what one wants, what one can do, and what the likely effects of one's actions are. Perceptions can also be simply defined as views held by the states concerned and the effects of these views on their behavior. A study of views is no different from a study of perceptions; there is no need for jargon.

One factor, however, justifies the use of the concept of perception. A study of perception places in sharp focus the problem of misperception and calls for an analysis of the difference between misperceptions and reality. An investigation of the gap between misperception and reality carries the implication that if misperceptions are subjected to an educational and re-educational exercise, these misperceptions can be corrected.

In this study, "perceptions" and "misperceptions" are applied in a particular sense. A central point of this study is that the nonproliferation debate in several Western societies, particularly the United States, Canada, Japan, Sweden, the United Kingdom, and Australia is based on the misperception that

the only thing standing between the millions of pounds of plutonium, to be produced by the world's reactors,

> and the hundreds of thousands of atomic bombs that
> can be produced from the plutonium, will be the
> adequacy of safeguards and other international agree-
> ments to insure the peaceful use of this material.[15]

This perception (misperception) is widely held in the United States
at the public level. Given this definition of the problem (which ignores the self-restraint in the security and foreign policy decision
making of many Third World states), the logical policy implication
is that one ought to strengthen safeguards and international inspection. This view becomes tied to the other perception (misperception), as expressed by Glenn Seaborg, the chairman of the U.S.
Atomic Energy Commission, that the NPT represents a

> major step forward in our common effort to end
> the peril of nuclear war and to further advance inter-
> national cooperation in the peaceful uses of nuclear
> energy.[16]

Finally, there is the perception that

> the atomic energy developments in these nations
> which can be made subject to control today are those
> dependent on material or equipment transferred be-
> tween nations or groups of nations or those develop-
> ments which individual nations may voluntarily sub-
> mit to such control.[17]

In the last instance, the perception that safeguards constitute a control mechanism is strong. There is the implication that a supply
relationship is meant to create dependency, which can sustain the
control of the relationship.

It is debatable whether each perception corresponds to reality
as other experts view it. If it does not, its use may result in faulty
problem definition and thereby lead to faulty policy prescriptions or
recommendations. To provide a corrective, alternative viewpoint,
so that the nuclear nonproliferation debate is not one-sided, this
study examines the perceptual aspect at three different levels.

First, the NPT and international safeguards are not the only
barrier to nuclear proliferation. A number of important potential
proliferators are outside the NPT and yet they have not moved toward nuclear weapon production and deployment. Even though India
tested a nuclear device in May 1974 and thus demonstrated its capacity to make crude nuclear weapons, the decision of the Indira Gandhi
government, as confirmed and publicly reiterated by Prime Minister

Morarji Desai, indicates that there is no decision to move toward nuclear weapons. Adherence to the NPT signals the existence of a contractual obligation, but the absence of a contractual obligation does not imply proliferation. In the same way, the presence of a contractual obligation does not necessarily signal the existence of a barrier against proliferation. In regard to the latter point, it is pertinent to mention that the NPT can be renounced and so can the safeguards, whether these are safeguards signed in compliance with the NPT provisions or safeguards signed with the IAEA outside the NPT regime. Admittedly, IAEA safeguards cover the life cycle of the nuclear items supplied. Nevertheless, if a state deems that international inspection is a matter of national peril, or if the NPT is renounced because of national security (as is permitted under Article X of the treaty), a legalistic view of the importance of safeguards is not a credible view of international life. The acceptance of IAEA or NPT safeguards represents a contractual commitment that is revocable if national security conditions so require. Without casting doubt on the safeguards obligations at present of Iran, Pakistan, Brazil, South Korea, and Taiwan, it is conceivable that these governments may be forced to repudiate their safeguards obligations in the 1980s. Furthermore, certain agreements—for example, the Canada-India agreement regarding RAPP I—terminate after a given period of time unless they are extended or renegotiated. Here a state does not even have to withdraw with as much fanfare as the withdrawal clause of the NPT entails.

If this line of inquiry has merit, a belief in safeguards as a control mechanism—as the barrier to proliferation—is a false and misleading one, which raises public expectations unnecessarily. This is one area of misperception where bureaucratic and public re-education in certain Western societies is needed.

Second, it is a mistake to regard the NPT as a major step forward in slowing, controlling, or stopping proliferation. It is readily conceded by experts that the NPT failed to stop proliferation; witness India's 1974 test. Now expectations about the NPT are that it slows proliferation. The shift in expectations from stopping to slowing proliferation is a significant index of erosion in the confidence about the NPT. Currently, roughly 20 percent of the world's nuclear industry is safeguarded; this may increase to 80 percent in due course. One needs to balance the security provided by the safeguarded nuclear industry against the prospect of revocability of existing safeguards agreements if the strategic environment of certain NPT parties deteriorates in the 1980s. One should also stress the extra-NPT activities of states not party to the NPT (particularly of South Africa, Israel, and India), as well as the extra-NPT activities of states party to the NPT, to assess the viability of the NPT regime.

These extra-NPT activities are not illegal under the NPT or under international law. Consequently, no legal rules are being broken. Still, the spirit of the NPT is being violated. These activities are barometers of the pressures, which are growing in volume and scope, against the existing NPT regime. Loss of fissionable material in shipment within the United States and on the high seas; diversions of U.S. uranium to Israel; commercial sales that transfer sensitive nuclear technology, equipment, and materials to potential proliferators; denials of nuclear supplies to NPT parties, which foster resentment against the nuclear suppliers for not keeping their side of the bargain; linkage in bargaining of nuclear supplies and nonnuclear items of interest to the nuclear suppliers, where the buyers of nuclear supplies exercise a veto—these are examples of areas in contemporary international relations where new tensions are gradually taking shape and impinging on the NPT regime. It is a tautology, as advocates of the NPT frequently maintain, that all those who adhere to the NPT abide by it and that therefore the NPT is a success. Of course, those who adhere to the NPT abide by it. But does this lead to a conclusion about its success? The question really is whether the NPT regime is globally effective in controlling the threats of nuclear proliferation.

There is another way to study the effect of the NPT. The public debates the NPT generated in several potential proliferation or threshold countries have done disservice to the nonproliferation cause because the debates led to the development of public consciousness and a commitment against a discriminatory treaty. Philosophical objections were blended and reinforced by political and security concerns. An actually discriminatory international document (NPT) led to the stiffening of the public attitude in many Third World countries against the nuclear weapon states and in favor of activities to strengthen the nuclear option. The point is that hitherto most of these options existed in secret bureaucratic debates but after the public NPT debate these options also became public. The objection to the nuclear option and indeed to nuclear weapons was diluted by resentment against a discriminatory treaty. Hence, there is a larger question of style involved. Might the cause of nonproliferation have been served better through quiet diplomacy than through noisy public diplomacy, which enabled the bureaucratic in-fighting to acquire the support of public opinion against renunciation of the nuclear option and against giving nuclear pre-eminence to the NWS? In other words, did the NPT generate a public mood in many Third World societies that stiffened the opposition to the antihorizontal proliferation game? Is the mood still present even though the issues vary? For instance, when an influential German analyst casts doubt on the wisdom of Canadian insistence on prior consent to the use of uranium supplied by Canada to the Federal Republic of Germany, even though the latter has signed the NPT and placed all its nuclear facilities under international inspection, the German resentment against a nuclear supplier's behavior can easily gain sympathy from the Indian resentment in a similar situation vis-à-vis the United States and Canada. The two situations are not entirely comparable but there are similarities. West Germany is a NPT party, whereas India is not. However, the point needs to be made that actually discriminatory behavior, or even behavior that has the appearance of blackmail or denial of what one state thinks is its due, if it becomes a matter of public knowledge and public debate, is likely to strengthen the public commitment and the bureaucratic sentiment against subjecting national decision making and the national industry to external bilateral or international controls. If this line of inquiry has merit the implication is as follows. The damage done by the NPT negotiations during the 1960s cannot be undone. But for the future politicians need to restrain their enthusiasm for antiproliferation public speech making. They need to consult their allies before taking to the public forum to goad them into acting.

There is another sense in which the NPT has done a disservice to the nonproliferation cause. The treaty is a cut and dried document. It permits no ambiguity, no subtlety, and no flexibility in its application. A nuclear explosive test is a nuclear weapons test, says the NPT, and a single nuclear test is the signal, according to the treaty, that proliferation is underway. Intentions do not count and unilateral policy statements about peaceful intent do not count. A purely scientific nuclear test is not permitted. By investing a single test with political and military significance the treaty invests it with international importance. Each test after January 1, 1967 by a new nuclear power is supposed to have the same importance— that is, it is a step forward toward nuclear weapons development and deployment. What happens after the first test by a new nuclear state does not matter. Virginity has been lost and the state is henceforth presumed to be galloping toward proliferation. The NPT is insensitive to the distinction between intent and effect; the former does not count because the effect is the same; one test is the sign of horizontal proliferation. Ironically, a single test gives a new nuclear power the international visibility of joining the club, whether or not the state in question wants to join it. Presumably, the logic of the NPT was that by codifying the notion that a peaceful test was a military test, a state contemplating nuclear testing would be deterred for fear of incurring the wrath of the world community and for fear of becoming an international outlaw. Yet, if the challenge is met and the bluff is called, the NPT has no means to ignore the test or to minimize it. If the new nuclear power escapes being dubbed an international outlaw—indeed, if it succeeds in gaining some prestige and improves its bargaining capacity—the NPT offers no choice except to upgrade a one-shot scientific experiment and a one-shot political act into an act of considerable international significance. While the need is for downgrading the importance of military nuclear power, the NPT does the exact opposite. It can be argued that, instead of being seen as a step forward, the NPT ought to be seen as a step backward. The NPT rules of the game are apparently nonnegotiable and, hence, cannot be brought in line with reality.

Third, in some policy perceptions external controls by the IAEA and/or the nuclear suppliers are viewed as the primary controls over horizontal proliferation. This perspective misses the quality of self-restraint in the behavior of the Third World societies, several of whom have the capacity to go nuclear but do not perceive the need to do so. It is worth debating, therefore, that Western policy makers and scholars not only overestimate the dangers of imminent proliferation, but also underestimate the sources of restraint within the threshold countries in the Third World. Overstressing the role of external controls can have the opposite effect of what is desired; instead of fostering nonproliferation, such an action can easily foster resentment against the discriminatory antiproliferation strategy. The point can be made that, while Western societies concerned about threshold states' proliferating tendencies misperceive the situation because of their ignorance of the decision making and perceptions of the objects of their analysis, the Third World societies do not feel compelled to move toward proliferation because of their accurate perception that proliferation at present is unnecessary and may work against nation building and national security. In other words, there is misperception in Western thinking of the nature of the problem and of the proposed solutions. This study takes the view that slow and controlled proliferation occurs because of the perceptions and decisions that are internal to a society; that is, proliferation occurs despite the existence of restrictive supply relations, despite the prohibitions of the NPT, and so on. Indeed, it is even arguable that discriminatory supply relations increase the incentives toward proliferation; that is, proliferation can occur because of discriminatory policies and rules of the game. In other words, it is necessary in the current debate to shift the focus of attention. Instead of treating the suppliers' conduct as the key variable in the future of the NPT regime, it is necessary to view the quality of self-restraint and methods to increase the incentives toward greater restraint in Third World decision making as a new dimension in the study and practices leading toward nonproliferation.

In summary, there is a need to reassess the parameters outlined so far in U.S. thinking about proliferation. In the 1960s,

proliferation was viewed as a finite terminal condition where proliferation from the fifth to the sixth weapon state would, or could,
produce a chain reaction to the sixteenth weapon state. In the 1970s,
the speculation is that as a consequence of proliferation of nuclear
weapons a war is probable by the end of this century. Whether or
not such speculation is sound, one needs to think of proliferation as
an infinite process that is a highly complex mix of technological,
political, economic, military, and cultural factors and is subject
to domestic and external influences. This study argues that the
real danger of proliferation lies not so much in the growth of nuclear arms and nuclear wars initiated by irresponsible states as in
hysteria caused by unfamiliarity with the decision apparatus and decision psychology of states who possess nuclear options and nuclear
arms. Avoiding this danger requires empirical analyses of the decision patterns of these societies; of the influence of intraregional
and international conflict on nuclear decision making; and of the
effect of domestic politics and intra-elite competition on the foreign
policy and security decision making. The linkages are not merely
regional and the regional dimension should not be overstated.

The study sets out two perspectives about proliferation. The
first expresses the conventional wisdom and asserts that nuclear
capabilities have proliferated throughout the world; more and more
countries can make the bomb; world order and stability are threatened and nuclear war is likely. With this as the starting point the
prescription is that the flow of sensitive nuclear materials ought to
be slowed if not stopped. Regrettably, these prescriptions are not
based on country and regional case studies where the perceptions
and decisions that inhibit (or foster) proliferation can be identified.
In this connection this book is a plea for more empirical work to
assess the nuclear factor in the larger political, strategic, and economic context of the country in question. The book does not expect
to offer a comprehensive analysis but it hopes to point to lines of
new inquiry.

The other perspective will have to be faced now or soon. The
consensus against proliferation—if it is defined as proliferation of
nuclear capabilities and ambiguous nuclear options rather than
weapons decisions—is not clear-cut on a global basis. The NPT is
a fragile document. While new multilateral mechanisms have
emerged to cover the deficiencies of the NPT, these mechanisms
also are deficient and no promising method of managing proliferation is in sight. The problem is structural. Unless there is a
global consensus against weapons and options proliferation, the best
that one can say about nuclear weapons is that they seem now to be
less militarily useful but are useful because they can freeze conflicts. If this is the real message about possessing nuclear weapons,

there seems to be a theoretical consensus toward proliferation of nuclear options at least.

The PRC is the only country so far that says <u>publicly</u> that proliferation is good because it breaks superpower monopoly. Too much should not be made of their theoretical position because practically the PRC is a nonproliferator and it is now beginning to show some interest in disarmament matters. But the PRC position generates a momentum because there are many decision makers and opinion makers in the Third World and in North America, inside and outside government, who argue privately that proliferation may be good because the NPT was really a cultural document and possession of nuclear options and weapons alters the negotiating setting. Option building at present precludes investment in costly nuclear weapons and is good if it is a slow, controlled, and conscious activity; and if the element of surprise is taken out of the activity and the way to option building is paved by proper diplomatic preparations.

The cultural dimension reveals a need to work toward a global consensus with an open mind. The International Nuclear Fuel Cycle Evaluation (INFCE) is meant on a two-year (1977-79) basis to establish a dialogue among nuclear nations. But the problem is deeper than can be handled at the level of technical INFCE meetings. There is no real consensus in the United States today about proliferation. Carter's election rhetoric and antiproliferation "diplomacy" was a product of a doctrinaire view in the U.S. Congress. Such views were fostered by Senators A. Ribicoff, J. Glenn, and C. Percy and Congressman C. Zablocki and supported by influential scholars like Albert Wohlstetter, Victor Gilinsky, Jessica Tuchmann, and Theodore Taylor. The doctrinaire views have not resolved the controversy within the United States, between the United States and its allies, and between the United States and nuclear recipients in the Third World. Instead, there is confusion in U.S. public thinking because of the overemphasis on nuclear terrorism; this frightens the public but does not necessarily educate people to assess alternatives calmly. President Carter claims that INFCE is meant to be an educational exercise, but if the opinions of Senators Ribicoff, Percy, and Glenn are going to be difficult to change, how meaningful is a dialogue at INFCE that does not engage the U.S. Congress?

Some people argue that with the conclusion of the work of the Zangger Group, the London Nuclear Suppliers Group, and eventually the INFCE, the antiproliferation argument has been won through multilateral diplomacy where suppliers agree to work in concert. This is a short-sighted view. Because of the fragmentation in the U.S. decision structure on proliferation matters (and other issues), U.S. diplomacy is at the crossroads. It needs to reassess whether

antiproliferation advocacy should begin with the NPT and conclude—
in nuclear supply matters—with priority given to bilateral relations;
or if the advocacy is to begin and end with the NPT, full-scope safeguards, and antiplutonium stance. As such the multilateral diplomatic achievement at best means that the argument is half-won.
But on the other hand the argument is also half-lost, and time is
not necessarily on the side of the antiproliferators.

NOTES

1. A Short History of Non-Proliferation (Vienna: International Atomic Energy Agency, February 1976).
2. Hedley Bull, "Re-thinking Non-Proliferation," International Affairs 5, no. 2 (April 1975): 175-89.
3. Report on the Implementation of the Treaty of Tlatelolco
and Some Comments and Views of OPANAL with Respect to Article
VII and Other Related Provisions of the Non-Proliferation Treaty,
Review Conference of the Parties to the Treaty on the Non-Proliferation of Nuclear Weapons, NPT/CONF/9, February 24, 1975,
Geneva, pp. 5, 29-31.
4. Ashok Kapur, India's Nuclear Option: Atomic Diplomacy
and Decision-Making (New York: Praeger, 1976).
5. President's Message to the Congress Transmitting the
Proposed Nuclear Non-Proliferation Act of 1977, April 27, 1977,
in Presidential Documents: Jimmy Carter 13, no. 18 (1977): 611;
and accompanying fact sheet on the proposed bill, ibid.: 611-13.
6. London Economic Summit Communique, May 7, 1977.
7. "Missing US Uranium Sent to Israel," The Guardian,
August 20, 1977.
8. "Reducing the Incentives to Proliferation," Annals 430
(March 1977): 74.
9. International Herald Tribune, Paris, July 18, 1977.
10. For useful background, see J. I. Coffey, Arms Control
and European Security (New York: Praeger, 1977), pp. 3-16.
11. Hedley Bull, "Arms Control and World Order," International Security 1, no. 1 (Summer 1976).
12. For an overview of the negotiation literature, see I. W.
Zartman, "The Political Analysis of Negotiation: How Who Gets
What and When," World Politics 26, no. 3 (April 1974): 385-99,
and his "Negotiations: Theory and Reality," Journal of International
Affairs 9, no. 1 (1975): 69-77.
13. For a Soviet defector's viewpoint, see Boris Rabbot's two
articles in the International Herald Tribune, Paris, July 11 and 12,
1977.

14. "Peace and Power in India's Nuclear Policy," Asian Survey 10, no. 9 (September 1970): 779-88.

15. U.S., Congress, Senate, Government Operations Committee, Export Reorganization Act of 1976, Hearings, 94th Cong., 2d sess., January-March 1976, Senator J. Glenn's statements, p. 6.

16. Ibid. Cited in David Lilienthal's letter quoting Glenn Seaborg.

17. Ibid., Glenn Seaborg's testimony, p. 14.

2

WHAT IS PROLIFERATION?

Today proliferation is a top-priority concern in U.S. foreign relations. India's nuclear test in May 1974 has generated concern over whether India's behavior signals a trend in the Third World for the 1970s and the 1980s. While nuclear weapons in many hands threaten to become military instruments, proliferating nuclear options (weapons options or PNE options) threaten to become diplomatic instruments that require subtle diplomacy to induce nonconversion of weapons options or PNE options into weapons production and deployment. Such developments do not threaten U.S. or Soviet military security in the foreseeable future; the gaps between the superpowers and third parties are too wide. But just as the PRC is now able to complicate Soviet contingency planning, Moscow, more than Washington, needs to worry about proliferation in regions that border Soviet territory. Strong bilateral relations between the USSR and its neighbors may mute the nuclear factor but for Moscow and Washington the need to balance specific bilateral ties and interests with the general fear of proliferation will complicate their foreign relations.

Although it is clear that there is an urgent need to study proliferation and devise policies to slow it, the ideological and negotiating parameters of inquiry and action keep changing—that is, the preferred solution and its underlying premises keep changing. In the mid-1960s the NPC was the preferred solution. A number of diverse, indeed competing and contradictory, premises accompanied the NPT. First, it was assumed that the international acceptance of the NPT solved the problem. India's May 1974 test exploded that assumption. Second, it was assumed that a bargain could be struck and kept between NWS and NNWS—the NNWS were to accept discrimination in this military sphere and in return the NWS would promise nuclear disarmament and promotion of the peaceful uses of nuclear energy (including PNES). So far this assumption is in the realm of aspiration, not achievement. Third, the evidence of super-power parallelism and joint action in negotiating the NPT led to the assumption that superpower interests were closely similar if not identical. However, Nixon, Kissinger, and President Ford defected from a tough antiproliferation stance until India's 1974 test and the export of sensitive equipment and technology by West Germany and France to Brazil and Pakistan revived proliferation concerns. This raised speculation that Moscow rather than Washington was the real antiproliferator in the 1960s and early 1970s. If so, third parties were prone to exploit the disorientation in U.S. bureaucratic be-havior on nuclear supply and nonproliferation issues. Fourth, it was assumed by the NPT parties that proliferation by the sixth nu-clear power was bad. Several assumptions accompanied this view: the sixth proliferator would/could pave the way for the seventh and so on to the sixteenth; proliferators in the Third World were irre-sponsible, inexperienced, lacked a mature world view, and were prone to generate crises that might lead to a general nuclear war; and, finally, insecure nuclear capabilities held by countries inex-perienced in this area could make the countries prone to pre-emptive strikes by them or preventive action against them. These assumptions were never seriously debated publicly. The identity of the so-called irresponsible Third World leaders remains to date a matter of abstract speculation rather than empirical analysis. To date it remains unclear whether the operative assumption is against the irresponsible proliferators or against proliferation per se. In either case it would be useful to establish internationally recognizable criteria of responsibility or irresponsibility, and secondly, to de-fine proliferation.

At present the international proliferation debate in the Con-ference of the Committee on Disarmament (CCD) in Geneva, and also at the UN in New York is essentially a monologue: different sides use the same language but the meanings differ. To the nuclear superpowers, antiproliferation means that one ought to prevent further proliferation, that is, to check the spread beyond the present big two and the three small NWS. Antiproliferation strategies were summed up by a former IAEA official (now attached to the UN Center for Disarmament at New York), B. Sanders:

Anyway, if it is correct to see the NPT as merely one of a series of measures intended to prevent the prolifera-tion of nuclear weapons, it follows that the steps which preceded the Treaty were intended to have the same effect, and that all Agency safeguards are meant as

anti-proliferation measures. The fact that peaceful
nuclear explosions may not, at an earlier stage, have
been expressly listed among prohibited activities must
be ascribed rather to their still more or less theoretical character than to any conscious wish to ignore
them.[1]

Mr. Sanders' views merit analysis.* True IAEA safeguards
are by definition meant to be an antiproliferation measure, given
that the IAEA statutes forbid military uses of atomic energy. True,
PNES were not explicitly banned before the NPT, but it is also true
that PNES were neither excluded nor included—neither accepted nor
rejected—in atomic energy cooperation agreements before the NPT
came into effect. One needs to guard against a tendency to interpret the past before the NPT in the light of the NPT provisions.
Sanders is wrong to suggest that the NPT was a part of a phasal development. Because the case against PNES has never been a clear-
cut one able to command a truly international consensus, and the
debate on this point still continues at the IAEA in Vienna, the NPT
codifies the issue in Article V; this article permits PNES under
international controls. In other words, outlawing PNES is not
necessarily an antiproliferation measure in the IAEA statutes or in
the international debate on PNES in Vienna.
        If superpower views about Third World (not third party—that
is, French, PRC, British) irresponsibility and instability are the
central ideological or cultural motivating force behind their antihorizontal proliferation drive, Third World mistrust about superpowers' preference for "leadership" rather than "co-operation"—
the latter presumably involves greater attentiveness to the Third
World's interests—seems to be the motive force behind their anti-
vertical proliferation drive. Both sides act on the basis of self-
centeredness. The negotiating strategy stresses a need for change
in the other side's behavior, not one's own. Unilateral restraints
are usually avoided and, if they are offered, are based on the expectation that the other side will reciprocate. Even when unilateral
restraints are offered to improve the setting for future negotiations,
the maintenance of the unilateral restraint may depend on the offer
of a concession by the other side. Reciprocal trade-offs are the
preferred negotiating norm so that both sides can claim a gain. But

---

*Reading between the lines, one can see the possibility that
Mr. Sanders' view reflects the thinking in the International Atomic
Emergency Agency and that these are not merely personal views.

since it is hard to define and balance trade-offs (for example, how does one assess a trade-off between Soviet tanks and U.S. aircraft in Europe), it is easy to blame the other side for failure to agree.

Overall then, there is a fundamental cleavage between those who speak of controlling horizontal proliferation and those who direct their disarmament diplomacy against vertical proliferation. In both cases, antiproliferation and disarmament diplomacy has less to do with disarmament and nonproliferation and more to do with promotion of national foreign policy and national security. The international debate about proliferation and disarmament is essentially a cultural and a foreign policy activity, where the moves consist of talk.

The following section summarizes the main points of the debate between the opponents and advocates of vertical and horizontal proliferation so that the setting of multilateral and international nonproliferation or disarmament diplomacy can be established for subsequent chapters.

DIFFERENCES BETWEEN VERTICAL AND
HORIZONTAL PROLIFERATION

Studying and practicing nonproliferation is an enormous exercise. There are a number of alternative ways to study the subject and to find prescriptions to slow and, in the view of some, to stop horizontal proliferation. Controlling vertical and horizontal proliferation are real problems but the control of each is a different exercise. Vertical proliferation control is perceived by the superpowers as difficult to agree on, but the U.S.-USSR arms race is held to be less prone to accidental wars, miscalculations by irrational decision makers, the problem of violence within the nation leading to loss of control by the national decision makers, the problem of insecure military communications, and so on. Although finding "rational" decision makers in the Third World is a real issue, at least in some Western minds involved in arms control analyses, this is not a problem in the vertical proliferation debate.

In a sense the problems of vertical proliferation are less urgent and in a sense they are more urgent compared with horizontal proliferation problems. Given that both superpowers have secure second-strike military capabilities, given that both perceive a need to avoid nuclear war by accident and both have established secure hot lines for that purpose, the danger of war by accident is lessened if not eliminated. In this sense arms control has been achieved by having secure military communications and by securing

against the danger that irresponsible or unauthorized behavior by
military personnel might launch a nuclear war. In this case, arms
control means ensuring that only authorized nuclear activities are
permissible under the rules of the game that are enforced by the
political leadership vis-à-vis its military force. Comparatively
speaking, there is a case for instituting similar secure second-
strike command and control procedures in other horizontal proliferation cases, if and when nuclear forces come into deployment. This
aspect is applicable more today to the PRC's force, as presumably
all other nuclear weapons states (NWS) have secure second-strike
forces under national or allied command. Still, in the future, command and control issues are likely to focus more on horizontal
nuclear proliferators than on the vertical ones, even though in the
latter cases the need to upgrade command and control procedures
and capabilities is presumably constant.

The problems of negotiating controls over vertical proliferation nevertheless seem more urgent. Although there exists a negotiated code of conduct about accidental wars and against escalation
of conventional regional conflict into superpower nuclear conflict,
this code is not sufficient for a détente system. Clearly, the
superpowers cannot avoid dealing with each other because both have
global and regional interests and both have the ideological commitment and the economic and military capacities to pressure each
other and to fight each other. Their capacity to negotiate agreement, so far, is demonstrably less than their capacity to impinge
on each other. All the arms control agreements negotiated so far
since 1945 by the superpowers have dealt with issues peripheral to
superpower interests. In none of these agreements have the superpowers sacrificed any real part of their interests. Both superpowers have spoken the language of disarmament but their actions
reveal linkages not with disarmament but with their foreign policy
and security interests. Both sides are inextricably involved with
each other, and yet each deals with the other on the basis of mutual
distrust.

It is probably inaccurate for the Third World societies to take
the view that the superpowers have not negotiated in good faith with
regard to nuclear disarmament. While the Third World's frustra-
tion with the absence of progress in disarmament is understandable,
the history of mutual mistrust must be kept in mind. The superpowers have striven to negotiate in good faith but the perceptions
and experiences of the past and fears of the future have precluded
easy agreement. It is conceivable, as noted in the introduction,
that the emergence of bureaucracies mean that actors do not really
negotiate desired outcomes; instead, actors negotiate about the location of the policy issue close to their preferred source of decision

making. In this case the failure of disarmament can be attributed to the rise of bureaucracies in the United States and the Soviet Union. If Parkinson's Law precludes the demolition of the bureaucracies—President Carter's reorganization plans to the contrary notwithstanding—renewing the commitment to negotiate arms limitations between the superpowers is more urgent. But since negotiating superpowers arms reduction is a function of the negotiation of the superpower relationship—toward détente or away from détente—the urgency of the exercise is lost because it promises to be a long-range one, extending into years and decades rather than months. Negotiating the superpower relationships and hence negotiating their arms reductions does not appear to be a time-bound or a terminal exercise. It is an on-going process involving both conflict and cooperation. The process conveys diverse and at times contradictory signals to its different audiences and thereby produces diverse and at times contradictory reactions.

Because the world has not blown up because of continued superpower arms build-up, because superpowers arms reduction is a function of a negotiation of their détente relationship, and because this process is extended over time, a similar mood prevails (or ought to prevail) in the study of the process of horizontal proliferation. In studying vertical and horizontal proliferation one sees a similarity between the two, because both are essentially rooted in political and cultural problems. One cannot negotiate arms reduction in the superpower dialogue because there is mutual mistrust, because bureaucratic and public memories die hard, and because new generations lose some of the historical memory but then add layers of their own memories derived from their experiences with the enemy. If mutual distrust accounts for the failure to arrive at arms reduction, then a similar logic can be seen to prevail in the case of Third World societies who decline to negotiate away their nuclear options. If the superpowers are not willing to negotiate away their preference for self-sufficiency rather than dependence, how can the Third World leader be persuaded to take a different route? Alternatively, can all states be made to move away from debates of self-sufficiency versus dependence into conversations that result in the development of mutual interests appealing to a majority of the bureaucratic actors involved? Can avoidance of unilateral concession become a basis of negotiating arms reductions in cases of vertical and horizontal proliferation? Might studies of horizontal proliferation benefit from an analysis of the foreign and security interests and perceptions underlying disarmament and arms control diplomacy, the assumption being that such diplomacy is linked to foreign and security policy rather than to disarmament as such at present? In other words, is not the study of foreign policy essential to understanding disarmament diplomacy as a series of moves made by states and bureaucratic players to implement their interests or to forestall activities that might threaten these interests?

However, there are a number of reasons to separate the horizontal and the vertical proliferation exercises. First, vertical proliferation deals with two superpowers. It is a two-party exercise in its formal negotiating aspects even though the PRC is a part of the hidden agenda. The superpowers' perceptions of their global interests account for the two-party exercise. The presence of only two parties means that each side views the other as the primary audience and the primary adversary. However, this situation does not necessarily mean that the state is the primary actor. If the hypothesis is sound that international negotiations are less about securing desired outcomes and more about the location of the issue in the bureaucratic debate, bureaucratic power play is the real level of analysis. This power play can operate in two different directions. On the one hand, the liberals or hawks in one society may exert an influence on their counterparts in the other society. On the other hand, the power play may influence the location of the issue within a particular society. Therefore, "two-party" means that two states are involved, but, obviously, many bureaucratic players are involved.

The foregoing indicates that vertical proliferation control is based on a unique dyadic relationship between the superpowers. It is unique because it involves the interests of two global powers; the exclusivity of SALT symbolizes the uniqueness. However, because it is unique it is different from horizontal proliferation. Studying horizontal proliferation is more complicated than studying vertical proliferation because the former is a multistate activity. The objection to a two-party analysis is not simply that it is centered on the superpowers. Because of this characteristic, a two-state view obscures a study of: (1) the effects of superpower behavior on a third party or third parties; (2) the effects of third parties' behavior on the superpowers in situations where issues may be linked (for example, linkage between nuclear energy and arms control, between plutonium technology proliferation and nonproliferation, between bilateral nuclear negotiations and economic negotiations, and so on); and (3) the effects of the preceding factors on the evolving international system (the outcomes), with implications for stability or instability as the case may be. When negotiations have acquired multilateral dimensions, the cause-and-effect relationships between two-party negotiations and third-party interference, or between two-party negotiations and third-party acquiescence, or between third-party interference and superpower-acquiescence, and so on, offer unlimited and obviously complex opportunities to study the new patterns of international politics. For instance, it makes sense to study Pretoria-Bonn-Paris nuclear relations and Federal Republic of Germany-Brazil nuclear relations in the context of superpower détente relations and to determine if there are political economic, intellectual, or diplomatic flows that have implications for the evolving world order. The opportunities for such analyses are vast and untapped, and it will take a radical change in the contemporary strategic and political science literature to start conceptualizing Bonn-Tel Aviv-Paris-Pretoria-Washington-Rio nuclear relations and their implications for the new world order of the 1980s. Our minds are so acculturated to perceiving world events through American and Soviet eyes that we fail to see world politics through other eyes and thereby fail to see the changing reality.

The superpower view is not irrelevant but it is limited conceptually for this study's purpose of studying the new orientations in world politics and the foreign policy and security behavior of states who think and act differently from the superpowers. The superpower relationship is a product of assumptions from the cold war, of a nuclear strategy based on these and evolving assumptions. The mutual mistrust has been a central issue and factor in superpowers' negotiations and can be seen both as a cause and a consequence of the cold war. Indeed, the exercise of controlling horizontal nuclear proliferation is seen as an attempt to keep the world divided between the nuclear "haves" and the "have-nots." By failing to negotiate restraints on vertical proliferation and by working aggressively against horizontal proliferation—often but not always in a collaborative fashion—the superpowers seem to want to limit the nuclear game to as few strategically armed actors as possible. This may or may not have been a motive in the superpowers' thinking, but to many in the Third World it appears as the only motive. The theory that horizontal proliferation control is needed seems to many a cover to promote superpower national security rather than the security of other states.

The central element in cold war thinking is that both sides see themselves as the leading members of a global confrontation, muted now into a peaceful competition. They see themselves as the fountainhead of controlled political and military change in the world. It is debatable whether their capacities today match their perceptions of their importance and their sense of responsibility for negotiating a stable new world order. The need to find a new world order and particularly some control over the spiraling arms race is not at issue. At issue, however, is an assessment of the superpowers' concern for making themselves the linchpin of any new mechanism to reshape the world and making their policies the ideological parameters of the new thinking.

According to the superpowers, what counts is the consensus between the superpowers. The group attempting to reach a consensus is broadened to include allies and neutrals in the Third World only when the desires of the third party or parties affect the superpowers or because accommodation of third-party views and interests does not interfere with any basic superpower concerns. The two super-powers have different styles of behavior. The Soviet Union is less prone to discuss differing perspectives in an intellectual fashion; rather, it often substitutes its superpower status for the need to explain its reasons. The United States, comparatively speaking, is more open to engagement in an intellectual fashion with its dissent-ers abroad. But in both cases the effect is the same. Both nations tend to act defensively if their own fundamental issues are at stake. Invariably, the unwillingness to consider the third party viewpoint in negotiations unless forced to do so is a consequence of the cen-trality the superpowers attach to their views and roles. This centrality is a consequence of the attitudes and history of the cold war.

The cold war required the acquisition of nuclear weapons. Such weapons expressed the sense that global power was being em-ployed in defense of global interests; that nuclear power was one of the policy instruments along with global political, economic, and military diplomacy and cultural influence. Nuclear weapons were the ultimate defense of the two leading nations—an instrument to provide for national survival in a military crisis and to provide for international leadership in peacetime. Nuclear weapons were not only symbols; they were also, in select circumstances, such as the Cuban missile crisis, policy instruments of threat making. But even though the slogan of "not being a world policeman" was discontinued by President Nixon, reducing commitments abroad is more a ques-tion of altering style and of avoiding unfruitful foreign interventions as in Vietnam. A lower profile does not necessarily mean a lower commitment. For example, if the B-1 is out of use, the Cruise missile is used, and can be found on the ground, in the air, and under the sea. If U.S. troops from South Korea are withdrawn, the U.S. commitment is retained through the presence of an American general, with the gift of U.S. arms, and by expanding the U.S. naval and air detachments in the region. In other words, the sense of engaging the enemy continually remains a part of the policy pro-cess. To the superpowers, international or regional détente does not lead to reductions. It produces only a reshuffling of old and new cards. For a society that constantly strives to reduce the margin of uncertainty in a world where uncertainties are growing, this is a contradiction that can be met only by continually retaining military arms as an insurance against the unforeseen.

In part, horizontal proliferation is a response meant to guard against the implications a cold war led by a superpower would have for regional security; in part it is an attempt to find an alternative to superpower intrusions into regional politics. The superpowers see themselves as primary actors in regional politics, but the regional actors see the superpowers as intruders whose presence permanently disrupts regional peace and the pattern of regional politics. As the developmental capacities and conventional arms of regional powers grow, they are likely to look to the nuclear factor more and more. The conventional literature portrays the entrance of nuclear power, particularly nuclear explosive capability, as a disturbance to regional peace. This may well be true. Nonetheless it is worthwhile to study horizontal proliferation as an activity directed toward superpower intrusion into regional politics and motivated by a concern with the implications of such intrusion. As a hypothesis it is worth indicating that as the superpower intrusiveness into regional politics decreases, as the regional balance (or imbalance) of power asserts itself in accordance with the play of regional forces that are not a front for external powers and that are not artificially inflated with external aid, as the natural regional balance (or imbalance) is accepted by all parties concerned and a code of conduct takes root, then horizontal proliferation is likely to remain a slow, controllable exercise. It is likely to be slow and controllable in the thinking of the regional powers because its development will appear in the context of a mutually understood and agreed-upon code of conduct. Whether these rules are understood and accepted by external (nonregional) powers is another question, and is probably irrelevant if regional understandings about the code of conduct exist.

In other words, given the existence of a globalized and a nuclearized cold war, horizontal proliferation aims to raise the price of superpower involvement in regional politics. The acquisition of nuclear options—consisting of untested or tested nuclear explosive capacity and of a credible nuclear industry infrastructure—is worthwhile because it makes the further development of the option a consequence of the irresponsible behavior of the superpower; and in this case irresponsibility is defined by the regional actor. The successful development of gradually emerging nuclear barriers against superpower intrusiveness is based on the premise that <u>all</u> nuclear weapon states are not likely to be in favor of doing away with taking out the incipient nuclear states' capability to teach it (and other future aspirants) a lesson. Therefore, as long as even one superpower can offer tacit or explicit protection against such sanctions, the process of gradually building a nuclear option as a nuclear and psychological barrier against superpower intrusiveness is a credible strategy. The implication of the strategy is that it seeks to control the global dimensions of the cold war. It is theoretically conceivable that if each region had one regionally accepted nuclear power and if it were clearly understood that the object of the nuclear option was to keep the superpowers guessing and not to wipe out the friendly neighbor, insulation of the regions from superpower intrusiveness could result in more regional stability.

A shift away from the two-state framework of analysis also opens up interesting alternatives for the emerging new thinking about nuclear strategy. There are implications for style and substance in the emerging reorientations. In the context of the cold war assumptions, the superpower strategy necessitated a development of military capabilities that narrowed the margin of uncertainty and increased the margin of safety. There has been considerable stress on making commitments. "Get your back to the wall and communicate your commitments" is a slogan that is not simply restricted to Thomas Schelling's work but expresses the American ethos. Demonstrating the existence of military power to demonstrate the existence of a commitment has in a sense been the essence of Soviet and American nuclear strategy. The stress has been (and still is) on having a capacity to punish and to deter and on employing threats that are credible. The stress is on articulating, verbalizing, and precisely formulating the strategy and its underlying reasoning.

In contrast, the nuclear behavior of Third World societies has mixed characteristics: clear-cut verbal commitments, ambiguity in actual behavior, and the possibility and perhaps the probability of evolution, depending on perceived developments in international and regional politics. India's behavior expresses the new orientation. The behavior is clear-cut and straightforward inasmuch as the Indira Gandhi government and the government of Morarji Desai have declared that they will not make nuclear weapons. The Desai government has also declared that it does not perceive a need to carry out more peaceful nuclear tests. But on the other hand, the behavior is ambiguous because the willingness to publicly declare against nuclear weapons and peaceful nuclear tests is matched with an unwillingness to accept an international contractual obligation, that is, to accept international safeguards that would provide international verification of the Indian promise not to make nuclear weapons. Thus one can think about India's nuclear policy as a process of evolution in which nuclear weapons will "eventually" be reached. In this case the clear-cut verbal stance against nuclear weapons and the ambiguity (because of the unwillingness to accept international inspection of the entire Indian nuclear industry) are temporary phases in an inevitable process; namely, the development of Indian nuclear arms. Table 2.1 provides an overview of these three ways to study India's behavior.

TABLE 2.1

India's Nuclear Strategy (1950s to present)

Clear-cut and Straightforward	Ambiguous	Evolving
India will never make nuclear weapons whatever happens in the world, that is, even if the rest of the world goes nuclear.	—	India may decide to make nuclear weapons if there is a deterioration of the international security environment as India perceives it. India's making nuclear weapons is an unstated possibility, given the ambiguity in India's nuclear behavior.
India has no plans to have more peaceful nuclear tests and if further tests occur the world community will be consulted or at least informed in advance.	—	
	India will not accept international inspection of its entire nuclear industry; consequently its clear-cut verbal policy is based on a unilateral declaration and not on a contractual obligation.	

Source: Compiled by the author.

If one generalizes the Third World's nuclear behavior from India's nuclear behavior, if nuclear supply negotiating problems between the United States, Canada, and Australia vis-à-vis Japan or the Federal Republic of Germany are examined, if the dividing line is viewed more in terms of possessing a capacity to have nuclear weapons than in terms of demonstrating a nuclear explosive capacity versus not doing so, then the central task is to forecast if the evolving nuclear strategies and disarmament strategies of developing societies are deliberately kept ambiguous;* if the ambiguities will remain frozen for a determinate or indeterminate period in the foreseeable future; and if the present ambiguity is a logical and a necessarily inevitable step toward acquisition of nuclear arms. The bulk of the current Western literature refers to possibilities of the third kind but the other two possibilities are not explored. Yet it is the first two possibilities that tell us something about the new orientation of developing nuclear options that may not necessarily become weapons.

There are a number of ways in which ambiguity can be created. Israel's untested bombs accompanied by the statement that it will not be the first one to introduce nuclear weapons into the region are one example. The Israeli statement raises more questions than it provides answers. For instance, what does it mean by not being the first one to introduce nuclear weapons when the United States and the USSR have already introduced nuclear weapons through their military and naval presence in the Mediterranean? Is the Mediterranean not a part of the Middle East region? Or is the Israeli

---

*Conceptually, "ambiguity" means different things, and to avoid confusion the different meanings need to be spelled out. First, one speaks of ambiguity in relation to capability and intent surrounding the existence of a nuclear explosives option—in tested or untested form. India, Israel, and South Africa are the three hard-core cases. Second, there is ambiguity about the effects of dramatic changes in the international environment—meaning a deterioration in the strategic situation that slowly or rapidly increases the sense of vulnerability—on the nuclear behavior of states that are now considered to be safely under an NPT regime. The Federal Republic of Germany and Japan may be cases worth considering in this regard. This statement is not meant to imply that there is any deception inherent in current Federal Republic of Germany and Japanese policies—that is, their present stance against nuclear weapons is sincerely intended. Third, there are ambiguous linkages that at times involve nuclear issues. Thus, one can speculate about the ambiguity of a suggested link between interest vis-à-vis the EEC and Canadian cooperation in arranging a uranium supply in return for the cooperation of the Federal Republic of Germany in facilitating Canadian and Australian relations with the EEC, and so on. Here there is ambiguity because the threats are implied, privately explicit but not public. The linkages are not self-evident and are, according to some, logically artifical and contrived. Still, they are effective in serving particular purposes in negotiating desired outcomes.

statement directed against the introduction of Egyptian or Iraqi
nuclear presence? The Indian way of creating ambiguity is the
second way. This method has been noted earlier. Ambiguity may
be generated in yet a third way in the future. States like Iran,
South Korea, and Brazil may find that it is necessary for them to
renounce their safeguards obligations because conditions have
changed and their view of national security requires them to follow
either the Israeli or the Indian route. In other words, if ambiguity
between two known adversaries such as the United States and the
USSR is not always possible, and may not be desirable (given a desire to avoid miscalculations and problems in détente), then from
the perspective of Third World societies seeking to limit superpower
intrusiveness into their affairs it may make sense to utilize the
development of a nuclear option as an instrument to generate ambiguity.

Such nuclear ambiguity is cheap because it is not directed
against a particular target and hence it does not invite punishment.
At the same time the ambiguous development of the nuclear option
is enough to increase the attentiveness of the superpowers and other
external agencies toward the holder of the nuclear option. If it is a
part of a program that has well-established and credible civilian
components (for example, in health, agriculture, medicine, and
electricity production), a nuclear option is a cheap way to increase
the external attentiveness and to improve the bargaining setting for
nuclear and disarmament issues and other issues. In other words,
a nuclear option can emerge as a bargaining chip in international
negotiations because the onus of inducing an option holder not to
exercise its option depends on the ability of the external powers to
satisfy the option holder's aspirations in return for the option
holder's restraint.

Admittedly, this is a strategy of mutual blackmail, or, in
diplomatic language, a strategy of mutual satisfaction, of negotiating on the basis of reciprocal incentives. The strategy of proliferating nuclear options implies the existence of ambiguity with respect
to its military uses. The ambiguity is useful with respect to the
political uses of the option in dynamic bargaining situations, such
as the negotiations between India and the United States, or among
Brazil, the United States, and the Federal Republic of Germany.
There are, of course, differences between these examples. For
example, India disclaims any intention of making nuclear weapons.
India is outside the NPT while the Federal Republic of Germany is
an adherent. India is ambiguous about safeguards, having accepted
some inspection but not of its entire peaceful nuclear industry,
whereas the Federal Republic of Germany accepts safeguards on its
entire nuclear industry and has no reservations about these. Still,

the point can be made that the Federal Republic of Germany has the capacity, should international environmental changes require such a political decision, to make nuclear bombs. For both India and the Federal Republic of Germany (and other countries, like Japan), there are nuclear supply problems with the principal suppliers, such as the United States and Canada. There is no ambiguity or uncertainty at present about the military ambitions of the Federal Republic of Germany whereas there is a question about India's nuclear intentions. But in the case of the Federal Republic of Germany, and, particularly, in the case of Japan, there is a concern that strains in alliance relations might develop if nuclear supply conditions are held to be prejudicial to the sovereignty and economic well-being of the Federal Republic of Germany or Japan. Ambiguity, therefore, has a role to play particularly as it concerns renegotiations of existing nuclear supply contracts and agreements.

There are other important differences in the expectations for and perceptions of vertical and horizontal proliferation. Vertical proliferation attempts to slow the arms race, to negotiate limitations on existing technology, and to negotiate arms reductions and perhaps eventual disarmament. As noted earlier, it is much more difficult to undo something than to prevent something from happening. The former is the thrust of vertical proliferation control; the latter is the thrust of horizontal proliferation control.

Horizontal nonproliferation deals with a hypothetical contingency in the sense that it refers to a danger that may occur in the 1980s. It is based on the assumption that, having acquired nuclear capabilities, a number of states will be forced or induced to acquire nuclear weapons. Thus horizontal proliferation studies rest on an inference that nuclear weapons decisions will follow the acquisition of technological capacities. It is viewed as a phasal activity whereby technological developments of the 1970s will lead to nuclear weapons decisions in the 1980s. Similar inferences were made in the 1960s about decisions in the 1970s and the scenarios of sixth to sixteenth* nuclear weapons states have proven to be fanciful; these facts do not really concern the contemporary thinkers who worry about horizontal proliferation. The problem of explaining and predicting future proliferation is avoided by simply projecting concerns about proliferation in the 1970s to the 1980s. In no case is there a convincing attempt to explain how and why certain societies will go about making decisions on nuclear weapons

---

*This refers to scenarios that have the sixth NWS leading inevitably to the sixteenth NWS.

development and deployment. Insofar as nuclear weapon development is rooted in contemporary analyses of technological developments and nuclear commerce, insofar as horizontal proliferation is not viewed as an evolution of foreign relations and foreign policy of the societies considered (that is, the foreign policy and security motives and policies underlying proliferation are not sufficiently analyzed), proliferating <u>images of uncontrolled horizontal proliferation</u> permeate most horizontal proliferation studies. By contrast vertical proliferation is seen as essentially a controlled and controllable activity.

Vertical proliferation control is a many-sided phenomenon, having a number of requirements. It entails a capacity to demonstrate political will, to mute and remove the situation of mutual mistrust, to solidify the détente relationship, to establish a firm code of conduct, and, generally, to make the superpower relationship a central determinant in contemporary international relations. That is, moderating the superpower rivalry and confrontation is indispensable to negotiation of arms control and arms reduction. This is the conventional wisdom about the superpowers arms control negotiations. By contrast, it is not the conventional wisdom about horizontal proliferation that political problems need to be understood and negotiated before it is possible to come to grips with the fact that current negotiating positions of prominent Third World societies and the potential proliferators are attempts to express their foreign policy and security insecurities rather than to move toward disarmament. In other words, in vertical and horizontal proliferation cases, the process is similar: disarmament diplomacy is linked to foreign and security policy rather than to the goal of disarmament. Yet there is a difference in expectations. With respect to vertical proliferation it is desirable and practical that disarmament and arms control diplomacy be viewed in a total foreign policy and security context. It is considered impractical to ask the superpowers to move toward disarmament. It is unrealistic to force them with embarrassing UN resolutions or to confront them with proposals to alter the disarmament. It is argued that such Third World pressure will be counterproductive because recommending changes in the disarmament machinery is not too useful unless there is a superpower will to make arms cuts. Here the development of the political will is said to precede constructive disarmament or arms control negotiations, and there is an underlying sympathy for the superpowers' negotiating problems. For instance, the superpowers are held to be negotiating in good faith and thereby fulfilling their NPT obligations under Article VI. They are seen to want to negotiate arms reductions. It is felt that their interests in this direction are parallel but do not yet coincide. By contrast, horizontal proliferation pleas generally fail to stress the links between, on one hand, disarmament diplomacy and the underlying security and foreign policy issues and concerns of the threshold states, and, on the other hand, the need to negotiate stable change in regional politics before there can be a movement toward nuclear or conventional disarmament. In the case of horizontal proliferation the importance of settling political problems, of creating political trust, is overlooked or underestimated, as it clearly is not in the case of vertical proliferation studies.

Another difference emerges from the foregoing discussion. In the 1940s and the 1950s a hysterical view about the consequences of a failure to disarm was present in the public consciousness. The sense was strong that if the nuclear arms race between the superpowers and other nuclear aspirants was permitted to go on, the world would blow up. Fortunately, the predictions of doom were wrong with respect to the 1950s, the 1960s, and up through the present. Predictions that the world would blow up have now been modified. Now the doomsday scenario is based on a notion that a crazy president or a military officer may get it into his head to blow up the world. Overall, the world has learned to coexist with the fully armed missile in the hands of the nuclear weapon states. With the passage of time, the educational process has been effective. Initially, there was a concern in Western thinking about a Soviet madman launching a nuclear war. As Soviet command and control procedures became firmly established this concern was eroded, only to be replaced with a concern about an insecure PRC nuclear liquid-fueled missile force that could be involved in a pre-emptive strike or a preventive war. It was feared that an insecure PRC force would be (or might be) a tempting target for the ambitious Soviets, who might want to secure their pre-eminence and also perform an international service by destroying PRC nuclear installations or missiles through a conventional attack. Conversely, given PRC insecurity, it was argued that the PRC might launch a pre-emptive attack against the Soviet Union. Today, the irrational Chinese, however, have become rational. The label of irrationality has now been transferred to the irrational Indians, Brazilians, and so on.

There are three lessons to be drawn from this process of fixed but transferable image. First, the perceiver always thinks of himself as rational and the other as irrational; that is, the perceiver overestimates his own rationality and underestimates that of his enemy. Secondly, once the perceiver is engaged in dealing with the object of his perception, once the perceiver becomes attentive to the verbal and actual behavior of the perceived object, a process of self-education sets in. The educational process may be externally induced or self-induced. In the former case the perceived object may continually and consciously transmit accurate signals to alter what it thinks are wrong impressions and wrong images held by the other side. But if the other side refuses to take note of the signals and acknowledge them, the transmission of accurate signals has no practical effect. It is important, therefore, that the signals be picked up and analyzed and that lessons be learned. It is important that the analyses of these signals be confirmed through the perceivers' other sources of information.

Thirdly and finally, if the practical experience of engagement between two adversaries results in a rectification of false images, inasmuch as interactions between two adversaries are unique, the same process must be repeated with another unique dyad of adversaries. For example, initially the United States saw the USSR as an irrational and expansionist actor but subsequently, in the light of interactions with it, the United States altered that initial view. Still, the imagery of the other side's irrationality and expansionism was repeated with the PRC until Sino-U.S. interactions led to its modification. It can be argued that it took the United States more time to shift its imagery of an expansionist and irrational nuclear PRC (1949-72) than it did for U.S. imagery of a nuclear armed USSR (1953 to the late 1950s). It can be argued in another case—that of India—that it took the United States even less time to alter its view about India's nuclear plans than it did for the USSR and PRC.

The cases are not entirely comparable. The Soviet-U.S. and Sino-U.S. cases involve fears of irrational use of nuclear weapons. The case of the United States and India involves fears about the irrational development of Indian nuclear weapons and its subsequent effect on horizontal nuclear weapons proliferation, which disturbs the regional and global peace. Nevertheless, given the difference in the content of the three situations, the point to be made is that the notion of irrationality is usually first applied to the other side. If the act (a nuclear explosion) has been sudden and unexpected (as was true with Soviet and Indian explosions and less true for the PRC one), the absence of interaction probably accounts for the initial response—that there is a danger of irrational behavior by the new actor. However, after the event, as interactions emerge, the educational process sets in.

Consequently, this difference between vertical and horizontal proliferation is somewhat as follows. The greater the understanding in the contemporary literature and in the public consciousness of Soviet-U.S. relations, the greater the likelihood that perceptions of the prospects of nuclear conflict are more refined and more accurate. Similarly, more is now known about the PRC than was in the early 1950s. The imagery of an irrational and an expansionist PRC has been

muted, probably transformed, into an expectation that in the next
five to ten years, through the growth of PRC self-education and the
evolving perceptions of its elites, it will gradually participate in the
international security debate in a mature fashion. The expectation
is that the PRC is currently domestically involved with the problems
of shaping its economy, modernizing its military forces, to balancing
its international trade, to solidifying its elites, and giving a better
shape to its political institutions. A generally sympathetic view of
the PRC is now being taken and the old imagery of an irrational and
expansionist PRC has been discarded.

With India, Western assessments have been aided by India's
open society, by the access and personal ties that Westerners have
generally enjoyed with the Indians, and by India's parliamentary
traditions. These features make the West see consensus building
and compromise as more feasible with India. In this respect, India
much more than PRC has been prepared by its postwar experience
with international conference diplomacy to articulate its concerns
and to seek to alter the other side's misperceptions. But even
though India is large and full of domestic problems, even though
most informed foreigners think that it would be idiotic for India to
contemplate territorial expansion (which would only add to India's
existing problems), the theory of Indian expansion has been popular-
ized by certain circles in the West. The 1971 Nixon-Kissinger
theory of Indian expansionism, and the old Pakistani belief in this
emotion-filled notion, are obvious examples.

True, the idea was discarded quite quickly just as it was
adopted rather quickly in the United States. Still, since the idea
has entered the public consciousness it cannot be far from the
minds of those who study Indian nuclear intentions. In other words,
if experts can fall prey to the theory of Indian expansionism and
its possible implications for future Indian nuclear decision making,
if this imagery can gain root in the public consciousness even about
an open society like India, how much more complex is the problem
of the imagery associated with closed societies like Brazil, Iran,
and Taiwan? Among the list of potential nuclear proliferators in
the 1980s are societies of which there are few scholarly analyses.
The media coverage is sensational and geared to convey the bad
news. Lord Beaverbrook's advice that good news is bad news and
bad news is good news is valuable for selling copy, but it does not
aid in the task of explaining and predicting nuclear behavior and
the foreign policy and security setting in which nuclear decisions
will be made.

It may be worthwhile, therefore, to recognize that ignorance
about the compulsions and barriers against horizontal nuclear proliferation accounts for proliferating images about this type of

proliferation. This is an important difference between studying
vertical and studying horizontal proliferation. Therefore, it is
urgent not simply to negotiate a slowing-down of horizontal proliferation in the Third World but also to negotiate the emergence of
an educational process that favors accurate studies of nuclear decisions and the barriers against them in Third World bureaucratic
debates along with the incentives toward proliferation.

TWO MODELS OF "GOING NUCLEAR" HORIZONTALLY

"Going nuclear" is an imprecise phrase. It is conceptually
weak for the purpose of predicting proliferation but is useful to explain proliferation in the past. "Going nuclear" contains a range of
possibilities. In the conventional sense it means the acquisition of
nuclear weapons by states that did not possess them. In terms of
the conventional meaning there are only five cases to consider,
namely, the United States, USSR, the United Kingdom, France, and
the PRC. Each case is different in terms of the circumstances
underlying the decision or decisions to make nuclear weapons. The
United States made the bomb before the Germans did and the initial
decision was geared to perceptions about the implications of German
atomic arms. Soviet atomic arms development was an on-and-off
exercise but it eventually took shape in the context of Soviet perceptions about the cold war with the United States. For the United
Kingdom prestige seemed to be an important element. Having col-
laborated with the United States and Canada on atomic research
during World War II, the United Kingdom and Canada felt left out
after the United States decided against sharing secrets about military applications of atomic energy with its wartime collaborators.
For France, prestige and security underlay the decision to acquire
the technological basis for atomic weapon development and production even before General Charles de Gaulle assumed the presidency.
French acquisition of nuclear arms is defensible in terms of French
views of the need for an independent defense but the acquisition is
usually regarded in the Anglo-Saxon West as a product of Gaullism.
For the PRC, the fear of the Soviet Union and the need for an independent voice in strategic policy, both within the communist world and
internationally, accounted for the development of its nuclear arms.
In short, the circumstances underlying the acquisition of
atomic weapons in these societies are varied and unique. Consequently, there is a need to examine the interplay in the decision
process among politicians, scientists, and bureaucrats (civil and
military) in the steps leading each state into the atomic and nuclear
weapons club. Generally speaking, the motives for acquiring atomic

or nuclear arms can be classified as security and prestige considerations. The processes, however, vary. In the case of PRC and
the Soviet Union, a political decision to have nuclear or atomic
arms preceded the technological developments and the allocation of
human, budgetary, and other resources toward that aim. In France,
technological decisions paved the way for the political decision to
have an independent French atomic deterrent. In the United States
and the United Kingdom, technology and politics apparently went
hand in hand.

According to the conventional meaning of going nuclear, nuclear proliferation is a phasal activity. One step leads to another,
resulting in a decision to make nuclear weapons. Nuclear weapons
development, production, and deployment are the end condition of
the phasal process, as far as proliferation is concerned. That is,
proliferation has occurred once nuclear weapons have been acquired.
Thereafter, the phasal process involves an upgrading of existing
nuclear arms so that the strategic balance is not impaired in the
eyes of the adversaries.

The second model for going nuclear, like the first one, involves the acquisition of capability to make a nuclear device. This
model does not reject entirely the first model but it raises new
possibilities, which have implications for the study of proliferation
in the 1980s and the 1990s. The Second model proposes the same
motives as the first one—namely, security and prestige. However,
the process and its implications vary. The process (judging by the
Indian case) consists of the political decision to acquire and the
acquisition of the scientific, human, material, and industrial infrastructure to make a bomb. There may or may not be a demonstration of a capacity to make the bomb. For instance, in Israel's case
there has been no such demonstration but in India's case there has
been. The process, from deciding to develop the infrastructure to
making a device, is phasal whether or not there is a demonstration
of the capacity through a nuclear explosion.

The second model is complicated because it directs one's
attention to two sets of evidence. The first set is quantifiable and
hence most visible. This set is the one that is usually stressed in
the nonproliferation literature. This set includes evidence of the
following type: the number of reactors in a threshold state; whether
reprocessing of spent fuel can take place in unsafeguarded facilities
under national control; whether uranium enrichment can take place
in unsafeguarded facilities under national control; whether the nuclear program is dependent on external sources for fuel; and so on.
According to one view, this type of evidence is meaningful for a
state that intends to explode a nuclear device or is said to be on the
verge of doing so (and, of course, for a state that has already done

so one). This view is inherent in the NPT. According to another view, in view of the weaknesses of the NPT proliferation capacity is measurable not only in terms of the actual occurrence of a nuclear explosion; that is, according to the first view proliferation occurs if and when a state explodes a device, whereas according to the other view proliferation is occurring even before a nuclear explosion is actually carried out.

The second model directs one's attention to a second set of evidence, which is not quantifiable and public but is relevant for an understanding of why certain states in the future are likely to develop nuclear weapons or nuclear options to promote their national interests. The first set of evidence, mentioned above, points to the technological base in a country's nuclear program that constitutes the foundation for a phasal evolution of a program from decision to weapons development and deployment. That is, if a decision to make nuclear weapons exists, what are the material requirements for doing so? This is the focus of the first set of evidence. The focus of the second set of evidence, however, is this: even if the technological basis for nuclear explosives capacity or nuclear weapons development exists, what are the strategic, foreign policy, domestic politics, cultural, and historical conditions that make less likely a political decision to make nuclear weapons as distinct from a decision to develop a nuclear option and stop right there? The range of evidence sought in the second set is vast. It involves an assessment of the foreign policy and security policy history of the country in question, and of the country's cultural norms, its value structure, and its perceptual base for decision making. A study of the country's views of the world (generally and in the thinking of its decision makers and opinion makers) is an instructive contribution to the second set of evidence. It may also be useful to determine, in the case of a nonexpansionist country, whether the restraint is externally or internally induced. A comparison of the roles of internally and externally induced restraint contributes helpful information to the second set of evidence.

The second model, therefore, does not necessarily involve the making of nuclear weapons even if there is a demonstration of a nuclear explosives capability or undemonstrated evidence of such capability. The first model involves the acquisition of nuclear weapons and then requires the nonuse of these weapons in a deterrence format. The second model involves the acquisition of a nuclear option (that is, no decision to make nuclear weapons but a decision to have an explosives capacity) and then requires the nonuse of the option. Conceptually, the idea of nonuse is common to both models, but there is one obvious difference. The first model requires acquisition of nuclear arms; this entails eventually the acquisition of a secure second-strike nuclear force. However, the second model requires only the acquisition of a credible nuclear option. In short, going nuclear now has two different meanings: acquiring nuclear weapons and practicing deterrence; and acquiring a nuclear option and then practicing a strategy of nonconversion into nuclear weapons.

What are the implications of the two models for the state itself, its neighbors, and the international system?

Implications of the First Model

For the state itself an enormous investment of human and material resources and political commitment is needed. Diplomacy is needed to practice the nonuse of nuclear weapons in crises; this entails considerable coordination between the foreign policy and the defense machineries of a state—a complicated task in pluralistic societies. It is necessary also to have constant upgrading of the strategic arms, which involves the existence of a controlled or an uncontrolled arms race. Ambiguity about the nature of the deterrent is not desirable, because it might allow room for the enemy to misunderstand the other side's behavior and read weakness when weakness does not exist (or at least is not intended for display). Because of the heavy commitment to military spending, fewer resources are available for fostering economic and social change domestically and internationally. Because deterrence becomes more difficult to practice as the number of parties involved increases, the NWS try to keep the superpower game as closed as possible. The resulting elitism also results in resentment in the world community about the undemocratic nature of international security policy management by the superpowers. Hence the superpowers have to expose themselves constantly to the allegation of Third World and nonaligned states that they ought to stop temporizing about international security and make practical moves toward arms reduction and eventual disarmament. To check such diplomatic pressure the United States and the Soviet Union have had to invest diplomatic resources to meet the challenge.

If a state acquires nuclear weapons, a neighboring state seeks to equalize the distribution of power by developing its own nuclear weapons (for example, the PRC in relation to the Soviet Union and the Soviet Union in relation to the United States). Alternatively, the weaker neighbor may learn to live under the nuclear umbrella of its bigger neighbor and accept the protection of an alliance or to repudiate the protection at its own peril (for example, Canada in relation to the United States).

As for the international system, a superpower arms race is a threat to international peace if there is a danger of a nuclear confrontation, as in the case of the Cuban Missile Crisis. An arms race is a waste of valuable human and material resources that could assist world development. Acquisition of nuclear arms by one nation sets a bad example for nations with nuclear aspirations. The attachment of prestige to nuclear arms fosters the sense of inequality in the international system because of the perception that those who have these weapons have special responsibilities in world affairs and are therefore entitled to a special voice in the councils of world affairs. The notion that those who have the latest nuclear technology are greatest invites resentment by those who do not possess the latest technology, and thus the latter are compelled by the rules of the game to acquire this technology. Furthermore, since nuclear technology transfers have slowed down in the 1970s because of lessons learned from the Atoms for Peace program of the 1950s, the slowdown fosters the sense of discrimination in the Third World perceptions and is reflected in UN majority decisions.

Implications of the Second Model

This appears to be the model for the future if the following premises about the modes of interstate relations are valid; that is, if there is a gradual but no radical deterioration of the influence of the superpowers; if the present trend of diffusion of resources and influence is controlled; and if competing subnationalism does not erode state authority and the state remains the principal actor in international relations. Central to these assumptions are the notions that possession of nuclear weapons does not necessarily provide the possessor with influence over those who do not possess nuclear weapons; that nuclear weapons can become frozen assets unless their use is calculated to generate some sort of nuclear diplomacy—the making of threats in crises; that there will be continued use of bargaining chips to induce arms reductions, thereby generating some movement toward nuclear disarmament; that the superpowers are negotiating arms reductions to codify the superpower relationship; and that they are also negotiating to bring PRC and France into the disarmament diplomacy dialogue but generally are not rethinking the end uses of nuclear weapons in national, regional, and international security thinking so that superpower behavior can serve as an example for the rest of the world to follow.

The second model is new (that is, innovative) and hopeful, but also complex. Since it is built on the notion that new nuclear aspirants are likely to see their interests served _more_ by a nuclear option coupled with a strategy of calculated nonuse, the development and the maintenance of the nuclear option requires a mixture of restraint in enemy behavior and restraint (self-restraint) on the part of the nuclear option holder, which is induced by its external enemies and its supporters. In other words, internally and externally induced unilateralism has a role to play. Each actor attempts to improve the other side's sense of security, and here this is an ongoing process rather than a static condition to be reached. Such other-directedness generates a feeling of mutual confidence and an enhanced sense of security.

This model has three variants. The first route sees the development of a nuclear option, which is converted into nuclear weapons. Here the acquisition of a nuclear explosives capability leads to weapons development and deployment and the adoption of a deterrent posture that is public and requires minimal ambiguity about the nature of the enemy threat and the required response. The second route (the Israeli route) involves undemonstrated evidence of a nuclear explosives capacity but also ambiguity about the circumstances (if any) in which the demonstration makes sense. However, this route is real because the infrastructure underlying the undemonstrated capacity exists and there is psychological manipulation involved in the capacity's presence. The third route (the Indian route) requires a demonstration of a capacity to explode a nuclear device followed by self-restraint and externally induced restraint. It requires diplomatic, political, and military concessions toward neighbors (Pakistan and Iran in the case of India) to enhance their sense of security and faith in the nuclear option holder's good will; that is, the concessions are recognized by the neighbors as well as by other major actors.

So far the model conveys optimism. Its dual-stranded approach (acquiring the nuclear option and practicing self-restraint and community building through concessions to neighbors) is an innovative way of viewing contemporary international affairs. This approach repudiates the notion of maximizing one's gains through military means—through coercion or by threat making. Reciprocal concessions are not sought if the other side is politically unable to offer these at a particular time. The process does not end with the achievement of a military victory or with the demonstration of a nuclear option.

However, the model can also easily deteriorate. For instance, assuming that Pakistan is not convinced of Indian nuclear intentions despite Indian concessions in bilateral relations, then Pakistan may decide to take the Israeli or the Indian route to acquire a Pakistani nuclear option. India, sensing that Pakistan is on the verge of exploding its nuclear device, decides that it must stay ahead of Pakistan, then decides to follow the first route described above—to move from its nuclear option to nuclear weapons development—and thereby starts a nuclear arms race. On the other hand, however, if Pakistan takes the Israeli route and keeps its nuclear option hidden and undemonstrated, then India may or may not decide to move toward nuclear weapons development and deployment.

This analytical mold suggests a need to consider a number of case studies so that circumstances favoring a movement from one route to another can be discussed. In the abstract, a movement from one status to another suggests a number of possibilities, as follows. Pakistan might move from being a nonnuclear weapon state to following the Israeli route. No phasal activity is indicated here. In this case there is technological momentum but no technological determinism. Political decisions favor refraining from a demonstration of an explosives option. In a variation of the above, Pakistan might decide to move from its present status and to follow the Indian route. A demonstration of Pakistan's explosives capability is followed by self-restraint like India's. There is continued technological momentum but no technological determinism. Political decisions prevent further nuclear explosions and any movement toward nuclear weapons development and deployment. If Pakistan acted in one of those two ways, India might react (or overreact) and move to the nuclear weapons development and deployment route taken by the NWS. This would indicate the phasal activity described in the first model of going nuclear.

So far the discussion has been based on the premise that once a state has acquired nuclear weapons it is reluctant to relinquish them. In the abstract however, it is worth speculating about the possibility of a NWS shifting from the first route described here to the third—namely, phasing out the momentum toward nuclear weapons development, slowing the arms race, cutting down on existing stockpiles, reducing nuclear arms with a view to eventually eliminating them from defense forces and moving to a nuclear weapon-free world. This scenario is totally unrealistic at present but analytically it ought to be considered as a phasal downward development. If the habit of seeking security through arms reduction rather than an arms race takes root in the thinking of the existing five NWS, if SALT II paves the way to SALT III—with movement from arms limitations to arms reductions—this route would have the effect of slowing the arms race among the five NWS as well as reducing the proliferating tendencies among the potential proliferators.

Research Implications

This chapter indicates a need to rethink the approach to the subject of nuclear proliferation. Usually nuclear proliferation studies are antiproliferation exercises, which take proliferation as a given and which then set out to devise multilateral controls and technological barriers for slowing proliferation. The bulk of the North American literature focuses on antiproliferation. The psychological and decision-making dimensions of the question "what is proliferation?" are not addressed. The North American approach, high on policy content but low in empirical work, is deficient as an explanatory tool. More work is needed in problem definition before there is policy prescription.

However, new approaches are beginning to emerge. The second approach is not as neat and logical as this section indicates but its parameters may be described as follows. Proliferation is inevitable; it is happening and too much should not be made of antiproliferation studies that see a rapid momentum toward nuclear weapons proliferation. Nuclear weapon proliferation by N countries is manageable, just as proliferation by the five nuclear weapon states has become manageable over time.

This chapter sympathizes with the second approach, but the approach has deficiencies. The merit of the second approach is that it tones down the antiproliferation hysteria; its disadvantage is that it really argues a weak case skillfully and pushes under the rug a number of important questions. Consider the following points. The second approach is based on the premise that Nth country nuclear weapons doctrines and force structures can be accommodated into superpower thinking just as French and PRC nuclear weapons postures have been. There are several weaknesses in this approach. First, if French nuclear weapons are not relevant in the Soviet-American military balance, the accommodation of French diplomacy in the London Nuclear Suppliers Group and in the Geneva disarmament debate is a cosmetic and, strategically speaking, a marginal activity as far as SALT is concerned. The real significance of the French induction into the antiproliferation dialogue is this: French nuclear weapons do not contribute to proliferation but French nuclear exports do threaten to promote Third World proliferation. Second, PRC nuclear weapons are important with respect to the Soviet-American strategic relationship, but here no one can say with certainty that an accommodation, even between Washington and Peking, has been reached. All that can be said with certainty is that the issue has been shelved until such time as the PRC acquires intercontinental missile capability. Thus Pentagon planners can hardly be expected to ignore the future implications of a nuclear PRC with global capability. Also, if PRC détente strategy with the United States improves the PRC negotiating position with the Soviet Union, the danger of a PRC double-cross hardly suggests a Sino-U.S. accommodation. A final consideration: the second approach is premised on the view that there will be Nth country nuclear weapons proliferation, and that the proliferation will have primarily regional, rather than international, implications. Both premises are questionable if proliferating nuclear options (which do not necessarily have weapons as their terminal condition) are viewed by decision makers as diplomatic, psychological, engineering, scientific, and potentially military resources rather than as primarily military resources. It hardly makes sense for India, South Africa, and Brazil to use nuclear threats against their neighbors when other means are available.

This study departs from the second approach studying proliferation by modifying and expanding it substantially. It indicates that proliferation in the coming decade is best seen as a slow, controlled, and conscious activity leading to proliferation of ambiguous nuclear options and nuclear diplomacy rather than unambiguous nuclear weapons force structures with nuclear doctrines, and command and control apparatus. The ambiguities lie in the strategic environment as perceived by the decision makers of the potential proliferators. Ambiguity is a hallmark of contemporary diplomacy, including nuclear diplomacy, and is likely to continue to be so until the superpowers can decide irrevocably whether they want a bipolar or a multipolar world, and who the essential actors in the latter instance ought to be. The problem with existing multilateral antiproliferation diplomacy is that it cannot really come to grips with strategic and diplomatic ambiguity. On the contrary, ambiguity is something it does not want to deal with in shaping the antiproliferation regime. Even if it is true that American interests fully accommodated French and Chinese interests (a statement this study does not accept), the example is irrelevant because the post-PRC proliferation perspective seems to focus more on option proliferation and less on weapons proliferation. Therefore a third possible approach to studying proliferation recognizes that the sources of restraint and of change reside in the Nth party decision making rather than (or more so than) in the behavior of the antiproliferators. Safeguards are seen in this approach as good treaties for good times, but if and when the strategic environment deteriorates the role of international restraints is doubtful.

To summarize: the first approach sees proliferation as a rapidly evolving process that increases the number of horizontal proliferators and enhances the dangers of nuclear war and regional arms races that can have international consequences. This view has been somewhat discredited by the fanciful nature of sixth to sixteenth proliferation projections in the 1960s. The second approach suggests that proliferation is happening but that it is manageable. This approach has its use in toning down the antiproliferation hysteria but does not come to grips with the international, national, and

subnational forces that favor nuclear option proliferation and the
diplomacy of ambiguity in the coming decade. The third approach
modifies and expands the second approach, particularly in the area
of the underlying factors and consequences of proliferation. This
book is concerned with the development of a framework for studying
the third approach.

NOTE

1. B. Sanders, Safeguards Against Nuclear Proliferation,
International Peace Research Institute monograph, Stockholm, 1975,
p. 12 (emphasis added).

3

MULTILATERAL DIPLOMACY
AND NONPROLIFERATION:
THE BACKGROUND

Efforts to control nuclear proliferation by international means started in 1946 with the Baruch Plan but the NPT, in the late 1960s, was the first nearly universal regime. It is, today, the heart of the antiproliferation drive. The history of the drive against horizontal nuclear proliferation has been outlined extensively in relation to the public efforts.[1] The task of this chapter is to focus on the expectations underlying the NPT and the developments after 1970.

Several points are central to an assessment of the NPT. First, as R. Imai points out, it was meant by its sponsors to be an intermediate condition to promote European security.[2] In particular it represented a U.S.-USSR consensus to put an international lid on the nuclear aspirations of the Federal Republic of Germany. Secondly, even though the treaty is touted as a major step in promoting international and regional security, it has little or nothing to say about Asian security. It makes sense primarily to those who view international affairs through American, Soviet, and European eyes. The NPT, like disarmament diplomacy, is about security, not peace. Peace refers to the absence of conflict and arms in interstate relations—security does not. Asian security involves, primarily, the use and threatened use of conventional arms in regions of conflict. The role of nuclear strategy is still evolving: (1) from possession of insecure nuclear force to its conversion into a secure second-strike force (in the case of China); (2) from possession of the nuclear option to its possible conversion into nuclear weapons (in the case of India); (3) from nonpossession of the nuclear option to its possible possession (in the case of Pakistan, South Korea, and Iran); and (4) from possession of advanced nuclear technology, materials, and equipment to possible decisions to "go nuclear militarily" if alliance relations and the strategic environment deteriorate (in the case of

Japan and Australia). By contrast, European international relations have evolved to the point that the military uses of nuclear weapons are becoming less relevant today. The trend in this direction should continue unless strategic conditions deteriorate in the coming years. In Europe, nationalism is being muted by the EEC experiment; in Asia, regional political and economic institutions have not taken shape (except for ASEAN)* and competition through nationalism and subnationalism is still the major driving force in the processes of political and social change within societies and in how societies deal with each other. In Europe, industrialism and consumerism require more economic and social change and less evidence of militarism; in Asia (except Australia) the renunciation of the military as a crucial component of nation building has yet to take place. The U.S.- USSR nuclear umbrellas are central in European military relations but this is not so in Asia, except for U.S. ties with Japan and Australia. Given such disparities in the evolution of political institutions and regimes, the NPT is not, and cannot be, a truly international document. The context or setting provided by Asia is too different from that of Europe. Even though European perspectives can be applied to Japan and Australia, what is relevant for these two nations is not relevant for other Asian societies. Also, whether the contemporary policies of Japan and Australia will persist during the 1980s and the 1990s is an open question.

Secondly, as B. Goldschmidt[3] points out, Article IV of the NPT encourages the world's nuclear trade but it favors the largest nuclear traders—the United States and the USSR—who still dominate the trade despite challenges by the nuclear industries of the Federal Republic of Germany, France, and Canada. In other words, the NPT regime is meant to stop or slow proliferation but it also assists the superpower nuclear trade. Consequently the commercial and the moral imperatives are hard to separate. The clash between the two motives is present in certain European perceptions of U.S. antiproliferation strategies and has been present in negotiations in the London–based Nuclear Suppliers Group (1974-) and in the Zangger Committee discussions (1970-). In other words, the NPT is not entirely an altruistic, other-directed, world-order proposition; it also has been, and still is, self-serving in a big way for the primary nuclear traders. It is noteworthy that the superpower promoters of the NPT do not sacrifice anything real militarily in their commitment to the NPT; furthermore, they gain commercially from the moral and legal

---

*Association of Southeast Asian Nations consisting of Indonesia, Singapore, Malaysia, Thailand, and the Philippines.

prescriptions of the NPT regime. The charge of hypocrisy and double standards is therefore a real one. The commercial motive should not be overstated but it also should not be understated.

Thirdly and finally, the NPT was really intended by some to be a statement of principles, rather than a list of definitions and procedures. There are two views on this interpretation. The first view is that, given the negotiating history from 1964 to 1968 in the Conference of the Committee on Disarmament (CCD) and elsewhere, each word in the treaty was carefully chosen; the NPT was meant to be the last word on the subject; the treaty codified a particular bargain between the NWS and the NNWS; the treaty emerged with a set of expectations.* In short, the NPT is seen as a legal instrument, a contractual obligation between NWS and NNWS. According to this view, in implementing the NPT one needs to go by its specific language, and deviations will undermine faith in the treaty.

The second view takes <u>parts</u> of the NPT as given and treats it as a useful starting point. But in fact, although not in words, this view has already repudiated the NPT as a whole while paying lip service to the NPT as the best instrument, the central mechanism to control proliferation. This view accepts Articles I, II, and III as the heart of the NPT. Article III of the treaty has been implemented, according to this view, through consultations and agreement on safeguards and the different trigger lists of the Zangger Committee and of the Nuclear Suppliers Group in 1974 and 1976 respectively. Proponents of this view, however, are not enthusiastic about implementing Articles IV and V, which deal with transfers of peaceful nuclear technology and with the establishment of an international PNE service respectively. Implementation of Article VI—where the NWS states state their intention of seeking disarmament, and particularly nuclear disarmament, at an early date—has also been pushed into the 1980s, assuming that SALT II gets negotiated and paves the way for SALT III. The implications of this approach are that the NPT is partly repudiated and by-passed (Articles IV-VI), and partly strengthened (Article III [1][b]) in its implementation. Finally, after the safeguards provisions of the treaty have been implemented, a new controversy has been raised by the antiproliferators. In the early 1970s, the NPT was the main instrument for

---

*Specifically this refers to the importance of denying the Federal Republic of Germany's national control over nuclear weapons; to encourage nuclear disarmament by the NWS; and to encourage peaceful technology transfers to NNWS in return for their renunciation of nuclear weapons.

nonproliferation.* The central premise was that nuclear transfers and nuclear trade were acceptable provided the transferred goods were safeguarded through international inspection. The post-NPT orientation emerged in 1975 and 1976 in the debate on nuclear exports. The NPT orientation was to discuss the conditions of nuclear supplies. The post-NPT orientation is to discuss restraints in supply of sensitive equipment and technology. The first orientation is based on the view that it implements the NPT. The second is based on the conviction that safeguards are not totally safe, the NPT is "best under the circumstances" but not good enough, and that nuclear suppliers need to slow, if not stop, transfers of sensitive nuclear technology and equipment. The new orientation is to stop or slow proliferation of reprocessing and enrichment technology and equipment even though the NPT does not prohibit these transfers provided they are safeguarded. A look at the evolution of the "NPT System" from 1970 to the antiproliferation drive of the Carter presidency is needed to provide the background.

POST-NPT DEVELOPMENTS

The NPT system refers to the regime initiated by the NPT in 1970. It is currently the principal instrument accepted by the international community, and particularly by the United States, the United Kingdom, and the USSR, to implement the goal of horizontal nonproliferation. France and the PRC have refused to sign the NPT. France claims that it will act as if it were a party to the NPT. This usually means that it will not supply nuclear exports without safeguards on the items involved. The practical effect of French policy is to implement Article I, which forbids a NWS to disseminate explosives technology or to encourage a nonnuclear weapon state to go nuclear. But it does not insist on Article II, which means that no state shall go nuclear in the future. The latter question is for each state to decide, according to France, and it is not for any other state to infringe on another state's sovereignty. France participated in the London-based Nuclear Suppliers Group but it did not insist on full-scope safeguards as the United States, the USSR, and Canada did.

---

*The NPT went into force on March 5, 1970. During the 1960s the main instruments for nonproliferation were a growing set of trilateral agreements (Supplier State/Customer/IAEA) or bilateral agreements (Receiver State/IAEA) based on the original IAEA safeguards system defined in INFCIRC/66.

At present France did not participate in the Zangger Committee (see discussion below).

The PRC also has stayed out of the NPT even though the practical effect of this is unclear. The PRC's practice is to favor proliferation verbally but it has not, so far, encouraged any of its allies—for example, Indonesia in the 1960s or Pakistan today—to advance their nuclear plans through PRC nuclear assistance. It is speculated that the PRC is a member of a joint board with Pakistan on atomic energy. Presumably under the auspices of this umbrella, PRC scientists have visited the Canada-supplied reactor complex near Karachi (KANUPP) and thereby gained access to CANDU technology. Whether this results, or is likely to result in the future, in a pay-off to Pakistan in the nuclear area is a matter for speculation.* Overall then, three of the five NWS formally adhere to the NPT and actively implement it and the remaining two oppose it verbally and implement it partially through their actions. The treaty enjoys considerable international support because of the large number of adherents but it is not a universally accepted document. Israel, India, Pakistan, Egypt, South Africa, Brazil, and Argentina, among others, have refused to adhere to the NPT even though they have not actively lobbied against it. The arguments of both the advocates and the detractors of the NPT continue to have merit in their particular contexts. The case for or against the NPT has never been settled and the treaty exists, therefore, without a genuine ideological consensus in the world community. If the number of states that are parties to the NPT is the criterion, the majority of the world community favors the NPT. On the other hand, however, if the population of the countries against the NPT is taken as the criterion, the bulk of the human population is against the NPT.

---

*According to the New York Times, September 11, 1977: "The Pakistanis told the French last week that if they did not fulfill their bargain 'other sources,' taken to mean China, a close Pakistani ally and a vigorous opponent of limitations on nuclear arms, would." Other reliable sources suggest that the PRC is not likely to be the "other source" because PRC proliferation advocacy is more talk than action. A more likely external source of help for Pakistan's reprocessing plans would be a combination of Libyan funding and acquisition of the cutting machine for the reprocessing plant from a West European source. It is estimated that in view of the cancellation of the French contract with Pakistan, the completion of Pakistan's reprocessing plant is likely to be delayed by at least two years; this is based on the assumption that the blueprints were delivered by France to Pakistan under the contract.

The NPT itself is neither dead nor alive, but the system that carries its name has evolved since 1970 in a manner that partly repudiates the NPT and by-passes its provisions, partly implements certain treaty provisions, and partly goes beyond those provisions. At present, pending the implementation in any measurable manner of Article VI of the NPT (stating that the NWS shall negotiate in good faith toward nuclear disarmament), this article stands repudiated, if one shares the pessimistic view that the SALT dialogue is not likely to lead to arms reduction until the 1980s at the earliest. Article IV calls for the peaceful uses of nuclear energy and an acceleration of peaceful energy transfers from the NWS and the IAEA to the developing countries. If the complaint of states like Yugoslavia and the Philippines has merit, this provision of the NPT also remains unfulfilled, as does the provision to establish an international peaceful explosive service (Article V of the NPT).

The NPT system has seen a subtle yet fundamental transformation. The changes appeal to the treaty supporters while its detractors think that the changes are inadequate or go in the wrong direction. The implementation of the treaty started with the work of the Safeguards Committee (1970-71).[4] Table 1.2 identifies the scope and the location of the committee in the evolving scheme to strengthen the safeguards function of the IAEA and the responsibilities of the parties to the NPT. At the same time, because of the recognition that the NPT did not go far enough with regard to safeguards and supply conditions, since 1970 a small group of states first met as the Zangger Committee and thereafter as the Nuclear Suppliers Group. Table 3.1 shows the membership of the two groups.

France, however, did not join the Zangger Committee discussions, because the meetings were an offshoot of Article III (2) of the NPT and France had ideologically rejected the NPT. The group drew its name from its chairman, Professor Claude Zangger of the Swiss Federal Office of Energy in Berne. The British Embassy in Vienna serves as the secretariat of the Zangger Committee. This group derived its mandate from a wish to implement Article III (2) of the NPT, which called for negotiations to establish conditions of supply of nuclear equipment and materials. The details of this committee are discussed later in this chapter. The scope and location of the Zangger Committee is identified in Table 1.2. The Zangger group was essentially, and still is, a discussion (negotiation) and reporting mechanism on members' export policies. It does not have a decision-making focus and is not likely to have one. It reports before April every year. It does not have any formal relationship with the London suppliers' group although the Zangger Committee was a jumping-off point for most (but not all) of the members who joined the suppliers' group. The Zangger Committee's work has been extended until at least 1978.

TABLE 3.1

Members of the Zangger Committee and the Nuclear Suppliers Group

Zangger Committee	Nuclear Suppliers Group

Present members:
  Australia
  Austria
  Belgium
  Canada
  CSSR
  Denmark
  Finland
  Federal Republic of Germany
  German Democratic Republic
  Ireland
  Italy
  Japan
  Luxembourg
  Netherlands
  Norway
  Poland
  Sweden
  Switzerland
  United Kingdom
  United States
  USSR
  South Africa
    (observer status)
	Original members:
	  United States
	  USSR
	  France
	  United Kingdom
	  Canada
	  Japan
	  Federal Republic of Germany
	
	Subsequent additions:
	  German Democratic Republic
	  Poland
	  Czechoslovakia
	  Belgium
	  Netherlands
	  Italy
	  Sweden
	  Switzerland
	
	Probable new members:
	  Australia
	  Austria
	
	After new members join, then enlargement by adding threshold countries to get a balanced relationship is possible, following a review initiated in 1975 of the basic suppliers document. This review was completed in 1976 and made public in 1978.

Source: Compiled by the author.

South Africa was dropped from the suppliers' group (formed in 1975) because of Soviet objections on ideological grounds. France, however, joined the suppliers' group because its initial task, strictly speaking, was to secure a consensus on imposing conditions for nuclear supply. Theoretically, it was not to be a closed group. Any nation could join it to define conditions of nuclear supply and nuclear trade. Still, practically, the suppliers' group has suffered from a major and perhaps natural limitation—a stigma of secrecy. On one hand, secrecy is needed and membership of a group should be kept small if quick results in controversial matters are to be achieved. But on the other hand, decision making by a small, and at times unrepresentative, elite group, with self-serving interests, can become counterproductive. The Zangger Committee discussions that led to the suppliers' group consensus were never submitted to the scrutiny of the membership of the IAEA. Hence it was never truly an international document that commanded the respect of the world community. The secrecy and the elitist nature of the Zangger Committee and the suppliers' group led the latter, in 1975, to take steps to review its proceedings with a view to making them public and expanding the membership. The review was carried out inconclusively during 1976 and the exercise is now complete. The basic guidelines were approved for publication in the September 1977 meeting but the group failed to accept the notion of full-scope safeguards when the guidelines were made public in February 1978. This topic was to be taken up later in 1978 but as of the time of writing no progress has been made.

Still, in retrospect, the Zangger Committee and the suppliers' group represented a new ideology and a new mechanism to help in moving toward the goal of nonproliferation. True, these mechanisms did not forbid PNEs by NNWS, as did the NPT. The question of PNEs was not a part of either group's agenda because its composition was of like-minded states who all believed in nonproliferation, in the NPT, and in nuclear exports. Of course, not all members of the suppliers' group were actually suppliers. For example, Japan, Czechoslovakia, Poland, Sweden, and the Netherlands are involved in the group on the basis of their qualities of likemindedness and their commitment to nonproliferation, and not because of their present supply capacity. Both groups functioned on the notion that a small and select membership was needed to make progress. In the suppliers' group, the demand for secrecy came particularly from the USSR and France, each for a different reason. The former wanted to hide its undemocratic behavior and the image of collaboration with the capitalists in a trade that involved discrimination against Third World states. France wanted to mask its public rejection of the NPT, which was coupled with a willingness to implement the NPT privately, without the glare of public scrutiny.

The ideological consensus of the two groups was rooted in the NPT, namely, that there was to be no dissemination of nuclear exports without tight safeguards. Nevertheless, the ideological consensus also contained a major ideological split about the level of safeguards to be required on exports. The first type of safeguards deals with safeguarding the "end use" of items supplied by a foreign supplier.* Suppliers, recipients, and the IAEA accept these safeguards. These require safeguarding of the entire peaceful nuclear industry of the recipient. In the suppliers' group the following states advocate the acceptance of full-scope safeguards: the United Kingdom, the USSR, Sweden, the Netherlands, Canada, and the United States. But there is no consensus on full-scale safeguards. The third type of safeguards seeks as conditions of nuclear exports that there be no more reprocessing or enrichment by the recipient, and that re-exports also be safeguardable and subject to prior consent. Advocates of this position are not talking simply about the safeguardability of nuclear exports. Instead their focus has shifted to a new approach, namely, restraining particular types of nuclear exports and reprocessing and enrichment. Included in the former approach is the promotion of nuclear exports provided these are safeguarded. According to the last approach, sensitive exports are to be restricted, on the grounds that safeguards are no longer sufficient.

Two variations of proposals for the third type of safeguards exist. The existence of the variations points to the absence of an ideological consensus even among the hardliners against proliferation. The first variation is expressed by Carter's April 27, 1977 proposed bill to Congress, which sought to discourage—strongly—reprocessing and enrichment by recipients of nuclear exports. This move is directed against Euratom states and Japan, as well as against states like Brazil, Pakistan, and India who are outside the NPT. Because it was directed in part against Euratom, the bill had the effect of bringing France into the picture even though it is a NWS. The second variation is expressed by Canada. Canada does not favor proliferation of reprocessing capabilities in threshold states, but its objection is to uneconomical reprocessing plants (as in Pakistan) rather than to economical ones (as in Japan, the Federal Republic of Germany, and France). Presumably the Canadian stance is open to discussion in practice on a case-by-case basis.

---

*INFCIRC/66 safeguards were facility-oriented safeguards and before India's 1974 nuclear test required "peaceful use" of the safeguarded facility. A problem with these safeguards was that defining "peaceful use" exactly is difficult, and the safeguards are not comprehensive over the entire nuclear industry.

The Zangger Committee is an informal, secret, and impersonal committee. It has played a prominent role in implementing Article III (2) of the NPT and yet its origin and evolution is hardly known. An examination of this committee's work sheds light on the nuances of multilateral nonproliferation diplomacy. The discussions in this committee paved the way for the Nuclear Suppliers Group. It is useful to have a sense of the recent past as a basis for understanding contemporary trends and possibilities for the future. The committee's work has ongoing linkages with the work of other multilateral organs like the Suppliers Club, although there are also important differences. An examination of this committee, therefore, can be useful as a basis for assessing and comparing the work of different organs dealing with nonproliferation. Such an assessment can be helpful in indicating the ideological parameters and the limitations of the group in question. The primary task here is to focus on group outcomes rather than on the use of the group in the foreign policy and security behavior of its members. The latter task is worthwhile but beyond the scope of this work.

The NPT came into force in March 1970, and the question of the adherence of Switzerland to the NPT was raised in December 1969. In Berne, Switzerland, a question arose about the meaning of Article III of the NPT. Professor C. Zangger, deputy director of the Swiss Federal Office of Energy, was (and still is) in charge of the international work of the Office of Energy and was asked to inquire about Article III. As a participant in the Safeguards Committee of the IAEA (1970-71), he was involved in deliberations with regard to Article III (1) of the NPT. He proposed a get-together of 14 industrialized countries to discuss Article III (2)(b). The zero meeting (to plan a working meeting) was held on July 22, 1970 and included Austria, Belgium, Canada, Denmark, France, the Federal Republic of Germany, Italy, Japan, the Netherlands, Norway, Sweden, Switzerland, the United Kingdom, and the United States.

The zero meeting's first purpose was to define the real content of Article III (2)(b), concerning exports of nuclear equipment. This clarification was important for several reasons: to avoid the danger of distortion, and to avoid the risk of exploitation of safeguards by NPT parties to gain commercial advantage. The 14 states were invited and were participants in the first meeting (March 11, 1971). France attended the zero meeting as well as the first meeting. The principal task was to examine the scope of equipment to be controlled. (There was some sentiment, on the part of Switzerland, Austria, and Sweden, in favor of involving the USSR in the committee's work right at the beginning. Others, however, wanted to bring the USSR in after the work started; the idea was first to get the consensus among Western states and only then to involve the USSR.)

The first extension of the group concerned Australia and South Africa and was motivated by the second purpose: to define the real content of Article III (1)(b), concerning exports of nuclear materials. By September 1972 both these states were participating in the committee but South Africa's official status was that of an observer. By June 1972 the work of the committee was in principle completed and the Zangger Memorandum, in two secret parts, was drafted to cover the supply conditions with respect to materials and equipment. Since 1974 the public part of the Zangger Memorandum has been known as INFCIRC/209. Still secret is the reporting mechanism whereby members of the committee communicate details of their nuclear exports to each other so that national reporting can function as a basis of unilateral verification of compliance with the supply conditions agreed to by members of the committee. The system of providing annual returns has been in effect for some countries since 1974. In practice the reporting mechanism is based on trust. There is no formal verification mechanism and no central evaluation. Given the ideological diversity of the committee membership, the willingness to share such information seems to be a step forward in interstate cooperation across East-West-European neutral state lines.

After the completion of the Zangger Memorandum in 1972, three questions arose. First, France was involved in the zero and the first meetings but, being a non-NPT state, did not feel entitled to influence the work of the committee. As such it asked to receive the minutes of the meeting and to decide on a case-by-case basis about adherence to the committee's work. France did not attend the committee after the first meeting and is not committed to the work of the committee.

Secondly, it was necessary to get the members' reactions to the June 1972 memorandum and there was enough support to warrant enthusiasm. Except for the moves made toward France and the USSR (see below), the only other activity during 1972-74 was the making of two decisions: members would approach the director-general of the IAEA and would start to report their nuclear exports to each other.

By June 1973, apart from inducing France to play the game, the other problem was to induce the USSR and East European countries to enter the committee or to accept the content of the Zangger Memorandum. Moscow was probably not informed about earlier Zangger Committee meetings and so its reactions were slow. It was necessary for Professor Zangger and his British secretary to explain the basis of the memorandum, especially the part dealing with nuclear equipment supply conditions. After back-and-forth discussions in June 1974 Moscow approved the content of the memorandum, but it also made proposals regarding interpretations. The interpretations in the letters to the director-general of the IAEA (discussed below) are Soviet in origin. In the summer of 1974, when Moscow agreed to play the game, it was not clear whether the USSR would participate in the committee's work. The other members wished that it would. The last official meeting of the committee before INFCIRC/209 was finalized was in June 1974. Moscow did not participate in this meeting. The first time Moscow participated in the Zangger Committee was in February 1977, that is, after Soviet participation in the London-based Nuclear Suppliers Group. Moscow's acceptance of the Zangger Memorandum in 1974 is clear, but the extent of its participation in the committee work in 1977 is unclear.

With Soviet support, the committee considered making the formal step to adopt the Zangger Memorandum. It was agreed that members of the committee would write to the director-general. Not every member-state could adopt the same obligations at the same time. In separate but nearly identical letters (with interpretations in certain cases), the first series of letters (also known as the Zangger trigger lists) were sent and published in August 1974. This is now known as INFCIRC/209 with additions of subsequent communications. Certain member-states accepted the supply conditions at the time they wrote to the director-general of the IAEA because their laws contained the legal basis for doing so. Other member-states, however, promised to implement the commitments at a later date.

South Africa's role in the committee is interesting. It was not in the committee at the outset because it was invited to join in 1972 at the first enlargement of the committee. Since 1972, South Africa has remained officially an observer but has participated actively in the committee's work. Because it has not signed the NPT it did not accept the Zangger trigger lists. With the political and military background of the Paris-Pretoria nuclear supply links, South Africa's presence generated some tension in the committee, but an attempt was made, apparently successfully, to keep nontechnical aspects in the corridors. Still, it is a measure of Pretoria's strategic perceptions and bargaining strategy that its position remained ambiguous—in terms of its observer status in the committee and in terms of its unwillingness to commit itself to the Zangger Memorandum. At the same time, however, Pretoria's participation is a useful point of contact between an "international outlaw" and industrial democracies. It is reasonable to argue that Pretoria should not be driven into complete isolation to the point that it feels it has nothing to lose by "going nuclear." On the other hand, Pretoria was on notice by the Zangger Committee (since September

1976) to decide whether it wants to play the game, to clarify whether it is in or out. South Africa's ouster from the Board of Governors of the IAEA in 1976-77 was an obvious psychological and political blow. To nonproliferation advocates the move was ill-timed, because Pretoria was on the verge then of signing the NPT and placing its enrichment plant under safeguards. However, even in the spring of 1977—after its ouster from the board of governors—there were private indications that Pretoria may decide to adopt the Zangger recommendations. At present, therefore, there is evidence of movement on the issue but nothing is finalized yet. Nothing happened at the October 1977 meeting of the Zangger Committee.

These "209" letters represented the first major breakthrough in the effort to get the principal nuclear suppliers to accept the notion of establishing common conditions for the supply of nuclear equipment and materials. The basic idea was that competition among nuclear suppliers ought not to lead to a relaxation of supply conditions to the detriment of the nonproliferation effort. The Zangger trigger lists did not deny the need for nuclear export; they only sought to establish the criteria for nuclear exports. The lists served a principal nonproliferation aim because they sought to impose safeguards conditions on supplies that could be used for nuclear explosive purposes. In a sense, India's peaceful test of May 1974 contributed, in part, to closing off the loophole in many nuclear supply agreements that, prior to 1974, made nuclear supplies conditional on peaceful purposes but left open the possibility of a peaceful nuclear explosion. After the Indian test, among nuclear suppliers willing to accept the trigger lists, the prohibition was against nuclear weapons and nuclear explosives uses. The loophole of PNEs was, therefore, closed by the 1974 trigger lists.* As such, these lists can be viewed as an evolution of bilateral and multilateral nuclear supply agreements.

---

*The impact of India's 1974 test on the Zangger Committee, however, should not be overestimated, because the basic documents were accepted in principle before India's test. The June 1974 meeting was the key meeting because a decision was made then to go forward to adopt formally the Zangger trigger lists. India's test was in May 1974. Undoubtedly it lent an urgency to the committee's work. By May 1974 the committee was ready because the USSR had signaled its approval of the Zangger Memorandum of 1972, and most members of the committee wanted to get the USSR and other Eastern countries into the committee's work as a condition of going forward themselves. The motivation was a desire to generate nondiscrimination in the nuclear market, to get the countries committed to avoid competition on safeguards.

The task of implementing the trigger lists, however, was not easy. It was easier to negotiate new nuclear supply agreements using the trigger lists as a basis. It was, however, a difficult, and in some cases an impossible, task to renegotiate retroactively pre-1974 agreements. Confrontation was possible if contractual obligations were unilaterally changed by the suppliers vis-à-vis politically sensitive nuclear buyers. There was also the question of credibility of the nuclear suppliers if old contractual agreements could be altered at will by the supplier. In 1976 the London Agreement expanded the trigger list contents. Table 3.2 gives comparative assessment of the evolving suppliers' regime.

A number of general observations about the Zangger Committee and the Nuclear Suppliers Club should be made to offer a perspective about the scope and limitations of these suppliers' groups in relation to the NPT. Lessons for other suppliers' groups (say, in the matter of negotiating restraints in conventional arms exports) may also be noted.

1. In the Zangger Committee it was relatively easy to establish the trigger list of materials requiring safeguards but it was hard to establish the trigger list of equipment for safeguards purposes. The types of equipment offered by the nuclear exporters complicated the issue. Canada was selling heavy water reactors; the United States was selling light water reactors (LWR); and the issue of exporting of breeder reactors was raised. Each reactor type contained components that had to be on a certain list. The precise meaning of the words "especially designed" in Article III (2)(b) of the NPT was difficult to define. The solution agreed upon in INFCIRC/209 was to list the different pieces of equipment that all members agreed were "especially designed." But not all issues were resolved, and there are differences that are still pending in the Zangger Committee minutes. For instance, heavy water exports were on the trigger list but heavy water plants were excluded, and there was general unanimity on the latter point in the committee in 1972. The question of heavy water plants has, however, been revived in the Zangger Committee. The committee seems to be divided over whether heavy water plant exports need to be safeguarded in terms of Article III (2)(b) of the NPT. As mentioned above, the committee has been extended up to at least 1978. Apart from the question of upgrading enrichment-related trigger items, the question of heavy water plants requires a decision. A larger question is posed: Should the Zangger Committee's work stay within the scope of the NPT provisions, or should it go beyond the NPT as the London group has already done? Should the Zangger Committee take in as much as possible? There may be a decision not to take in as much as possible,

TABLE 3.2

Suppliers' Group Activity

INFCIRC/209 of 1974 (public version of secret Zangger Memorandum, 1974	London Agreement, 1976 (guidelines published in 1978)
seeks to implement the NPT (Article III [2][b])	seeks to go beyond the NPT
stresses the NPT obligations of NPT parties who are also the major nuclear suppliers	stresses the antiproliferation obligations of the NPT states and particularly of the great powers
views the NPT as the terminal condition, which first requires an implementation of the NPT bargain (namely, the balance between Articles III and IV, and between Articles II and VI); sees the NPT as the framework for negotiating a balance between nuclear supply and nuclear safeguards relations	avoids a specific commitment to implementing these bargains and at least puts the debate about bargains aside; views the NPT as the starting point for establishing a nuclear suppliers' consensus against particular supplies to potential horizontal proliferators
stresses agreement about the conditions of supply, including reprocessing and enrichment technology transfers and equipment sales	requires suppliers not to offer sensitive equipment and technology relating to reprocessing and enrichment. So the focus is on strengthening, through a multilaterized regime, the existing unilateral restrictions on supplies rather than on strengthening the safeguards conditions of supplies including sensitive items
is satisfied with the acceptance of IAEA safeguards instead of the full-scope NPT safeguards; hence absolutism and rigidity are avoided	is motivated by a concern to move toward full-scope safeguards, but at present the suppliers have failed to reach consensus on this point
sees the importance of fulfilling treaty obligations; hence stresses the role of the NPT as an international legal instrument where the bargain must be kept	views the NPT as a political rather than a legal instrument because circumstances underlying NPT negotiations in the mid- to late 1960s changed in the 1970s; hence there is a need to strengthen the antiproliferation regime that covers the NPT's weaknesses, that is, its withdrawal clause
stresses the role of trust	downplays the role of trust in nuclear matters

Source: Compiled by the author.

with the exception of heavy water plants. One objection against safe-guarding of heavy water plants is that it opens up the question of safeguarding production of uranium pellets, fabrication of fuel elements, production of nuclear-grade graphite, and so on. The question of light water pumps is also still pending in the minutes of the committee. The question of heat exchangers was also raised but it was argued that if this item was included, then for boiling water reactors the turbines would also have to be included.

2. The London Nuclear Suppliers Club takes the Zangger trigger lists as its starting point, but the London lists give more specificity to the definition of uranium enrichment items. Consequently, in the February 1977 review meeting of the Zangger Committee some members who are in both groups sought to upgrade the Zangger lists and to bring these into line with the 1976 London trigger lists. This upgrading was accepted at the October 1977 meeting of the Zangger Committee. INFCIRC/209 is specific enough with regard to reprocessing that upgrading in this area was not needed.

3. In the NPT, nuclear technology and scientific knowledge is not safeguarded. Leaving aside the question of whether it should be, there is the question of whether it can be, given that there is no easy way to safeguard the human brain against learning. As early as 1972, Canada made a plea to safeguard and control technology transfers in the trigger lists but the idea was rejected by the Zangger Committee. Still, the issue of controlling and safeguarding technology transfers has been dealt with at the London Club.

4. Functionally the Zangger Committee and the London Club are connected. The former has given shape to the NPT. The latter has sought to eliminate the loopholes in the NPT. The problem of technology transfer has been noted. But there is another major legal loophole in the NPT. Article III (2)(a) and (b) triggers safeguards on all materials and equipment in customer states on supplies that are exported but not on the entire peaceful nuclear industry. The London Club has tried to fill such loopholes but the guidelines of the London* Club contradict NPT rights. For example, Article IV of the NPT permits uranium enrichment and plutonium reprocessing if safeguards are accepted by the NNWS. But one guideline in the London trigger list (1976) urges restraints on exports of heavy water plants,* and on exports of enrichment and reprocessing capacity. These guidelines (the first draft) were finalized in November 1975—one year before the Carter election campaign. Consequently, they should not be viewed solely as a Carter contribution to the new nonproliferation strategy.

---

*This was in particular a Canadian idea.

5. The work of the Zangger Committee seems to be on firm legal ground because its purpose is to implement the NPT, whereas the London Club has deliberately deviated in a big way from the NPT. Both committees suffer from the image of secrecy and "back room dealings" that take place without public scrutiny by the world community. The Zangger Committee has minutes of its work, and if the decision to publicize its work were ever made its deliberations could be opened to public inspection. On the other hand, the London Club keeps no minutes and its past history is known only on an oral basis to participating member-states. Only the guidelines (initially leaked in the press but not made public until 1978), the basic document, and proposed amendments have been under review; these were published in 1978. A move has been under way since 1975 to finalize the basic document of the London Club, to make it public, and to enlarge the club on the condition that the new members accept the basic document. One way to enlarge would be to ask all members of the Zangger Committee to join the London Club. Another way to enlarge would be to ask important customer states to join the club. This might be preferable because the invitation would avoid the discrimination between NWS and NNWS that is inherent in the NPT. On the other hand, incoming customer states (for example, Brazil and India) might wish to renegotiate the basic document and inject new ideological parameters into the technical discussions. The addition to the club of newcomers to the nuclear materials market—such as Gabon and Niger—may be easier than that of old customer states who are not presently in the club.

Overall, the evolution of the NPT regime is rooted in a number of circumstances. The fear of horizontal proliferation is the obvious motive for the development of the regime. The need perceived by the three nuclear weapon states (the United States, the USSR, and the United Kingdom) is to strengthen international controls over the nuclear industry of NNWS through stronger safeguards. The underlying premise is that international inspection can lead to verification of national claims about peaceful nonexplosive activities; and verification can, through fear of detection and of possible international sanction, lead to prevention of a diversion from peaceful to military uses. The approach is to convert a unilateral claim of an intent not to make nuclear weapons or other explosive devices into a legal commitment through adherence to the NPT or the IAEA regime. Many NPT parties still prefer to see universal adherence to the NPT even though it is recognized that the NPT is a discriminatory document and hence politically objectionable, notably to several Third World societies. Given that NPT safeguards are weak because an NPT party can withdraw from the treaty on national security grounds, the general aim is to bring as much of the world's nuclear industry as possible, outside that of the NWS, under international control. This approach to nonproliferation is rooted in discussions of the mid-1960s. But it is also true that the general fear of proliferation was radicalized by the Indian test and led to activity to promote NPT safeguards.

Nonetheless the NPT regime has never been able to escape the fact that it lacks an ideological consensus; that is, there is no real community interest between its adherents and its principal opponents. The demand for NPT safeguards emphasizes the need for a contractual obligation in a one-sided manner; in legal and practical terms, the nuclear have-nots do the giving and the nuclear haves do the receiving. Political trust as a basis of interstate relations and for community building is downgraded. The NNWS have been treated as the objects of control by the NWS, with the exception of the PRC, which is not known to offer nuclear aid and has denounced the NPT.

Two variations of the control mechanism have evolved. The NPT/IAEA safeguards emerged directly out of the NPT. Since the NPT safeguards could not apply to those who did not sign the NPT, a distinction emerged between the much more stringent NPT safeguards (where the entire nuclear industry of the treaty signer is safeguarded) and the facility-oriented IAEA safeguards for the non-NPT parties. Given the contrast, a pressure has grown to upgrade IAEA safeguards and bring these into line with the NPT safeguards. The demand for an upgrading comes from the NPT parties, particularly from the NWS. It is facilitated by the fact that the IAEA administers both NPT and IAEA safeguards, although there are two different regimes to administer as far as their scope is concerned. The first variation, therefore, is to cause acceptance of the safeguards on the entire nuclear industry of NNWS by inducing acceptance of the NPT.

The second variation in the evolving NPT regime shifts the focus but the purpose is the same: to safeguard the nuclear industry of states other than the five NWS. The second approach is a product of the early 1970s. Although it is an elitist exercise, to describe it as a cartel is inaccurate. It commenced as a grouping of a few like-minded states who believed in nonproliferation. Its aim was to regulate the nuclear competition among the nuclear suppliers. Its aim was not originally to cast a judgment on the political wisdom of particular nuclear export. That would violate national sovereignty. Instead, it established supply conditions for particular items where supplies or exports would automatically involve safeguards. The selection of the items that made up the lists (called the Trigger Lists of 1976) was the result of interstate bargaining. The Suppliers Group was important because it was able to bring France into its deliberations even though France has never signed the NPT. Presumably the French declaration that it would behave as if it had signed the NPT was useful; presumably, it was enough to provide a starting point for giving contractual shape to French policy. This acknowledgment that the unilateral policy declaration of a state is a tentative substitute for accepting a contractual obligation by signing the NPT is itself a precedent.

The London Nuclear Suppliers Group is not a cartel because it is not in the business of dividing up the world's market among its members; nor does it establish a price structure. Instead, the aim is to preclude lowering of safeguards standards, which could help nuclear buyers, particularly the NNWS outside the NPT, to hasten their nuclear weapons developments. The group functions on the basis of consensus. The final version of its basic document was published in the beginning of 1978. So far its work is a product of the minimum consensus. The club members have failed to agree on the necessity of full-scope safeguards. France and the Federal Republic of Germany, as major exporters to Brazil and Pakistan, believed in minimum controls over nuclear exports; their position reflected their concerns. Canada, the United States, and the USSR, on the other hand, believe in full-scope safeguards even though their theory and their practice may vary. For instance, Moscow agreed to supply India with 200 tons of heavy water after Canada cancelled a similar deal with India. India was sent 50 tons of heavy water on the condition that India negotiate a safeguards agreement. In September 1977, negotiations resulted in a safeguards agreement for the end use of the heavy water. Oddly enough, Soviet supplies reached India before the safeguards were negotiated. Apparently, the left hand and the right hand of the Soviet bureaucracy are not well coordinated. One hand stresses nonproliferation concerns but the other hand stresses Indo-Soviet bilateral relations.

The group was stung by criticism about the secrecy surrounding its work and there was a move within the group to make its work public and to expand the group. Since 1975 the group has been reviewing its basic document; this review was completed in September 1977. It is possible that the group would be expanded. It is unclear whether acceptance of the NPT is the precondition for the new members and whether the group is to be changed into some sort of group of suppliers and buyers. If adherence to the NPT is not required (as it was not of France) for the new members, there is still the requirement that NNWS place their entire nuclear industry under safeguards. This problem does not apply to French membership in the group because it is a NWS in terms of the NPT. This point could, therefore, pose a problem for prospective members who have chosen to stay outside the NPT.

The thrust of the first variation is to get the NNWS to accept the NPT, through threats, cajolery, or pressure. The thrust of the second variation is to make the nuclear supply relationship an instrument of nonproliferation, by inducing dependency through a supply relationship; thus this variation makes cooperation among nuclear suppliers a basis for achieving nonproliferation. Whether such a supply dependency can be made permanent is, however, an open question.

Overall then, regulating the conditions of nuclear exports and inducing universal acceptance of the NPT or at least its principal provisions are the principal avenues for strengthening the NPT regime. The first method requires the cooperation of the nonparties of the NPT. The second method relies exclusively on cooperation among the nuclear suppliers. Both methods stress the central importance of strengthening international safeguards—and enlarging the role of the IAEA—in controlling, stopping, or slowing proliferation. If one thinks of policy perceptions, interests, and motives as the "front end" of nuclear proliferation, and existing and future technology as the "tail end" of proliferation, the NPT regime tries to control the tail end. The regime does not attack the front end—that is, the sources of insecurity that lead to nuclear proliferation.

These approaches—namely, universalizing the appeal of the NPT, widening the net of international safeguards on the peaceful nuclear industry of nonparties to the NPT, and securing cooperation among nuclear suppliers with regard to supply conditions and restrictions in supplies—were the principal achievements of the advocates of nonproliferation through the NPT regime. This mix of strategy prevailed up until the end of 1976, when a new administration took over in Washington and other developments occurred. Carter criticized, as a candidate, the Ford-Kissinger nonproliferation policy. But even before Carter stated his views on nuclear and foreign policy,[5] Congressional hearings and the U.S. press had started a nuclear debate in the United States in 1975.* The debate was still without conclusions when the Carter regime came to power, but it had shaped the principal parameters of the debate. On one side of the spectrum were the views of the House International Relations Committee, National Regulatory Commissioner (NRC) Victor Gilinsky, University of Chicago Professor Albert Wohlstetter, Hudson Institute futurologist Herman Kahn, and U.S. Arms Control

---

*The Senate Government Operations Committee and the House International Relations Committee took a lead in debating nonproliferation issues.

and Disarmament Agency Director Fred Ikle. This group was very skeptical of the need for reprocessing of plutonium, and it was obviously skeptical of PNEs. The other side of the spectrum consisted of the lonely voice of Dixie Lee Ray, chairman of the U.S. Atomic Energy Commission and subsequently a member of the Department of State. Dr. Ray took the view that there was no problem about nuclear energy. No one of any consequence admitted to holding such an opinion. Even the U.S. nuclear industry would not take this view. The centrist and the dominant position in 1976 reflected the Congressional debate in the House and the Senate during 1975-76 and revealed its impact on candidate Carter's nuclear policy. The Carter philosophy is discussed briefly below and in Chapter 4. The new orientation was revealed in Secretary of State Kissinger's UN speech on September 30, 1976 and in President Ford's statement of October 26, 1976. The new orientation expressed a concern against national reprocessing in the Third World and proposed the development of regional nuclear fuel cycle centers. It banned reprocessing in the United States for three years. Reprocessing advocates in the Energy Research and Development Administration were unhappy with the Ford announcement.

The 1975-76 Washington debate became international after Carter became president. It could be seen that Carter the candidate and Carter the president had the same views on nuclear policy. The Carter announcement of April 1977 confirmed Ford's three-year ban on U.S. reprocessing and thereby sought to set an example against the plutonium fuel cycle. The Carter thrust was not simply against national reprocessing centers. The Kissinger-Ford policy had sought to meet this problem by proposing regional multilateral fuel cycle centers. The Carter thrust was against further reprocessing. In this respect it went beyond the Ford-Kissinger plan. It proposed measures of three different types. First, it sought to undo the export of reprocessing and enrichment capabilities from the Federal Republic of Germany to Brazil, and to prevent the export of the French reprocessing plant to Pakistan. Secondly, it sought to ban reprocessing and the plutonium technology, including fast breeders in the Third World, and also repudiated the Ford-Kissinger proposal for regional reprocessing fuel cycle centers. Finally, and perhaps more importantly, it sought to slow down, if not end, the reprocessing and fast breeder developments among several of its principal allies—namely, Japan, the Federal Republic of Germany, France, and the United Kingdom.

1976 was important not only because it revealed a new orientation in nonproliferation policy in Washington. It also signaled a new orientation in Canadian behavior and enhanced the prospect of active cooperation between the United States and Canada in this area. Still, on the reprocessing question, the Canadian and the U.S. attitudes varied. Canada kept an open mind about reprocessing whereas in the American official policy this was a closed issue. Canada was willing to discuss the reprocessing question on a case-by-case basis, arguing that reprocessing that was economical was justified whereas uneconomical reprocessing activity was suspect and ought to be prevented or penalized. Secondly, Canada's enthusiasm for nonproliferation was greater than that of the United States, given that Canada found itself burdened with the self-inflicted guilt for the Indian test of May 1974. Public opinion in Canada had tied the hands of Canadian politicians more than they had expected or wished for. Indeed, it was arguable that Canadian commitment to nonproliferation went deeper into the past than did the American commitment. In the Zangger group discussions, Canada had clamored for more control over nuclear technology and, in part, it took the Indian test to put some momentum into the U.S. nonproliferation policy. The pre-1974 Canadian and U.S. attitudes toward nonproliferation, therefore, were in strong contrast.

In December 1976 the Canadian government placed a moratorium on uranium exports to Japan and Euratom countries pending negotiations of its new policy, which required that joint consent of the seller and the buyer be obtained concerning the end use of uranium supplies. Negotiations with Japan and other countries were prolonged, complicated, and eventually the product of a bargain. The concerns of each side were met through a formula indicating temporary agreement pending further discussions in a bilateral and multilateral setting. The implications of the "joint consent" clause were far reaching. It added a new dimension to the nonproliferation debate. For countries that adhered to the NPT and thereby accepted safeguards on all their peaceful nuclear industry, the clause meant that the enrichment and reprocessing of uranium supplies provided by Canada and the United States could be open to a veto by the suppliers. In other words, Japanese, German, and French reprocessing plants (and those of other Euratom states) could become subject to decisions in Ottawa and Washington. This limitation clearly was beyond those of the NPT.

The purpose of the proposed limitation was unclear. Skeptical Germans asked why it was necessary to have this clause when the entire German nuclear industry was safeguarded and open to IAEA inspection. The Japanese asked how the United States could slow or even stop the production at the reprocessing plant when that plant had been built with U.S. consent and even encouragement preceding the arrival of Carter. Indians had similar questions about Tarapur because its reprocessing capacity had been developed with the aid, advice, assistance, and encouragement of the U.S. administrations before Carter. These instances revealed that the nonproliferation exercise in the United States and Canada was reaching a point where even NPT safeguards were apparently not enough, and unilateral controls resting in Washington and Ottawa were needed as additional guarantees. The latter approach was problematic. It made nuclear exports subject to the political whims of new leaders with new or different constituencies. These leaders felt they were not necessarily subject to the discipline and commitment of their predecessors; consequently they were willing to repudiate the contractual obligations of previous governments. In other words, while nuclear buyers were being asked to accept irrevocable contractual commitments beyond those of the NPT, the nuclear suppliers retained by definition their freedom to maneuver freely, interpreting the old agreements according to their perceptions rather than according to specific and commonly understood criteria accepted by both sides.

The Carter policy of April 1977 raised more questions than it provided answers. First, it raised the touchy issue of style, namely, whether the bureaucracy in the new administration had become a victim or a willing tool of Carter's moral philosophy, and whether it had failed to consult U.S. allies adequately in matters that affected their economic and political well-being. For Japan reprocessing was an economic question and not one of abstract political sovereignty; it lacks energy sources of its own and its dependence on nuclear energy is likely to grow. Similar considerations applied to the other, European allies of the United States. Secondly, there was the question of whether Carter's initiative had backfired. All the states involved were quick to repudiate Carter's call to decide against plutonium technology. Thirdly, Carter's policy raised doubts over whether his analysis of the situation and the prescribed solution were motivated entirely by moral and nonproliferation considerations. Carter's critics noted that if plutonium technology were slowed, or banned through a moratorium, the policy might have two effects. Given that European developments in reprocessing and fast breeders were ahead of American technology, the moratorium might enable the United States to catch up with its competitors in Europe and Japan. Furthermore, a moratorium would enable the United States temporarily to continue its lead in light water reactors; these worked on enriched uranium supplies from the United States primarily. That is, a double dependence on the U.S. reactor type and U.S. nuclear fuel seemed to be an implication of the Carter stance. Even if Carter's policy initiative is viewed as sincere, it is hard to deny that the commercial motive was a secondary or associated factor. Finally, Carter's critics noted that his April 1977 initiative had overshadowed the work of the Nuclear Suppliers Group; that it detracted from the important work of the group; that the goal of nonproliferation could be achieved more through the quiet work of securing better (safeguardable) conditions of supply (that is, through comprehensive safeguards as in the Brazil and the Pakistan deals) than through a controversial and perhaps fruitless debate about plutonium technology that seemed to be an inevitable development on the verge of commercial application.

How should Carter's April 1977 announcement be assessed? According to one perspective, just as the Zangger Committee and the London suppliers' group overshadowed the NPT, these groups were themselves overshadowed by the Carter announcement. It brought to a half the constructive work of the suppliers' groups by diverting attention to the issue of plutonium technology and the fuel cycle. It forced many Europeans to defend their nuclear programs against the Carter challenge. The quiet diplomacy of the suppliers' groups had had several achievements. The French position had evolved since 1975 or 1976 and the gradual emergence of an Atlanticist rather than a Gaullist France was important for U.S. foreign relations. Exports like the nozzle technology (still in an experimental stage) were accompanied by stringent safeguards. It is widely acknowledged that the Federal Republic of Germany negotiated the best safeguards deal with Brazil that was possible. This is a considerable nonproliferation measure because the safeguards agreement places Brazilian nuclear industry practically under full-scope safeguards even though Brazil does not adhere to the NPT. In this sense, therefore, the deal between the Federal Republic of Germany and Brazil was a nonproliferation measure. By stressing the dangers of reprocessing plant export rather than the safeguards that were agreed upon, Carter's public diplomacy had the effect of undermining the quiet diplomacy. Quiet diplomacy was effective not only in bringing the Brazilian nuclear industry under safeguards but also in reorienting the French and German views about the danger of sensitive nuclear exports, so that the suppliers groups' consensus could be upgraded over time.

According to another perspective, however, Carter's April 1977 announcement forced a number of states to re-assess the implications of plutonium technology for the proliferation issue. It is argued that the Carter policy did not overshadow the suppliers' groups but rather pointed to the natural limitations derived from their exclusivity, secrecy, and narrow mandate to discuss the conditions of supply rather than the political wisdom of supplying sensitive nuclear materials, equipment, and technology. Accordingly, the natural limitations of the suppliers' groups were bound to emerge once the groups' significant work was completed. Thus, the overshadowing of the suppliers' groups should be viewed in the context of their significant achievements.

There is still another way to assess the Carter announcement. It is true that Carter overemphasized the dangers of plutonium technology, that is, of reprocessing and fast breeders. It is also true that Carter's dramatic announcement, made without consulting his European allies, paved the way for an ideological confrontation with Japan, the Federal Republic of Germany, and France, in particular. These states rejected the Carter view that a plutonium economy was unacceptable. Such a confrontation may overshadow the suppliers' groups, or if the European viewpoint prevails in the nuclear fuel evaluation program in the next two years (1977-79, the period during which the exercise is to take place) then Carter may have to backtrack from his public position or sulk and go his own way. According to one assessment such dangers were acceptable because the price was small for high stakes. Carter's bold statement was guided by a careful calculation. It was rooted partly in a concern with morality and nonproliferation, but it was also rooted in a concern with protecting the rapidly decreasing U.S. monopoly in light water reactors fueled by enriched uranium. This was one effect of Carter's bold and dramatic initiative even if the commercial aspect was not central in his intent as some of his critics suggest.

Furthermore, the Carter stance also meant that he had shelved, not killed, U.S. plans for reprocessing and fast breeders. In inducing the Europeans (who were ahead of the Americans) to go slowly, Carter could buy time for his own industry to catch up to the Europeans and Japanese. The commercial concern, mixed with a layer of nonproliferation, was a motive. By setting the stage for an ideological, political, and technical debate, Carter developed new parameters and a new mechanism for an international debate. The NPT was a discriminatory mechanism because it divided societies into NWS and NNWS, all because some had tested a device before January 1, 1967. This discriminatory document had probably accounted for India's refusal to participate in the suppliers' group work. At the same time, the history of the Nuclear Suppliers Group and the Zangger Committee and their obvious connection with the NPT point to these groups' natural limitations as a truly international forum for furthering nonproliferation. The International Nuclear Fuel Cycle Evaluation (INFCE), on the other hand, was a truly international device that had nothing to do with the NPT. It had the potential to become the basis for slowing proliferation through the development of a technical consensus about the economics and technology of plutonium. Whether or not INFCE can break new ground in the new nonproliferation debate is the subject of the next chapter.

Little has been said so far about the role of nuclear disarmament in promoting nonproliferation. Article VI of the NPT saw nuclear disarmament or preliminary arms reduction by the nuclear

superpowers as steps in curbing the nuclear arms race and setting
an example for the world community. The promise regrettably has,
to date, remained unfulfilled. The chances of curbing the arms
race in the 1980s are at best slight, if the current trend in superpower relations persists. Consequently, superpower disarmament
does not appear to be feasible as the central strategy toward nonproliferation. Yet there are two noteworthy possibilities. First, if
a comprehensive test ban accompanied by a ban or a moratorium on
peaceful nuclear tests (or a time-bound CTB/PNE agreement) is
agreed upon by the superpowers without any insistence on universal
agreement, such a step may cool the enthusiasm for PNEs; it would
take the momentum out of the issue in Third World thinking while
retaining the PNE option in the form of an international PNE service
as a theoretical option. This would have the effect of theoretically
implementing Article V of the NPT without actually implementing it!
It would also have the effect of muting Third World criticism of the
superpowers' intentions and yet take the steam out of the Indian and
the Egyptian interests in a theoretical PNE, however residual such
interest may appear at present. The prospect of a CTB/PNE ban or
a moratorium rests on the prospect of an evolution in the Soviet position on PNEs. Until 1977 Moscow was the principal advocate of retaining PNEs for developmental uses, and this obviously strengthened
the Third World argument. During 1976-77 it was intimated that
Soviet scientists had started to consider seriously environmental objections to PNEs and may therefore have lost some interest in PNEs.
However, there are other, equally convincing intimations that tell a
different story. The Carter-Brezhnev controversy during 1977 over
arms control and détente suggests that the political climate at present favors a token arms control agreement involving a chemical ban
rather than the bolder and more controversial CTB/PNE moratorium.

Nevertheless, in the U.S.-Soviet strategic dialogue a Soviet
shift on the CTB/PNE issue signals several changes.* Moscow's
willingness to move away from its earlier insistence on a universal
CTB agreement signals that it is willing to take a chance that a
moratorium will not give much advantage to Peking militarily. Yet
if Peking decides, as it is expected, to stay outside a CTB/PNE
moratorium or a ban, that would isolate the PRC in the disarmament
and nonproliferation community. An element in the Soviet calculation
in 1977 was the feeling that France would take a seat at the CCD and
thereby further isolate the PRC on this internationally visible issue.

---

*For details see Ashok Kapur, "Negotiating the Comprehensive
Nuclear Test Ban," International Perspectives, Ottawa, forthcoming.

Secondly, the acceptance of the notion of verification by challenge and on-site inspection, as outlined in the Gromyko letter to the U.N. secretary-general,* was an important step forward given that the United States attaches considerable importance to verification and on-site inspection in its arms control agreements. Last but not least, Soviet movement on the PNE issue would inevitably strengthen détente between the superpowers and reveal a difference of opinion in Soviet-Third World relations. If it is true that Moscow worries about potential proliferators on its borders—from South Korea to Iran—movement on the CTB/PNE issue is warranted. The CTB/PNE issue is finite and not necessarily linked to SALT II. However, it is also arguable that a CTB/PNE agreement could improve the political climate for negotiating SALT II and perhaps even SALT III in the 1980s. Chapter 6 discusses the disarmament aspect of nonproliferation multilateral diplomacy.

The foregoing discussion has presented a brief overview of the evolution of post-NPTmultilateral diplomacy. It reveals a selective implementation of the NPT provisions. Whereas the Zangger group sought to implement Article III (2)(b), the London Nuclear Suppliers Group went beyond the language of the NPT to devise concerted supplier policies to fill the NPT loopholes. The exercise was meant to find multilateral solutions to highly technical and highly political problems. In a sense the evolution was a phasal activity—beginning with the NPT in 1970 and ending with the INFCE in 1979. In another sense it marked the failure of the NPT parties, and particularly of the United States, to formulate an approach to international negotiations that reflected a solid domestic and international consensus. In the latter perspective the evolution from the NPT to the Safeguards Committee to the Zangger group formed a package that implemented the NPT provisions. To this extent the evolution was a phasal one. But the work of the NSG and the INFCE suggests a departure from the letter and spirit of the NPT. If NPT parties themselves have defected from the NPT their plea to non-NPT parties to help make the treaty a universal document is hardly credible.

---

*The Soviet Union is convinced that no particular difficulties should arise in elaborating such a compromise basis for an agreement as would ensure a voluntary framework for taking decisions relating to on-site ascertaining of relevant circumstances and, at the same time, impart confidence to all parties to the Treaty that the obligations are complied with. The Soviet Union stands ready to participate in a search for a universally acceptable understanding on this basis."

The defection from the letter and the spirit of the NPT reveals two structural problems in efforts to shape a sound antiproliferation regime and to define the role of the NPT in this regard. The first structural dimension is that consensus in the U.S. (as the foremost antiproliferator) decision structure is needed before there can be an international consensus; a corollary of this dimension is that consensus among the Americans, Europeans, and Japanese is needed before the antiproliferation argument can be emphatically presented to important Third World threshold states. At a time when the international elite network is small and cosmopolitan with respect to nuclear matters, and evidence of fragmentation in decision making is hard to hide, such fragmentation in domestic debates accounts for the absence of an international consensus. The orientation of President Carter's diplomacy and its implications for the international antiproliferation drive are the subject of Chapter 4.

NOTES

1. For background see The United Nations and Disarmament, 1945-1970 (New York: United Nations, 1970); and William Epstein, The Last Chance (London: Free Press, 1976).
2. R. Imai, "The Non-Proliferation Treaty: The Japanese Attitude Three Years After Signing," in Nuclear Proliferation Problems, Stockholm International Peace Research Institute (SIPRI) (London: The MIT Press, 1974), p. 245.
3. B. Goldschmidt, "International Nuclear Collaboration and Article IV of the Non-Proliferation Treaty," in ibid., p. 209.
4. A useful survey is in SIPRI, Safeguards Against Nuclear Proliferation (London: The MIT Press, 1975). This monograph was prepared by B. Sanders, then an official of the International Atomic Energy Agency.
5. See for instance the coverage in New York Times, May 14, 1976; New York Times, May 23, 1976; New York Times, June 24, 1976; New York Times, July 7, 1976; Washington Post, August 15, 1976, September 30, 1976, and October 6, 1976; US News & World Report, July 26, 1976, and September 13, 1976; Congressional Quarterly Weekly, July 17, 1976; New Republic, July 17, 1976.

4

MULTILATERAL DIPLOMACY AND NONPROLIFERATION: THE CARTER STANCE

Unlike the antiproliferation advocacy of the Kennedy presidency, Henry Kissinger had accepted nuclear proliferation as inevitable. The consequent lack of enthusiasm for nonproliferation by the Nixon-Kissinger-Ford administration is well known. During 1976, however, President Ford's nonproliferation policy started to evolve in light of the congressional pressure to tighten U.S. nuclear exports restrictions to curb the national development of repprocessing and enrichment abroad, particularly in the Third World threshold states. Since 1975, the well-publicized hearings of the Senate Government Operations Committee and the House International Relations Committee pointed to a sharpening of the exchange between the congressional and executive branches of the U.S. government. But until France and the Federal Republic of Germany started selling sensitive materials to Korea, Pakistan, and Brazil, and until Carter during his candidacy started to speak out on the subject of proliferation, Kissinger's enthusiasm for nonproliferation was, at best, lukewarm.[1] Furthermore, the Ford-Kissinger nonproliferation strategy stressed regional rather than national nuclear fuel centers, thus sanctifying the growth of self-contained fuel centers abroad. The regional fuel center idea was mainly a U.S. idea, promoted by U.S. academic circles and financed by the United States. But after Carter became president, the United States was embarrassed by the regional fuel center idea. Carter had concluded that the use of plutonium was undesirable, and that a change of U.S. thinking was needed. In 1977 regional fuel cycles had to be avoided under the new orientation because an essential part of regional fuel cycles was the reprocessing of plutonium. The new orientation was reflected in the view of J. Nye, deputy to the undersecretary of the

State Department.* A summary of the main points of his statement to the Senate Committee on Foreign Relations on June 29, 1977 follows:

1. Our task is to slow, if not stop, the spread of nuclear explosives.
2. If proliferation progressed rapidly, many states that have decided not to make nuclear weapons despite their ability to do so would reassess their decision.
3. The widespread commercialization of plutonium is at least ten years away, but we need to improve our institutional framework before we enter the plutonium economy.
4. In seeking to limit the number of nations with nuclear explosive capabilities, there are two crucial components of the problem: a country's motivation to build a bomb and its technical ability to do so. Just because a state can build a bomb does not mean that it will choose to do so.
5. In addition to security guarantees (for example, to Japan) the NPT is an important instrument to affect motivation because it has helped create a regime in which states feel their security is better served by avoiding the further spread of nuclear weapons.
6. The NPT is a delicate instrument. In essence, it is a compromise whereby discrimination in the military sphere is accepted for benefits of the atom in the energy sphere.
7. We are acutely sensitive to the political and security motivations that lead states to acquire nuclear explosive devices. Consequently, this means

ensuring the credibility of existing security guarantees, making progress in achieving meaningful and verifiable arms control agreements limiting or prohibiting nuclear testing, strengthening our alliances, and behaving in our foreign policy in a way that devalues the prestige identified with a nuclear weapon capability.

8. The second element of the proliferation problem—technical capability—presents us with a different set of challenges. If possession of sensitive enrichment and reprocessing facilities that can

---

*Contrast this with his article in Foreign Affairs, April 1978, and his conciliatory statement to the Uranium Institute, London, July 12, 1978. See David Fishlock's assessment of Nye's latest views in Financial Times (London), July 14, 1978.

produce weapon-usable material spreads, then the number of states near the nuclear weapons threshold increases.

9. The U.S. nonproliferation policy has gone through four phases. The Baruch Plan was the first one. After it failed, the second phase was to restrict export of technology. This did not prevent the USSR and Great Britain from obtaining the bomb. Consequently, the third phase, in December 1953, came with President Eisenhower's atoms for peace program, whereby civilian nuclear energy proliferation was encouraged in return for an assurance that it would be used for peaceful purposes. There have been problems in implementing the third phase. Sensitive technologies were declassified prematurely and guarantees of peaceful use were sometimes loosely written. But the approach had two achievements: the commercial fuel cycle was isolated from nuclear weapons uses; and a norm emerged against further spread of nuclear weapons capabilities. After India's explosion of 1974, U.S. policy shifted into the fourth phase. This is premised on the following view:

> If the world used only the current type of reactors and the low enriched fuel for them, and enrichment facilities were limited and we never reprocessed the spent fuel to extract the plutonium, our current international safeguards system would work very well, and our problems of keeping commercial and military uses of nuclear energy isolated from each other would be considerably reduced.
>
> Unfortunately for such a neat solution, technology does not stand still, and its diffusion is difficult to restrict. If countries are able to buy or develop enrichment plants . . . if countries are able to buy or develop reprocessing plants, [they can have the capacity to use these materials for bombs]. This is why President Carter objected to the German sale to Brazil. . . . Our view is that such facilities are not yet economically necessary or adequately safeguardable. In the long run, the number of such facilities should be restricted, redesigned to incorporate more proliferation resistant technology, and embedded in carefully designed and effective multinational institutional settings.

10. It is not assumed that the commercial fuel cycle is the only path or the best path to nuclear weapons capability. It is, however, assumed that

in situations of extreme tension, states may turn to second or third best instruments to get their hands on weapons they regard as essential to their security.

11. The proposed policy of the United States rests on three elements: controls (asking nations to accept safeguards on all three elements: controls (asking nations to accept safeguards on all their civil nuclear programs); denials (asking nuclear suppliers to exercise self-restraint in the export of sensitive nuclear technology, materials, and equipment; and incentives (offering secure uranium fuel supplies and enrichment services to foreign buyers). The last category consists of bilateral fuel supply commitments and may include multilateral arrangements (assuring access of fuel supply to reactor exporters not having their own fuel supply) and other international arrangements such as an international fuel bank. The international fuel program must have three characteristics: it must remove incentives for acquisition of full fuel cycles by nations; it must be nondiscriminatory to consumers in full fulfillment of their nonproliferation obligations; and it must not increase the dependency of recipient nations on a capricious supplier nation.

12. As President Carter called for an International Nuclear Fuel Cycle Evaluation (INFCE) on April 7, 1977, there is a need to avoid premature commercial commitment to new technologies.

Carter's motives in revising U.S. policy were unclear. They were, and still are, guided by morality and a desire to halt proliferation. In the Carter view, adherence to the NPT and acceptance of safeguards and conditions on nuclear exports are insufficient. The new baseline must be drawn against the further proliferation of the plutonium economy through either nuclear exports or indigenous development in the threshold states. The NPT speaks against the spread of nuclear weapons or nuclear explosives, but the Carter administration stresses control over proliferation capabilities. Instead of asking states to fulfill their NPT obligations, now the stress is on nonproliferation obligations. The scope of the latter is broader than the scope of the former, and it partly narrows the rights permitted by the former by curbing the access to sensitive technology under safeguards.

The moral imperative may, however, just be a part of the Carter orientation. It is arguable that Carter's motives may rest on more domestic and less foreign policy considerations. For instance, the absence of pressure from the U.S. atomic energy industry on reprocessing and fast breeder developments may account for a willingness of the industry to accept a moratorium on these items for a few years. But, on the other hand, a number of other commercial motives may be present in U.S. thinking at present. First, the United States has a major stake in the future of the light water reactor. Secondly, the breeder in the United States is temporarily dispensable and it makes sense for the United States to try to put maximum distance between the LWR and the breeder. Given these two considerations, it makes sense that the future of the plutonium economy has been thrown to the environmental wolves to save the LWR from international competition and from continued advancement in breeder and reprocessing technology by France, the Federal Republic of Germany, and Japan. Admittedly, Carter's policy is not motivated entirely by commercial greed. The more charitable viewpoint is to view the commercial imperative as secondary in comparison with the moral one. There is a genuine concern for preventing or slowing the unrestricted spread of small and uneconomical reprocessing facilities, a concern that Canada has also expressed. In the latter case, however, the distinction is between the acceptance of economical reprocessing units and the rejection of uneconomical ones. Canada's position, therefore, expresses an open-mindedness but no real enthusiasm for reprocessing. Carter's policy in 1977 revealed no such open-mindedness and no willingness to be convinced otherwise.*

During 1977 the United States administered shocks to its allies in Europe and Japan. In part, U.S. allies have been at fault for failing to see that Carter during his candidacy was sincere in his beliefs and that his views were not merely electoral rhetoric. In March 1977, the allies received a hint regarding the altered U.S. views. After the Nixon shock on the PRC in 1972, Carter administered what is now known as the plutonium shock to Japan when Carter raised questions about the future of Japan's Tokai Mura reprocessing program. (See Table 4.1 for information on reprocessing capabilities.) Japan's energy dependence on imports is total because it has no domestic coal, no oil, no hydroelectric power, and no domestic uranium. Japan, therefore, has no economic alternative to the reprocessing and the fast breeder route. France is in a similar position, but is less exposed than Japan. The Federal Republic of Germany is also in a similar position, but is less exposed than France. The United Kingdom is the least dependent of

---

*Canada's open-mindedness on reprocessing, however, does not obscure the point that its views on proliferation, even more than Carter's, are those of a zealot and fundamentalist. Canada overemphasizes goodness and, by implication, Canadian goodness. According to European and Japanese sources, Canada is not the model to follow.

TABLE 4.1

Existing Capabilities, Production, and Pilot Scale: 1977
(Eastern Europe, United States, and the PRC not included)

Country	Facility	Type of Fuel	Design Capacity (MTU/Y)
United Kingdom	British Nuclear Fuel Ltd.	Magnox metal	2500
	Windscale Works	Oxide, LWR type	400[a]
France	La Hague (HAO)	Magnox metal	2000
		Oxide LWR type	800[b]
	Marcoule	Natural, metal	1000[c]
Belgium	Eurochemic–Mol[d]	Metal and oxide low enrichment	75
		High enrichment (shut down in mid–1974)	1.25
India	Trombay	Natural	50
	Tarapur	Oxide	135
Japan	PNC	Oxide, LWR type	210
	Tokai Mura		
Federal Republic of Germany	W & K	Oxide	40
Italy	CNEN	Oxide	10
	Rotondello (CNEN)	Oxide (used also for thorex process)	2[a]

[a] Not operating.
[b] Is being tested. Full operation not for at least three years.
[c] This capacity has not yet been reached in practice.
[d] Consideration is being given to reactivating the plant under Belgian ownership and expanding its capacity.
Source: IAEA, private communication to author.

all these states because of the prospects of North Sea oil. Brazil's position is like Japan's because about 95 percent of its energy needs are met by imports. In short, there are differences between the energy pictures of European states and Japan on one hand and those of the United States and Canada on the other hand. This situation's implications for the future of nuclear power account for the adverse reactions of U.S. allies to the Carter announcement in April 1977. That the Carter policy statement did not involve detailed consultation with the allies prior to the announcement of the policy added fuel to the fire.

The initial reaction to Carter's policy was emotional and occurred in the conference hosted by Iran at Persepolis on nuclear technology transfer issues in April 1977. The reactions at the Salzburg conference in May 1977 were more intellectual but still they reflected the isolation of the United States from its allies, and the IAEA, and the Third World. However, at Salzburg the United States started the dialogue by raising the issues, and the INFCE exercise, the next two years (1977-79), was meant to raise alternatives. In the Canadian and the U.S. view, INFCE is meant to be a purely technical evaluation to study the technical and economic aspects of nuclear fuel cycles.

The INFCE dialogue may be seen as a continuation of the antiproliferation strategy of the United States, but it is actually, or is meant to emerge as, different from the work of the NPT, IAEA, the London Nuclear Suppliers Group, and the Zangger group. The Zangger group dealt with nuclear export conditions, but the London Nuclear Suppliers Group shifted its focus to establish a mechanism for restraining nuclear supplies. Both are multilateral exercises, but the groups are small. The London suppliers' group has discussed the possibility of enlarging itself since 1975. The proposed enlargement was not based on the notion that consumers are to be brought into the group or that it is necessary to further a supplier-consumer dialogue. Such dialogue has been going on since the London suppliers' group started its work. For instance, France, the United Kingdom, the Federal Republic of Germany, and Japan are consumers and suppliers and as such provided both perspectives. Third World spokespeople, however, wonder if the London suppliers' group has become an East-West, North American-European exercise where Third World viewpoints are singularly absent.

Partly in response to criticism about the secrecy of the activities of the suppliers' groups and partly because of Carter's antiplutonium stance, INFCE can be viewed as something different from other groups seeking nonproliferation. Its principal task, initially, was to assess fuel cycles to find the one that lends itself best to nonproliferation. This question the suppliers' groups could not ask.

Moreover, INFCE is not focusing on safeguards, with which the NPT, the IAEA, the London Nuclear Suppliers Group, and the Zangger Committee have been preoccupied. Neither is INFCE meant to restrict nuclear trade or to control the conditions of nuclear supply. It is meant to be a multilateral exercise, to examine the means to further nuclear cooperation but also to agree on what is desirable regarding nuclear power. Any state with a stake in nuclear energy was permitted to participate in the INFCE exercise, and 40 states and several international organizations attended the organizational meeting in Washington in October 1977.*

The motives of states promoting the INFCE exercise vary. The United States sees the exercise as a way of justifying its opposition to plutonium and furthering Carter's policy, but others take different ideological directions. Canadians feel that ideological differences should not enter the INFCE exercise, yet it is likely that the exercise will be confused and complicated by the entry of political aspects. Several governments including the United Kingdom want to see alternative nuclear fuel cycles examined. Still, there is a reluctance to put much effort into INFCE because, after all, for years atomic energy commissions and industrial and foreign policy bureaucracies have been examining alternative aspects, many of which have been discarded over time. One approach to the exercise is to make activities more safeguardable, including those involving the plutonium fuel cycle. Another is to repudiate the plutonium technology and make other fuel cycles more safeguardable.

There were differences of opinion among a number of the countries that had been involved in the initial preparations following the London economic summit of seven European and North American states on May 7, 1977. Initially, France and Japan reserved judgment, neither agreeing nor declining to participate in the INFCE. The United Kingdom, the Federal Republic of Germany, and Italy, on the other hand, agreed to participate with preconditions: the INFCE was to be an open-minded exercise, and there was to be no suspension of existing programs. Canada took the view that the INFCE should be opened up to anyone concerned with nuclear power. They were to be committed only to studying the problem from a technical point of view. According to Canada, success in INFCE depends

---

*For details see INFCE/TCC/1/2, December 12, 1977. Israel attended the organizational meeting. This surprised many, but it said little. South Africa was invited by the United States but declined to attend the organizational meeting because of the short notice. It subsequently joined the group and is playing a constructive role.

on the level of consensus achieved regarding plutonium economy. What the consensus is does not matter as long as there is a consensus that puts limits on plutonium economy and does something about the problem of diversion of plutonium. Given the Canadian distinction between economical and uneconomical reprocessing, a fine distinction between the Canadian and the U.S. stance seems to exist, but its practical effect is far from clear.

What is likely to appear out of the INFCE exercise during the coming two years and what can emerge out of it are questions to which there are no real answers. Indeed, it is probable that many, if not all, governments currently involved in promoting INFCE are not aware of all the issues and parameters. There is disagreement on basic questions, for instance, in Working Group III, which is the most political, the least understood, and yet deals with a key aspect of nuclear energy policy—namely, security of supplies. Given the problem of the limited expert manpower that is available to manage the staff work on INFCE, given that the ideological parameters of even Western positions are in flux and at variance with each other, no firm predictions about INFCE outcomes can be made yet.

The task is complicated because at least three groups can be distinguished in INFCE: the United States with its commitment to an antiplutonium stance; the Europeans, who feel that they have no real options as far as reprocessing and fast breeders are concerned; the Third World countries like India, Brazil, and others, who remain suspicious about U.S. motives in promoting INFCE. A subcategory can be added to the first group: Canada. It takes the view that its policy, unlike Carter's, is not based on any ideological premise. Canada claims to have a flexible policy core and to be still open on the reprocessing question.* It is not convinced that the breeder is the way to energy satisfaction and to nuclear development. It does not think that plutonium technology and economy is desirable. But, on the other hand, its policy is nondiscriminatory because it is willing to see a distinction between economic and noneconomical reprocessing plants. Furthermore, even though Canada's policy is not based on ideological premise, Canadian policy making must take into account the moralistic view of the Canadian public. The public view is highly critical of nuclear energy and contains an ideological prejudgment that Canada's leaders need to respond to. If INFCE is seen as an alternative to other nonproliferation exercises of recent years,

---

*An argument exists in Canada that it may itself need to reprocess Canadian spent fuel during the next 20 years. So a reprocessing ban is premature.

and Canada is pleased to have taken the initiative in support of INFCE, the ideology-free rationale for INFCE is that it ought to be able to produce some internationally acceptable criteria for judgment of the technological and economic dimensions of alternative nuclear fuel cycles.

In 1977 the consultations about INFCE have proceeded slowly because building a consensus on such a controversial subject takes time. The original decision, announced May 7, 1977 at the London Economic Summit (also called the Downing Street Summit), attended by the United Kingdom, France, the Federal Republic of Germany, the United States, Canada, Belgium, and the Netherlands, was to establish a process to consult and prepare a preliminary report for two months from then. The study group was set up because of U.S.-European differences of a substantial nature on President Carter's April 7, 1977 policy and the proposed bill he sent to Congress to govern U.S. nuclear exports. The matter gained considerable urgency because initially the Carter bill was expected to become law by September 1977 and even if it was delayed, the congressional attitude was likely to strengthen and not weaken Carter's hand. The INFCE exercise over a two-year period emerged as an escape mechanism to cool tempers on both sides of the Atlantic and to provide interim solutions for a number of pending issues. For example, Canadian uranium exports to Euratom countries were suspended starting December 31, 1976 because of Canada's insistence on its prior consent regarding the end use of its uranium. At the Schmidt-Trudeau meeting in 1977, Canada agreed to reconsider its position and resume deliveries on an interim basis pending the outcome of the INFCE exercise.* This bilateral understanding could pave the way for a permanent change, because INFCE is likely to ratify the notion that there is really no alternative to a plutonium economy. As such, INFCE is a useful mechanism to divert negotiations from frozen positions by providing a mechanism for interim solutions during which attitudes and policies may evolve on one side or the other, or on all sides.

But diverting negotiations away from frozen positions into new channels, however, does not necessarily imply agreement. Taking the Canada-Euratom uranium supply case, a number of procedures and potential barriers had to be crossed before agreement was reached in 1978. The idea of resuming Canadian uranium supplies

---

*According to the communique of July 13, 1977, reprocessing of Canadian-supplied uranium to West Germany and other Euratom countries was permitted pending the outcome in INFCE by 1979-80. See also Communique, Department of External Affairs, Ottawa, January 16, 1978.

on an interim basis pending the outcome of the INFCE exercise was an agreement in principle in the Schmidt-Trudeau meeting. It had to be put to the Euratom states and it then had to be translated into a formal agreement. The view in 1977 that Canada and Euratom states would not try to find a permanent solution to the notion of prior consent but would leave it up to INFCE later found support in Euratom, but there was still a problem of finding suitable negotiating language. For instance, Canada was willing to talk on an interim basis before the Trudeau-Schmidt meeting, but, on the other hand, Canada wanted to retain, in a theoretical sense, a veto to be applied at Canadian discretion. The Canadian stance was ambivalent. On one hand Canada has nothing in particular against reprocessing, but, on the other hand, it wants a veto—theoretical against Western allies like Japan and the Federal Republic of Germany and more real vis-à-vis states like South Korea. One item on the negotiating agenda, therefore, is how one defines a "theoretical veto." The European preference is obviously to have a highly or absolutely theoretical veto. Perceptions of issues vary from the political level to the bureaucratic. At the political level, Canada agrees to exercise considerable discretion in exercising its theoretical veto vis-à-vis the Federal Republic of Germany and other Euratom states and Japan. According to informed sources, in 1977 the speculation was that the criteria would be likely to consist of two parts. The final criteria are to be internationally acceptable guidelines established after INFCE (after 1979). In defining the interim criteria, however, the old Euratom agreement (1959) had to be taken into account. Thus the element of prior consent was involved, but the criteria were not spelled out in the 1959 agreement. Now the Euratom concern was to spell this out or, better still, to eliminate the notion of prior consent.* It is probable that the German and Euratom arguments were directed against the Americans rather than, or more than, against the Canadians. Europeans have been suspicious that Canada's prior consent argument is simply a front for the Americans, given the history of Canadian cooperation with the United States in a number of international security issues.

The mechanisms for beginning operation of INFCE were complicated. Initially, a report prepared by the United States was circulated to a number of governments. This report was essentially a

---

*The 1978 agreement requires "notification" to Canada and "consultations" to ensure that "adequate safeguards" are in place before reprocessing occurs. This means that Canada failed in its attempt to require "prior consent" for European reprocessing.

U.S. document based on Carter's policies and premises about plutonium and antiproliferation. The launching of INFCE pointed to a need to discuss alternatives. The first meeting of the study group was inconclusive. The second one, however, produced a report that was submitted to governments of the seven nations participating in the London economic summit of May 1977. The reactions of the majority of the seven states favored continuation of the INFCE exercise without any precondition by the United States and with the West European precondition that participation in the exercise did not mean that existing programs were to be suspended. France agreed to participate in INFCE, having initially taken a noncommittal view. In early autumn 1977, the United States sent out invitations and the report of the seven states to the 40 participants. The first organizational meeting was held in Washington during October 19-21, 1977. The basis of discussion, therefore, was the second report, because it reflected a consensus of the seven states and deviated sharply from the first report, which was based on Carter's policy.* Moscow participated in the INFCE exercise, but it seemed to be unwilling to discuss its own nuclear fuel cycle; still, it was willing to comment on that of other nations. Moscow was not involved in the London economic summit, but it was approached informally about INFCE. Initial reactions indicated that it is not enthusiastic about the exercise. It did not want to get caught up with an international exercise that could open up its own reprocessing program to international scrutiny and discussion. It was agreed that while INFCE was in progress, the Carter nuclear export bill would go forward. All parties to INFCE had the right to go forward with their decision making, to go slowly in the light of INFCE or accelerate their programs if they so desired, or to adapt subsequent decisions to a post-INFCE environment. The majority expectation probably was that INFCE would legitimize reprocessing, with modifications such as coprocessing or a plutonium fuel bank. The stress is on finding new institutional mechanisms to slow proliferation and to curb na-. tional decision making that does not conform to multilaterally acceptable criteria.

---

*In his statement after the meeting, U.S. Ambassador G. Smith expressed the hope that there would be an "educational effort" and that U.S. nonproliferation proposals would be supported. See USIS Backgrounder, American Embassy, London, October 26, 1977. Mr. Smith's optimism was not shared by most INFCE participants.

INFCE AS A MULTILATERAL CONFERENCE

INFCE has a variety of justifications, not all of them mutually supportive. For President Carter, it was an effort to obtain an international consensus to support his antiplutonium stance. For Carter's opponents in Western Europe, INFCE is a way to ratify the notion that even if according to Americans uranium is plentiful, even if enriched uranium is offered by the United States to its consumers, even if Canada is willing to moderate its position on "prior consent" in its uranium contracts, nuclear consumers are unwilling to have their industrial and economic interests and security depend on bilateral political relations for an unspecified period. For the Europeans also, INFCE may be the mechanism to ratify once and for all the view that there is really no alternative to a plutonium economy in the foreseeable future. Lastly, if the exercise is directed more toward the Third World threshold states, it may turn out to be ineffective if, for instance, Brazil and others decline to participate or drag their heels in doing so. Also, if countries like Brazil participate, it is an open question whether the exercise can or will remain apolitical, as Canadians and others may wish.

Plainly, INFCE is meant to be an educational exercise. According to present thinking, the approach that might work is to view issues thematically rather than on a case-by-case or country-by-country basis. It is not meant to be a prescriptive exercise. The results are meant for consideration by national governments. There are to be no votes; it is hoped that a consensus will emerge.

But a look at the list of invitees reveals that the exercise was geared to bring together most of the hard-core cases, including some of the outlaw cases like South Africa and Israel. It is still unclear whether INFCE will be able to persuade these cases to change their nuclear policies. India has potential military concerns with the PRC, and diplomatic concerns with the superpowers. South Africa worries about strengthening its ties with the United States by getting Washington to choose between "apartheid with a bomb or without it." Taiwan is outside INFCE and Israel just listens, not committing itself unless there is peace and security in the Middle East.

The other real problem of INFCE is that many states attend the meetings but few are really interested in examining alternative nuclear fuel cycles. Although there are about 20 alternatives that can be discussed, there is little enthusiasm for re-examining items that have frequently been examined internationally and in national bureaucratic debates. The current mood favors making existing technologies work and improving their safety because much time, effort, and money has already been spent on these. True, public opinion in a number of industrialized societies has slowed nuclear developments in the energy field, and the role of public opinion cannot be denied in democracies. INFCE may have the effect of slowing down nuclear developments at the bureaucratic level. Still, in many instances, the opposition to nuclear energy is based on local rather than national and international perceptions. For instance, if a German farmer does not like a nuclear waste storage site because it is too close to his farm, his opposition has nothing to do with the merits or disadvantages of nuclear energy development and nonproliferation; it is based on perceived self-interest and nothing more. In short, the INFCE scenario is one of a big gathering in terms of numbers, big issues to be resolved, and politics that involve fighting all the way because of the presence of a mix of technical and foreign affairs experts. Given these factors, it is difficult to separate the technical from the political issues.

Dealing with the issues of education and plutonium can be loosely called the primary task of INFCE. There are three separate audiences to consider:

1. President Carter, congressional antiproliferators, and those in the National Security Council and the State Department who are totally committed to Carter's views as stated in the April 7, 1977 announcement

2. the Western Europeans, and the Japanese, who think there is no alternative to reprocessing and fast breeders in the 1980s and the 1990s

3. Third World societies that have soiled their hands in plutonium technology, who see no alternative to it in the foreseeable future, who are deliberately going slowly with it for domestic and international reasons but who are not likely to see themselves giving in to Carter or anybody else.

The roots of behavior of the second and the third group vary. (This applies more to Argentina and Brazil and less to India because India has partly given in to the Carter stance, in practice but not theoretically.) The Western Europeans see themselves acting in defense of their industrial and commercial interests. Even if they are willing to restrain themselves in their nuclear exports (as in the case of the Federal Republic of Germany and France, which have promised to restrain themselves in export of sensitive technology for an indefinite period), the industrial options, particularly in Japan's case, provide no escape from reprocessing and fast breeders. In the thinking of the Europeans and the Japanese there is also mistrust about the motives of North Americans. Because the United States could go on for many years without reprocessing and breeders, because Canada is secure in its energy policy, because Carter really gives up nothing by shelving American reprocessing and breeder development, the sentiment is strong in the second group's thinking that Canada and the United States have no business laying down the nuclear laws and that unilateral decisions are no way to do international business.

INFCE makes sense for resolving the current nuclear controversy between the first and the second groups of states. It assumes that the controversy is essentially about the role of nuclear energy in industrial and commercial relations. Further, it assumes that Carter and his advisers failed to consult their European allies and thereby failed to estimate their genuine concerns and interests. INFCE can remedy these failures and the new technical-economic consensus of INFCE can offer "international" criteria for judgment that have trans-Atlantic validity. In this perspective a number of issues can be examined in a calm, dispassionate manner. What, for instance, is likely to be the international supply position of uranium and at what price? What are the perceptions of the nuclear buyers in Western Europe and Japan about coordination of policies by the United States, Canada, and Australia with respect to conditions of uranium supply? What if Australia takes the view that bilaterals are not the way to go? Will Australia's defection from the Canadian position make obtaining uranium supplies easier? Will South Africa and Namibia continue to be secure suppliers without safeguards to societies like the Federal Republic of Germany and with what sorts of consequences for the Federal Republic of Germany's economic and political relations? What are the prospects of building self-contained nuclear parks that minimize transportation of fissile materials within a single national jurisdiction and thereby minimize the problem of subnational nuclear terrorism, violence, or theft? Can the public be educated about waste disposal issues? What are the consequences of breeder developments, assuming that breeders are here to stay? What are the consequences for Western industrialized democracies of a "no growth" policy? (Since the role of nuclear energy is premised on growth, this is a basic assumption worth examining. Furthermore, such an examination could expand the parameters of domestic debates by revealing how a policy of no growth can reduce dependence on nuclear energy but also exact social and economic costs—for example, higher unemployment.) These are questions that INFCE, if it consists of the United States and the Western European nations, might constructively debate in an attempt to reach a trans-Atlantic consensus. This view implies that the purpose of INFCE is educational. The strategy is to utilize a multilateral conference setting to confront experts with the issues and alternatives. The method is thematic: members of a working group express their concerns; thus national perspectives can be analyzed and points of consensus identified. This scenario assumes that considerable national research is needed to prepare for such an intensive and extensive debate.

Bringing in the threshold Third World societies raises a different set of questions. It is worth exploring whether INFCE is the right medium for these societies. There are two views about the role of Third World societies, both unevenly developed and less developed ones. The first view draws lessons from the steam-roller effect of Third World majorities at the United Nations. There are two objections to such majorities: that they lead to confrontation with the Western minority and reduce the Western incentive to work through multilateral conference diplomacy, and that the majorities respond to emotional and political considerations and thereby fail to engage their opponents in a reasonable dialogue about the underlying issues. Atomic energy issues in the IAEA have so far been free, relatively speaking, from the impact of Third World majorities. However, in 1977, Third World countries were able to oust South Africa from the board of governors of the IAEA on grounds that had little to do with atomic energy and more to do with Afro-Asian international politics. Given this experience, it is felt by Western societies that there is danger in introducing unrestrained Third World countries into a technical and professional multilateral nuclear exercise such as INFCE. The second view, however, correctly notes that inasmuch as several of the threshold states are located in the Third World (even though India and Brazil are hardly less developed societies), there is an urgent need to bring such societies into the security dialogue through bilateral and multilateral conference diplomacy.

Within the second group of countries (namely, the Western European industrial nations), INFCE is more of a discussion about the role of nuclear energy, as far as the domestic programs of these nations are concerned. It deals to a smaller or negligible degree with nuclear proliferation. There is, however, a connection between European reprocessing and enrichment plants for domestic use and exports of products of these plants to Third World societies. One consequence is that European reprocessing and enrichment can set an example for Third World societies. This view may be oversimplified. For example, India and Brazil did not decide to have reprocessing plants under national control simply because the industrialized nations had them. Rather, their decision was based on national considerations where the foreign example provides a parallel but not necessarily a cause for copying. But the second consequence is real. It lies in the emergence of supply relations between European industrial democracies and Third World societies in the field of nuclear energy development. The nuclear deal between the Federal Republic of Germany and Brazil; continuing and growing nuclear ties between France and South Africa, and the Federal Republic of Germany and South Africa; and growing nuclear ties between France and the Federal Republic of Germany and India are examples that indicate a major transformation in the nuclear trade. It does not signal the end of the traditional nuclear trade patterns between Canada and the United States and their old clients. Still, the entrance of the Europeans into the international nuclear trade market signals the emergence of a new pattern of European/Third World nuclear trade that challenges the dominance up to this time by the North American states. In other words, with regard to the domestic uses of reprocessing and enrichment plants, the interactions between the North American societies and the Western European ones are concerned more with a study of nuclear energy and the economic wellbeing of national society. However, the same European domestic industry may also be geared to promotion of exports. In the latter sense the European industry emerges as the tacit collaborator of Third World societies who aspire to proliferate. Thus, it makes sense to bring the Third World buyers of nuclear exports into INFCE. That is, if the Europeans are to be brought into the exercise on the premise that INFCE is really about nuclear energy, then their partners in the Third World need to be brought into the exercise, but on antiproliferation grounds.

This diversion to discuss the possible motives for participation in INFCE is necessary to make one point. The desirability of bringing the Third World societies into INFCE is based more on proliferation control and less on a discussion of the alternative nuclear fuel cycles. Or, to put it differently, debates of alternative fuel cycles, as these address bureaucratic audiences in Third World societies, are meant to raise the level of consciousness of problems of nuclear energy development. In raising the consciousness level, the strategy is to slow the decision-making process in the Third World societies, at least for the duration of the INFCE dialogue—until 1979 or (probably) 1980.* This strategy may work with respect to countries that

----

*The report of the seven countries participating in the London summit was due two months after the end of the summit on May 7, 1977. This report was late. INFCE was launched by Carter in early autumn. Many delegations at the Washington meeting in October 1977 stated firmly that INFCE should not last beyond the end of 1979 and that the uncertainties raised by it should not be allowed to continue beyond this time.

are not firmly committed to nuclear energy in their development plans. Thus, Pakistan may be assisted by INFCE in its bureaucratic debate about more nuclear reactors versus more oil rigs. The Brazilians may lose interest in the still-experimental German Becker jet nozzle technology after a few of their technicians have been trained and after they recognize on their own that the technology is still too experimental for application. The Iranians may similarly learn from the INFCE dialogue and not push for reprocessing under Iranian control. These are the types of countries that will provide the most promising targets for the North Americans to work on.

The underlying premises in this approach are that "soft" threshold states (or states on the threshold of the threshold) ought to be confronted in multilateral conference diplomacy; that confrontation rather than inertia is the necessary strategy; that a widening of the debate internationally can meaningfully provide a widening of the debate domestically in these threshold states; and that domestic opposition can be externally induced and can slow proliferation in conjunction with existing international controls (through safeguards). This line of argument is a calculated gamble. It fails to take into account that a widening of the nuclear debate domestically and internationally also produces a larger number of experts with on-the-job training; if some experts know how to slow nuclear developments there are other experts who know how to create situations to justify an increase in nuclear development. The latter experts also have covert supporters among so-called horizontal proliferation controllers. (For instance, Moscow on one hand insists on full-scope safeguards in the suppliers' group meetings but on the other hand offered India a supply of 200 tons of heavy water under safeguards— but not full-scope—after Canada canceled its agreement with India in May 1976.) Furthermore, raising the level of consciousness and casting a wider net within the bureaucracy of a target country can have a spillover effect. The communication revolution is taking place in the Third World also and, as the Indian case demonstrates, a secret bureaucratic debate (1950s-1964) can pave the way for a public nuclear debate (1964-68) and swing public opinion to the side of advocates of nuclear self-reliance leading to nuclear self-sufficiency.* At present, therefore, it is unclear if the calculated gamble will work.

Two types of problems are central to the antiproliferation exercise and INFCE may not be able to influence outcomes in the direction that Carter wants. First, the ideal way to stop proliferation would be

---

*Self-reliance is an attitude, and a strategy of having several suppliers so that dependency is minimized.

to have the nuclear suppliers ban all exports or carry out a moratorium for a given period. David Lilienthal proposed this in 1975, but the proposal was rejected outright.[2] Commercial greed clearly cuts into nonproliferation. Consequently, the policy in North America and in Western Europe is clearly to balance the promotion of commercial greed with the aim of nonproliferation. Carter wishes the Europeans to avoid exporting their sensitive technology, equipment, and materials even with safeguards, whereas the Europeans wish that Carter would stop moralizing about their behavior and stress mechanisms that improve safeguarding of existing technologies. The second dimension of the problem is that many of the hardcore threshold cases have escaped international controls. It is debatable whether they can be brought into line through INFCE or related multilateral or bilateral conference diplomacy. The latter question merits attention because if the hard-core threshold cases have in fact escaped control, then "slowing proliferation" can have different meanings: (1) slowing the pace of proliferation of nuclear capabilities in the "soft" threshold states like Iran, Pakistan, and South Korea; (2) inducing the hard-core threshold cases like India and Israel to avoid PNEs, whether the test would be the nation's first (as in Israel's case) or would not (as in India's case); and (3) inducing South Africa to adhere to the NPT, to place its enriched uranium capacity under international safeguards, and generally to use its nuclear power as a tool to bargain against South Africa's further isolation from the Western community. In the first instance, INFCE is a mechanism to utilize a technical and economic discussion to appeal to the Third World bureaucracies to make the correct decisions, using internationally accepted technical and economic criteria. In the second instance, the search has shifted from the bureaucratic-technical-economic level of debate to the highly political. This is based on the recognition that even through the Israeli and Indian strategic circumstances vary, the two cases now have one element in common: the Jewish lobby in the United States is now India's best and probably only friend in nuclear matters and in Indo-U.S. nuclear relations! There is recognition that the demand for safeguarding India's entire nuclear industry carries no pressure. The willingness of the United States to fulfill old contractual obligations regarding fuel supply to India's Tarapur reactor is no large matter and adds no new element to the situation. Israel is protected by its relationship with the United States and there is no new element in U.S.-Israeli relations to induce an Israeli willingness to place its Dimona reactor under safeguards. Consequently, unless a new element is found at the highest political levels, a low-level INFCE exercise is not likely to alter existing attitudes. India's program parallels that of France and the Federal Republic of Germany, and it is too late now to turn back the technological clock on fast breeders and reprocessing plants.

This sketch offers a pessimistic view about the prospects of proliferation control in the hard-core cases (which, incidentally, are located in regions of conflict). It is probably a coincidence that this is so, and the importance of the coincidence ought not to be overstated. Nuclear proliferation is not rooted in regional disputes. For instance, Indian proliferation had nothing to do with its problems with Pakistan. Conceivably, Pakistani proliferation may be a response to a nuclear threat it perceives from India. One can hypothesize that proliferation is rooted in regional rivalry. Yet it is debatable whether Pakistan is indeed developing its capacity to move toward proliferation. According to current estimates, it is at least a decade (perhaps more) away from acquiring an explosives capacity. That Pakistan is slowing down (Bhutto did not renounce the reprocessing plant deal with France; his successors might) has nothing to do with India, just as a decision to accelerate would have nothing to do with India, even though perception of a threat from India would probably provide the rationalization for such an action.

If regional disputes are not the central motives for regional proliferation, one can speculate that the motives are international ones. The Indias and Brazils are therefore reacting not to their neighbors but to their principal (but not always obvious) international threats. The threats may include their principal supporters, their arms suppliers, their sponsors in international conferences, their supporters in military crises, and their godfathers in U.N. Security Council meetings. It is not, therefore, unrealistic to assume that India's nuclear behavior may be rooted in reactions to both superpowers, whereas Brazil's and the Federal Republic of Germany's (that is, the Federal Republic of Germany-Brazil deal) may be directed against the United States. The point to be made is that if proliferation is rooted in a country's international rather than regional perceptions, the solutions must also arise at the international rather than the regional level. If the solutions seek more and more controls, without setting limits on the controls, the tolerance for externally imposed conditions will be reduced by growing nationalist sentiment. The history of externally imposed solutions in the post-1945 international environment of the Western industrial nations and the Third World supports this contention.

AN OPTIMISTIC VIEW ABOUT THE HARD-CORE CASES

Actually, there are only a few hard-core proliferation cases to consider. Brazil and Argentina are, for all practical purposes, under safeguards. Argentina may suffer a societal collapse because

of a deterioration in its economic situation and in its political institutions. In the 1980s there may be no Argentina and, hence, no
problem of a nuclear Argentina. For those who worry about a nuclear Argentina, this can be optimistic news. Brazil is under safeguards because of the excellent safeguards negotiated by the Federal
Republic of Germany for 20 years. But it is possible to consider a
Brazilian renunciation of safeguards in a case where its supreme
interests (which are not defined under the NPT) dictated such action.
Spain has some unsafeguarded facilities but it wants to join the Common Market and can therefore be persuaded to bring its entire nuclear industry under safeguards. This leaves India, Israel, and
South Africa as the hard-core cases for proliferation because of the
presence of unsafeguarded activities. There is a big problem regarding Dimona in Western thinking. Ideally, to control proliferation in the Middle East, Dimona facilities should be under international safeguards but Israel and the Jewish lobby in the United States
will not permit this. Everything in Pakistan is under safeguards,
and Pakistan would have to break an international agreement, as
would South Korea and Taiwan, to go nuclear. Indian nuclear facilities are either entirely unsafeguarded or under what can be called
(for want of a better term) "partial full-scope" safeguards; for instance, the facilities at Tarapur and Rapp I and II. South African
nuclear facilities are at present unsafeguarded because it has declined to sign the NPT but has kept the question of signing open.
Even though South Africa's rejection of the NPT initially was based
on arguments similar to India's, India's rejection of the NPT is total,
but South Africa's is not so clear-cut even at present. By keeping
the matter under review, it leaves open the possibility of signing the
NPT, as clearly India and Israel do not (except under impossible
conditions—India is willing to sign the NPT if the superpowers renounce nuclear arms, and so on).

The India-South Africa similarity does not hold for another
reason. South Africa is in a difficult situation in terms of its nuclear and racial politics. It had bought two nuclear power reactors
from France but the enriched fuel comes from the United States.
There is a question about the reliability of U.S. fuel supplies; that
is, can the United States politically sanction fuel supplies to South
Africa? The contract was signed before Carter became president
and Carter has tried to exercise his leverage to move South Africa
into the NPT. According to unconfirmed reports, South Africa was
on the verge of signing the NPT before it was expelled from the
Board of Governors of the IAEA. In addition, South Africa has some
problems with its enrichment plant. As a commercial proposition,
the plant faces problems of finance. Also, certain bits of technology
have to be imported from the United States because the local industrial

infrastructure cannot support the production of these supplies. Such circumstances, therefore, make South Africa responsive to U.S. pressures. Moreover, South African and Indian attitudes toward the United States vary. South Africa wishes to negotiate an improvement in its commercial and political ties with the West and particularly with the United States. India wishes to negotiate a marginal improvement of ties with the United States without coming too close and without upsetting the balance in its ties with Moscow. India is too large, too self-contained to be a target for the United States or for any other nation, whereas South Africa is more vulnerable because of its racial policies and the consequent outlaw status it has acquired in Africa and in the world. India's nuclear ties with the United States are geared to fulfilling an old contractual agreement that the United States will supply enriched fuel for Tarapur. Overall, Morarji Desai's moderation and cooperation with the United States is meant mostly to buy time until India's fast breeder program is completed with French help.

The NPT has been ratified by the Federal Republic of Germany (in 1975) and Japan (in 1976). Now, according to the optimistic view, the NPT can become universal* if South Africa, Israel, and India are made to become parties. It is argued by many experts that South Africa would be the first to be induced into the treaty, along with its safeguards system, as a part of its bargain to retain and to strengthen its ties with the Western industrial nations. This presumes the continued presence of South Africa in the Western fold. Once South Africa joins the treaty, the next round becomes more complicated. There are two schools of thought on the step to be taken next. The first one argues that there is a need for India to set an example by joining the NPT, thereby creating a situation in which Israel is the sole dissenter in the world. The second school of thought argues that there is a need for Israel to set an example by joining the NPT, thereby leaving India as the sole dissenter in the world.

Proponents of the first view present two arguments. First, India's leadership position in the Third World and in international affairs generally requires that it set a good example in the nonproliferation area. If it does so, its influence will not be limited to South

---

*This perspective ignores two questions: Can there be a truly universal regime without the People's Republic of China? Until the PRC accepts curbs on its testing program through participation in a comprehensive test ban and the Partial Test Ban treaty, even if South Africa enters the NPT, the PRC and India will be the two main Asian dissenters to the NPT.

Asia or Asia alone, according to this assertion. Secondly, India's supply position with the United States in nuclear negotiations and in functionally separate but politically linked negotiations for World Bank loans can be considerably aided by Indian adherence to the NPT or by acceptance of full-scope safeguards. One justification for proceeding with the Indian case is that it is easier to work with India because Israel's problems are tied to a permanent Middle East settlement and that may take a few years. Another justification is that India's nuclear energy program is much too highly motivated by politics and does not have adequate economic justification. The Indian plea that the Tarapur reactor program is for generating electricity primarily does not carry much conviction, because, according to one study, only about 30 to 40 percent of the installed capacity is being used. If engineering or management problems result in such low utilization of a power plant, it makes sense to argue that such plants are economically inefficient. Thus parts of India's nuclear energy program, like the Tarapur power plant, could be closed on economic grounds.* In such instances, INFCE can be useful in revealing the ratio of economics to politics in the decision-making process. In the Indian case, it might lead to an investigation of a need, caused by engineering and scientific leadership problems, to rely more on Indian coal (which is in surplus) and less on nuclear power.

The list of prescriptions for India to fill vary from small steps to big ones:

1. sign the NPT and place all Indian nuclear industry under safeguards

2. leave aside CIRUS for the moment and negotiate other agreements

3. permit publication of IAEA inspection data either by the IAEA or unilaterally. This proposal is meant for India and all other inspections elsewhere.

4. negotiate a series of INFCIRC/66 agreements with the IAEA on facilities not involving third parties. This would place CIRUS under safeguards without Canadian involvement in the safeguarding.

5. adopt the IAEA's partial-full scope agreement according to the IAEA's text

---

*This school ignores the basic point, namely India's nuclear policy is influenced by the policy of the People's Republic of China and even India's PNE option is a diplomatic and a political resource—for external and domestic politics—rather than an engineering resource.

6. bring RAPP II under safeguards through a safeguard agreement on the use of Soviet heavy water supplies to RAPP; make RAPP I agreement permanent by continuous infusion of Soviet heavy water into RAPP I

7. Place all Indian plutonium under safeguards or into an international plutonium fuel bank.

The stress on the force of India's example is also considered relevant for Indian subcontinental relations. Even though the pattern of Pakistan's civilian nuclear development is largely foreseeable in the future, the role of its reprocessing plant is unclear. The reprocessing plant, if and when it is developed and installed, is expected to have an output of 100 tons, whereas the output of Pakistan's single nuclear reactor (supplied by Canada)—KANUPB, in Karachi—is only 16 tons of spent fuel for reprocessing. To be economical a reprocessing plant must have an intake of at least 500 tons. Therefore, if India placed its entire nuclear industry under safeguards, Pakistan would be reassured and would, therefore, go slowly on its nuclear development.

MULTILATERAL DIPLOMACY AND NONPROLIFERATION

Multilateral diplomacy is a double-edged sword. It can help convince others by persuading them with better arguments or by isolating them and pressuring them to recognize the implications of international isolation. But on the other hand, multilateral diplomacy can lead to strong disagreements and strong pressures, and it can become an unhappy exercise if it means a fight all the way. This is particularly a danger if consensus in international and domestic politics is absent, if the basic definition of the problem, the approach to the problem, and the strategy to implement the approach are confused, ambivalent, changing, and contradictory. President Carter's call on April 7, 1977 to have the nations engage in INFCE and his proposed bill to Congress, which was released on April 27, 1977, indicate the problem of public initiatives that go beyond accepted international consensus. Consider the following:

The executive branch of the U.S. government is moving now against proliferation of nuclear weapon capabilities whereas the central element in the NPT was to guard against testing of nuclear weapons or of any nuclear device. The prohibition against testing—which was the yardstick to measure proliferation in the NPT—has now been expanded through the added prescription against national development and export reprocessing and enrichment capabilities even if these are fully safeguarded under conditions acceptable to the IAEA.

There is a nascent theme in U.S. statements—namely, the United States will offer secure supplies to recipients who fulfill their <u>non-proliferation obligations</u>. Here again, a shift from <u>NPT obligations</u> to nonproliferation obligations has occurred subtly. NPT obligations refer to a commonly understood regime where safeguard obligations are monitored by the IAEA. But nonproliferation obligations refer to unilateral policy changes that exceed NPT obligations.*
The assurance of the U.S. government that it will be a reliable supplier of enriched uranium or of enrichment services is undermined by the Japanese, German, and Indian experience. Old contractual obligations have become renegotiable, thus casting doubt on the credibility of the U.S. government. If agreements signed in the past are open to renegotiation because of the views of a new government, might this not set a precedent (where lead time for the industry and trade are long but electoral politics have a normal span of 4-5 years) by which successors to the present government might consider its agreements also negotiable? Lastly, there is a growing sentiment that there will be no end to the need for renegotiating agreements—technology is in constant flux, political attitudes underlying proliferation are unpredictable, and solutions are being sought today for a political, economic, and nuclear environment at least a decade hence. Perhaps it is time to reassess the assumptions on which policy prescriptions are being built.

Two lines of investigation are worth pursuing. If proliferation control is to be achieved through multilateral diplomacy (supplemented by bilateral diplomacy), managing a mix of secret Zangger group and London Nuclear Suppliers Group negotiations and the proposed public INFCE is going to be difficult. Either one chooses to be elitist and secretive, and hopes to be effective; or one abandons the pretense of promoting the common good of the world through the behavior of a small group and broadens the international dialogue by bringing in the major military and industrial nations. The INFCE is founded on a compromise. As a meeting of about 40 states and several international organizations as participants, it is big enough to reflect problems of a polarized world, and yet it seems small when one considers that there are today about 140 nation-states. But if INFCE is meant to be an educational exercise, it is an open question whether the education is to be carried out by exposing delegates (mostly experts) to the enlightened discourses of their colleagues

---

*As noted earlier, nonproliferation obligations also narrow NPT rights by restricting access to sensitive technology under safeguards.

(most of whom know each other through previous contact); or whether the target of education is to reach a wider public audience, which, in turn, might—like the ecologists in the Federal Republic of Germany and France in recent years—pressure its leaders into re-examining the alternatives to nuclear power, either by proceeding slowly with their nuclear programs or by the drastic method of placing a moratorium on licensing of further nuclear plants for a few years. If INFCE is meant to be a closed government-to-government exchange (meaning a monologue among the deaf and the committed, according to some skeptics), then secrecy in the proceedings may be justified and there will be no great pressure on other multilateral forums (such as the suppliers' groups) to declassify their actions and the basis of their actions and to secure worldwide approval for their work. Assuming a secret INFCE and given that almost a third of the likely INFCE participants are also participants in the suppliers' groups, the pressure to open the proceedings to public scrutiny could be quashed. The question of secrecy versus public debate is, therefore, one question about multilateral diplomacy, given that the tasks now at hand require not merely education of the public but also, more importantly, reeducation of the bureaucracies and the leaders. This aspect ought not to be underestimated. The task is not merely to educate or reeucate the decision makers in the threshold states. It is also to educate or reeducate the decision makers in most influential nuclear supplier states,* because their self-centered images and behavior induce them to overemphasize the irresponsibility of the other side's actions and to underemphasize the effects of their own behavior on the others.

Secondly, it is unclear right now if INFCE is meant to complement the existing multilateral mechanisms or to replace them, or indeed if INFCE is meant to be the last multilateral exercise in the antiproliferation game. One solution is to discourage the asking of such questions by denying the formal existence of the Zangger Committee and the London Nuclear Suppliers Group. There is some justification for such a stance. After all, the Zangger Memorandum of 1972 is a private memorandum and its public version (INFCIRC/209) is a document of the International Atomic Energy Agency. Furthermore, even though the principal work of the Zangger group was completed in 1974, it continues to exist. Its dual status enables it to exist and yet have a nonexistent character. This group was able to

---

*According to European, Japanese, and certain Third World sources, the United States and Canada, in particular, need re-education with regard to the style and substance of their antiproliferation diplomacy.

provide a bridge between the consensus among its members and its formalization through INFCIRC/209 (by the mechanism of separate but identical letters sent by members to the director general of the IAEA beginning August 1974) of the IAEA. This group is in limbo at present but some uses may be found for it.

As for the London-based suppliers' group, there are arguments both for and against its continuation. The justification for discontinuing it is that its trigger list is quite comprehensive, and since the basic document was published in 1978 there is no need to keep the group alive or to consider expanding its membership. A public document is there for all to see. New members cannot re-negotiate the basic document; they can either accept it or reject it. If the bridge between this document and the IAEA is established according to the INFCIRC/209 pattern, the dismantling of the suppliers' group would have a dual effect. It would publicly internationalize the consensus among nuclear suppliers and leave this as a fait accompli for the rest of the world to see and, at most, to verbalize against. It would save the present members from the trauma of having to explain their secretive actions, to explain why they were afraid to test their position through the scrutiny of the IAEA, and so on.

There are, however, a number of reasons for keeping the London Nuclear Suppliers Group alive. Even though its job is finished at present, it afforded an opportunity for Soviet participation, which has been most valuable. If Moscow is unlikely to have much enthusiasm for INFCE, its participation in the suppliers' group could provide a valuable forum for continued private diplomacy without betraying Soviet confidence through public disclosures or public diplomacy. Secondly, if there are new discoveries concerning safeguards technology, the existing comprehensive trigger list could be upgraded and linked to the IAEA. Thirdly, if the suppliers' group is expanded by the addition of nonaligned states from the Third World, it might gain respectability. This measure might introduce new ideological dimensions into the debates, but, at the same time, might ratify, for instance, the consensus against the transfer of sensitive technology to unstable societies. For instance, at present India has expressed no interest in joining the suppliers' group, but, at the same time, it has taken the view in the past that it will not export sensitive technology. If the conditions of entry into the suppliers' group were right (they would have to differ from existing ones), then it would be possible to think of India's participation. Fourthly, the group plans to meet occasionally for a general exchange to consider the prospects of securing a consensus by suppliers on full-scope safeguards; to examine how the 1978 guidelines are implemented and whether interpretations of the language need consideration; and to consider collective action if a country breaks an agreement.

In conclusion, whether or not multilateral conference diplomacy succeeds in slowing nuclear proliferation, one point is certain. Since President Carter has introduced a new ideological and economic dimension in his crusade against the plutonium economy, he should be prepared to receive a counterdose from his European and Third World counterparts. If multilateral diplomacy can induce self-centered societies to rethink the effects of their behavior and to alter both the style and the substance of their policies, if secret diplomacy of the past can be made public to remove the suspicions of the nonparticipants, and if antiproliferation rhetoric can be replaced by quiet and expert diplomacy, then perhaps there can be a movement away from confrontation politics and toward consensus building on a slow, case-by-case basis.

NOTES

1. Joseph Kraft, "Foreign Policy on Ice," Washington Post, September 30, 1976.

2. Testimony of David E. Lilienthal, former First Chairman of the U.S. Atomic Energy Commission, in U.S. Congress, Senate, Government Operations Committee, Export Reorganization Act of 1976, Hearings, 94th Cong., 2d sess., January–March 1976, p. 10.

5

PROBLEMS OF
NUCLEAR SAFEGUARDS

INTRODUCTION

The antiproliferation drive is based on four strategies of control. The first seeks to universalize, to standardize, and to upgrade the application of internationally verifiable safeguards on the nuclear industry of all nonnuclear weapon states; the purpose of this approach is to prevent the diversion of materials from peaceful to military (defined as explosive) use. The second strategy aims to curb the flow of sensitive equipment (reprocessing and enrichment plants), materials (uranium enriched over 20 percent), and sensitive technology to countries that currently do not possess these. The third strategy is to conduct a public debate at the international level so that bureaucratic and societal debates in threshold states are radicalized, fragmented, and paralyzed by a coalition of domestic and international antiproliferation forces. Finally, the fourth strategy is to utilize supply relations to slow the growth of the plutonium economy in Europe, Japan, and the Third World.

The second approach produced an agreement in 1976 when the London Nuclear Suppliers Group made an agreement on curbing sensitive flows to Third World nations. France was the primary target of this approach in American diplomacy. France was induced to act like the British and to abandon its Gaullism and commercial opportunism. By changing France's position, the approach succeeded in exposing the Federal Republic of Germany, which had protected itself under the French umbrella in nuclear export matters. This approach can be regarded as successful inasmuch as the Federal Republic of Germany-Brazil nuclear deal is not likely to be repeated by the Federal Republic of Germany and the transfer of a full fuel

cycle to countries like Iran, Pakistan, and South Korea is not likely
in the foreseeable future in view of the London Suppliers Group consensus. The France-Pakistan deal for the supply of a reprocessing
plant is unlikely to be implemented in view of domestic conditions
in Pakistan today. Pakistan is in the throes of a chronic identity
crisis and the wave of Pak-Islamism is supposed to be a substitute
for social and economic reform. Its economy is weak and Indian
exports tend to produce a trade imbalance rather rapidly. If Pakistan's economy cannot absorb Indian civilian goods and if its industrial infrastructure is weak with respect to intermediate technology,
it is debatable whether Pakistan can absorb sophisticated nuclear
technology. So until Pakistan can come to grips with its psychological problems it is hardly a viable threshold state. Under these circumstances, Indians welcome opportunities for Pakistan to become
a Third World and Islamic leader and to lead the disarmament debate against the superpowers. But the lesson of the above-named
second strategy is that if countries want to achieve nuclear fuel
cycle independence, they will have to do so through their own efforts
rather than by relying on Article IV of the NPT, which promises
more technology transfers. Since commercial reprocessing in several nations that are industrialized (Western European countries and
Japan) or industrializing (India, Brazil, and Argentina) is still in the
future, the effect of the second approach was not really to postpone
reprocessing in these countries. Instead, it is argued that, in emphasizing the second approach, the United States revealed its hand
and aggravated suspicions about the true nature of the American
commitment to Article IV of the NPT.

The third strategy is not usually studied in the nuclear proliferation literature but it is an important side effect of the public antiproliferation diplomacy of the Carter administration. The targets of
this diplomacy are India, Pakistan, Israel, South Africa, Brazil,
and Argentina. Apparently this diplomacy has had no effect on
Brazil, Argentina, South Africa, and Israel, because these societies
are domestically cohesive with respect to antiproliferation pressures.
But the strategy has had some effect in India (as Chapter 8 reveals).
In the absence of domestic cohesiveness, the Indian decision-making
structure is open to external pressures, which can increase Indian
dependency on foreign nuclear aid and make India more responsive
to Western antiproliferation prescriptions. But on the other hand,
fragmentation can become polarization. When this becomes a public
phenomenon the effects may be different from what was originally
intended. Carter's diplomacy radicalized Indian nuclear nationalism
at the public level and at certain points in the decision-making structure. At the same time it exposed publicly the advocacy of the NPT
and full-scope safeguards in the Indian decision structure. With

respect to South Africa, it seems that its nuclear scare in the summer of 1977 took the heat out of the American antiapartheid drive and forced Washington to take seriously the implication of a nuclear South Africa. American thinking in 1978 indicated that the choice was between "apartheid with the bomb or without it." Thus some movement in favor of South Africa seemed to have occurred in the South African-U.S. nuclear dialogue. So, on balance, with the exception of the South African case, which has yet to produce an agreement, the third strategy had on the whole reached a conclusion. The debates may go on but the parameters are established and the lines are, with some flexibility, firmly drawn.

The second strategy stressed technological denials to weaker members of the international system. The strategy can work precisely because the targets are weak. The second and the fourth strategies overlap but there is a difference: whereas the second one seeks to deny access to reprocessing and uranium enrichment technology and equipment permanently by restricting these supplies (and not merely safeguarding them as provided for in the NPT), the fourth approach seeks a temporary slowdown of supplies provided under existing contracts. The temporary slowdown is an attempt by the suppliers to use leverage explicitly to renegotiate the terms of the supply and also to change the rules of the game by forcing the other side to accept restrictions on their freedom to develop an independent nuclear fuel cycle. The primary targets of the fourth approach have been Western European nations, Japan, India, and South Africa. However, renegotiations between North American states and these states have not been successful to date in changing the rules to fulfill the original American and Canadian aims. Canadian-Indian negotiations during May 1974 and May 1976 resulted in failure.[1] U.S.-Indian renegotiations over Tarapur to date have been acrimonious; there is no negotiated solution in sight and threats by both sides continue to mar the bilateral relationship.[2] Renegotiations between Canada and EURATOM, and Canada and Japan led to agreements in 1978 after Canada embargoed shipment of natural uranium supplies to these countries in January 1977, but the new agreements revealed weaknesses in Canadian viewpoints.* European

---

*The renegotiations revealed that the outcome depends on the negotiating history and the current bargaining capacity of the states involved. A comparison of the agreements finalized between Canada and the European Economic Community (EEC) and between Canada and Japan in January 1978 reveals that Canada was less able to satisfy its demands vis-à-vis the EEC than vis-à-vis Japan.[3]

and Japanese advocacy of the plutonium economy and criticism of the self-centeredness of the North American states in their anti-plutonium stand led to a softening in the American and the Canadian attitude toward plutonium reprocessing. In 1978 the Carter administration started to soften its antireprocessing posture. The new argument is that American concern was not in principle against re-processing but instead referred to the timing of commercialization of reprocessing. For the present it seems that the North American states have recognized the bargaining strength of European and Japanese advocacy of a plutonium economy and how important it is to these nations to have nuclear fuel cycle independence particularly by those nations who already have access to the fuel cycle. Nevertheless, supply relations are likely to remain tempting levers in the North American antiproliferation advocacy until the debate about INFCE is settled. Thus, the fourth strategy is likely to remain on the agenda until at least 1980, and probably longer—until the analysis of INFCE has thoroughly penetrated national bureaucracies.

INFCE may be described as a process that eventually shapes North American positions or it can be seen as a terminal condition that concludes with a report by February 1980. The first perspective may be more important than the second one. As of this writing (fall 1978) it is unclear whether INFCE will be anything more than an evaluation. A great deal depends on how American objectives evolve and at present this is unclear. Recent American statements[4] indicate that the United States recognizes the need for accommodation rather than confrontation. As of the time of writing, the conciliatory mood is being shaped but until INFCE is completed there are no real issues that can be taken to the ministers and political leaders for resolution.* The ministerial decision process is likely to begin in

-----

*It is noteworthy, for instance, that nuclear proliferation received little attention at the Bonn summit (summer 1978) compared to the attention given to the subject at the London summit in 1977. 1978 was the time for officials to negotiate and deliberate behind closed doors through INFCE. The expectations at the time of writing are that draft reports of INFCE working groups will be ready in May 1979; they will be finalized in autumn 1979 and the concluding INFCE conference will take place in February 1980. In the reports it will be interesting to see the Soviet position in Working Group (WG) V and the American position in Working Group III. WG V deals with breeders and WG III deals with the question of security of fuel supplies. In the latter the United States as of August 1978 had not disclosed its position.

late 1979 or early 1980. At present, however, a constructive mood
has already emerged to resolve issues through a process of accommodation. It is generally recognized that it is wrong to think of proliferation issues in absolute terms. Even Carter's thinking seems
to have evolved during 1977-78. He now is said to claim that his
mind is not even closed to the fast breeder program after 1980-81;
that he is not against the breeder in principle but is concerned about
its timing. It is possible that the questions can be approached more
clearly now because the questions themselves are clearer today than
the questions of 1977 and 1976 were. In this sense the charitable
view is that the position of the Carter administration has not shifted
during 1976-78 but has evolved and consolidated, in the sense that
in 1977 and 1976 the United States was less conscious of the needs of
others and now it is more conscious of other parties' needs. Overall then, the question now is primarily one of timing. There is
agreement in the making about the necessity to have, at the very
least, security of nuclear fuel supplies, if not access to the fuel
cycle.

The foregoing suggests that solutions seem negotiable as the
questions become clearer to the political leaders and the officials.
But it is premature to argue that solutions have been found. One
type of question is central to the future of multilateral diplomacy:
can countries gain access to independent national fuel cycles under
international arrangements concerning plutonium fuel banks or some
other form of international fuel management that utilizes provisions
(such as Article 12[A][5] of the IAEA statutes) of existing international legislation? In 1978 the IAEA circulated papers outlining such
ideas for consideration by its members. It is possible that fuel
banks will become the means to manage the flow of sensitive materials throughout the world. However, the issues are complex and
have political overtones. [5]

The outcome of the fourth strategy is, therefore, different
from what was originally intended. It was intended to slow the implementation of the plutonium economy. Instead, the outcome is that
there is no real danger of runaway proliferation but on the other hand
there are no clear-cut solutions to the problem of the full fuel cycle;
and this problem is now ready for solution. So the fourth strategy
has in essence emphasized the difficulty of striking a balance between Articles III and IV of the NPT, with Article V being pushed to
the sidelines and Article VI as the focal point of the 1978 United Nations Special Session on Disarmament. (See Chapter 6 for discussion
of the significance of the session.) In short, this argument is now
alive: it is necessary now to implement the balance between Articles
III and IV because the superpowers did accept the balance in the NPT;
that is, nuclear safeguards and peaceful nuclear technology transfers

should move hand-in-hand if a credible international nuclear regime is to be established with any prospect of permanence. The notion of implementing Articles III and IV together has two implications. On one hand it means that a balance has to be struck against total fuel cycle technology transfers that create proliferation risks, but, on the other hand, it is necessary to work much harder to engage in meaningful technology transfers at a controlled rate; that is, Article IV will have to come closer to being carried out if the NPT system is to have greater credibility in the light of the post-NPT developments, and given that the superpowers have failed to achieve arms reductions as promised in Article VI of the NPT. Another aspect of striking this balance is to retain the commitment to have an international PNE service in terms of Article V of the NPT. Such action would take the steam out of the PNE issue; this means in effect a practical renunciation of the PNEs but a theoretical retention of PNEs until the world community (particularly the major military powers) is ready to accept a complete ban on PNEs.

If a balance between Articles III and IV is to stand at the center of post-NPT diplomacy in the coming decade, the two elements of this balance should be noted. The first element is that technology transfers will have to be increased to implement Article IV. Articles I and II of the NPT should no longer be used as excuses to avoid meeting the obligations of Article IV. Secondly, in achieving this goal the suppliers are expected to improve the safeguardability of the transfers. Improving safeguards is therefore, the crux. The role of the Standing Advisory Group on Safeguards Implementation (SAGSI) merits attention because little is known about this group, and its work raises important questions about the premises and implications of the contemporary international nuclear safeguards regime. The group's work is still going on. The following section, therefore, sets out only to outline in a general form the parameters of the group's thinking.

STANDING ADVISORY GROUP ON SAFEGUARDS IMPLEMENTATION

This group is a secret enterprise that was organized in response to a Japanese initiative (principally by R. Imai) at the end of 1974. It emphasized a need to rethink the premises on which IAEA and NPT safeguards since the late 1960s were based. The old Safeguards Committee (1970-71) which met under the auspices of the IAEA had wide representation. SAGSI is a small group that represents all types of interests. The group is chaired by Dr. Jon Jennekens of Canada and includes experts from Japan, Mexico,

France, the United Kingdom, India, the United States, the USSR, and the German Democratic Republic; the membership is on an individual basis. It first met in December 1975 and it is supposed to meet twice a year.* It is an advisory group to the director-general of the IAEA. Its main purposes are to rethink the technology of safeguards; to re-examine the principles underlying safeguards; and to formulate ways to develop and to strengthen the NPT safeguards system (known as the INFCIRC/153 system). Whereas the Safeguards Committee dealt with technical questions with respect to Article III of the NPT, SAGSI's mandate is wider. In its technical aspects it seeks to examine the totality of safeguards technology. In its political aspects it seeks to focus on the utility and limitations of safeguards in relation to proliferation issues. Perspectives vary among members of the group. This signals that a debate about all aspects of safeguards is now under way in the international Atomic Energy Agency and its membership.

SAGSI takes the evolving safeguards system as the point of departure of its work. The INFCIRC/26 and 66 safeguards systems were written in broad terms in the 1960s before the NPT came into being. INFCIRC/153 (the NPT safeguards system) was more specific. The use of containment and surveillance as safeguards instruments was not mentioned in the 66 system; it is mentioned specifically in the 153 system. SAGSI in a sense reflects the continuation of the work of the Safeguards Committee. But in another sense it reflects dissatisfaction with the 153 safeguards system. At the least it expresses a need to have independent advice and in-house IAEA research on safeguards. It is a product of diverse pressures. The Japanese, for instance, emphasize a need to explore technical, political, and legal aspects of safeguards implementation. The Italians wanted a management board for safeguards. The IAEA Secretariat produces safeguards implementation reports, but these are confidential and some countries wanted more information (than is currently available publicly) to be published about safeguards implementation. For instance, Americans want a lot of details to be known to them privately and publicly, and U.S. legislation requires that information be made available unless it is against the rules of an international organization. U.S. congressional sources are known to be unhappy about the availability publicly of existing safeguards information.

---

*As of fall 1978, the group had met in December 1975, May/June 1976, October 1976, November 1977, January 1978, April 1978, and October 1978.

SAGSI's work is guided by two important considerations. First, it is necessary to check the effectiveness of safeguards. To oversimplify, the IAEA is moving away from the accountancy approach (see discussion below), which was intended to be complemented by containment and surveillance. The new conclusion is that, as reprocessing and plutonium fabrication facilities enter the national fuel cycles, the uncertainties in the accountancy approach are so high that it is necessary to supplement it with other means of surveillance (including physical means). This was not foreseen in 1971 when the NPT Safeguards 153 system was devised. In this context, the key SAGSI recommendation to date is to focus on the concept of "critical time," that is, the time required to make a bomb. The point emphasized by SAGSI is that safeguards should be applied so that the diversion of materials to make an explosive device should be detected within the time required to make a bomb. This requires facility-by-facility assessment rather than abstract criteria for safeguards. Furthermore, the facility assessment makes sense if it is evaluated in the context of the national nuclear fuel cycle.

Secondly, since the pattern is to take each facility assessment in the context of the national cycle, SAGSI's work, logically speaking, requires it either to skirt the question of the political intentions of the country possessing the national fuel cycle, or to have a technical agency such as the IAEA to make political judgments. So far SAGSI has not gotten to the point of discussing political intentions, but there is already a discussion of what can happen. This important area needs more work. What can happen and what will happen are, or can be, two entirely different matters, and there is a problem if an international agency bases its work on possibilities rather than probabilities. This is clearly an area where SAGSI, in conjunction with the IAEA and the United Nations Secretariat officials, could establish parameters for actually predicting proliferation activity in the threshold states. Solid research of the threshold state's resource allocation activity and psychological parameters, the nature of its experimental work, and so on could produce internationally acceptable intelligence. The UN Disarmament Centre and the UN Secretariat were recently given a strong mandate by the UN General Assembly to strengthen their analytical and research activities in the disarmament and related fields. The mandate was offered by the UN Special Session on Disarmament and had the blessings of the UN Secretary-General and the United States. This could be the precedent for SAGSI and the IAEA Secretariat to strengthen their analytical role in conjunction with the UN Secretariat.

At present SAGSI has started to define the main questions but has not yet reached the stage where it can provide concrete answers. The aspects that have been identified for analysis include the following:

1. In the 153 system there is too much emphasis on the material accountancy approach. The terms MUF (material unaccounted for) and MBA (material balance accountancy) are used. But MUF can be positive or negative; materials may be lost, misplaced, or diverted. There may be less accounted for than is indicated in the documentary information about the amount that should exist; or the material may actually exist in the inspected facility but for various reasons it may not be accounted for at the time material accountancy is established. In the latter instance, if the material exists in the safeguarded facility but is being processed and hence is in the pipeline, it would take a plant clean-out to locate the unaccounted-for material—a costly measure.

2. What amount of fissionable material unaccounted for (which might be lost, diverted, misplaced, or in the pipeline) is significant in terms of convertibility into a bomb or bombs as far as a single facility is concerned?

3. Should the definition of "significant strategic quantity unaccounted for" be assessed in relation to one facility or in relation to multiple facilities? What is the significant strategic quantity for one facility in relation to that for many facilities?

4. What is the critical detection time for establishing that diversion of materials from peaceful to military use has taken place? How soon after the diversion must the IAEA be able to verify that such a diversion has in fact occurred? The detection time has to be in relation to the conversion time—that is, time needed to divert materials from peaceful to military use and in particular to make a bomb. Is it feasible technologically to have a detection time that is less than conversion time?

5. If the technology exists to ensure that the conversion time is slower than detection time, is it practical to have the IAEA utilize this technology if it imposes intolerable inspection requirements IAEA members consider undesirable?

6. Should the size of the nuclear industry be scaled to increase its safeguardability?

7. Should IAEA's safeguards system be regionalized? This was a Canadian suggestion almost a decade ago. At that time INFCIRC/26 and 66 safeguards agreements were oriented to individual facilities. The limited manpower needed to carry out inspections did not justify regional safeguards operations. However, with the growth of IAEA's work during the past decade and with the

travel required of Vienna-based inspectors, there is a danger that operational effectiveness of the inspectors is reduced. Do such problems make a case for regionalization of IAEA's operations?

These questions hide two possible different, and at times overlapping, approaches to safeguards. The first approach stresses the technical dimension. It seeks to balance the accountancy approach with containment and surveillance techniques, and investigates the relationship between surveillance by human and by instrumental resources. Accordingly, the new safeguards technology does not replace the accountancy approach but modifies the earlier reliance on accountancy. It is an evolutionary development of safeguards technology. It is a cautious approach that seeks to manage on an ad hoc basis.

The other approach raises some of the more fundamental questions about safeguards. It suggests a need to come to grips with the political dimension of a safeguards regime. This approach may not succeed in offering answers but it is interesting that it is now raising questions about the limitations of safeguards.

This approach directs attention to the shortcomings of the key premises in the INFCIRC/153 system. One key premise was that the operator of a safeguarded facility would want to improve the efficiency of his facility and to increase his control over the materials. The second premise was that sound measurement methods were available and technology would continue to improve. In retrospect both premises are questionable. In practice it appears that the operators cannot optimize safety and measurement standards; and there are limits to the growth of sophistication of measurement equipment. As a result the accountancy aspect of safeguards now is less important than it was expected to be in the late 1960s. Yet the safeguards regime is based on the concept of material accountancy through national means, which are then verified by the IAEA. In short, the concept stressed in the 153 system is, in practice, hard to realize.

Furthermore, the new emphasis on containment and surveillance means that the IAEA has to be more involved than before in implementing safeguards. The accountancy approach meant relying on national means primarily, with the IAEA verifying that the national means were satisfactory. The INFCIRC/66 approach was facility-oriented. It tried to catch the operator in the act of diverting materials from peaceful to military use. There was criticism about this approach and the 153 system was supposed to be the solution. Now the conclusion is that both approaches, while desirable, are still inadequate.

A comparison between the 66 and the 153 systems reveals the deficiencies and the negotiating problems. Paragraph 16 of the 66 system "hoped" that parties would continue safeguards using the principle of "end pursuit: or "contamination"; that is, all material, equipment, and fuel that touched a safeguarded item would, according to the hope, become safeguardable. This hope was, however, negotiable. Moreover, the 66 system did not include nuclear explosions that occurred through the use of unsafeguarded nuclear facilities. Thirdly, the duration of safeguards in the 66 system was for the length of the agreement, that is, until there were no items for safeguards under the agreement.

The 153 system, on the other hand, forbids nuclear explosions. Implementing the principles of pursuit and contamination is now a nonnegotiable matter for countries accepting the 153 system of safeguards. For instance, even though India did not sign the NPT, in September 1977 it accepted safeguards as the condition of supply of Soviet heavy water for the Rajasthan reactors. This deal, as approved by the IAEA board of governors, rests on the 153 system. The Federal Republic of Germany-Brazil nuclear agreement of 1975, however, has elements of both the 66 and the 153 systems. Generally speaking, the system applied to parties to safeguards agreement who are not parties to the NPT contains a mixture of 66 and 153 systems, depending on how well the countries negotiate. In practice the differences may be more theoretical than real, because subsidiary agreements make the safeguards uniform for each country (as for instance in relation to Spain and India, and for Japan until it agreed to the 153 system upon ratification of its safeguards agreement with the IAEA in 1977).

Still, the negotiating histories of agreements of the 66 and 153 types have varied. In negotiating a 66 agreement it was recognized that the IAEA secretariat was a weak vessel and that the outcome depended on the relative bargaining powers of the IAEA and the country concerned. The advantage of the 153 system was that the IAEA secretariat had little room to change the basic agreement because there was a standard negotiating model. It covers all nuclear activities, unlike the 66 system, which is facility-oriented. The 66 system is a useful instrument to fall back on in instances where a country wishes, for propaganda reasons, to maintain an appearance of political independence. But at the same time the 66 system is full of holes, in the sense that it requires renegotiation because of the lack of standardization. The IAEA has to be alert to the opportunities to renegotiate, particularly if factional bureaucratic disputes in safeguarded countries create opportunities for renegotiation and external pressure. The disadvantage of the 153 system is that it becomes at times too rigid; then the IAEA is called upon to use the exceptions provided in the 153 agreements. The 66 system offers a better balance of technical and political considerations, and at the very least an opportunity exists to find such a balance on a case-by-case basis. But usually the disadvantage is that the IAEA is a technical agency and politics takes second place.

This review of the 66 and the 153 systems is useful because it reveals that at present both systems are in use in the IAEA safeguards regime. Thus the debate about the correct balance between the technical and the political approaches to safeguards is still unsettled; this provides the essential background to SAGSI's work. On one hand this group is sympathetic to the demand for safeguards, not merely because the world community (particularly the United States) lacks trust in nonsafeguarded facilities but because it is up to the recipients of nuclear supplies to implement safeguards and to show that their hands are clean. Yet, on the other hand, SAGSI recognizes the problems of the material accountancy approach to safeguards, as noted earlier. In a way, the existence of SAGSI reveals a dispute between the IAEA and the United States on the one hand and the rest of the world on the other hand. The United States and the IAEA, in general, follow a pattern of going excessively into details and of downplaying the role of political trust in implementing and fashioning safeguards.

SAGSI, like the 66 and the 153 systems, suffers from a bureaucratic problem: namely, it is a prisoner of the past. In shaping future alternatives it cannot ignore past negotiation experiences. In preceding sections it was established that the accountancy approach with containment and surveillance methods has become the heart of the present safeguards regime. But there are physical limits to measurement accuracy. For instance, suppose 0.3 percent of the fissionable material is unaccounted for. Even if the measurement is 100 percent accurate (which it is not), the critical time to make a bomb is less than the detection time, assuming the proliferator has the technology to make the bomb. Existing safeguards using the accountancy approach assume the good will of the operator and the existence of complete accountancy records. The 153 system (unlike the 66 system) requires countries accepting safeguards to have an acceptable national system of accountancy; the state and the IAEA have to agree on the accountancy system. Yet if the significant quantity required to make a bomb is less than the permissible level of material unaccounted for, no matter how cooperative the operator is, proliferation control is not possible with the accountancy approach. Still, this system was adopted in 1968 because it followed the Euratom agreement and Euratom/IAEA negotiations were so difficult that no one wanted to change the old approach.

As noted earlier, SAGSI is moving away from the accountancy approach. SAGSI takes the view that it is not useful to focus on the same, abstract safeguards techniques for large reprocessing plants in Japan and West Germany and a small reactor in Israel; different safeguards are needed and more complicated systems analysis is required. This suggests a trend away from abstraction and standardization and a trend toward solving problems empirically.

In terms of the potential implications of its work, SAGSI's approach seems to be more sophisticated than what exists in the current safeguards regime. The problem with the accountancy approach is that it views "material unaccounted for" as the significant parameter in assessing diversion from peaceful to military use. This is not a sufficient technical basis on which to make political judgments. The accountancy approach does not necessarily examine the entire nuclear fuel cycle, whereas SAGSI is trying to examine all the parameters of the system, including political ones. In its technical work it is trying to get away from safeguarding reactors to safeguarding reprocessing and enrichment facilities. It does not attack the question of whether there should be reprocessing and enrichment. Instead, given that such facilities will enter national fuel cycles, it seeks to examine the best methods to safeguard these. SAGSI's approach creates some problems for the IAEA in view of the primary focus on reactor safeguards by the IAEA so far. SAGSI also points to a need to limit one's imagination and to avoid safeguards discussions by those who are not practicing engineers. It also opens up the discussion of the utility of sanctions against diversions when the technical basis to assess diversion is unsound. To date no diversions have been reported and the question of sanctions remains hypothetical. But the NPT says that if there is a diversion it must be reported to the IAEA Board of Governors and to the UN Security Council. International sanctions are, therefore, accepted legal norms in the sense that procedures exist to punish violations. But suppose now that a certain quantity of plutonium is unaccounted for, and that the accountancy system is 95 percent accurate. A real question then arises in international law. Is it safe to assume the plutonium has been diverted? Can a system based on 95 percent probability become a reliable basis for international sanctions?

Instead of viewing diversion as the central parameter of the safeguards regime, SAGSI (or some of its members) sees a need to examine all the symptoms of weapon-directed activities. The parameters are still being discussed because the IAEA has still to be fully convinced. It took almost two years to convince the IAEA director general and others in the agency about the need for such an exercise. But it is a part of the rethinking process that bureaucratic interests intrude upon and slow, if not paralyze, rethinking. In this particular case the inspector general of the IAEA (R. Rometsch) was difficult to deal with—presumably because of his commitment to the existing safeguards system and the bureaucracy over which he presided. Rometsch, a Swiss, has now left the agency, and his successor is an Austrian. He and the IAEA in Vienna are likely to be more amenable to the influence of the Austrian government and thereby, possibly, more open to persuasion by SAGSI members.

In conclusion, the debate by SAGSI about all the parameters of nuclear systems has broadened the scope of safeguards discussion. The search now is for technical answers that are relevant to conditions in the contemporary world. At the same time, by implicitly warning against the dangers of overelying on technical solutions and technical parameters, SAGSI indicates a need to take into account viewpoints from politics, industry, and law.

NOTES

1. Ashok Kapur, "The Canada-India Nuclear Negotiations: Some Hypotheses and Lessons," The World Today 34, no. 8 (August 1978): 311-20.

2. Ashok Kapur, "India's Nuclear Debate," The Bulletin of the Atomic Scientists, forthcoming.

3. For details see Canadian Department of External Affairs, communique, January 16, 1978 (for Canada/European Economic Community agreement), and communique, January 26, 1978 (for Canada/Japan agreement). For an assessment by a Canadian external affairs official, see J. J. Noble, "Canada's Continuing Search for Acceptable Nuclear Safeguards," International Perspectives (July-August 1978): 42-48.

4. In particular, see the statement by J. S. Nye, "Balancing Non-Proliferation and Energy Security," speech at the Uranium Institute, London, July 12, 1978, official text; and a commentary on the change in the U.S. viewpoint by David Fishlock, "U.S. Thinks Again," Financial Times (London), July 14, 1978.

5. For instance, see "International Management and Storage of Plutonium and Spent Fuel," IAEA Secretariat Study, July 1978.

6

NUCLEAR PROLIFERATION AND DISARMAMENT: SOME REGIMES AND PREMISES

INTRODUCTION

International communications are saturated by the variety of recommendations and proposals seeking arms control, arms reductions, arms limitations, a stable central balance, and generous and complete disarmament.[1] Nothing much has come of such initiatives. To be sure, a number of arms control agreements have been signed in recent years,[2] but none of these have significantly affected the process of gradual militarization of a growing number of peacetime economies in the world today.[3] In the post-1945 system of competitive and cooperative interactions, military strategies have dominated the quest for international and regional security in the thinking and behavior of the great powers and the lesser powers. Today the character of the "war system" has changed from how it was during the pre-1945 period, when military force was utilized as an all-out exercise to win the peace by getting the enemy to surrender.[4] With the emergence of the deterrence concept and atomic power in the military and political diplomacy of states, the "war system" has become a "threat system." A credible threat system requires the possession of nuclear and conventional arms, of strategic and tactical arms. Thus a transformation of the national economy in peacetime, to ensure that national resources maintain and enhance the threat system, is also entailed. Peacetime mobilization of these resources is meant to ensure that threats continue to be perceived by the enemy as visible and viable.

The existence of nuclearized and nuclearizing military and strategic regimes is a prerequisite of national life as long as wars and threat remain a feature of international, regional, and national life. As anarchy (defined here as the absence of a central, worldwide authority structure rather than as the existence of a lawless world) characterizes the present world order, the war system and the threat system are two separate but complementary ingredients of national sovereignty and survival. Conceptually, the nuclear threat system presumes that the primary use of nuclear weapons is to deter rather than to fight small or large nuclear wars; there is, however, a possibility that some technological advances may be geared to achieve war-fighting capabilities that exceed the requirements of deterrence. The war system presumes that the primary task of conventional arms is fighting wars. The boundary between the threat and the war systems is not clearly defined; conventional fights involving violence could escalate into small (tactical atomic weapons, neutron bombs) nuclear wars or large-scale wars. U.S. and Soviet military doctrines recognize these possibilities. The boundary is also blurred because threats of escalating a conventional conflict into the nuclear realm could dampen the conventional conflict. Whether or not the crossing of the boundary between nuclear and conventional conflicts is desirable, the presence of the war system (using conventional arms) and the threat system (using nuclear threats) means that the uses of force and threatened force have expanded over time and are imbedded into contemporary diplomacy and strategy.

If peace is defined as the absence of war, at present there does not seem to be an alternative to the threat system. It is possible that the diplomatic uses of nuclear weapons are curtailed through a pledge against the first use of nuclear weapons or a pledge against the use of nuclear weapons against nonnuclear-weapon states. It is possible that high ceilings on Soviet-American nuclear arms will be kept in terms of the Vladivostok agreement of 1974. This may be done on the premise that high ceilings preserve superpower equilibrium and offer a cushion against unexpected advances in new military technologies. But at the same time, because such insurance is available it is feasible to consider dampening the technological arms race and to place restraints on qualitative advances. But even if the arms race is so redirected, even if war-fighting potentialities are curbed or eliminated in terms of future developments, there must be structural limits against dismantling the threat system, inasmuch as the threat system is the preferred alternative to a nuclear war system.

For some, the presence of a nuclear hierarchy led by the superpowers[5] is stabilizing because it can dampen international and regional conflict; that is, even if the superpowers' competition complicates their bilateral military relations, their concert stabilizes international and regional security. For some the notion of hierarchy is applicable even <u>among</u> the nuclear weapon states and not only between the nuclear weapon states and the nonnuclear ones. Thus, the United States and the USSR are the top level of the nuclear hierarchy, while France, the PRC, and the United Kingdom represent the lower rung. The relevance of the distinction in terms of raw military power is doubtful if the central purpose of possession of nuclear force is narrowly defined as deterrence. Thus PRC, French, and British nuclear deterrents (particularly PRC) may minimize the relevance of the qualitative and quantitative superiority of the nuclear superpowers in areas of conflict management outside their bilateral relations. This is particularly so if the superpowers have a policy dispute between themselves. For instance, it is noteworthy that just as the PRC needs U.S. support against the USSR today, the United States needs the PRC's support against the Soviet Union also. It is the identity of interests rather than the size of the nuclear arsenal that is likely to determine the scope of cooperation among the nuclear weapon states. Hierarchy among the nuclear-weapon states therefore may be less important in determining outcomes than might seem to be true at first. The stress by the superpowers on the importance of hierarchy may be for self-serving reasons. Self-images involving the importance of hierarchy thus may not necessarily confer influence in multilateral bargaining situations between nationalistic states in the world today. If images of the implications of hierarchy are self-centered rather than relevant in terms of the adversary's perceptions, the hierarchical distinctions among the nuclear-weapon states may be less of a control mechanism. Consequently, the scope of threats made by powers situated at the lower rung of the nuclear hierarchy may be greater than the nuclear superpowers may be willing to admit publicly. This means that as the proto-PRCs and proto-Frances reach the minimum deterrent status, the implications of the nuclear hierarchy are less clear-cut than quantitative and qualitative figures may suggest.

The growth of the threat system can also be examined from another angle. One line of argument is that nonnuclear-weapon states outside the NPT are likely to go nuclear because the Soviet-American arms race has not been toned down and because Soviet-American strategic arms are a threat to the nonnuclear-weapon states. The implication is that because Soviet-Americans arms threaten the others and the threat is perceived by others, the tendency is to proliferation of nuclear arms with a view to creating minimum deterrents against the superpowers. Here the threat is of nuclear arms and the counterthreat is to proliferate nuclear arms in a group of unspecified size—up to the "sixth plus" party. In other words, the action and reaction are in terms of nuclear arms, and explicitly so. However, there is another way to assess the

impact of nuclear proliferation on the superpowers and in extending
the scope of the threat system. According to this view, the threat
of Soviet-American nuclear arms is not inherent in the arms themselves, but rather in the rule-making rights that possession of
nuclear weapons offers to the nuclear weapon states. Possession
of nuclear weapons (indeed possession of weapons) seems, rightly
or wrongly, to create hierarchical distinctions; it provides the
possessor with the right to veto a consensus among a majority of
states. Hierarchical distinctions, as for instance in SALT, can
mean the exclusion of lesser powers; those who see themselves at
the top of the hierarchy acquire the "right" to manage international
and regional security conflicts and thereby the right to intervene in
defense of their own interests in the name of preserving stability
and balance. Thus there is a clash between the nuclear superpowers,
who stress the benefits of inequality, and the nonnuclear-weapon
states, who seek to minimize the implications of hierarchy by
stressing the benefits of equality. The quest for equality can be
pursued by enunciating declaratory goals; UN majorities can exert
pressure on the superpowers to induce them to break up exclusive,
club-like negotiations where third-party and Third World interests
are not given prominence. And insofar as talk is cheap and not
always effective, and inasmuch as ambiguous nuclear options (which
are neither clearly military nor peaceful in nature) are first steps
toward, or substitutes for, nuclear weapons, the growth of third-
party and Third World nuclear options or weapons signals the rise
of counterthreats from the nonnuclear-weapon states, directed
toward the nuclear-weapon states. But such growth of the threat
system in this instance should be seen in terms of proliferation not
only of nuclear arms but also of nuclear options. If the emerging
nuclear regimes in the world today are seen in terms broader than
the possession of nuclear weapons, * the rising threat of proliferation
in certain Third World regions outside the industrial heartland
(North America, Western Europe, and Japan) points to a growth of
the threat system because of a declining capacity of the superpowers
to stop nations from building options. Ambiguous nuclear options
are not subject to technological and institutional restraints although
efforts in this direction continue to be made in post-NPT diplomacy.
Proliferating nuclear options are not exclusively or even primarily
threats to regional conflict pairs (such as India and Pakistan, Israel

---

*The Council on Foreign Relations' 1980s project does not
come to grips with proliferation as an option-building rather than a
weapons-building activity.[6]

and Egypt, Brazil and Argentina); one only has to examine the evidence between pairs where proliferation of nuclear arms did not occur. For instance, India seems to be in no hurry to catch up with the PRC since the latter exploded its first device in 1964. The situation of Pakistan is similar, as Chapter 8 reveals. Proponents of the argument that horizontal nuclear proliferation is a threat to world order are looking in the wrong direction, because the real threat is to the right capacity of the superpowers to manage international and regional security. Moreover, Third World experts argue that current conceptions about world order require re-examination in terms of a different argument. Existing hierarchies in the world today are a threat to the Third World's external and internal relations. The hierarchies and the threats from the superpowers are not lessening, and the gaps between the industrialized and industrializing nations on one hand and the poor nations on the other are growing. Newer rationalizations are emerging to justify the conduct of the superpowers. Proliferation is to some a process of gradual escalation of nuclear option development, with the aim of sensitizing the superpower bureaucracies about the need to rethink the implications of their actions. The longer it takes the superpowers to moderate and to modify their bilateralized approach to keep order in the world, the greater the possibility that the nuclear factor will enter the bureaucratic and public debates of proliferation-prone Third World societies. The greater the likelihood of Third World nuclear proliferation, the greater will be the growing sense of uncertainty in superpower thinking about the implications for the superpowers of a proliferating world. Admittedly, in the foreseeable future Third World proliferation is not a threat to the military security of the superpowers, but it is a threat to their capacity to win approval for their policies in multilateral forums. Inasmuch as these forums are instruments of national policies, this is the real threat of horizontal proliferation.

American officials stress that nuclear weapons in irresponsible and unstable hands are likely to lead to nuclear war. In the words of Joseph Nye:

> Some have argued, for example, that proliferation
> does not matter or could even have a stabilising effect
> on world politics. . . . Just as nuclear weapons have
> produced prudence in U.S.-Soviet relations, they argue,
> so may nuclear weapons stabilise regional balances.
> But this assumes stable governments with established
> command-and-control systems; the absence of strong
> destabilising motivations such as irredentist passions;
> and the discipline to resist the temptation for preemptive

strikes against adversaries during the early stages
when new nuclear weapons capabilities are soft and
vulnerable.[7]

These views contain several dubious premises that border on
racism. The overemphasis on regional implications diverts attention from the effect of proliferation on superpower interests. Although superpower management of the world order can mean stability, it can also mean that the superpowers feel it necessary to guard
against pressures to make real sacrifices to compensate for the
sacrifices the lesser powers are asked to make in the name of
"world order." The confusion between what is good for the world
order and what is good for Soviet-American interests is real in
superpower thinking. Unless one assumes that industrial elites are
intelligent and Third World elites are stupid, it is hard to assume
that Third World elites are proliferating much against their interests; instead it is reasonable to assume that nuclear proliferation
in the coming decade is a conscious development of the threat system by Third World elites. Furthermore, only if nuclear options
development becomes nuclear weapons production and deployment—
and this is a big leap forward in terms of national security planning
and budgeting—does the scenario of a nuclear war by "irresponsible"
and "unstable" states become worthy of consideration. When such
a danger arises, the real answer is not to necessarily curb proliferation but to educate the so-called irresponsible leaders about
the importance of reliable command and control procedures. This
was done by President Kennedy in his dealings with Khrushchev.
In short, there are two separate arguments to consider: first,
that nuclear proliferation itself is undesirable because it complicates superpowers' policy planning and challenges their preference
for retaining their primacy in world politics; and second, that
horizontal proliferation into irresponsible hands is undesirable
because it could destroy the peace. Here nuclear weapons themselves are not bad and can be controlled by responsible leaders.
These observations point to the growth of a threat system in
the contemporary global scene. Nevertheless, it is possible to differentiate conceptually among a number of variants of nuclear regimes. The following discussion is cast in terms of projections into
the future. A discussion of the analytical mold of different nuclear
futures is useful to assess their implications for disarmament.[8]

FIRST REGIME

This regime is the current regime. It rests on the notion that
although nuclear weapons may be morally objectionable, their

presence produces a moderation in the existing conflicts. The line
of argument is somewhat as follows. Nuclear weapons freeze conflict by creating a stalemate. They compensate for conventional
asymmetries; weaknesses in conventional war-making capabilities
are compensated for by the addition of nuclear deterrence capability, which permits avoidance of war. However, ambiguity is needed
for an effective deterrent, and the first use of nuclear weapons
against nuclear-weapon states can neither be accepted nor renounced.
Nuclear arms also build barriers against escalation of conventional
conflict into general wars that might involve the superpowers. So
nuclear arms serve a dual purpose: they set limits to the upward
escalation of conventional conflict into general wars that might involve the superpowers. So nuclear arms serve a dual purpose:
they set limits to the upward escalation of conventional conflict for
fear that it might become nuclear war; and because of this danger
they invite superpower attention, which facilitates superpower intervention in local conflict to dampen it. Given such uses, there
are benefits to inequality, according to superpower thinking. The
approach requires the maintenance of the hierarchy not only between
the nuclear superpowers and the nonnuclear-weapon states but also
among the nuclear-weapon states. The approach is based on the
view that the international system is anarchical but not lawless.[9]
It is necessary to maintain the Soviet-American strategic equilibrium
through controlling the pace of the arms race, and to have a margin
of safety that can cushion innovations in advanced military technologies. Superpower hegemony vis-à-vis the rest of the world is
desirable and necessary to maintain global stability. Denuclearization of existing nuclear-weapon states is not desirable, although it
is desirable to keep the rest of the world nonnuclearized. Article VI
of the NPT promised superpower negotiations in good faith toward
"cessation of the nuclear arms race at an early date"; it also sought
to move toward nuclear disarmament and a treaty on general and
complete disarmament. According to the logic of the first regime,
Article VI was never seriously intended and is not so now. On the
contrary, the prevailing premises are that the Soviet-American
arms race is stable now; that it is likely to remain so; and that the
central threat is not of the superpower arms race but of horizontal
nuclear proliferation.

SECOND REGIME

This regime is similar to the first one, with one difference.
An attempt is made to tone down the utility of nuclear weapons by
limiting their uses to nuclear deterrence only. This is done by

proposing the acceptance of no first use of nuclear weapons and nonuse of nuclear weapons against nonnuclear-weapon states; the former notion would bring superpower declaratory policy in line with the PRC position and the latter would or could enhance the sense of security of nonnuclear-weapon states. The approach opens up a debate on trimming the uses of nuclear weapons today by restricting these weapons primarily or even exclusively to deterrence purposes. But at the same time, the trimming exercise sanctifies the continued utility of the deterrent function of nuclear weapons, thus casting doubt on the views of some Third World leaders who consider it an illusion to think that nuclear weapons offer protection to any nation. In stressing the utility of reducing the uses of nuclear weapons, the approach opens up the possibility of also reducing the high level of superpower nuclear arms at present. The latter may not be a necessary consequence of the former but it could be the case if and when the current difficulties with the Soviet-American détente are resolved by removing the linkage between Soviet behavior in the Third World and the bilateral negotiations. In abstract terms, it is possible to suggest that the toning-down approach could lead to the acceptance of the notion of minimum deterrents of the proto-PRC or proto-French type and thereby dilute, if not eliminate, the current superpower emphasis on the benefits of hierarchy.

This regime is rooted in several premises:

1. High level of Soviet-American ambiguity about the uses of nuclear weapons—as manifested by the refusal to accept no first use of nuclear weapons against a nuclear adversary or a nonuse of nuclear weapons against a nonnuclear-weapon state (which may nevertheless permit the deployment of nuclear weapons on NNWS territory even though the NNWS may have no control over its use)—is no longer necessary for superpower diplomacy.

2. The gap between the superpowers' nuclear arms and those of the PRC is very wide, and the PRC cannot realistically expect to bridge it in the next five to ten years. Consequently, in their relations with the PRC the superpowers can live with a no-first-use pledge.

3. The French nuclear deterrent is manageable in Soviet-U.S. nuclear planning.

4. Because the prospect of nuclear proliferation is a greater danger to superpower planning than to the Soviet-U.S. arms race, it is necessary for the superpowers to tone down the arms race by making gestures that appear to minimize the uses of nuclear weapons. No-first-use and nonuse pledges under certain circumstances do not affect the mutual assured destruction (MAD) doctrine and capabilities. Yet by appearing to rethink the uses of nuclear weapons, the

superpowers could induce potential nuclear proliferators also to
rethink their plans to go nuclear. By toning down the implications
of the Soviet-U.S. nuclear hierarchy, the superpowers could also
induce a toning down of the bureaucratic debates in proliferation-
prone societies by giving the opportunity for moderates in these
societies to point to the rethinking processes in superpowers' bureaucracies and argue that it ought to be encouraged by third-party
restraint.

5. Superpower duopoly can and should be modified in the
world today. By limiting the use of nuclear weapons to deterrence
purposes only, the implications of hierarchy can be, and should be,
muted in adversary perceptions among the nuclear-weapon states.
When the focus is exclusively on the deterrent function of nuclear
weapons, the utility of a minimum deterrent (proto-PRC in particular) is enhanced. This point is strengthened if toning down of the
uses of nuclear weapons is followed or accompanied by a toning
down of the level of superpower arms.

The foregoing premises indicate superpower sensitivity to
Third World concerns and to the perceived effects of nuclear proliferation on superpower interests.

THIRD REGIME

For the reformer and the disarmer, the third regime is the
most interesting and challenging. It posits a denuclearized world
with two distinctive variants. The terminal condition is an internationalized regime where the citizen's loyalty to the national government is transformed into a loyalty to an international body or
bodies. This variant involves far-reaching international controls
over all national nuclear arms and presumably over all nuclear
transfers. So the focus is not simply on preventing diversions of
nuclear supplies from peaceful to military purposes but on having
an international authority monitor the world-wide structure of the
nuclear industries. This variant may eventually produce a Kantian
international society with an ideological consensus, but at the very
least this variant renounces the existence of a nuclear hierarchy;
ethnic and ideological conflicts may continue to exist but these are
likely to be manageable. Undoubtedly, inequalities would be likely
to persist in terms of economic performance, diplomatic skill, and
ideological appeal of different "units" or "regions" in the world,
but a crucial difference between this variant and the present-day
world is that the citizen's loyalty would be shifted to an internationalized regime and the regime would involve itself in securing
local change.

The second variant in this regime views it as an incremental growth of internationalization and a progressive phasing-out of the nation-state. Another qualitative difference between the third regime and the present-day world is that nonmilitary issues are meant to provide a stronger motivation for change than would military issues. This is particularly so in the internationalized variant and less so in the incremental one because in the former the deterrence concept is liquidated, whereas in the latter the process is to water it down. In the incremental variant, a comprehensive nuclear test ban and a ban on peaceful nuclear explosions (a moratorium, however, would not be enough) could become an intermediate step toward eventual denuclearization. Under contemporary conditions and thinking, incrementalism rather than an internationalized regime seems more likely, for two reasons: the former can be viewed as an extension of the nation-state. The current human rights campaign, for instance, reveals citizen consciousness and loyalty to a human and an international idea. Moreover, the appeal of international bodies can become closer to reality in citizen consciousness as it becomes increasingly clear that complex problems require solutions that are beyond national capacities; the role of international functional agencies in raising citizen consciousness is instructive in this regard. Secondly, incrementalism is of greater interest to the superpowers because it means a continued utilization of the state as an international institution. This allows the superpowers an opportunity to minimize their loss of control over international relations. For the nuclear-weapon states, incrementalism is desirable as an intermediate condition toward an internationalized world for another reason. Even though nuclear forces are eliminated in a denuclearized world, the nuclear technology continues to exist in the form of the nuclear talent of existing personnel in the former nuclear-weapon states. Thus the danger of renuclearization exists potentially, and until that danger has been put to rest the incremental method of reaching denuclearization may be preferable to the internationalized mode.

FOURTH REGIME

This regime highlights a number of pessimistic assumptions about nuclear proliferation. It sees the probability of nuclear war as a consequence of an increase in the number of nuclear-weapon states. Deterioration of the strategic environment is thus defined as the likelihood of a nuclear war as a consequence of proliferation. This implies a failure of the current Soviet-U.S. antiproliferation strategy. It means that the superpower hierarchy is undermined. It means that because the emotional reaction against nuclear weapons concerns their use rather than their possession, the superpower manipulation of the public fear about more nuclear arms fails to stop the elite from furthering proliferation; indeed, it is possible to speculate about the emergence of an international and intranational, elite network that tacitly recognizes a need to break the superpower hierarchy. The emergence and persistence of such a network implies that nuclear decisions, even when these are carried out in the glare of publicity, are relatively immune from public pressures at the time decisions are made. Once the decisions are made and trends established toward development of nuclear options, the trends are hard to reverse. Finally, once nuclear forces are established, they are immune to political change and social conflict. This regime points to a deterioration not merely in the strategic environment because of nuclear proliferation but, more importantly, to a deterioration in the influence of the superpowers in building technological and institutional or legal constraints against horizontal proliferation. In the past, judging by the experience of the French and the Chinese, third-party threats to the superpower hierarchy were immediately repudiated by the superpowers but eventually accommodated. A strategic deterioration scenario, however, implies that no further accommodation of other proliferators is feasible.

Strategic deterioration perspectives have two variants. The first one visualizes a substantial deterioration of the NPT regime, arguing that it has already started to deteriorate. Unless there is a SALT III the failure of the Second NPT Review Conference in 1980, in the context of the failure of the first one in 1975, will confirm the death sentence of the NPT. In addition, this variant has a mix of several views: safeguards will not work to prevent proliferation because proliferation is not a question of diverting materials from peaceful to military uses; rather, it is a question of not being able to control legitimately—that is, in terms of existing institutions, regimes, and policies—the capabilities of states that are near nuclear weapons acquisition. The Soviet-U.S. détente will fail to produce a meaningful reduction of their arms race and without a real détente it will not be possible to have agreement between the superpowers on antiproliferation. Nuclear weapons may fall into irresponsible and unstable hands, and the new entrants into the nuclear club may not have the capacity to learn about command, control, and communications aspects of nuclear weapon management even if they have the opportunity to do so. Bureaucratic and resources-allocation debates will fail to slow proliferation debates. Consciously or unconsciously, national decisions will be pronuclear instead of being in favor of fossil fuels or other energy alternatives. Finally, explicit nuclear weapons programs will appear to be more useful diplomatically and militarily to the proliferating states than ambiguous nuclear options, which are less costly financially and militarily even if they are costlier diplomatically.

The definition of "strategic deterioration" in the above variant seems narrow—namely, it rests on the emergence of policies, doctrines, and weapons that increase the number of nuclear-weapon states and thereby increase the chances of war. Yet there is another way to conceptualize strategic deterioration. A mix of the following comprises the second variant. Ambiguous nuclear options pass into multiple hands; governments hover on the brink of nuclear weapons acquisition but consciously decide not to allocate resources to weapons production; they consciously decide not to develop doctrines and military postures, and their actions and declarations remain ambiguous because the policy is ambiguous. In a sense, an ambiguous nuclear option represents a merger of two types of seemingly contradictory decisions: whereas the first decision prepares for possible weapons production and deployment, the second decision builds national barriers against a decision "at present" against production and deployment but repudiates efforts at international controls. This variant represents strategic deterioration because nuclear options create uncertainties in superpower thinking and imply a loss of superpower control. Such a loss reduces the existing influence of the superpowers in managing the proliferation tendencies of the group that extends to the Nth nuclear power.

FIFTH REGIME

The fourth regime posits strategic deterioration of the international environment because of nuclear weapons or nuclear options proliferation. The fifth regime takes the growth of proliferation as an inevitability but reassesses its implications. It argues that proliferation can be stable and even, from some points of view, desirable. It takes comfort from the PRC example, arguing that nuclear forces that are insecure and located in a region of high tension can still be in stable and responsible hands. In the fifth regime, proliferation is a controlled and conscious activity. Its main purpose is to sensitize the nuclear-weapon states to the dangers of thinking about the benefits of hierarchy and to the virtue of avoiding discriminatory international nuclear rule-making, which has implications for the pattern, distribution, and sources of power and influence in the foreseeable future. In this regime, nationalism remains intact as the basic unit of analysis and as the basic center of power; the vision of an internationalized central body or an incremental devolution of the nation-state is therefore excluded in this regime. Nuclear options compensate for the lack of economic clout in the proliferation-prone societies; and since the nonaligned states among the proliferation-prone societies desire not to join military alliances, nuclear options are also meant to reinforce nonalignment. The threat of nuclear proliferation is also a bargaining chip. But unlike U.S. bargaining chips, which are utilized from a position of military or technological superiority, a proliferation threat is a bargaining chip utilized by nonnuclear-weapon states when they are dealing with the nuclear superpowers from a condition of inferiority. The fifth regime leaves the Soviet-American MAD system intact, but adds to it the layer of proliferation threat. The threat becomes a part of the system because it requires, at the very least, diplomatic engagement of the superpowers in multilateral and bilateral diplomacy with the proliferation-prone societies. The underlying premise is that nuclear-weapon states, and particularly the superpowers, genuinely fear poliferation. The threat of proliferation is useful if it can sensitize the superpowers to the necessity to curb their arms race and not to get too comfortable with it through rationales about the benefits of inequality. Otherwise, proliferation in the 1980s will just make the international life of the superpowers more complicated. Just as French and PRC proliferation in the 1950s and the 1960s facilitated American accommodation with these lesser powers in the 1970s, similarly Third World proliferation can be a sensitizing and bargain-inducing activity. The following notions are implicit in this regime: that Third World societies need to alter the inequality of their status and bargaining position; that images about nuclear hierarchy and power do affect the bargaining situation in multilateral negotiations; and that bargaining from a position of military weakness with a nuclear superpower is possible if an actor can inject itself into the middle of a situation where policy is being decided. If it can do so successfully, it can lessen (for the superpowers) the impact of their hierarchical status, and, conversely, can alter the implications of its own presumed weakness. Also, the utility of bargaining chips to the weaker actors is an innovative idea. Usually, the stronger actor will offer not to escalate the threats if the weaker side desists from a particular line of action. For instance, the neutron bomb is a possible bargaining chip for the United States if the USSR becomes willing to make concessions in the SALT dialogue. Bargaining chips are useful to the stronger party, but they may also prove useful to a weaker actor that is able to become a party to a discussion and is not willing to deny its opportunities and obligations to engage in power politics. Proliferation threats are crisis-prone activities, and crises create both dangers and opportunities. Unlike many other crises, the proliferation crisis allows ample time for decision making among the nuclear-weapon and the nonnuclear-weapon states. Crisis outcomes could be of two different kinds. If the nuclear superpowers persist in their view of the benefits of hierarchy, and the proliferation-prone societies remain unwilling to accept hierarchy as a basis of world order, then proliferation from nuclear options to nuclear weapons seems difficult to contain. On the other hand, if the nuclear superpowers are willing to be educated about Third World nuclear concerns and to limit if not eliminate the implications of nuclear hierarchy, then the rate of proliferation activity and the number of countries involved can be controlled. Because the crisis is slow and manageable in national and international terms, the thesis of "drift" toward nuclear weapons is suspect.

SIXTH REGIME

Usually proliferation activity and proliferation control activity see the state as the source of activity and the object of control. Multilateral diplomacy seeks to restrain the proliferation-prone state by inducing it to accept a contractual obligation. One approach is to raise technological barriers against proliferation; the other approach is to develop institutional mechanisms that constrain state activity. In the latter it is assumed that legal instruments and multilateral interstate diplomacy can be a sufficient and necessary defense against proliferation. President Carter's approach, as defined by J. S. Nye,[10] takes the technological-legal-multilateral approach. It implies that, given time, if new technological and institutional mechanisms can be evolved (a terminal condition), then the proliferation process can be stopped or slowed.

In stressing the utility of interstate contract as the method of stopping or slowing proliferation, the above-named approach fails to visualize proliferation as a consequence of a synthesis between subnationalism and science, where the political, bureaucratic, scientific, and intellectual elites are divided within themselves and the factions for and against proliferation have international as well as domestic constituencies. Such a framework of inquiry provides a new perspective on nuclear decision making and its effect on emerging nuclear regimes in the foreseeable future. The sixth regime involves neither an internationalized nuclear regime (one variant of the third regime) nor a progressive phasing-out of the nation-state (the second variant of the third regime). It is not internationalized because it does not permit the emergence of an antihorizontal proliferation international culture; the "world community" lacks a real consensus on the subject. National nuclear debates remain ineffective in deciding among the arguments for and against proliferation. The sixth regime is characterized by a growing awareness of the importance of avoiding secrecy in nuclear decision making; of the importance of fulfilling publicly acceptable criteria for health and safety in the matter of civil uses of nuclear energy; and of the importance of ensuring that factional activity within a government does not prevent the government, in its declaratory policy and actions, from presenting a unified view that represents public opinion. Thus, if more time is needed to find international solutions for slowing proliferation, the delays also assist the emergence of the sixth regime. To hypothesize: given the existence of factional (subnational) activity in domestic debates of proliferation-prone societies, and given that the debates are gradually becoming public, the longer it takes to achieve an international consensus about the proper means to slow or stop proliferation the greater is the probability that factional activity in domestic nuclear decision making will persist and paralyze the international proliferation-control exercise. Furthermore, given the presence of factional activity against proliferation control, the greater the external pressure on a domestic faction to conform to a proliferation-control position, the greater is the likelihood that the particular faction will seek traditional domestic support and cultural roles. As traditional cultural roles pose the danger of cultural insularity rather than promising internationalism, the combination of insularity and scientific subnationalism (or nationalism if the factional activity is justified in national terms) directs attention to a level of analysis and behavior that is not usually stressed in the literature.

This combination casts a doubt on the utility of securing an interstate agreement to control nuclear proliferation without first establishing a consensus among the competing factions in domestic politics. Furthermore, the combination can produce two variants, one of which aids the antiproliferation cause and one of which does not. If the factional activity in a proliferation-prone society is characterized by self-centered, self-serving, and secret activity, the faction may be willing to serve the international cause of antiproliferation in return for external support for this faction in the domestic debates; this support can be made meaningful through the transfer from abroad of much-needed nuclear materials that preserve the bureaucratic base of the domestic faction, with its foreign links. The other variant, however, visualizes insularity as intense cultural centeredness that has public appeal. This variant pleads for a greater amount of debate and debate that is more public whereas the first variant pleads for less debate and less public debate. The second variant therefore constitutes a pronuclear subnational culture that seeks contact and support for like-minded subnational

cultures in other societies. In the world today, globalized communications facilitate interpersonal contact across continents, which
can result in the rise of an "international social elite network."
Such a network is not formally constituted; in fact, if it were a
formal gathering it would probably lose its effectiveness as a coalition of like-minded science-oriented experts who are able to impinge on the policy processes in different societies and who keep the
nuclear debate alive. In each variant, national boundaries are
crossed, and each variant constitutes a unit of analysis and behavior
that nations and states simply do not reach. In short, in the second
variant, the central forces driving toward nuclear proliferation are
not based on a combination of nationalism and science. Rather,
they are the products of a combination of competitive subnationalism,
science, and the emergence of an international social elite network
of compatible subnational elites who participate in a society whose
existence is facilitated by world-wide communications.

DISARMAMENT IMPLICATIONS OF
NUCLEAR REGIMES

In the first regime, the disarmament of nuclear weapon states
is not feasible, because of the perceived need for nuclear deterrence;
nor is disarmament considered desirable. In bringing France back
to the disarmament table, the French president noted that "the
immediate goal for disarmament cannot be to achieve a zero level
of weapons the world over."[11] Earlier France noted that the "goal
sought by France cannot be a utopian world completely without
weapons."[12] French re-entry into the disarmament debate was
useful because France had declined earlier to join the debate in the
Conference of the Committee on Disarmament (CCD) in Geneva, on
the ground that the proceedings were dominated by the superpowers.
The French entry signaled a slight change—a democratization of
the dialogue among the nuclear weapon states—but the above-noted
French positions also revealed that France today shares in part the
superpower thinking and that the prospects of implementing Article
VI of the NPT are remote as ever. In any case, inducing French
and PRC participation in the strategic dialogue with the United States
is more important for the United States than implementing Article VI
of the NPT.

But at the same time, although nuclear disarmament of the
nuclear-weapon states at present is neither feasible nor desirable
in U.S. thinking, disarmament and nonnuclearization of others by
the superpowers is of obvious interest to them. For instance, the
superpowers support in principle the utility of nuclear weapon-free

zones in the efforts against proliferation. Nuclear weapon-free zones mean that certain continents or regions are precluded from making nuclear weapons; here nonnuclearization has the same effect as disarmament of existing armed states. But the focus is not on dismantling existing overarmed military machines; rather, it is on preventing the proliferation of new centers of nuclear power.

The disarmament idea has other marginal uses for the nuclear-weapon states. Talk about disarmament is popular. Talk about disarmament can also help manipulate public opinion: unacceptable demands made on the adversary are rejected; then the rejections strengthen the sentiment in favor of self-serving regimes and higher levels of arms. Disarmament proposals are also useful sources of diplomatic intelligence. They reveal the pattern of rejections and acceptances, and these patterns can reveal the mix of bureaucratic and societal forces of the target country.

Overall, the first regime at best generates pressures toward nonnuclearization of the existing nonnuclear-weapon states, but these pressures still do not necessarily kill the proliferating nuclear debates in these societies. By sanctifying nuclear weapons and their military and political uses, the first regime sets an example exactly opposite to what is desired by the advocates of disarmament and denuclearization of the existing nuclear-weapon states.

The second regime has a dual thrust. One aspect seeks a pledge of "no first use of nuclear weapons," aimed at moderating and regulating the nuclear behavior among the nuclear-weapon states. This aspect strengthens the centrality of the deterrence concept in defense of nuclear weapons. This aspect is potentially a disarmament measure, insofar as limitations on the uses of nuclear weapons except for deterrent purposes strip nuclear weapons of ambiguity. Through restricting nuclear weapons to a deterrent role, the way is paved for accepting "eventually" the policy and strategy of the minimum deterrent. However, a minimum deterrent is useful mainly as a retaliation measure against an enemy attack using nuclear weapons, and a second-strike nuclear force cannot be used, if the no-first strike pledge is kept, to compensate for weaknesses in the conventional defense. Thus it is arguable that the no-first-strike pledge could encourage conventional wars and threats.

The second aspect, namely, a pledge by the nuclear-weapon states not to use nuclear weapons, or threaten to, against nonnuclear-weapon states, seeks to moderate the behavior of the nuclear-weapon states. Both pledges would have psychological value because they would imply a sacrifice in the declared position of the nuclear-weapon states even though the pledges could not be enforced by the nonnuclear-weapon states. Such pledges would reveal a responsiveness to Third

World and nonaligned nations' concerns, and would imply a willingness to rethink existing doctrines, policies, and strategies. In and
of themselves the pledges do not produce denuclearization and disarmament of existing force structures, but they imply an improvement in the psychological setting in which denuclearization and
disarmament proposals in the future can be discussed.

The third regime, with its plan of a denuclearized world, has
major disarmament implications. It is based on the premise that
the nuclear-weapon states need to pave the way for global disarmament. It is a plea to achieve the denuclearization of the nuclear-
weapon states first and then to expect nonnuclearization of the
nonnuclear-weapon states.

The reasoning behind the plea for denuclearization, however,
is not always clear. For instance, Alva Myrdal, former Swedish
ambassador to the CCD, and a recognized international authority on
disarmament, concludes that: (1) the escalation of the arms race
is a "flagrant miscalculation"; (2) it endangers the security of us
all; and (3) there is a need to demilitarize our societies.[13] It is
unclear whether the third point is necessarily a consequence of the
first and second points. Controlled escalation of the arms race by
the superpowers may in fact be a sound calculation. For instance,
overarmament and pursuit of the arms race by the United States
keeps Soviet resources committed to wasteful military expenditures.
This means that fewer resources are available for the consumer
industry. It means more prospects for encouraging internal dissent
in the USSR. Given that the superpower détente is in part built on
the premise that Soviet-U.S. interests are not harmonious, the U.S.
arms race has its uses. Secondly, the notion that the superpower
arms race threatens the entire world is overstated. Given that
nuclear weapons today are all in stable hands, and given that such
weapons exist primarily for deterrence purposes, surely countries
like Sweden, India, and Brazil, among others, are not threatened
by the U.S. or Soviet nuclear threat. The quest for demilitarization
of societies rests more on moral concerns: a quest to divert military expenditures into developmental purposes; a quest to rely less
on wars and threats for mediating disputes; a quest for re-educating
the bureaucracies about the importance of conflict resolution by
peaceful means; a quest to demonstrate that pleas in favor of
nonnuclearization make sense if nonnuclearization is seen as a consequence of denuclearization of existing arms. The present analysis
suggests that there is a psychological linkage between vertical and
horizontal proliferation: the superpower arms race strengthens
proliferation advocacy in the bureaucratic debates of proliferation-
prone societies, and toning down of the superpower arms race could
also tone down the prospects of horizontal proliferation. In short,

societies that are already militarized and nuclearized need to demilitarize and denuclearize or face the prospect of further militarization and nuclearization of the international and regional environments.

Obviously denuclearization and nonnuclearization cannot happen overnight, but a case exists to devise proposals that achieve both through a reciprocal process. One approach is to ban all nuclear weapons testing.[14] To close the loophole of peaceful nuclear testing, which the superpowers kept open for themselves in their 1974 agreement, the ban could be expanded to include all nuclear testing in all environments and to cover all states. A ban would freeze existing asymmetries but it would not prevent theoretical work. It would freeze the bureaucracies that tend toward vertical and horizontal proliferation, and freezing can become a first step toward arms reduction. Another proposal seeks to place all nuclear transfers under international safeguards. A third proposal would place the entire nuclear industry of the world under safeguards.[15] Cumulatively, such proposals could inject a balance in attempts to shape simultaneously the linkage between denuclearization and nonnuclearization, on the premise that all sides must make real sacrifices. Efforts to emphasize denuclearization or nonnuclearization, without balancing the two activities, are likely to remain one-sided and hence objectionable in bureaucratic debates. If denuclearization and nonnuclearization can emerge through the foregoing proposals, a nondiscriminatory, international political culture aimed at proliferation control would emerge. Furthermore, the willingness of the nuclear-weapon states to subordinate their rivalries and power politics concerns to the goal of controlling vertical and horizontal proliferation would become clear. Alternatively, if the nuclear-weapon states appear unwilling to mediate their power rivalries, then the message will be clear that ideological and power disputes are more important than policies to control nuclear proliferation.

Unfortunately, as of the time of writing there is no significant evidence that the nuclear-weapon states are willing to seek a balanced linkage between denuclearization and nonnuclearization. Alva Myrdal is right in saying that the Partial Test Ban Treaty (1963)—widely touted as an arms control measure—was "never intended" to curb nuclear weapon development.[16] She further claims (from her experience as the former Swedish ambassador to the CCD disarmament talks) that the NPT was meant to put a "seal on superpowers' hegemonic world policy."[17] Furthermore, she convincingly indicates that the "consensus" at the NPT Review Conference in 1975 (at which the conference president, Inga Thorsson, made the best of a bad situation) referred to the need to maintain the "balance" of mutual obligations—"as if such a balance existed."[18] In other words, insofar as the NPT was imbalanced to begin with, insofar as the imbalance was perpetuated by the failure of the nuclear-weapon states to implement Articles IV through VI of the treaty, to keep the existing "balance" in effect meant to perpetuate the existing imbalance.

This history of Soviet-U.S. insincerity—only talking about disarmament and denuclearization—indicates that a skeptical assessment of current superpower disarmament diplomacy is warranted. In recent years the task of achieving a comprehensive test ban (CTB) has been on the agenda. After India's nuclear test in 1974, the effort was to secure control over nuclear testing that could be carried out under the guise of PNE testing; at least Soviet-U.S. agreement in 1974 made a distinction between sites for PNEs and those for military tests. Some progress has been made in discussions among the United States, the USSR, and the United Kingdom in the matter of CTB/PNE control, but the details are shrouded in secrecy. Is this issue to be viewed as a step toward denuclearization of nuclear-weapon states and therefore an inducement to encourage nonnuclearization of the nonnuclear-weapon states? Or is this another ploy in a continuous superpower game that is guided more by international power politics than by antiproliferation and disarmament concerns? Consider the following assessment, which is derived from confidential interviews.

On November 2, 1977 President Brezhnev offered to suspend the Soviet PNE program in order to pave the way for a CTB agreement between the United States, the USSR, and the United Kingdom.[19] This was an important development; in the past the Soviet Union had been willing to discuss a CTB agreement but was not willing to close the PNE loophole. Moscow's concern for PNEs was justified on the grounds that PNEs had potential engineering uses in such areas as mining, excavation, and changing the course of rivers. Soviet statements at scientific and governmental conferences were emphatic on this point before Mr. Brezhnev's dramatic announcement. It opened up the possibility of a three- to five-year moratorium on military and peaceful nuclear testing.

The Soviet announcement was good news for those who wanted an evolution—leading to a repudiation of PNEs—of Moscow's excessive commitment to PNEs. It was argued that this commitment kept alive the PNE options in proliferation-prone Third World societies. Thus, it was argued that Soviet commitment to PNEs lent credence to the Indian argument in defense of PNEs, and that the combined Soviet and Indian approval strengthened the Third World plea to establish an international PNE service under Article V of the NPT. Whereas Third World societies feel that the nuclear-

weapon states are obliged to provide this service as a part of their
bargain, the United States and the United Kingdom take the view
that their commitment was and is conditional; thus, if the nuclear-
weapon states are convinced of the virtues of PNEs for themselves,
then these can also be offered to satisfy the Third World demand.
Prior to the Brezhnev announcement, the Soviet attitude kept the
Third World demand alive. The Treaty of Tlatelolco created a
nuclear weapon-free zone in Latin America (even though the treaty
is not yet in effect), but it also recognized the possibility of peaceful nuclear explosions' taking place and recognized a difference
between PNEs and military tests. This is significant because the
NPT does not recognize such a difference. In 1974, however, just
as India was testing its peaceful device, the superpowers accepted
a bilateral agreement recognizing a difference between PNEs and
military tests. Even though the United States itself had no particular interest in PNEs, the agreement ratified the notion that, while
it was acceptable for the superpowers to have PNEs, this was not
so for the lesser powers. Furthermore, in sanctifying the existence
of a PNE option for the Soviet Union, the agreement kept the PNE
option alive for other states also.

   Even before the Brezhnev announcement, the PNE issue was
academic for most Third World societies. For instance, Egypt has
had an interest in PNEs for engineering purposes even though it may
be said that Egypt needs a million shovels rather than a PNE if the
purpose is to build a dam. Leaving that aside, even if an international PNE service had been set up under Article V of the NPT, and
the Soviet Union had been the country offering the PNE service,
Egypt could hardly have sought or accepted Soviet assistance in
view of its strained relations with Moscow after the breakup of its
friendship treaty. This example illustrates the point that the PNE
option was a theoretical one for most Third World societies even
before the Brezhnev announcement. The announcement made it
even more theoretical, and in this sense it aided the antiproliferation
cause.

   But did it help control the superpower arms race and take
steps toward denuclearization of the international environment? The
arms race involves billions of dollars; the excessive military spending does not buy more military security and it means that there are
fewer resources for economic development and peaceful social
change. During summer 1977, there were tripartite discussions
among the United States, the Soviet Union, and the United Kingdom
to negotiate a CTB/PNE ban. The negotiations were secret, but it
seemed that the public purposes of the negotiations were to achieve
a PNE ban (to kill the PNE argument in the Soviet Union and in the
Third World) and to achieve progress on the CTB (to produce arms

reductions). The former aim was directed toward the nuclear pro-liferation problem and the second one seemed to imply a need to alter the infrastructure of the superpower arms race. Thus the CTB could be seen as the first step toward denuclearization of the international environment, and could therefore be construed as a step in an extended process with no time limits.

The Brezhnev proposal, however, raised the question of whether the foregoing view of the CTB as a step in an extended process leading to denuclearization really expressed the strategy of the Americans, the Soviets, and the Western Europeans. The Brezhnev announcement's timing and scope revealed that it was an exercise with definite, limited goals. Moscow continues to have geostrategic and geopolitical disputes with the PRC; the PRC's internal power struggle is still unresolved; the PRC's internal de-bate now is about who is more anti-Soviet and who is less so. Until the Sino-Soviet relationship is settled, neither Moscow nor Peking can afford to freeze its arms race. A finite moratorium on CTB/PNE testing (as distinct from an indefinite ban) is tolerable for Moscow because the PRC is not likely to be able to bridge its military gap with the Soviet Union for at least ten years. But even though a moratorium for three to five years is tolerable on military grounds, the issue is really political. Moscow will not and cannot offer unilateral concessions to the PRC, so as to put the PRC's mind to rest, unless the PRC is willing to start normalizing Sino-Soviet relations.

The timing of Mr. Brezhnev's announcement was interesting. It occurred when Americans and Western Europeans were having growing doubts about a CTB. U.S. strategists were arguing pri-vately in 1977 that Soviet behavior reflected the psychology of the expansionist principality of Muscovy, and that bargaining with Moscow was not feasible because the negotiating behavior and the political philosophy of the Soviet Union and the United States are substantially different. Today, this line of argument has hardened into a debate about the linkage between SALT and Soviet "expansion-ism" in Africa. Moreover, say these Americans, the Soviet Union cannot catch up with U.S. military technological advances. The United States is ahead and ought to continue to be. For the United States, therefore, arms reductions are unnecessary and undesirable. A PNE moratorium is fine inasmuch as it brings the Indias and Brazils under control and thereby fosters a nonnuclearization re-gime. But if PNE control also entails a permanent ban on military testing (of new technology) and retesting (of deployed weapons sys-tem), the balance of the argument rests in favor of a moratorium and against a ban.

The Western Europeans seem to have a different set of doubts. They want a cruise missile and the neutron bomb for European defense, according to one viewpoint. Even if Eurocommunism was a passing phenomenon in European international relations, the rise of communist-linked regimes in Europe creates a danger that military secrets will pass from NATO hands into communist hands. Disputes between NATO parties (for example, the Greek-Turkish dispute) raise a question about NATO's effectiveness in these areas. Moreover, if NATO is becoming dated as the mechanism for European defense, and if the Common Market decision makers also are slowly focusing on defense, the trend may be to strengthen the European defense industry and policy-making infrastructure based on Anglo-French-West German cooperation. Today, the Federal Republic of Germany has established a major space effort in Zaire under private auspices, and there is talk of setting up an Anglo-French cruise missile project with German financial backing. Growing European interest in the cruise missile and in the neutron bomb suggests that in European thinking limited rather than open-ended denuclearization and disarmament proposals are preferred. Moscow knows this and wants the blame for the failure of a CTB ban to shift to the Americans and the Western Europeans. Meanwhile, Moscow gets a public relations advantage and keeps Peking guessing about Soviet military and political intentions.

Of course, it can be argued that as Sino-U.S. links become stronger, as the Taiwan issue is subordinated to Sino-U.S. global strategies, the Soviet Union will need to make concessions to strengthen its U.S. connection for fear of weakening its hand vis-à-vis Peking. Certainly the link between PRC rightists and Western ones indicates that global strategy rather than ideology is the hallmark of PRC diplomacy today. What count, however, are the consequences of actions and not merely their motivation. Today the PRC has emerged as an honorary member of NATO, but if NATO is becoming weaker, the PRC's advocacy of Western positions and interests in Africa and in the Third World may alienate the PRC from the Third World without adding much strength to Western diplomacy in trouble spots. Such maneuverings indicate that the great-power diplomacy is not necessarily meant to pave the way toward denuclearization and disarmament, but rather to prevent the crystallization of opposing coalitions in a world dominated by power politics. Seen in this light, Brezhnev's "concession" relieves the pressure on Moscow and leaves the next move up to the West.

The foregoing discussion indicates that at best a CTB/PNE moratorium can emerge as a finite exercise (dealing with a limited period and limited circumstances). One can argue that a limited agreement may continue for an indefinite time—that is, if the three-to five-year moratorium is extended from time to time. But on the other hand, a superpower moratorium cannot become an unlimited agreement unless the PRC and France also enter the CTB/PNE agreement. The PRC is not likely to do so unless it completes its military modernization program. The PRC's anti-Soviet policies today make more sense as a nation-building exercise than as an expression of fear about the imminence of war; but the domestic rationale is sufficient to preclude its participation in an international agreement to ban further testing. Furthermore, unless the PRC participates in a ban, even if it joins a moratorium, India is not likely to enter into a limited agreement. For India the question is, What happens after the moratorium ends? India does not fear a military threat from the superpowers at present but it has a concern—however marginal it may be at present—about the future of Sino-Indian relations, where a balance exists at present between a "have" and a "near-have." Moreover, if the search for a ban takes the form of a moratorium, the latter would leave mostly intact the Soviet PNE bureaucracy and the revival of the PNE argument in the Soviet Union cannot be excluded in the post-moratorium future. Thus buying time, not negotiating denuclearization and disarmament, seems to be the central purpose of the current disarmament diplomacy of the superpowers.

The fourth, fifth, and sixth nuclear regimes discussed above signal the deterioration of the international and regional strategic environment. Nonnuclearization seems hard to achieve because of the failure of denuclearization. The fifth and the sixth regimes, however, reveal a need to sensitize nuclear-weapon states about the implications of their behavior as these are perceived by the nonnuclear-weapon states and about the necessity of establishing a link between denuclearization and nonnuclearization. In addition, the fourth regime points to a need to sensitize proliferation-prone nonnuclear-weapon states to ensure that their activities are a consequence of conscious decision making at the highest level and not merely products of what is known as technological drift. To the extent that proliferation is a consequence of a cultural reaction to the behavior of nuclear-weapon states, proliferation cannot be stopped until the cultural distances are bridged. But still it is possible to ensure that nuclear decisions are carefully and publicly debated; that effective command and control mechanisms are established and national safety mechanisms are upgraded to conform to international standards; and that nuclear activity conforms to authorized governmental regulations and standard operating procedures. Proliferation is dangerous in part because the roots and the effects of the activity are not familiar to Western culturally bound perspectives. So growing familiarity by the nuclear-weapon states with the processes underlying Third World proliferation can help contain overreactions to the proliferation activity. At the same time, familiarity with the command and control implications of nuclear weapons and of slippery nuclear options can inject caution in the planning and decision making of proliferation-prone societies. Such caution is desirable, but it will not stop proliferation unless the cultural and political disputes among rival nations are mediated. Only if denuclearization and nonnuclearization are linked into a simultaneous negotiating process, one that involves give and take, can we look forward to a world managed by nondiscriminatory and universally relevant constraints that require real sacrifices by both the nuclear-weapon and the nonnuclear-weapon states.

NOTES

1. The interested reader is directed in particular to the extensive documentation issued by the United Nations General Assembly, by the Ad Hoc Committee on the Review of the Role of the United Nations in the Field of Disarmament, and by the Preparatory Committee for the Special Session of the General Assembly devoted to Disarmament. The latter documentation includes useful background papers prepared by the United Nations Secretariat.

2. These are: The Antarctic Treaty, December 1, 1959; The Treaty Banning Nuclear Weapons Tests in the Atmosphere, in Outer Space and under Water (Moscow Treaty), August 5, 1963; The Treaty on Principles Governing the Activities of States in the Exploration and Use of Outer Space, including the Moon and other Celestial Bodies, January 27, 1967; The Treaty for the Prohibition of Nuclear Weapons in Latin America (Treaty of Tlatelolco), February 14, 1967; The Treaty on the Non-Proliferation of Nuclear Weapons, July 1, 1968; The Treaty on the Prohibition of the Emplacement of Nuclear Weapons and Other Weapons of Mass Destruction on the Sea-Bed and the Ocean Floor and in the Subsoil Thereof, February 11, 1971; and The Convention on the Prohibition of the Development, Production and Stockpiling of Bacteriological (Biological) and Toxic Weapons and on their Destruction, April 10, 1972.

3. For the basic data see the annual Yearbook prepared by the Stockholm International Peace Research Institute.

4. Michael Howard, Studies in War and Peace (New York: The Viking Press, 1972), p. 201.

5. See M. Mandelbaum, "International Stability and Nuclear Order: The First Nuclear Regime," in Nuclear Weapons and World Politics (1980s Project/Council on Foreign Relations), edited by David C. Gompert et al. (New York: McGraw-Hill, 1977), pp. 15-80.

6. See Gompert's "Introduction," ibid., p. 6, for the narrow focus.

7. "Nonproliferation: A Long-Term Strategy," Foreign Affairs 56, no. 3 (April 1978): 602.

8. The first four regimes rely heavily on the discussion outlined in Gompert et al., op. cit.

9. See Hedley Bull, The Anarchical Society (New York: Columbia University Press, 1977).

10. J. S. Nye, "Non-Proliferation: A Long Term Strategy," Foreign Affairs 56, no. 3 (April 1978): 601-23.

11. Address by Valery Giscard D'Estaing, president of the French Republic, before the 10th Special Session of the United Nations General Assembly, New York, May 25, 1978, official text (offset), p. 6.

12. "France's Position on Disarmament," French Embassy, New York, March 1978, official text.

13. Alva Myrdal, The Game of Disarmament (New York: Pantheon Books, 1976), p. 334.

14. Ibid., p. 133.

15. Ibid., pp. 186-87.

16. Ibid., p. 95.

17. Ibid., p. 168.

18. Ibid., p. 175.

19. The Guardian, November 3, 1977.

7

NUCLEAR POWERS OF THE FUTURE: AN OVERVIEW

Acceptance of the NPT by a majority of states after 1968 created an impression that the danger of further proliferation—beyond the five nuclear weapon states (the United States, the USSR, the PRC, the United Kingdom, and France)—had been put to rest. India's "peaceful nuclear explosion" shattered this impression and pointed up the danger of proliferating nuclear options, if not nuclear weapons. The list of potential proliferators has changed from the 1950s to the 1970s and may continue to change in the 1980s. Israel (and, according to some views, India) are on the list, but others like Japan, Australia, South Africa, Brazil, South Korea, Taiwan, and Argentina must be added if proliferation is defined as a process of growth of nuclear technologies and capacities (research and development, and industrial applications) in industrially advanced and less advanced societies, including areas of tension. This chapter asserts that proliferation, while unstoppable, is slow, and not because the NPT is necessarily working, but because the military and economic security perceptions of potential proliferators do not dictate a higher rate of proliferation. Yet the possible deterioration of the strategic environment in the 1980s may induce faster proliferation. The new stress may not be on the acquisition of nuclear arms, but rather, because nuclear arms are becoming militarily less useful, on development of nuclear options coupled with a strategy of their nonuse or nonconversion into weapons.

In the 1960s the general perception of nuclear proliferation was that the NPT would serve to contain the danger. Dealing with the problem of proliferation was then defined primarily as safeguarding reactors. The evolution of the safeguards regime (see p. 6, Table 1.2) shows that as new equipment, materials, and technology were transferred beyond the North American/Western European/

Japanese network of industrially advanced nations, the scope of the international, bilateral, and multilateral safeguards regime was gradually expanded to cope with the threat that was perceived. Most of the safeguards agreements (bilaterals and trilaterals) required "peaceful uses" in the application of transferred technology, equipment, and materials. The agreements specifically forbade development, acquisition, and testing of nuclear weapons. But by and large, "peaceful use" was left ambiguous; in agreements adopted during 1956-74 (before the Indian PNE), PNEs were neither included nor excluded. In safeguards agreements made after the Indian test, the injunction against PNEs became a condition of nuclear supply. Chapters 2-6 discuss the evolution of multilateral diplomacy after the NPT came into effect, and in light of the Indian explosion.

A new trend in American thinking was revealed in congressional hearings* in the United States and in other developments, namely, the reassessment of nuclear exports policy by the Ford/ Kissinger regime, culminating in the Ford policy statement of October 26, 1976; the statements by Carter in 1976 during his candidacy; the April statements by President Carter on nuclear export policy and the setting forth of the nuclear export bill to the U.S. Congress; the writings, some secret and some open, by prominent Americans like Albert Wohlstetter of the University of Chicago and of groups assembled by the Ford Foundation and the Mitre Corporation, and so on.

The new trend had several features, as follows:

1. The old trend was to see adherence to the NPT as the principal barrier to future nuclear proliferation; the new trend in the United States was to develop restraints against future supplies of reprocessing and enrichment capacities to countries not already possessing them, and to make reprocessing difficult for countries already possessing these facilities.

2. The old trend was to think of partial safeguards, that is, safeguards on items supplied to a recipient, as a fulfillment of the requirements of the safeguards regime. Partial safeguards seemed to be the fair and right thing to do, considering it was natural to ask that propriety rights be extended from one nation to another, from

---

*Particular mention should be made of the role of Paul Leventhal, counsel to the Senate Government Operations Committee. The interplay between Leventhal and Senators Ribicoff, Percy, and Glenn is worth exploring to determine how the initial questions and initial perspectives were established, and with what sort of biases.

the seller to the buyer, for items supplied but not for indigenous production. The new trend, however, sought full-scope safeguards; that is, it tried to place indigenous production of the recipients under international inspection, thus eroding the distinction between safeguards for items supplied and no safeguards for items that were not supplied.

3. The old trend, as represented by the philosophy and language of the NPT, was to regard the plutonium fuel cycle as natural provided it was safeguarded. The new trend is represented by the thinking outlined in a study by the Ford Foundation and the Mitre Corporation:

> The process by which a country could move toward nuclear weapons through acquisition of processing facilities need not involve conscious national decisions to pursue weapons capability. The political thresholds which stand in the way of nuclear weapons are lowered by reprocessing and by use of mixed oxide fuels. The timetable on which weapons could be developed is also shortened. A country without weapons may thus find itself in a situation in which the political, social and economic costs of taking the final steps toward weapons are small at a time when external threats to national security are high. This possibility in one country may also induce it in another. Plutonium availability, as a result of reprocessing or domestic use of mixed oxide fuels, would thus amplify and destabilise conflicts.[1]

The study concludes that "there is no compelling national interest to be served by reprocessing."[2]

A number of problematic premises exist in the Ford study. The first is that the nuclear weapon acquisition process need not involve conscious national decisions. Thus technological determinism is assumed. A decision (or decisions) to acquire nuclear weapons is a grave matter. It involves making budgetary commitments that face competing resource-allocation and power-distribution issues in a developing society. Such a decision requires evaluation of the political, economic, military, and psychological costs and benefits of making nuclear weapons versus not making them, and of making nuclear weapons versus investing in a vague nuclear option. Assuming that a decision to acquire nuclear weapons is not conscious is assuming that such elements can be ignored consciously or unconsciously in bureaucratized societies like India, Brazil, Argentina, and Pakistan (and there are others). A study of the debate in India, for example, indicates a high-level, conscious debate, not only about the economic implications of nuclear weapons decisions, but also, and this is usually not stressed in American antiproliferation thinking, about the strategic and tactical purposes that can or cannot be served by nuclear weapons at present or in the foreseeable future. The premise of technological determinism lacks evidence with respect to Third World nuclear decision making. One would think that Western intellectuals trained in the art of reason and empiricism would want to prove how the process of technological determinism operates (if it does) in these societies and whether or not the opposite premise is the more sound; namely, that the process of acquiring nuclear weapons is likely to entail conscious and public decisions now that the world is alarmed about proliferation and many societies are going through intense public hearings on all aspects of nuclear energy development. Even in societies like India, Iran, Pakistan, South Korea, and Taiwan (among others), where environmentalists and nuclear safety lobbies have yet to emerge and to make a national impact, the Ford/Mitre study's plea should be for more national debates and not less reprocessing. Thus, unless one assumes that Third World leaders are fools and the public is naive, it seems better to contain the hysteria about unconscious nuclear decision making so that the U.S. public is not unduly alarmed into an emotional reaction on the subject.

Secondly, the point that reprocessing capacity lowers the political/technological thresholds makes sense. In the late 1970s and the 1980s, the technological barriers to weapons development and proliferation may lessen. But from this fact it is merely abstraction to assert that as the technological, economic, social, and political costs of moving toward nuclear weapons decline, and as external threats to national security are high, the combination of lowered thresholds and a perception of greater national security threats leads to a nuclear weapons acquisition decision. It is quite valid to study the circumstances that lead to a lowering of the threshold of weapons decisions, but the crucial variable is that the national security threats must not only be "high" (whatever that means) but they should be such that there is no other viable and visible alternative to nuclear weapons as a means of managing security.

The framework of inquiry of the Ford/Mitre study is excessively narrow. It sees "lowering" thresholds and "high" perception of national security threats as the two variables, with an "unconscious" nuclear weapons decision as the result of this mix. It ignores a number of circumstances, though. First, conventional military arms today are still very relevant for conflict and security management, in the perceptions of nuclear threshold states like India, Israel, South Korea, Taiwan, Brazil, Argentina, South Africa, and so on. Second, in Africa, the Middle East, and Latin America, subatomic strategy, interelite competition (among subnational elites), and intraelite competition are part of the national security picture; and a bulk of the political, social, economic, and military activity of such societies is executed at the subnational level. Indeed, it can be argued, as in the case of India's peaceful test in 1974, that attempts to develop nuclear explosives capacity were motivated in part by the desire of one subnational elite (the ruling group, in this case) to win out over perceived threats of competing elites. Thus the national security argument should not be overstated, simply because in many advanced and developing societies, including those with sophisticated strategic arms, the real phenomenon is competing subnationalism rather than merely threat making and deterrence of external enemies through a defined national interest or through a national security consensus.

The premise that external threats to national security are high today is probably fanciful and is at least debatable. Many Americans are prone to see high national security threats, and one cannot think of a time in the postwar American international relations and strategic literature when the threat was said to be low. The premise of a high external threat makes for good politics, but it should not be portrayed as the thinking of responsible leaders in Asia, Africa, Latin America, Europe, and even the Middle East. Asking whether there is a link between lowering thresholds to nuclear proliferation and perception of a high level of national security threats fails to ask or answer several important questions. For example, what does the leader or the ruling elite in question perceive to be the threat? Is it high or low in its perceptions? How much reliance can be placed on the public posturing of the leader or ruling elite, recognizing that Third World leaders also have domestic and international audiences to cope with? Does the actual pattern of decision making in security policy suggest irrationality of a type that threatens the world order? Are Americans overreacting to the outside world because of their self-centeredness and because of their ignorance of how others think and behave? Might cross-cultural analyses of Third World decision making help the cause of American public education and re-education? Is not evidence of "normalization," or the search for normalization in the thinking of many leaders (the promoters of Ostpolitik, the builders of ASEAN, the advocates of a South Asian peace zone and a common market, the practitioners of "no war, no peace" Soviet-Chinese and India-China borders, and so on), a basis for optimism? It can be argued that as societies become preoccupied with quality-of-life questions, as economic concerns impinge on defense and nuclear resource allocation issues, as nations look inward and become self-contained and less prone to external interference, the current trend toward normalizing external relations may emerge as a trend in world politics in the 1980s. It may not, but in fairness to its readers the Ford/Mitre study and others ought to sketch both an optimistic and a pessimistic setting for proliferation analyses.

Lastly, the premise in the Ford/Mitre study that if one country goes nuclear it may induce another country to do the same seems to rely on the notion that the interstate system is a society of fools where an example is contagious. This perspective fails to account for one crucial element. Leaders respond to their domestic enemies and their international enemies as they see them. It is naive to assert that Indians copy the Israelis, or Brazilians copy the Indians, and so on. All that can be said is that one country may adopt another country's rationalization to justify changes in its behavior. Still, the onus is on the researcher to investigate the underlying motives for a particular decision and to assess the interplay between pressures of competing subnational elites and external developments.

Predicting proliferation trends is a hazardous activity. Because national intelligence estimates of capabilities, and particularly of intentions, are imprecise, our conceptions and images* are culture-bound. Ambiguities not only characterize the world order but, furthermore, are deliberately fostered in the negotiating behavior of the major military powers. Deliberately fostered ambiguities serve to prevent the acquisition of intelligence just as improved communications aid in acquisition of intelligence. Still, the exercise must be undertaken if the margin of uncertainty is to be reduced and if realistic solutions are to be found that appeal both to the major military powers and to potential powers.

Incentives and disincentives for going nuclear vary from one state to another. For this study's purpose, incentives to explode a device or to possess one in an untested form could be any of the following: to achieve a deterrent against a potential nuclear enemy; to neutralize the conventional military superiority of an enemy; to gain international, regional, or domestic prestige; to participate in international or regional security policy making; to reduce dependence on a great power; to stay abreast of modern technology so that scientific or technological dependence on great powers is avoided or minimized; to create ambiguity in enemy calculations; to induce the enemy of a

---

*Images are loosely defined as one's view of the other side's expected behavior and its expected consequences. Included also in the definition is one's self-image; what one is, wants, and can do, and what the likely effects of one's actions are.

potential proliferator not to force the latter to decide in favor of making nuclear weapons; to experiment with the potential economic prospects of PNEs; and so on.[3] Disincentives for going nuclear (defined as developing and deploying nuclear weapons systems) could be any of a number of factors. Premature decisions to produce and deploy nuclear weapons could increase regional and international tension and could interfere with normalization of relations. There are budgetary and political advantages to the noncommitment implied in continuing nuclear research and development without moving toward weapons production. If nuclear weapons are becoming less useful militarily, weapons with long lead times may be prone to obsolescence and be costly for national development, and yet may not add to national security. Threats to proliferate can aid negotiations of conventional arms transfers; and so on. This study assumes that security assurances by great powers are worthless in the perceptions of potential nuclear powers. The prospects of nuclear disarmament (defined as zero level of arms) are nonexistent at present and perhaps are even undesirable in contemporary international relations. Finally, morality has practically no role in a highly nuclearized, militarized, and commercialized world.

Overall, at present, the incentives to go nuclear exceed the disincentives. The message of this study is that no one is really interested in negotiating disarmament because states, even the developed ones, continue to be dissatisfied—politically, militarily, and economically. While militarily powerful states want to negotiate arms control (meaning stable military relations with no necessary reduction of arms), to regulate the dangers of unlimited competition rather than to reduce their arsenals, many potential powers want to improve their bargaining position vis-à-vis their competitors by altering the structure of contemporary international society. This means a desire to diffuse further, to distribute more widely, power and influence in the world today. As long as nuclear power is an element of power and influence, its growth will continue to be motivated by political, economic, and security considerations, irrespective of how the growth is rationalized. It may be important for the evolution of world order that many of the potential powers are located, or are likely to be located, in the southern half of the globe. The trend clearly points to a southward orientation of international nuclear relations. The North America-South Asia nuclear ties in the 1950s started this focus, but today one needs to consider a number of North-South nuclear linkages, such as between the Federal Republic of Germany and South Africa, the Federal Republic of Germany and Brazil, South Africa and Taiwan, India and Argentina, Japan and Australia, and so on. Some of the linkages are more significant than others, but the growth of nuclear power in the southern half of the globe points to a reordering of power and influence world-wide.

In a sense then, the problem of slowing proliferation in the less satisfied states in the Third World requires a prior understanding of the policy perceptions in these societies and the effects of the behavior of the industrialized and westernized societies in the Third World. The problem is not merely one of educating or re-educating Third World elites. It is also one of expanding the range of public education in developed societies and of re-educating the elites in the developed societies. Conceptualizing the relationship between horizontal and vertical proliferation using detailed case studies is, therefore, a desirable underpinning of scholarly and policy activities. The point here is not that potential nuclear powers will seek nuclear explosives capacity just because five states have nuclear weapons. The point is that if nuclear weapons remain useful as military and diplomatic instruments for five nuclear-weapon states, the nuclear factor may enter the in-house bureaucratic debates of nations aside from these five in a big way in the 1980s. In a sense, until the existing five nuclear-weapon states are able to define publicly the end uses of atomic and thermonuclear weapons (assuming they continue to be militarily and diplomatically useful) and to reduce their nuclear arsenals in a manner that reflects a process of making real sacrifices, the in-house bureaucratic debates in Third World societies are not likely to be impressed with, say, President Carter's "open mouth" antiproliferation speech making. What counts to them is behavior, not talk. Thus, even though many share the goal of slowing vertical and horizontal proliferation, goal achievement depends on how the present nuclear-weapon states behave, and how their behavior is perceived by their audiences in the threshold states.

SCENARIOS OF THE FUTURE

As indicated previously, the future will be shaped by a number of factors, many of which are unrelated to nuclear proliferation. Even in that context, not all relevant factors may be desirable, and those that are desirable may have diverse and sometimes contradictory impacts; for example, a normalization of relations between the USSR and the PRC may make strategic arms limitations (and hence acceptance of curbs on proliferation) more likely, but it may also arouse fears among the Japanese (and others) that could induce them to seek nuclear weapons. Nevertheless, it is possible both to define active trends that could slow proliferation and, in light of these, to assess the likelihood of proliferation, just as it is possible to assess that likelihood under other, less favorable circumstances. This section deals with that task.

An Optimistic Scenario

The central lesson about proliferation to be learned from a study of French, PRC, and Indian behavior is that proud and powerful societies are unwilling to exempt themselves from the opportunities and obligations of power politics. This motive has the potentiality of creating stability or instability, depending on whether the superpowers are willing to share their prerogatives or whether their policy is to exclude other major military powers from the decision-making process in strategic affairs—for example, in SALT and the CCD. A primary assumption underlying this optimistic scenario is, therefore, that the global powers begin to recognize the implications for proliferation of their efforts to duopolize power and to determine outcomes by virtue of that power. As the superpowers succeed in loosening their stronghold on international security policy making; as SALT gradually becomes a multilateral exercise in the 1980s; as the CCD is reorganized and brought closer into the UN machinery to permit discussion of the links between disarmament and development (thus going beyond the current discussion of limited arms control measures), with a revised agenda and revised negotiating mechanisms, it may be that potential nuclear powers will decide to slow or to abandon attempts to acquire a nuclear option, on the grounds that they can obtain the political benefits of proliferation without incurring the political (and other) costs.

Another assumption underlying the optimistic scenario is that as the PRC is brought into closer and more beneficial contact with the rest of the world, the exercise can aid the normalization tendencies within the PRC. This is on the premise that the PRC's first priority is to modernize rather than to generate revolutionary upheaval in the world, or even in Southeast or South Asia. At least one superpower now recognizes the importance of bringing the PRC into SALT. According to L. I. Brezhnev:

> Certainly the time will inevitably come when the question of associating other nuclear powers with the process of strategic arms limitation will come up on the agenda. Any powers that refuse to join would be assuming a grave responsibility before the peoples.[4]

If this statement is seriously intended, one implication is that the future of SALT depends on PRC participation. Another implication is that eventually both superpowers may desire PRC participation in the SALT dialogue and thereby pave the way for involvement of the other major military powers as well in SALT III in the 1980s. This may even lead to a merger of the SALT dialogue and the work of the CCD in the 1980s. This scenario assumes that some sort of normalization between Moscow and Peking may occur and that, if the frontier dispute is bypassed, if Sino-Soviet trade and military ties are restored to an extent, the PRC may become willing and able to participate constructively first in the UN Special Session on Disarmament in 1978 and then in the SALT dialogue in the 1980s.

If Moscow and Peking can mediate their rivalry through bilateral means, the normalization process (according to this optimistic view) is likely to aid normalization in regions neighboring the USSR and the PRC, particularly in South Asia. Thus, if Sino-Soviet normalization occurs, if it leads to (or is preceded by) Sino-Indian and Indo-Pakistani normalization, some of the incentives to go nuclear (beyond exploding a nuclear device) are reduced. Here the nexus of PRC-India-Pakistan normalization is held to account for slow and controlled proliferation of nuclear options in South Asia, with the implication that complete normalization (an ideal state) could conceivably lead to no proliferation. Likewise, the prospect of the PRC's active participation in the disarmament dialogue at the UN special session in 1978 could result in arms limitations, and perhaps arms reductions by the great powers, and thereby improve the climate for slowing of proliferation among at least some of the potential nuclear powers. Overall, in this scenario, once the PRC's entry into the superpowers' nuclear dialogue has been arranged, then a momentum toward arms reduction may grow because the underlying security issues, or at least some of these, will have been resolved or shelved. A spillover effect of this change will be to induce other major military powers to avoid complicating the international security agenda by continuing programs for the acquisition of nuclear weapons.

Another factor in the optimistic scenario is the expectation that France can be induced to alter its present position on the NPT and its present policy of promoting nuclear sales of reprocessing plants and other sensitive technology to potential proliferators in the Third World. Because of the French position in the London Agreement (1976), three issues are at stake. The first involves an exploration of the prospects of upgrading the safeguards requirements with a view to moving toward full-scope safeguards that apply to the entire peaceful nuclear industry of states not presently nuclear-weapon powers. The guidelines published in 1978 by the London Nuclear Suppliers Club reveal a failure to agree on full-scope safeguards because of French and West German opposition, but the issue is still on the agenda. The second issue is the question of the political wisdom of sales of sensitive items like reprocessing plants. Pending the outcome of the INFCE exercise (1977-79), the Federal Republic of Germany and France agreed in the summer of 1977 to ban "at present" future exports of these items but not to renounce existing contracts. This ban is likely to continue indefinitely. Thirdly, inasmuch as the Federal Republic of Germany is held to be hiding behind the French position, a shift in the latter could conceivably induce a shift in the former also so that there will be no repeat of the Federal Republic of Germany–Brazil nuclear deal. This scenario is optimistic inasmuch as there is a hope, if not an expectation, that the French position has evolved and may continue to evolve to the point that it coincides with policies of the United States and Canada. Optimism is warranted in North American thinking inasmuch as further technological barriers can be realistically created against the potential nuclear powers in current and future nuclear sales.

A fourth factor is rooted in the view that certain Third World societies may be credited with innovative strategic thought and behavior. This scenario suggests that analytically it is possible to differentiate three types of nuclear strategies for states to follow. The first type, as practiced by the superpowers, is to engage in a constant arms race on the assumption that incremental change in the adversaries' capacities has the potential of shifting the balance or of increasing the uncertainties. The second type is the one that the PRC appears to follow; namely, to avoid an arms race to seek a minimum deterrent but not to endeavor (deliberately or inadvertently) to bridge the gap in capabilities, because bridging this gap is difficult or unnecessary. The third type, which India is probably practicing, is to engage in nonconversion of its nuclear option into a weapons system. The first type may be said to express a preference for nonuse of nuclear weapons; the third type expresses a preference for nonconversion of an option into deployable weapons.

A fifth factor is the perception that certain potential nuclear powers are beginning to reduce their enthusiasm for nuclear proliferation and have become receptive to some extent to Western discussions about the dangers of proliferation. Whether this shift in attitudes will continue depends in part on continuing efforts by these countries to learn, coupled with efforts to create more technological and political barriers against sensitive nuclear exports. In part, it also depends on a real movement toward arms reduction, so that an international lessening of the arms race can aid bureaucratic and public debates in favor of regional and national reductions also. Thus, the impact of this factor on proliferation, like that of others, is dependent on deliberate policy choices by both existing and potential nuclear powers.

Regional Outcomes under an Optimistic Scenario

If proliferation is seen as a process rather than a terminal condition, five regions bear scrutiny. These are South and Southwest Asia, Northeast Asia, the Middle East, Southern Africa, and Latin America. Because the range of inquiry is vast and each society has its own set of perceptions and circumstances, what follows is a rash attempt to paint a picture in bold brush strokes. The task here is to provide a sense of the future and to offer summary overviews in subsequent chapters, leaving detailed case studies for future research.

India is a useful starting point for the consideration of South and Southwest Asia, not because it is actually the sixth proliferator in the world but because it appears so to many observers. Proliferation in Pakistan will validate the theory of nuclear chains.[5] Western thinking is somewhat as follows: Just because India tested one PNE, Pakistan will be induced to copy India. (It is noted that Pakistan reacted in many ways to India's test: by developing its indigenous nuclear option; by seeking external guarantees against nuclear threat or aggression; by seeking conventional arms as a trade-off to a threat to go nuclear; and so on. But the implications of alternative strategies are not spelled out in these analyses.) Secondly, India tested a nuclear device to demonstrate its political will. Its purpose was not achieved and hence India will need more nuclear tests. Hence Pakistan will need to continue to copy India until Pakistan and India have a mutual deterrent. It is assumed that given technological momentum Indian PNEs will gradually and eventually become nuclear weapons, if they have not already.

There are problems with the foregoing analysis. If "action-reaction" is central to explaining Indo-Pakistan nuclear relations, why was Pakistan's nuclear development stifled or slowed during 1958-72, when Pakistan's diplomats actively argued about the dangers of "Indian proliferation?" Plainly, President Ayub Khan was more interested in Pakistan's economic and military development. Thus, the domestic political barriers to proliferation must be noted in the case of Pakistan up to 1972, if not later. True, Bhutto wanted to be innovative by renouncing Ayub Khan's policies, hoping thereby to impress the public. But surely today someone in Pakistan is arguing about the utility of having more rigs to tap oil against the utility of having more nuclear reactors. This is not to predict that Pakistan will not explode a bomb after it establishes convincingly its reactor and reprocessing program. The concern here is to suggest that in Pakistan, as elsewhere, there are competing resource allocation issues and arguments. With the downfall of the Bhutto regime, civilian bureaucrats in Pakistan find it easier to work with their military counterparts, and thereby they could accelerate the nuclear program with a view to considering again the Kashmir issue and to diverting the public's attention from pressing problems of domestic, economic, and social reform. But on the other hand, if Pakistan's military knows the military score with India, if the future of the new regime depends on no more adventurism with India, if the future depends on a gradual evolution in India-Pakistan-Iran affairs (starting with improvement of official and nonofficial ties between the Punjabs and ending with an open Kashmir border and a South-Southwest Asian common market), then the nuclear factor may slip into the background.

Admittedly, Pakistan's atomic energy talent is now first-rate. With the French sale of a nuclear reprocessing plant,* or if Pakistan is able to secure a reprocessing laboratory from a West European source or if it gains technology through clandestine contacts with South Africa (which South Africans deny), Pakistan may be able to have, by the early 1980s, a capacity to explode a device. Yet someone in Islamabad may be arguing today that it is sufficient to have a capacity to explode a device but not to use it, since Pakistan, unlike India, does not distinguish between peaceful and military explosions; that leaking information about that capacity through the pages of Pakistan Times will be sufficient to induce Indian restraint; that since the reprocessing capability will be heavily safeguarded by the IAEA, the burden and the opportunity for violating the safeguards should rest on Indian action that threatens Pakistan's national security—for example, an Indian invasion of Pakistan. In other words, it may make sense for Pakistan to follow Israel's example rather than India's.

There is also a problem with those who argue that Pakistan will need to go nuclear because India will continue to test because its first test failed in its primary goal, which was to impress the major powers who needed impressing. But who is to say that the test was not an exercise in political signaling? As the Far Eastern Review notes, "one bomb can be enough to shift your strategic posture—and that of your neighbours, allies and enemies—in unexpected and significant ways."[6] Instead of arguing that a nuclear test by a poor country devalues the impact of a test, perhaps the reasoning should be as follows: India's test proves that an unevenly developed society, with food-population problems but with a decent scientific establishment and a strong-willed leader, can explode a device.

---

*This was canceled in 1978.

Testing a device still requires much political commitment and scientific or technological prowess. India's test proves that the major powers were impressed with the fact that India would dare to flout their prescriptions in such a subtle and yet explicit fashion, and damage the NPT.

Conceivably Gandhi's test had a variety of audiences. Her first audience (indeed, some say, her prime audience) was a domestic one—and it is possible that the May 1974 test was meant to divert attention from Gandhi's growing domestic problems by arousing Indian nationalism through an Indian test. A second audience was the PRC; here the message was to signal India's intention to take the nuclear route unless the PRC was more accommodating in India-PRC and subcontinental relations. The third audience consisted of the superpowers. To these the test signaled that India ought not to be taken for granted in international security affairs. These were Gandhi's signals, but she also received a signal from her supporters in the Aid India Consortium. The message was clear that if India exploded one more test that might be the end of foreign assistance to India.

In other words, if the messages were sent and received, the acknowledgment implied two things. First, India was not going to be in a hurry to keep exploding nuclear devices unnecessarily. Prime Minister Desai stated this publicly in 1976, and this was implied in Gandhi's behavior after June 1974, even though she was reluctant, as is Prime Minister Desai, to offer a binding contractual pledge in this regard. Secondly, as the message was converted into "action" by the receiver, the result was a search for normalization of subcontinental relations. The question at present is not if there will be normalization, or if there is normalization. Rather, the question is about the speed, scope, and permanence of the normalization. In Indian thinking the sense is strong that protecting Pakistan as a strategic buffer is in India's self-interest. India has no wish to seek common borders with the Soviet Union and Iran, a sentiment which Iranians probably share. As such, advocates of nuclear explosions in Islamabad will need to assess carefully the foreign policy and defense implications. This does not mean that India is against Pakistani proliferation. It means that India prefers that proliferation in Pakistan be slow, as is India's, and predictable, as it should be, so that South Asia's constituents abroad have a chance to comprehend fully the geostrategic realities and to adjust their sanctimonious perceptions to realities.

Given the Indo-Pakistan "nuclear chain" proceeds slowly, if at all, the addition of Iran to this chain is even more difficult to assess. Iran had adhered to the NPT. This meant little since the Shah of Iran had already declared the possibility of changing the policy should circumstances change. Iran has a modest atomic energy program and it imports nuclear items from the United States, France, and West Germany, among others. Neither India nor Iran can benefit from the disintegration of Pakistan (but still the possibility of disintegration cannot be excluded should Pakistan become adventurist over Kashmir), but Iranian nuclear arms (or an option) could relate to two theoretical contingencies: to deter a troublesome Soviet presence in the Persian Gulf, and to catch up with India and Pakistan if these countries acquire a nuclear-weapons status. The Shah's and the Iranian elite's plan to make Iran the world's fifth great power could be a motive.

However, these motives are not realistic at present. Given anti-Soviet fears in Iran, even if these are seriously intended and are not merely nation-building and alliance-building activities, its conventional capacities are better means to police the Persian Gulf. The role of status is important if Iranians perceive India as the emerging dominant power in the region. Yet this is not an issue now. The dominant trend in Indian and Iranian thinking is to develop Iran and India as the two pillars of the South and Southwest Asian community. The presence of Iran is Pakistan's insurance that India will not dominate the region. It encourages moderate Indian thinking to secure interdependencies through official and nonofficial relations in cultural, academic, trade, and investment spheres with Pakistan and Iran, so that all parties develop the habit of cooperation and see the benefits of partnership in regional growth. The Iranian concern with India's nuclear status, however, could become meaningful if the Indo-Iranian détente fails and if the two regional powers come to disagree about the future of the Indian Ocean. In view of domestic disorder in Iran in 1977 an Indo-Iranian clash seems to be only a remotely hypothetical possibility.

But if Iran, unlike India and Pakistan, is still at the prenuclear option stage, it nevertheless has strong nuclear concerns. At present these are expressed in its disarmament diplomacy. If they are not clarified, they could conceivably enter the Iranian bureaucratic debate in a big way, as they could in debates in certain Arab societies during the 1980s. At present Iran does not need PNEs. But at the same time it does not want its hands to be tied with extensive rules. Israel's nuclear bombs do not bother Iran. Still, it prefers a Middle Eastern nuclear weapon-free zone (NWFZ) to become a stepping stone toward the NPT, with a view to inducing Israel to join the NWFZ.

Talk about an Indian-Pakistani-Iranian nuclear chain is considered highly speculative at this stage. Instead, the Iranian stress is on getting the nuclear-weapon states to accept in principle a willingness to discuss security guarantees. The exact details, sequence of moves, and eventual outcome of moves are imprecise. For instance, what are the geographical limits of a Middle East NWFZ? Does it include North Africa and South Asia? Conceivably Iran's NWFZ diplomacy implies probing on Pakistan's behalf also, and a linkage is implied between a quest for security guarantees by the nuclear-weapon states and the definitions in a NWFZ. The concern about a NWFZ is directed to the nuclear superpowers but also to bureaucratic debates in Middle Eastern societies. If the United States stated that it would provide a strategic umbrella, the effect of the advocates of nuclear weapons would be neutralized.

Instead, the superpowers' attitude is purely defensive. While the United States appears to be more willing to debate than the USSR, neither is prepared to play the game on any terms other than its own. While paying lip service to the idea of a NWFZ, neither superpower is really willing to let a NWFZ hinder its freedom. For instance, until Sino-Soviet relations improve, the USSR is not even willing to consider a pledge not to threaten use of nuclear weapons against the PRC.

Given such tendencies, Iranians draw these conclusions: The whole exercise of finding a NWFZ in the Middle East and South Asia may be too late, and India, Israel, and Egypt remain suspicious. Still, the disarmament process is a long one and quick progress should not be expected. Even if some progress is made that may be worthwhile. Moreover, at present for Iran there is no alternative to talking about disarmament. The superpowers may come to a point where having a NWFZ could serve their strategic purpose. But until that happens Iran needs to resist U.S. pressure to seek more control through proposals such as regional reprocessing plants.

The area considered next is Northeast Asia. The foregoing scenario suggests that slow proliferation in South Asia is tied to an expectation of a slow normalization in Sino-Soviet and in regional affairs. This process can buy time, just as the implementation of safeguards under the London Nuclear Suppliers Club (1976)* can buy time. Buying time is useful if the time is to be put to constructive use to educate elites in developed and developing societies. The strategy of talking about nonproliferation should be discarded because posturing produces counterposturing. A more constructive strategy might be to stop talking about nonproliferation publicly but quietly to

---

*The Nuclear Suppliers Group agreed on guidelines in 1976 and made these public in early 1978. The group failed to agree to require the acceptance of full-scope safeguards, and this matter is still officially under review.

stress, for instance, the economic and technical problems of buying and selling reprocessing plants, in instances where the economic justifications of such a plant are hazy. But if Canada may need to consider reprocessing for its needs in a 20-year time scale, the antireprocessing argument cannot be pressed; it may already be a lost cause. It might be better to remove the odium of discrimination—to safeguard all nuclear exports similarly, irrespective of the status of the buyer in terms of the NPT. Prime Minister Desai has a point when he argues that he is willing to place the entire Indian nuclear industry under full-scope safeguards if the five nuclear weapon states will do the same with respect to all their facilities, and not merely a selected few facilities (as the United States and the United Kingdom offer at present).

A strategy of buying time may make sense for South Asia, but normalization in Central Asian relations may have adverse implications for Japan in the 1980s. At present Japanese views stress the following: Seoul does not face a nuclear threat from North Korea. If Seoul acquires nuclear weapons they would look provocative to North Korea and Japan. Seoul is not likely to acquire nuclear weapons, and if it has nuclear ambitions, Washington is likely to check these. Nuclear weapons for Taiwan are not probable, even though Taiwan, more than Seoul, can develop these. According to Japan there is no speedy solution for disarmament; it is still trying to create an atmosphere for disarmament.

Japan is clearly the key to proliferation in the Pacific area, not because it is more influential than the PRC but because it is more unpredictable. True, Japan participates in the London Agreement. Still, its position should be noted. The positions of Canada, the USSR, the United Kingdom, and the United States are similar (though the United States has a greater recognition of obstacles). They seek safeguards on the entire fuel cycle and, if possible, on all peaceful nuclear industry of a recipient state. France and West Germany seek safeguards on their supplies and this represents the London Suppliers Group's consensus. Japan's position is somewhere in between these positions. It has traditionally mistrusted standards unless these apply to all its competitors.

Several circumstances make Japan's nuclear abstention uncertain in the 1980s. The logic and argument against nuclear proliferation is not really clear-cut. As NPT safeguards requirements are constantly upgraded, the NPT safeguards will be used increasingly to interpret the work of the IAEA. This may increase resentment among IAEA members who resent IAEA/NPT safeguards. So far the NPT regime has barely survived despite the superpowers' effort to insulate the IAEA and the NPT from criticism in the NPT Review Conference (1975). If nothing tangible happens in the field of disarmament by the early 1980s the NPT regime could collapse. Some states have already threatened withdrawal, but the threats have not been carried out; and it may take 10-20 withdrawals to collapse the NPT. In such a tenuous setting, a trend toward Sino-Soviet normalization could create doubts about Japan's future, about the credibility of the U.S. commitments in the Pacific region, and about the effect of a shift of the Asian balance in favor of the communist states. Furthermore, the prospect of Sino-Soviet normalization could conceivably induce the USSR to take a harder line against the United States. In such circumstances, it may make sense for the Japanese to upgrade their defense expenditures, to invest more in maritime forces, and to make their nuclear option visible, with or without tacit U.S. concurrence. In addition, if Japan defects from the U.S. alliance, Australia may find itself preparing its nuclear option, if it already does not have a theoretical one at present. At present it has not decided on Australian uranium enrichment (with Japan's and/or France's collaboration) but the infrastructure to carry out uranium enrichment exists in Australia today.

This discussion turns now to Latin America and South Africa. The national circumstances of Brazil and Argentina with regard to proliferation vary from those of South Africa. The latter's future in Africa is bedeviled by the pressure of Black Africa. Argentina and Brazil carry no such burden of racism. Still, there is merit in examining these societies collectively. South Africa and Brazil are economic giants among pygmies. Brazil and Argentina are most active in disarmament diplomacy. Brazil and Argentina adhere to the Treaty of Tlatelolco (with reservations) but not to the NPT; South Africa rejects the NPT at present but officially is keeping the matter of adherence under review. All three have positions on the NPT similar to India's, and Brazil and Argentina have expressed themselves in favor of the PNEs. South Africa has first-rate enriched uranium technology but not reprocessing technology, whereas Brazil has gained access to reprocessing and German jet nozzle technology. South Africa participated in the Zangger Committee discussions but is not a party to the London Agreement.

The real impact of these societies at present lies not in the probability that they will develop nuclear weapons. Rather, it lies in their revisionist views about nuclear safeguards and their impact on the disarmament debate. The Federal Republic of Germany-Brazil nuclear deal is not viewed in Argentina as the first step toward a Brazilian bomb. Neither are South African nuclear bombs of much use against fanatical black guerrillas. The real point about Brazil and Argentina (and Mexico) is that they think that the superpowers are playing a double game, both consolidating their hold on the structure of power in the world and expressing phony concerns about horizontal proliferation. That is, the great powers agree on marginal disarmament issues or issues that can be safely ignored but not on issues that threaten the present structure of power. It is argued by Latin Americans that if NWFZs are to be promoted, there should be common treatment for all such zones; the rights and obligations should be identical or equivalent. Others however argue that the Tlatelolco Treaty is a useful model but not the only model. Even this treaty shows how the NWFZ concept cannot really be implemented until the views and interests of all involved parties are taken into account. Subsequent chapters discuss the problems of a NWFZ in Latin America and Africa.

A Pessimistic Scenario

Even under the optimistic scenario, there may be eight or ten nuclear powers a decade hence rather than the five (or six) now extant. The pessimistic scenario does not envision a rapid and uncontrolable increase in the number of proliferators, partly because the Third World societies most likely to proliferate have paid constant and careful attention to the external environment. It does, however, recognize that because these countries are relatively immune to Western pleading about the dangers of proliferation, there are likely to be considerable difficulties in negotiating nonproliferation in a complex international environment.

If, therefore, Sino-Soviet-Indo-Pakistani normalization fails to establish interdependencies in the political, security, commercial, and cultural areas, if intergovernmental and intersocietal habits of cooperation and interdependency fail to emerge within five to ten years, the weaker parties are likely to make visible their need to seek security through conventional and nuclear means, that is, to practice self-reliance and to seek minimal dependency on external partners. In this case, there may be controlled proliferation among continental (or subcontinental) Asian societies, while the process may be less pronounced or marginal in insular Asian countries, including Australia.

Even if normalization occurs in Sino-Soviet, Sino-Indian, and Indo-Pakistani relations (that is, among continental Asian states) this does not mean an end to proliferation. If these countries are able to negotiate and moderate their rivalries in a decade or so, given the long lead time for nuclear weapons development, will U.S. allies (namely, Japan, Australia, Iran, and perhaps even the Federal Republic of Germany) find themselves constrained to rethink their nuclear options? As a corollary, will Taiwan and South Korea be tempted to make their nuclear options visible, either to follow the lead of the other U.S. allies or to strengthen their negotiating stance vis-à-vis the United States? In short, will proliferation among the U.S. allies be a function of normalization between the USSR, the PRC, and India?

Even if it is not, one may see a trend toward a multipolar world because the danger of superpower nuclear conflict has lessened and because new centers of regional and international power and influence have emerged. From a Third World and a third-party perspective this is a desirable and inevitable trend. However, the superpowers' loss of political and economic control over third parties means also a loss of control over their decisions to create nuclear options or to build nuclear weapons. Hence, while some incentives to proliferation may diminish, so will some disincentives. One may, for a variety of reasons, see the emergence of 10 or 20 new nuclear powers, if not during the 1980s, at least in the 1990s.

IMPLICATIONS FOR THE SUPERPOWERS

A firm conclusion about the outcome of the relationship between "slow, controlled proliferation" and nonproliferation processes cannot be offered, because future foreign policy alignments are unpredictable. Still, superpowers' reactions to the optimistic and pessimistic scenarios may be briefly noted as well as policies that they might follow to bring about what each power regards as an optimistic future for itself.

To date, nonproliferation has been regarded as a goal shared by the superpowers since at least the mid-1960s. There are doubts whether the superpowers' commitment is real or whether bilateral and regional priorities signal a limited defection from nonproliferation and arms control. Thus, the USSR could not, and did not, complain too much about India's test because the USSR still needs India against the PRC. Likewise, the United States, unlike Canada, chose not to terminate its nuclear supply relationship with India because that would have meant a loss of leverage and of political and technological intelligence. It is debatable whether unwillingness to punish India reflects a superpower preference tacitly to support India or a recognition that punishment would serve no purpose. Overall, the superpowers' reactions are seemingly guided by a joint concern for slowing proliferation. This identity of views exists at the level of rhetoric and in the London Nuclear Suppliers Club meetings. But the identity is not total. The USSR believes in, and adheres to, full-scope safeguards in its supply policy. Before Carter became president, the United States believed in safeguards for items supplied—that is, the end use of those items must be according to the supply

contract but the entire nuclear industry of the recipient is not safeguarded. Therefore, historically speaking, Soviet safeguards are
more demanding that U.S. ones. Aside from this, if Sino-Soviet
relations do not improve, the superpowers are likely to continue to
defend the NPT, to seek improvements in the IAEA, to stress the
need to safeguard or prevent the export of sensitive technology, and
so on.

However, a real question exists over whether the USSR would
abandon its commitment to nonproliferation and arms control if the
bait was the prospect of Sino-Soviet normalization in the 1980s where
both the USSR and the PRC adopted a give-and-take policy. In such a
hypothetical situation, the joint and antiproliferation strategy of the
superpowers could change. The USSR, PRC, and France could begin
to pave the way for a merger of the SALT and the CCD dialogues.
Such an optimistic situation for the USSR and its partners could only
be pessimistic for the United States and its allies, if it meant a reduced emphasis on superpower détente—that is, keeping the PRC
out of SALT.

The policy implications for the United States are troublesome
for the 1980s. To encourage a slowdown of proliferation, for example in South and Southwest Asia, the United States ought to encourage the Sino-Soviet-India-Pakistan normalization process. But normalization and nonproliferation in South Asia are marginal to U.S.
security. Consequently, it makes sense for the United States to tol-
erate South and Southwest Asian nuclear proliferation as well as proliferation elsewhere, except perhaps among allies whose assistance
and dependence is needed to promote U.S. interests. It may make
sense for the United States to debate publicly the underlying interests
rather than to harp endlessly on a goal that may, in certain circumstances, run counter to U.S. interests.

Finally, it should be recognized that issues deemed to have
been solved or shelved could appear actively on the agenda again in
the 1980s.. It must never be forgotten that détente is a highly tenuous
activity in terms of what is sought and what is achieved. Neither
must it be forgotten that there is a constant interaction among
Europe, and Central Asia, and East Asia in the foreign strategies
of the major powers. [7] The NPT emerged in the context of a superpower concern to keep the lid on Bonn's nuclear aspirations and to
keep Germany divided. (Whether or not the concerns are justified
is beside the point.) If Sino-Soviet normalization takes root, the
German-Soviet Ostpolitik may become unhinged, with or without the
tacit approval of the United States. In such circumstances in Europe
and Asia, global and continental relations rather than regional or
local ones will have radicalized the shifts toward proliferation on a
scale much larger, and much more ominous in its implications, than
that of a controlled Indian test and its effects.

How do the regional actors view the trends and uncertainties in the international and regional environment, and with what implications for their economic, military, and political security? If decision makers must of necessity respond to overlapping and at times contradictory trends in their security environments, how does the mix of resources diplomacy, bilateral political relations, military concerns, and domestic politics impinge upon nuclear decision making? If proliferation is defined as acquisition of tested or untested capabilities to build the bomb through reprocessing and enrichment processes, is not the net of countries that are proliferation-prone wider than the group of states that are outside the NPT or states who do not accept full-scope safeguards? Current NPT parties are also proliferation-prone, because countries like Japan, Australia, and the Federal Republic of Germany already have bomb-making capabilities; the NPT regime is fragile because of the withdrawal clause; international safeguards, even with an ungraded regime, cannot provide "timely detection" of diversion into military use; there are no real sanctions if a diversion is detected, because imposition of penalties by the nuclear suppliers also entails costs for the suppliers; and the political and psychological commitment implied by adherence to the NPT is based on the premise that the NPT is a good treaty for good times but may not be so good for bad times. Under these circumstances the proliferation process is a function of the perceived deterioration of the security environment of the decision makers in the threshold states. To assess the circumstances that favor proliferation and those that inhibit proliferation, and to study the evolving trends in terms of the thinking of the potential proliferators are the tasks of the following chapters.

NOTES

1. Nuclear Power: Issues and Choices, Ford Foundation and Mitre Corporation study (Cambridge, Mass.: Ballinger, 1977), p. 332.
2. Ibid., p. 333.
3. The Annals 430 (March 1977): 85.
4. L. I. Brezhnev, Report of the CPSU Central Committee and the Party's Immediate Objectives in Domestic and Foreign Policy, 25th Cong. of the CPSU, February 24, 1976, p. 33.
5. See Lewis Dunn and Herman Kahn, Trends in Nuclear Proliferation, 1975-1995, Hudson Institute, HI-2336-RR/3, May 15, 1976. This study offers a worldwide perspective on nuclear chains.
6. Far Eastern Economic Review 99, no. 1 (January 6, 1978): 24.
7. Lionel Gelber, Crisis in the West: American Leadership and the Global Balance (London: Macmillan, 1975), p. 118.

8

SOUTH ASIA: NUCLEAR CHAINS, OR INTRAELITE POLITICS AND CREEPING DEPENDENCIES?

INTRODUCTION

In May 1974 India exploded a "peaceful" nuclear device, using a sophisticated implosion technique in an underground explosion. The only physical casualty of the test was an unfortunate crow who happened to be at the test site and died of shock! The test was controlled physically, but it sent psychological shock waves through many national capitals. Some people asserted that the test made India a nuclear weapon state.[1] Some thought that the test meant the beginning of a nuclear chain reaction in sensitive regions of the world, including South Asia.[2] Some questioned the credibility of India's statement that the test was peaceful in intent and in its impact.* Many pondered the implications of the spread of nuclear technology and of massive nuclear exports from the advanced industrialized societies to Third World societies.[4]

Reactions to the Indian test generally (but not completely) divided along rich/poor lines. Spokesmen for Third World societies

---

*The question of the peaceful nature of India's test arises because Article II of the NPT sees no difference between a weapons test and a PNE because the technology is the same. The meaning and implications of this definition are now problematic because it is also argued that India at present lacks the capacity to make and deploy nuclear weapons. According to the New York Times, "Although India has exploded a nuclear device, American experts said there was still a considerable way to go before it could be considered to have a nuclear arm."[3]

quietly congratulated India but also noted that the PRC had preceded India in taking the lead in shaping Asia's nuclear future, and in attacking the NPT. Among westernized industrial societies, only France (which had itself stayed outside the NPT) took a positive view of the test, and the French atomic energy chief congratulated his Indian counterpart. Canada, Sweden, and Japan took the lead in attacking the Indian test. The United States and the Soviet Union, while obviously displeased, took the diplomatically mature view that the Indian test lacked military significance, a point also accepted by Peking.

The Nixon administration, with Kissinger's encouragement, had generally downplayed the importance of the proliferation issue in American foreign relations, compared with the stress on the subject by the Kennedy and Johnson administrations. India's test intensified the interest in arms control and nuclear proliferation issues. National debates and international debates grew louder, often becoming heated without clearing matters up much. 1968 to 1974 had been a calm period, during which the NPT created the feeling that the danger of nuclear proliferation had been eased. India's 1974 test shattered the smugness.

The pressure to reconsider the danger and prospects of nuclear proliferation came from two directions. When the NPT was negotiated in 1965-68, it was essentially an elitist exercise: the national security planners of the nuclear weapons powers could speak the language of disarmament while continuing to increase their own armaments. Public talk and secrecy in action were parallel activities made possible by the insulation of international nuclear transactions from domestic politics. But as early as 1971, even before India's explosion of a device in 1974, environmentalists had started to question the utility, indeed the centrality, of nuclear energy.[5] The debate questioned the social and economic costs of nuclear energy. Rightly or wrongly, public opinion in certain states, such as the United States, Sweden, Canada, and Japan, had an effect on nuclear policy. Some groups proposed a moratorium on domestic and international uses of nuclear energy, while others proposed continued sales, even intensified sales, supported by stricter safeguards against diversion from peaceful to military uses. The debate still continues. But it has had the effect of causing popularly elected governments to ponder the impact of nuclear politics on electoral politics.

The second source of pressure came from the Indian test. In 1956, when Indo-Canadian atomic energy cooperation started to take concrete shape, Dr. Homi J. Bhabha (the father of India's atomic energy program) had discussed openly but privately his plans to develop Indian explosives technology. A decade later in the Eighteen Nations Disarmament Committee in Geneva, India's Ambassador V. C. Trivedi repeatedly emphasized India's right to carry out PNEs. Such statements had prime ministerial sanction, and in late November 1965 the Indian Prime Minister, L. B. Shastri, talked publicly about nuclear explosions being peaceful. Indeed, there is speculation that before his death Prime Minister Jawaharlal Nehru sanctioned work toward PNE development, as did his successor, Shastri. But Prime Minister Indira Gandhi in early 1966 canceled the project sanctioned by Prime Minister Shastri. Thus, during 1966-71 Indians talked about India's right to explode a peaceful nuclear device, but India's actual decision was not to take such action. This revealed a zigzag in India's nuclear decision making.[6]

The 1974 test undoubtedly was a new policy act that contrasted with the earlier talk about India's right to have a PNE. It was widely regarded as evidence of a new course or a new set of priorities by the Indira Gandhi government. But what exactly did the Indian test signal to India's neighbors and to the world at large? Was this India's real defection from the spirit of the NPT, given that earlier, even while refusing to sign the NPT, India could still abide by its provisions (that is, by actually behaving like a nonproliferator without signing the treaty)? Was the test the first decisive step toward a nuclear weapons policy, or was it a strategy of stretching out the nuclear option to use diplomatically and politically to the fullest extent the ambiguity and threat inherent in the very existence of a nuclear option? How does Pakistan, in particular, perceive Indian nuclear intentions? Overall, should India's test and Pakistan's new commitment to nuclear development be viewed as the beginning of a nuclear chain reaction in South Asia or elsewhere? Is the nuclear decision-making oligarchy vulnerable to external influences that limit the actual and potential autonomy of Indian (and Pakistan) nuclear development?

DEFINING SOUTH ASIA

The first problem in discussing nuclear proliferation in South Asia is to identify the geographical scope of the region. The issue is not solved simply by adopting an arbitrary definition of South Asia. The choice of the geographical boundary has conceptual implications. For instance, if South Asia is defined simply as India and Pakistan for the purpose of nuclear proliferation studies, problems arise with such a limited two-party view. India rejects Pakistan's effort to define South Asia in a two-party sense. For instance, the nuclear suppliers in South Asia are outside the region and the potential nuclear threat from the PRC to India is also extraregional. Furthermore, in the post-1971 context, the Indo-Iranian détente has taken shape and consequently "South Asian" international relations must now include Iran. So bilateral Indo-Pakistani nuclear interactions should be assessed but in the regional and the international context of the diplomacy of India—the dominant actor in the subcontinent. Finally, inasmuch as Iran is moving to acquire nuclear reactors as a part of its campaign to modernize itself rapidly, its nuclear development has more to do with the Shah's views of the world and Iran's position in it than with merely reactions to India's nuclear developments in recent years. And yet the political analyst cannot ignore the effects of Indian and Iranian nuclear development on Pakistan's perceptions. This is particularly relevant in the following sense. If Iran protects Pakistan against what Pakistan perceives as the possibility of an Indian takeover, at the same time, in a scenario where feudalistic Pakistan breaks up, the idea of Iran taking over a part of northwestern Pakistan worries its planners.

Such a scenario at present is merely fanciful, and if attempted would in practice be fraught with dangers for all parties concerned. In sketching it, however, the point is made that today there is boundary-crossing activity: the line between South Asia and Middle East is hard to draw, as linkages between these regions, which in the not-too-distant past could be called different, take shape.

One framework of analysis suggests Indian "action" and Pakistani "reaction." Another framework sees Iran-Pakistan-India interactions as suggesting something different: Pakistan's geopolitical fears of Indian and Iranian threat potential are magnified by the image of two nuclear (or potentially nuclear) neighbors; the prospect of neutralizing the adversaries' excessive power (in Pakistani perceptions) through development of Pakistan's nuclear option is a reaction to India and Iran that seems desirable to Pakistan. In this case, Indian and Iranian nuclear developments encourage Pakistani development of its nuclear option. Yet a third framework suggests that, as evidence of Pakistan's nuclear growth increases, India and Iran in turn may feel the need to stay ahead or to keep pace with Pakistan.

If the starting point of analysis is India's behavior, Pakistan's reactions can be traced easily. In the Indian perspective of the 1970s and 1980s, South Asia is defined for nuclear purposes to include the PRC as a relevant factor. The PRC's military power extends to the Himalayas. Its political influence penetrates to certain parts of the subcontinent; Even as it has diminished in Pakistan, it has increased somewhat in Bangladesh and Burma. This has implications for India's northeastern provinces. Its nuclear armed missiles overshadow the subcontinent, and its claims to a doctrine of no first use of nuclear weapons is revocable. One can argue that India's first underground test was a reaction to the emergence of the PRC's nuclear power. But is this true? If Indians were afraid of the PRC's nuclear weapons, which Indians claim they are not, it would have made sense for them to develop, produce, and deploy nuclear weapons in the mid-1960s, when the capacity (in undemonstrated form) and opportunity (in demonstrated form) existed.* Who in India or abroad could have objected to Indian nuclear arms decisions in the 1960s, when most objective observers did, and still can, easily accept the view that India does have a political and a security problem with the PRC? That it has taken India so long (a decade) to explode one nuclear device and that India has then not followed it up with a substantial testing program can only mean one of two things: either that the Indian government and, particularly its atomic energy establishment, is incompetent and unable to explode more devices, or that there is no immediate strategic need to do so. If the latter perspective has merit, the hypothesis of action and reaction is for the present inapplicable to the study of India-PRC nuclear interactions. Whether or not this will remain so in the foreseeable future is an open question. Thus, a narrow geographical view of South Asia is inadequate and can be conceptually misleading. To trace the flow of actions and reactions, to explain and predict causality between strategic adversaries, it is essential to identify a wider range of actors and concerns. So far, three analytical sets have been noted: (1) the PRC acts and India reacts; (2) India acts and Pakistan reacts, and Iran acts and Pakistan reacts, and vice versa; and finally, (3) India reacts to Pakistan's reactions to India's nuclear behavior.

----

*If Indian nuclear planning is viewed primarily in the India-PRC context one line of argument is that India could have exploded a nuclear device shortly after the PRC exploded its first device in 1964. But India did not because it was not able to match the PRC's achievement. However, events in the 1960s—the 1962 war, the superpower détente, the NPT debate—caused the Indian test. In part India wanted to induce the PRC to negotiate with India. But the PRC has not been responsive to India. Therefore, India may have to "turn the nuclear screw further."

South Asian and several other interviewees pointed out to the author that India could have exploded a device before or after the PRC did if Nehru had wanted to do so. "Turning the nuclear screws further," these sources pointed out, was a political and a diplomatic question and not primarily one of military strategy toward the PRC.[7]

The first analytical set (Indian reaction because of PRC action) is hard to demonstrate when the Indian government claims not to worry about PRC nuclear intentions, asserting that PRC use or threatened use of nuclear weapons would constitute an international crisis. The second analytical set concerns future activity but the following pages reveal that the India-Pakistan nexus is not the central "system." Iran's nuclear proliferation capacity, like Pakistan's, exists potentially with respect to the late 1980s if the safeguards system fails to detect diversion from peaceful to military uses. The third set is at the moment purely hypothetical.

THE NUCLEAR CHAIN MODEL

The work of Lewis Dunn and Herman Kahn[8] of the Hudson Institute asserts that the Indian test of 1974 is the beginning of a nuclear chain reaction that may lead up to proliferation decisions in Pakistan, Iran, Brazil, Argentina, Taiwan, South Korea, and so on. The nuclear chain involves crossing of national, regional, and continental boundaries. It suggests the triggering influence of a single event.

A number of premises (not spelled out by Dunn and Kahn) exist in the nuclear chain scenario. First, technological determinism is the central dynamics in the proliferation process. Secondly, politicians, scientists, and officials (decision makers) are easily impressed with the behavior of their adversary. If A does something, B (its adversary) will venture to do the same to negate A's achievement. Thirdly, a single nuclear bomb test signals a decision to go in for nuclear weapons; indeed, a single explosion signals the existence of nuclear weapons status. Fourthly, once a state decides to explode a nuclear device it cannot stop; the decision to make nuclear weapons is irreversible. It cannot stop for a number of reasons: if the purpose of the decision to explode a device was to impress the great powers, and the great powers are not impressed, then the decision to explode a device has to be repeated time and again, with further nuclear tests, until the great powers are impressed. As repeated nuclear testing occurs the adversaries (B, C, and so on) are also aroused and then they must also start testing; as the adversary (B) starts to move toward nuclear option or nuclear weapon proliferation, then A must react to the perceived threat from B's testing, and so on. Fifthly, the proliferation process is linear or phasal and undimensional; there is little or no probability that there are ups and downs in the decision-making process. That is, once a decision to explode a device is made, competing subnational groups are not likely to be able to reverse or suspend the decisions of a preceding competing subnational group; determinism describes the events that occur. Sixthly, the decision-making apparatus of the proliferating state is monolithic; it is not open to external penetrative linkages whereby a competing subnational elite within a state could decide to collaborate with an external elite (the CIA or an international organisation) to sabotage and paralyze the decision making of the proliferating state. Lastly, the nuclear chain begins with the sixth nuclear proliferator and not with the first, second, third, fourth, or the fifth nuclear-weapon state. Dunn and Kahn do not explain why the sixth proliferator constitutes a coupling link, in a way the other five did not and in a destabilizing manner.

There is some evidence to support the nuclear chain model. India's test in 1974 can be regarded as a delayed reaction to the PRC test of 1964. Secondly, there is some sort of technological determinism underway. India continues to work on its space technology.[9] Today it depends on the USSR for launching its space satellites but it has developed satellite technology. The forthcoming space launch will also depend on Soviet rocketry. It is possible that the third launch could depend on Indian launching capacity if the satellite weighs about 45-60 kilograms.[10] One can also imagine that work continues in the ballistics laboratory[11] that developed the trigger mechanism for the 1974 test. The pilot plant that reprocessed fuel for the 1974 test was closed for expansion and decontamination,* but if all goes well, by the 1980s Indian reprocessing capacity should be adequate for making several plutonium bombs. Technological determinism can also exist, theoretically, in the realm of Indian development of the cruise missile, if one assumes that by the 1980s this cheap missile will become widespread.† If it did, it would bypass the necessity for expensive strategic delivery systems with a heavy industrial and political infrastructure to support the numerous components of rocketry, warhead production, and its political and military management.

Cheap Indian cruise missiles in the 1980s could make technological and fiscal sense and save India from the danger of an Aid

---

*It is estimated that the Trombay reprocessing plant functioned during 1964-72.[12]

†According to SIPRI 1977 Yearbook, a number of Third World countries like Argentina, Brazil, India, Israel, and Taiwan could make these missiles. Others which can develop these in collaboration with others are Egypt, Indonesia, North and South Korea, and Pakistan.[13]

India Consortium embargo if India explodes a device again. In this
scenario, technological determinism does not begin with the May
1974 test and end up with an International range ballistic missile
(IRBM) or Canberras/plutonium bomb nuclear force. The 1974 test
may be reviewed as a one-time event even in Indira Gandhi's thinking. The uniqueness of this test has been underscored by Prime
Minister Desai's statements in 1977[14] that his government did
not intend to conduct more PNEs. (It is arguable that Desai's
repudiation of the 1974 test neutralizes Gandhi's achievement. But
it is also arguable that Desai wishes to have the cake and eat it too.
He and his government benefit from the world's greater attentiveness to India after the 1974 test, and his repudiation of Gandhi's
action shifts attention to Desai's personality and his policy views;
there is no way to undo the 1974 event.)

The terminal condition of this sort of technological determinism is not another nuclear explosion but activity that does not invite
the censure of Article II of the NPT and in part falls in the realm
of modernizing conventional defense forces in the light of technological developments of the 1980s. This kind of technological determinism also means there is a link between the Indian route to
proliferation (testing one device and letting the world know) and the
Israeli route (not testing anything; neither confirming nor denying
anything; not taking a "no comment" position; and taking advantage
of ambiguity). The link exists because the process adopted by India
is to follow the single test phase with a nontesting phase and treat
the two as a continuum that is directed not to weapons building but
to the acquisition of multiuse capacity, which aids image building
and diplomatic signaling. This process suggests a conscious effort
to stay abreast of modern military technology; to find legitimate
conventional uses for technology that could also have possible nuclear uses; to keep the activity sufficiently ambiguous that nothing
is proven against India; to ensure that such Indian activity does not
induce an excessive reaction from India's enemies and that the
reactions are slow, controlled, and predictable; and, above all, to
ensure that global and regional opposition does not crystallize
against India at any point in time—that is, to ensure that, at all
levels, the conflict remain manageable.[15]

If this is India's approach, does Pakistan's reaction suggest
a chain reaction? The strongest public evidence that lends credence
to the chain model is Bhutto's statement that Pakistan would make a
bomb even if the Pakistanis had to eat grass. This was in 1965[16]—
nine years before India's first test. The connection is not between
this statement and Pakistan's policy at that time. Then Pakistan's
diplomats abroad were counseling the world about the dangers of
Indian perfidy—implying that Indians were not to be trusted with

nuclear materials and that they were likely to explode a device and break their agreements. But still President Ayub Khan rejected the advice of his atomic scientists, and the external diplomatic talk had no real parallel in action on atomic issues. The advice was that Pakistan ought to soil its hands with plutonium technology.[17] The advice was not to build Pakistani bombs but to get the scientific know-how and to train some Pakistani experts in plutonium technology. President Ayub Khan's answer was that the priority for Pakistan lay in economic and military modernization and not in acquisition of plutonium technology. This suggests that there was no connection between Bhutto's view in 1965 (when he was foreign minister) and Pakistan's actual decision; nor was there a connection between the public statements of Pakistan's diplomats about Indian nuclear intentions and Pakistan's actual decision making on atomic energy matters. (As an aside, it is noteworthy that a military president in Pakistan gave preference to military and economic modernization and ignored the potential military uses of atomic energy in Pakistan, while a civilian concerned himself with the potential military implications of atomic energy in Pakistan.) But still a connection has to be made among Bhutto's pre-1974 views about the importance of Pakistani atomic development; the 1974 Indian test and its effects on Bhutto and Pakistan's public opinion; and the rise of the Bhutto presidency in 1971.

Pakistan decided to acquire the processing plant in 1976. In 1972, the Canada-supplied KANUPP reactor (125 MWe) started operation in Karachi. This agreement placed KANUPP under facility safeguards. (At the time KANUPP was signed and came into operation, the notion of full-scope safeguards had not come into being.) But after Pakistan signed the agreement with France to acquire the reprocessing plant, Canada insisted on placing the entire Pakistani nuclear industry under international safeguards. On December 23, 1976, Canada ended its nuclear supply program with Pakistan when Pakistan refused to accept the full-scope safeguards demand. According to Pakistan the demands were "unreasonable," and they entailed the imposition of perpetual safeguards even after Canadian nuclear supplies had ended.[18] The resentment over the Canadian decision was coupled with resentment over the American pressure on France to delay delivery of crucial blueprints for the reprocessing plant,* particularly of the sensitive cutting plant, which reduces the spent uranium fuel rods for reprocessing.[19] The Canadian-American pressure, along with the

---

*In August 1978, France canceled the agreement.

other points noted above, provided Bhutto with added incentive to
move along the nuclear path and to strike a blow for nuclear-based
nationalism and Pakistani nuclear self-sufficiency in the 1980s.
Pakistan's behavior in the nuclear field will be discussed later (see
pp. 196-211). Before this is done it is useful to explore further the
conventional wisdom about nuclear chains.

The conventional wisdom about the India-Pakistan nuclear
chain rests on the following set of views and assertions: (1) India
has a long-established nuclear community; (2) it expects to have
eight nuclear power plants in operation by 1982; (3) it can field a
credible nuclear force (tens of nuclear weapons) on a variety of
delivery vehicles if it wants; (4) India's position is that it seeks
peaceful uses of nuclear energy and will seek a nuclear weapons
program of substantial magnitude only if the superpowers fail to
curb their arms competition; (5) while it is premature to discuss
the difference between the nuclear policies of the Indira Gandhi and
the Desai governments, it is possible that India will show nuclear
restraint unless Pakistan develops a nuclear arsenal or if Sino-
Indian relations deteriorate to the point of conflict; (6) Pakistan
feels severely threatened by India and seeks nuclear weapons as the
great equalizer; Pakistan is one nation whose nuclear weapons
capability can be determined by its nuclear suppliers' sensitive
technology-transfer control.[20]

A review of India's nuclear performance[21] (as distinct from
proposals seeking increased budgets* and visions of the future) and
a random sampling of Pakistan's press materials since 1965, however, tell a very different story. The conventional wisdom consists
of dubious premises and facts. These can be categorized either as
propaganda (when one knowingly offers wrong information for the
purpose of achieving a desired effect) or as mistaken beliefs that
are honest errors and are nevertheless grist for the propaganda
machine. The premises and facts in the conventional wisdom bear
close scrutiny. No conclusion can be drawn from the "fact" that
India has a long-established nuclear community (see Figure 8.1).
Just as long-established professors are not necessarily productive,

---

*An example of this is the Sarabhai profile titled "Atomic
Energy and Space Research: A Profile for the Decade 1970-80,"
Department of Atomic Energy, Trombay, 1970. Because there is
no public scrutiny of this department and decision making is of a
czarist nature, the public statements of Indian atomic energy officials should not be taken at face value unless there is supporting
evidence. Indian atomic energy establishments will be discussed
shortly.

FIGURE 8.1

Atomic Energy Establishments in India

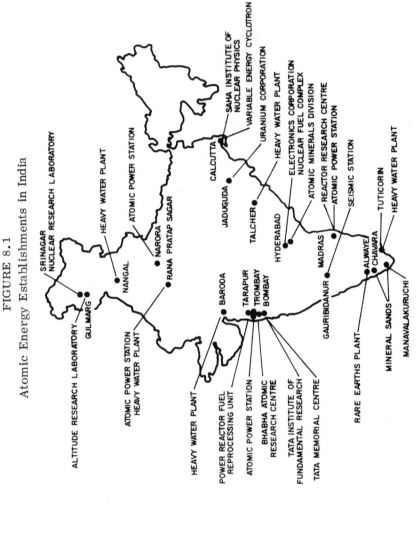

Source: Annual Report 1977–78, Department of Atomic Energy.

192

similarly a long-established nuclear community could be engaged in empire building rather than implementing programs successfully. The long-established community may be high on profile and low on performance, and it can continue this act by making itself immune from public scrutiny. True, India has plans to have a number of reactors by the early 1980s. But,

1. India's nuclear program has slipped badly since the mid-1960s.
2. U.S. enriched uranium fuel supply for Tarapur is problematic beyond 1979.
3. India is heavily dependent on heavy water imports—200 tons from the USSR and an unspecified amount was offered by President Carter in his visit to India in early January 1978.
4. The dependency on heavy water imports came about even though India's future program will operate on CANDU natural uranium heavy water and India speaks the language of nuclear self-sufficiency.
5. The dependency has led to a renegotiation of existing safeguards agreements concerning the RAPP I and II (Rajasthan reactors) in 1977. The philosophy of the Nuclear Suppliers Group of London (NSG) now applies to the only two commercial power reactors. Thus a facility that uses the heavy water imports is automatically safeguarded and anything that comes out of the safeguarded facility is also safeguardable. Therefore, the NSG now prefers that India depend on heavy water imports and prefers that the imported items be as widely used as possible so that the scope of safeguarded facilities will increase over time.
6. With the explosion in the Baroda heavy water production facility and the resulting setback, the already existing dependency on heavy water import has increased. The prospect of "early" indigenous production of heavy water has receded to a distance of perhaps two to ten years.
7. With the cancellation of the Canada/India supply agreement in May 1976 the commissioning of the RAPP II was delayed, and delays in the MAPP and Narora reactors are also likely because there is an inadequate industrial infrastructure to support indigenous manufacture of reactor components and supporting facilities. Consequently, India's atomic profile on paper and the image of India's nuclear prowess in Western thinking do not necessarily correspond to the realities.

True, that India can deliver tens of nuclear bombs on a variety of delivery vehicles such as:

1. a suitcase in the hands of an Indian suicide squad or through a PLO subcontractor that could enter Pakistan or the PRC

2. the aging Indian Canberra bombers, with its limited range, armed to deliver the bombs on Tibetan targets or on Pakistan, or to undertake a one-way suicide mission to Peking

3. Indian SLBMs after they are designed, constructed, and deployed sometime in the indeterminate future

4. Indian tactical atomic weapons, after these are deployed as mines on Indian frontiers and after the Indian army has been trained not to be blown up by its own tactical atomic weapons

5. Indian neutron bombs after lessons are learned about American deployments

6. Indian cruise missiles after these are developed, constructed, and deployed for use with conventional warheads (but plutonium warheads can be developed for emergency use)

An Indian nuclear bomb program also assumes that India's limited plutonium (one estimate suggests about 75-100 kilograms at present) would be used for weapons purposes even though there is a competing demand for retaining the plutonium for the fast breeder program due to start on pilot scale in 1980s (that is, if the program stays on schedule). Here the optimistic estimates of India's plutonium production capacity merit reassessment.[22]

A cursory look at this list indicates that the presumed variety of delivery vehicles with respect to Chinese targets is largely imaginary. A variety of delivery vehicles exist with respect to Pakistan but then the question arises of why Indians would want to bomb their Pakistani neighbors and create a situation whereby global opposition would crystallize against India. Furthermore, why would India want to deliver a nuclear bomb against Pakistan and rule out for the foreseeable future the prospect of normalization of relations? Finally, there are cheaper mechanisms to contain Pakistan—namely, seeking normalization through peaceful and bilateral relations; shelving the Kashmir issue for the present; encouraging a gradual trade relationship in a fashion that does not highlight the structural deficiencies of Pakistan's economy (which do exist, unlike the optimistic reports of the Harvard advisory group that dealt with Pakistan's economic development); encouraging growth of human relations among the peoples of Pakistan, India, and Bangladesh; and so on. In this case, an assessment of Indian delivery capabilities should be made in the context of Indian policy needs. Indian self-interests, rather than Indian altruism, require elaboration.

It is not India's position that it seeks a nuclear weapons program (let alone one of "substantial magnitude") if the superpowers fail to curb their arms competition. No Indian government has said that. The position of the Indian Prime Minister Desai is that it is an illusion to think that nuclear weapons offer protection to any country. The official Indian position at present rejects even the widely held view that nuclear weapons freeze conflicts in certain situations. Furthermore, a linkage between Indian behavior and superpower behavior is false because the superpowers do not pose a military threat to India. A rationale that linked Indian weapons production and deployment to lack of progress in SALT II and III would only crystallize Soviet and U.S. opposition against India at a time when India is trying to mend its ties with the United States and is in the process of slowly disengaging itself from the Soviet connection. India's disarmament diplomacy ("let us freeze nuclear testing, let us move toward arms reduction, let us eventually seek a nuclear weapon-free world zone")* is based on a quest for a world order that is antinuclear.

On the other hand, if a link is presumed between the nuclear arms of India and the PRC, one might ask why the Indian government has been so slow in establishing its nuclear arsenals since the PRC threat emerged in 1964. Is it that the Indians are just slow ("they cannot get their nuclear program going but just watch, they will") or stupid ("they don't really know what is good for them as far as China is concerned") or cunning ("they are hiding their nuclear arsenals and one day we are going to be surprised with what they have")? For scholarly and policy purposes, it may be useful to take another view. The problems with the PRC and with the superpowers are better served in Indian thinking by the ambiguity of their nuclear diplomacy. This means heavy disarmament talk, one PNE with no more to follow, continued research and development in military technology, and gradual adoption of intrusive safeguards on operational nuclear programs (except for CIRUS, the Trombay reprocessing plant, and a new research reactor). This behavior is accompanied by talk that as a matter of principle and national sovereignty, and because India is against discrimination, it will not accept full-scope safeguards on future Indian nuclear projects.

Is this the kind of behavior one expects from a society bent on making nuclear weapons? A country determined to make nuclear weapons would want gradually to erode existing international inspection of its nuclear facilities. India has behaved in exactly the

---

*Note here that India rejects a regional South Asian zone but seeks a stable one.

opposite way since 1966, when Homi Bhabha died.* Furthermore, since India's nuclear weapon program is presumed to be a consequence of the "failure of the superpowers to curb their arms competition," it is worth noting that there is no time limit placed on the "failure"; nor is there an operational guide to assess the failure.

It is not premature to discuss the difference between the nuclear policies of Indira Gandhi and those of Morarji Desai, but it is premature to discuss the permanency of the policies of the Desai government because the government is of a transitional nature. The point is valid that Indian nuclear restraint is a consequence of Pakistan's nuclear development and of trends in Sino-India relations.

Finally, it is useful to examine the interplay between two variables: seeking Pakistani nuclear weapons as the great equalizer vis-à-vis India; and using the NSG to determine or to control Pakistan's nuclear development. The first variable expresses verbal Pakistani perceptions, while the second one expresses (particularly the United States and Canada) desired strategy of some NSG members to control proliferation. An assessment of the roots of Pakistani perceptions and of the implications of the U.S.-Canadian strategy is warranted.

PAKISTAN'S VERBAL DIPLOMACY

Reactions of the Press and Government
before the 1974 Indian Test

In September 1965, after Western media circulated reports from New Delhi that it was "practically certain" that India would explode a nuclear device in ten months, the reaction in a major Dawn article, "We Must Make the Bomb, Too" (September 30, 1965), revealed the following perceptions and reasoning:

> This new surge of enthusiasm among India's war-
> mongers for the acquisition of nuclear-weapons is of
> course the product of the humiliation and dishonour
> India has just suffered as a result of the crushing de-
> feat inflicted on its intruding hordes by the heroic
> armed forces of Pakistan. New Delhi's reasoning
> seems to be quite simple: since Pakistan can beat

---

*At that time Bhabha was preparing India's nuclear explosive capability.

back an attack supported by the bulk of the conventional
arms possessed by India, the only course open to that
country is to acquire nuclear arms and keep them ready
for use against Pakistan.

But why is India, which is a signatory to the partial test ban treaty and which has made much of its opposition to the proliferation of nuclear weapons and to test
explosions, so eager to acquire the atomic weapon,
especially at a time when its economy is in such bad
shape and when it cannot even feed its hungry millions?
India surely knows that if it comes to a competition for
superiority in nuclear arms it does not have the slightest
chance of beating China which possesses a larger economic base and a sounder economy and which is far more
advanced in the scientific field. Such nuclear armament
as India is capable of accomplishing can only make sense
if it is directed against India's small neighbours, especially its declared enemy number one—Pakistan. Having
been put to the worst in the military confrontation with
Pakistan in which it enjoyed the advantage of a treacherous surprise attack as well as of numerical superiority,
India has suddenly realised the limitations of its military
power.

If India decides to let its nuclear ambitions have
free scope—and there is now little doubt that it will do
so—, its purpose will not be to neutralise the nuclear
strength of China, which country India's cowardly
rulers do not have the courage to challenge, but to
blackmail its small neighbours, especially Pakistan.

In the hands of the unscrupulous and treacherous
Indian jingoists, who harbour evil designs against their
small neighbours, the nuclear bomb will be a terrible
weapon indeed. There is little doubt that in order to
be able to defend its independence and territorial integ-
rity, this country needs an independent nuclear deterrent of its own. Pakistan must work for making an
atomic bomb of its own, irrespective of the considerations of cost. For when a country's freedom is in peril,
no price can be too high for defending it.

On October 20, 1965, Dawn echoed the call by Morning News,
a Dacca paper, in its article "Pakistan Should Also Make A-Bomb":

Recalling Mr. Bhutto's statement that Pakistan may have
"to eat grass" but should have her bomb if India gets hers,

the paper says "we must either destroy India's capacity
to manufacture the bomb now, or get busy manufacturing or acquiring our own atomic arsenal by ourselves,
or in concert with nations capable of helping us.

In his book The Myth of Independence[23] (1969), with a preface
written in November 1967, Bhutto, however, revealed sophistication
and agility in his thoughts in the chapter titled "Deterrent Against
Aggression." Bhutto's ideas merit close scrutiny because he is
commonly known to be the advocate of Pakistan's nuclear program.
In the mid-1960s he had asked President Ayub Khan to give him the
atomic energy portfolio, which he got. He was responsible for
promoting the KANUPP and PINSTECH nuclear facilities, although
he was unable to persuade President Ayub to authorize the acquisition
of a reprocessing facility. Bhutto was the leader of Pakistan when
India exploded its device in 1974, and the current Pakistani nuclear
program is very much a product of his leadership. What follows is
a paraphrase of the chapter mentioned above. (Emphasis is added.)

    1. Pakistan's security and territorial integrity are more
important than economic development.
    2. It would be unwise to think in terms of competing with India
in size of forces and quantity of equipment.
    3. Within the next few years, Pakistan cannot develop a local
industrial potential for equipping its armed forces with the more
sophisticated weapons; nor can Pakistan depend entirely on ingenious
diplomatic initiatives.
    4. There are set limits to diplomacy on account of certain
deficiencies in the structure of Pakistan's economic and political
organization. Without sufficient backing of national security measures, diplomacy cannot be considered safe.
    5. It must be made clear that aggression against Pakistan is
a very dangerous affair for the aggressor and Pakistan has the
means to find an effective deterrent.
    6. All wars of our age have become total wars and a war
against Pakistan is capable of becoming a total war.
    7. It would be dangerous to plan for less and our plans should,
therefore, include the nuclear deterrent. It is vital for Pakistan to
give the greatest possible attention to nuclear technology, rather
than allow herself to be deceived by an international treaty limiting
this deterrent to the present nuclear powers.
    8. India is unlikely to concede nuclear monopoly to others,
and judging by its nuclear program and her diplomatic activities,
especially in Geneva, she is determined to detonate a nuclear bomb.

9. If Pakistan restricts or suspends its nuclear program, it would enable <u>India to blackmail Pakistan</u> with her nuclear advantage and it would also cripple its science and technology.

10. <u>Pakistan is not immediately concerned with the question</u> of a nuclear stalemate. <u>Its problem is to obtain such a weapon in time before the crisis begins.</u>

11. India's progress in nuclear technology is sufficient to make it a nuclear power in the near future and it can provoke a crisis at a time of her own choosing. Pakistan must therefore embark on a similar program although <u>a nuclear weapon will be neither a real deterrent nor produced in a few years. Pakistan must therefore write it off as a practical deterrent in a conflict with India in the near future.</u>

12. The Vietnam war shows that a small, poor nation can fight the most powerful nation.

13. <u>Pakistan's best deterrent would be a national militia</u> following the Swiss example.

Bhutto's views revealed an elaborate thought structure with premises and conclusions that nevertheless did not disclose the strategy or its time frame. Moreover, the views were flexible enough to be interpreted differently by different audiences: as a sign of caution by a foreign audience and as a sign of nationalism by a Pakistani audience. Still, Bhutto had captured the Pakistani imagination with the vision of an atomic Pakistan. The press in Pakistan mounted a vigorous educational campaign.*[24] But one

---

*For instance, see articles by Azim Kidwai (<u>Dawn</u>, December 7 and 21, 1969). KANUPP built with Canadian assistance was advertised as the first nuclear power station in the Muslim world (<u>Pakistan Times</u>, August 25, 1970); the prospects and problems of a 400 MW nuclear power plant at Rooppur in East Pakistan received extensive editorial attention (<u>Dawn</u>, January 29, 1970). The theme that "there is no escape from nuclear power as an alternative source of energy" was stressed (see Pakistan Atomic Energy Commission Chairman Usmani's lecture, reported in <u>Pakistan Times</u>, January 8, 1971). Pakistan's uranium production was reported by Q. Aziz (<u>Christian Science Monitor</u>, June 10, 1971); and a plan to establish an atomic energy agricultural research center was reported (<u>Pakistan Times</u>, December 15, 1972). The inauguration of KANUPP on November 28, 1972 received strong editorial support as an "atomic

thing was clear. Press editorials and writers were the ones who openly asked for a Pakistani bomb program. Bhutto spoke in guarded terms about the importance of having a deterrent but his plea seemed to be more for intensifying the acquisition of nuclear technology (in the context of President Ayub's Khan's alleged refusal to promote nuclear technology and particularly plutonium technology) rather than for bomb development and production. Indeed, no urgency was revealed in connection with finding a nuclear alternative to the prospect of India's nuclear blackmail. Moreover, the issue was perceived not only in terms of Indian nuclear blackmail. The problem of conceding the nuclear monopoly to the present nuclear powers was also stressed. Thus, the threat to national security was seen in terms of the danger of Indian nuclear blackmail and the distribution of nuclear power in the world. In short, Bhutto's perception as revealed was not merely in anti-Indian terms. At the same time, the educational effort through the press required heavy reporting about the scientific and developmental aspects of Pakistan's atomic energy program by the chairman of the Pakistan Atomic Energy Commission and by other writers.

Reactions of the Press and Government
after the Indian Test, May 1974

After the oil crisis in 1973 and before the Indian test, Pakistan decided to set up a chain of nuclear reactors to meet its energy needs. This was done under the orders of Prime Minister Bhutto. Nuclear energy became attractive to Pakistan, as to many other developing societies, because Pakistan's oil import bill had gone up

---

landmark" for developmental purposes but the editorial in the Pakistan Times recorded a complaint.

> It is obvious that the vital importance of the nuclear programme is fully realised at the Government level: the President's keeping it in his personal charge is an indication of it. But this consciousness has yet to seep down far enough to the levels of the scientists and administrators involved in the programme. Freed of bureaucratic control, and also somewhat of financial constraints, they have no reason now not to devote themselves wholeheartedly to the mission before them. KANUPP is doubtless a glorious milestone. But it is only the first, and the journey is long.

to $400 million—four times the original estimate. The oil bill ate into 40 percent of Pakistan's foreign exchange earnings.[25]

After the Indian test, Pakistani reactions varied, both among different sectors of Pakistani society and within the government. The business community, through the Federation of the Chamber of Commerce, offered to help develop Pakistan's nuclear potential through subcontract work, in view of the challenge posed to Pakistan's sovereignty and independence by the Indian test. The federation noted that as far back as 1965 it had advocated association of private industry with defense work through subcontract work.[26] Pakistan's ambassador to Australia, however, called an unusual press conference to tell the Australians that Pakistan "will not jump on the bandwagon" even though he felt that India's test could upset the regional balance.[27] The president of Azad Kashmir felt that Pakistan and other Muslim states ought to go nuclear, but the Indian blast did not surprise him because Indira Gandhi had told India in 1971 about giving India "a good news." At the United Nations, Pakistan charged that India was working on a delivery system and challenged India to prove its intentions by accepting full-scope safeguards. (The Pakistan government, however, declined to place its nuclear industry under full-scope safeguards.) In Karachi, Bhutto's reactions to the Indian test were that Pakistan would develop its nuclear program as a result of the Indian test; its program would be restricted to peaceful purposes; Pakistan would not explode a bomb; India's test was meant to intimidate and blackmail Pakistan; India was brandishing the nuclear sword to extract political concessions from Pakistan and to establish Indian hegemony in the subcontinent; and India's test had set back the normalization process.[28] According to one report from Peking, Pakistan sent its foreign minister to seek PRC support for a world-wide move to stop India's nuclear program, to induce others to withdraw aid to India, and to impose economic sanctions. The report noted the Pakistani claim that India "may have more than one hundred kilograms of plutonium" (enough for 10-20 bombs).[29] But then a New York Times story filed from Karachi points out that "In Karachi, Nuclear India is Topic Z"; while some people thought that India might drop the bomb on Pakistan, others felt that the price of cooking oil and factional political and religious struggles worried the people more.[30] After the test, serious experts like the chairman of the PAEC and writer Azim Kidwai continued to advertise the scope of Pakistan's atomic energy program (without even hinting about its military implications), about the prospects of atomic power in general.[31] The chairman of the PAEC stressed again that Pakistan's dependence on nuclear energy was likely to grow manifold, to the extent of inducting 5,500 MW (nuclear) by A.D. 2000; that is, by the turn of the century almost one-third of the total generating capacity was expected to be nuclear.[32]

A long press conference reported extensively in Pakistan Times (December 27, 1974) established that in Bhutto's thinking there was no mad momentum toward Pakistani nuclear weapon development or a Pakistani nuclear explosion, but that the nuclear program of Pakistan was being accelerated. The following quotations provide the texture of top Pakistani thinking. First, on the matter of a nuclear-free zone:

> QUESTION: Does it not suggest that to your mind that to go nuclear in some way undermines your suggestion to make South Asia a nuclear-free zone?
>
> PRIME MINISTER: But you see, you put this question to me assuming that Pakistan will not be able to get conventional weapons. Now the point is that we believe that Pakistan will be able to get conventional weapons. We can get conventional weapons from the United States and, who knows, we might be in a position to mobilise and muster financial resources from friendly countries to be able to get military supplies.
>
> Who knows we might be in a position, in a year or two, to strike oil and we might have our own resources to get conventional armaments.
>
> Who knows some other countries, other neighbours, might have greater co-operation with Pakistan.
>
> We already have some military collaboration and co-operation with one of the great Powers and the door can be opened for others in the future.
>
> But finally and ultimately, if our backs are to the wall and we have absolutely no option, in that event, this decision about going nuclear will have to be taken.[33]

And on a peaceful nuclear program and the promotion of peace:

> QUESTION: This means that you are already going ahead with preparations for a nuclear programme if it becomes necessary?
>
> PRIME MINISTER: We are not going ahead with a nuclear programme for the explosion of a nuclear device which whatever India might say really means a nuclear device for military purposes. We are not going ahead in that direction. But our nuclear programme for peaceful purposes has undoubtedly been accelerated.
>
> QUESTION: Do you think that the enemy will give you time to go nuclear in case you need to?

PRIME MINISTER: Time depends on policies also
and our policy as the world has seen is to promote peace.
This country has concluded the Simla Agreement with
India which has been a major agreement for peaceful
purposes. That is consideration number one.

Secondly, we have taken the painful and difficult
decision of recognising Bangladesh which has also been
a decision to promote peace and goodwill.

I visited Bangladesh and that was also done to
stabilise peace in the Sub-Continent.

Thirdly, do you think that my reply to the very
first question put to me on Pakistan-Afghanistan relations was a warlike reply? I gave a reply which indicated that we are anxious to have good relations and to
remove tensions.

Fourthly, we have also improved our relations
with other neighbours. We have consolidated our relations with neighbours with whom we have good relations
and we have improved our relations with neighbours
with whom our relations were under a cloud during the
1971 war.

All these measures that have been taken are deliberately and conscientiously taken to promote the cause
of peace. At the same time, if our neighbouring country
India thinks that peace can only come by the total security
of India and the total insecurity of Pakistan, this is not
our interpretation of achieving peace. [34]

Overall, these statements revealed the existence of a number
of alternatives to promote Pakistan's security. One approach was
to get more conventional arms. Another approach was to increase
oil prospecting. A third approach was to accelerate the nuclear
program, with the disclaimer that Pakistan was not going in for an
explosion because there was no difference between a weapons test
and a peaceful test. A fourth approach was to signal India that it
ought not to adopt a position that meant "total security of India" and
"total insecurity of Pakistan" if both countries sought peace. When
asked if the enemy (India) would give him "time to go nuclear in
case you need to," Bhutto replied that "time depends on policies
also." All in all, there were no public signals that Pakistan intended to follow the Indian route of PNE development. Indeed, there
are plenty of signals in the foregoing statements to indicate that
Pakistan intended to explore alternatives to nuclear weapons development without ignoring the potential threat from India (which, of
course, Indians deny).

Still, the press in Pakistan continued its coverage of nuclear developments. A debate on the budget produced a statement that "Pakistan should go nuclear."[35] The chairman of the PAEC continued to stress the importance of transforming Pakistan through technology,[36] without a tinge of any military thought (much unlike the views of the late Homi Bhabha a decade or so earlier). IAEA's approval of the French reprocessing plant deal with Pakistan on February 27, 1976 was noted as "good news" even though it was also noted that Canada was being difficult on KANUPP because of the Canadian experience with India; and the Indian test had made "things difficult" for Pakistan even though Pakistan had a pressing need for nuclear technology because of its energy needs.[37] On the same day, in New York, Bhutto said that Pakistan had no plan to make atomic weapons and that the French reprocessing plant would be under safeguards.[38] On his return from a foreign trip, Bhutto made several important points in a press conference at the airport: Pakistan is a peaceful nation and it will not develop the bomb; Pakistan would use the reprocessing plant, "which can also be used for manufacturing a bomb" for producing nuclear power; there was an objection to the reprocessing plant because Pakistan had only one reactor (KANUPP); however, Pakistan planned to have a string of nuclear reactors to meet the rising energy needs of the country; Pakistan welcomed international inspection; Pakistan should not be punished for what India had done; India's policy was based on aggression and it had a record of breaking international commitments; India had launched a nuclear program in 1947 under the direct control of the prime minister; it took Pakistan seven years to set up its AEC but it was only a "paper commission"; in 1960, Usmani became the chairman of PAEC but he also did some paper work; as foreign minister he asked the government for the atomic energy portfolio and received it; his effort resulted in the establishment of PINSTECH and he had to go to the president to get the approval of KANUPP because the economic committee declined to approve it; in 1965 he pleaded for a reprocessing plant (costing Rs. 30 crores, about $4 million) but it was refused on the ground that Pakistan's economy could not afford the burden; finally, the principles of the agreement to upgrade the safeguards on KANUPP had been agreed to by him and the Canadian prime minister but details were being worked out and an agreement was likely "today or tomorrow."[39]

This review of Pakistani press and other public materials yields no firm conclusions but points to some tentative ones. Between 1965-71, if one assumes that Pakistanis were obsessed with India (this author does not hold such a view), then three arguments that could possibly lead to nuclear proliferation by Pakistan are

revealed by its press. These are: to guard against India's bombs
(in the plural), against its perfidious habits, and against Indian
nuclear blackmail; to acquire reprocessing capacity (which incidentally also produces a bomb, a point admitted by Pakistanis)
because of its energy needs; and to secure the progressive growth
of Pakistan's nuclear industry so that Pakistan has a network of
nuclear reactors by A.D. 2000.

It is far from clear, however, whether the three arguments
should be viewed as complementary or as competitive. For instance,
if the fear of Indian perfidy and nuclear blackmail is the central
motive for Pakistan's nuclear development, and particularly for
acquisition of the reprocessing plant, then Pakistan's public nuclear
diplomacy is misleading, if not dishonest. But on the other hand,
since 1965, Pakistan's real assessment (inferred from private conversation rather than public speeches) is not of overconcern about
India (because it is not India's advantage to wipe out Pakistan and
thereby to become the neighbor of Iran and the Soviet Union), [40]
then Pakistan's slow nuclear development is meant to place Pakistan, belatedly, on the atomic map of the world; it is also empire
building by Pakistan's atomic scientists, a practice not uncommon
in developed and developing societies. Bhutto radicalized Pakistani
public opinion about nuclear power in the mid-1960s and is rightly
called the father of Pakistan's nuclear program. His involvement
in nuclear power can be explained as a development of nuclear
politics, more than of nuclear power, in the power struggle of
Pakistan's domestic politics. Furthermore, Pakistan's willingness
to place the French reprocessing plant under strict IAEA safeguards—along the lines approved by the Nuclear Suppliers Group in
London—was reassuring. Pakistan, however, refused to accept the
Canadian demand for full-scope safeguards and suffered a penalty of
cutoff of Canadian nuclear supplies to Pakistan (KANUPP) for the
sake of preserving a principle.* But preserving the principle and
taking the penalty means either that there is greater nuclear self-
sufficiency by the sufferer of the penalty than is readily apparent,
so that the blow of the penalty is softened; or an alternative external
supplier is available; or the domestic program languishes and is
near death. The continuation of KANUPP after the Canadian nuclear

---

*Put differently, this action brought Pakistan's nuclear diplo-
macy in line with India's, in the sense that both have suffered the
penalty for the sake of the principle that conditions on propriety rights
ought to extend only to items actually transferred and do not apply to
domestic industry.

aid cutoff in 1976 suggests that Pakistan may have more nuclear self-sufficiency than had been apparent. The French reprocessing deal, on paper, suggested that an alternative supplier was available, but as that deal was killed, it may well mean the end of the Pakistani program. Theoretically then, Pakistan's nuclear nationalism, from the mid-1960s to the present, is rooted in two different concerns: anti-Indianism and an antinuclear suppliers' attitude.

The suggestion that Pakistan is moving irrevocably toward nuclear bomb development should also be examined in light of Pakistan's nuclear diplomacy. The diplomacy has been conducted in a fashion that does not suggest a mad momentum toward nuclear weapons development. In the 1950s and the 1960s the diplomatic exercise was primarily anti-India and the themes expressed were that India would explode a nuclear device; India would break international agreements; India would seek hegemony over Pakistan; Pakistan was the only target of a nuclear India because India could not, and dared not, take on China. A two-party view of the implications of a nuclear India was the hallmark of Pakistan's, and particularly Bhutto's, nuclear diplomacy. The net effect of this public diplomacy was to score a few points against India among those who already suspected Indian nuclear intentions.

Even so, at that time (from the 1960s until the 1974 Indian test) the public diplomacy did not produce a Pakistani initiative like the proposal to have a South Asian nuclear weapon-free zone (NWFZ); this was presented by Pakistan after the 1974 Indian test. To be sure, Pakistan talked about peace zones in India and South Asia before the 1974 test, but there was no real Pakistani initiative to control nuclear proliferation in South Asia. For instance, Pakistan could have followed up the Tlatelolco Treaty of 1967 (concerning a Latin American NWFZ) with a similar proposal for South Asia. Indeed, this could have been initiated in the mid-1960s when the Pakistani press and Bhutto started to worry publicly about Indian nuclear intentions; at this time Treaty of Tlatelolco discussions were under way. Even if one assumes that India would reject a South Asian NWFZ proposal (as it currently does), still Pakistan would have scored a diplomatic victory against India. The point being made here is that Pakistan did not pursue all available diplomatic channels to curb Indian nuclear diplomacy even though Pakistan's public was presented with view of the threat to Pakistan of a nuclear India. A gap between talk and action is clear.

Furthermore, even though Pakistan's concern with the possibility or a probability of Indian nuclear blackmail was predictable, the real surprise was that Pakistan's nuclear decision making was so slow. As mentioned earlier, Bhutto told the Pakistani press that up to the mid-1960s the PAEC's programs existed mostly on paper.

This allegation cleverly laid the problem at President Ayub Khan's doorstep. It is understandable that in a power struggle one always sees one's enemy as wrong. But although President Ayub Khan was responsible for not giving attention to nuclear energy, his attitude does not fully explain the slow development of Pakistan's nuclear development. President Khan left the political scene in 1969 and it is curious that the deal with France was signed only in 1976. In 1967/69 Bhutto wrote about the necessity of having a Pakistani nuclear deterrent.[41] He came to power in 1971,* but the decision to acquire the reprocessing plant was made after the 1974 Indian test and not in anticipation of it. This is odd, because Bhutto himself points out that he told the Canadians, among others, that India would explode a nuclear device anytime after 1965 and Indians could not be trusted with international agreements. Given such a publicly stated, and apparently deeply felt, sentiment (some might call it hatred), the absence of a decision not to acquire a reprocessing plant or even a laboratory-scale reprocessing facility (according to one witness who was shown a facility in 1975 there was not much in the room)[42] during 1969-74 is hard to explain.

One hypothesis that comes readily to mind is that Bhutto did not really believe in the prospect of an urgent Indian nuclear blackmail threat; that fears expressed in the Pakistani press during 1965 about India's nuclear plans were justified because Indian nuclear decision making in late 1965 by Prime Minister Shastri and Indian atomic energy chief Homi Bhabha did in fact signal a shift toward preparation for a peaceful nuclear explosion;[43] and that Bhutto's writings in the second half of the 1960s were motivated by a concern to present the Bhutto alternative to the Ayub Khan regime by emphasizing the theme of nuclear nationalism (among other themes) to the Pakistani public. Accordingly, expressing concern about Pakistan's nuclear safety was good national politics, but Pakistan's intelligence knew that the 1965 momentum toward an Indian PNE had been called off by Prime Minister Indira Gandhi in 1966 and consequently there was no real pressure on Pakistan to divert valuable economic and human resources toward nuclear development. In short, until two events—the energy crisis (1973) and India's test (1974)—impinged on Pakistan's thinking (according to this hypothesis no real link between the 1971 war and Pakistan's nuclear thinking is implied or is explicit), Bhutto's talk about nuclear matters differed from that of President Ayub Khan (1958-69) but his

---

*Yahya Khan was president from March 1969 until December 1971, and Bhutto was linked with General Yahya Khan.

actions were motivated by similar concerns. In general, both Khan and Bhutto felt that economic development and military modernization had prior claim to resources, but that atomic power could be slowly (as Ayub stated between 1965 and 1969, and Bhutto stated between 1965 and 1969, and from 1971 onward) introduced into Pakistan. The KANUPP came into operation in 1972. Many other atomic energy proposals for Pakistan are still on paper, as for instance the prospect of uranium refinement and plans to have a network of reactors in Pakistan by A.D. 2000.* What might be called the teething problems of a new industry, with the general world-wide slowdown of reactor installation, may have some bearing on the rate of growth of Pakistan's nuclear industry. Still, the point can be made that there does not seem to be a major push in Pakistan's decision making toward quick nuclear development.

The foregoing hypothesis is rooted in a number of features or premises about Pakistani behavior. First, it is assumed that Pakistan's intelligence about Indian capabilities and intentions is generally sound on nuclear matters and that for this reason there has been no visible overreaction in Pakistani nuclear planning. The implication is that the more complete is Pakistan's intelligence about Indian nuclear planning (actual performance rather than proposals seeking budget support and empire-building programs and visions of the indefinite future), the greater is the likelihood that Pakistan will not overreact and enter into a nuclear race in South Asia. Secondly, Bhutto played to the gallery using the nuclear issue, but he never aroused nuclear nationalism in Pakistan to such a pitch that he could not control it. Thirdly, there has been no visible urgency in Pakistan up to the present to move quickly and to accelerate nuclear development of Pakistan, as one would expect of a nation facing nuclear blackmail. Fourthly, even when nuclear development was justified for energy reasons, Bhutto recognized that oil prospecting was also a viable option; hence the incentives in favor of nuclear energy after the oil crisis were not one-sided in high-level Pakistani perceptions. Fifthly, as Bhutto disclosed, President Ayub Khan and Pakistan's Economic Committee favored resource allocation for economic development and military modernization. Bhutto has constantly had influential ties with the military general headquarters. One can infer, therefore, that the

------

*A casual examination of the annual reports of Pakistan's Atomic Energy Commission reveals the ambitiousness of atomic plans and the problems in implementing these. The target dates for commissioning facilities keep slipping.

military during the regimes of Ayub Khan, Yahya Khan, and Bhutto would not allow itself to be deprived of its military modernization needs, particularly when a civilian regime has to depend heavily on the military for political support.[44] In this instance, a quest for constant military modernization can slow proliferation.

Lastly (and this may well be the most significant proliferation-control activity), Pakistan's acceptance of safeguards on the French reprocessing plant is in line with the safeguards adopted by the Nuclear Suppliers Group in London, and the safeguards are monitored by the IAEA. The safeguards preclude a PNE and they apply to any Pakistani facility that uses French technology. For instance, if Pakistan were to establish a reprocessing facility using French technology, that facility would also become safeguardable, according to the NSG guidelines; this Pakistan understands. Therefore, it makes sense to prolong Pakistan's dependency on French nuclear assistance because technology transfer also leads to intrusive international inspection. The constant pressure by the United States— by Kissinger and Carter—therefore, induced rather than controlled proliferation in the sense that cancellation of the French-Pakistan deal would or could result in the growth of nuclear nationalism in Pakistan.* The possibility cannot be excluded that the U.S. strategy is to foster an India-Pakistan nuclear race and U.S. Machiavellianism in South Asian international relations has taken a new form after the U.S. failure in the 1971 crisis.

All this is not to suggest that there is no circumstance in the foreseeable future under which Pakistan will go nuclear. But it suggests that a number of psychological and self-inflicted constraints exist as barriers to Pakistani nuclear bomb development. If French nuclear technology had been slowly inserted into Pakistan, this would have delayed the rate of growth of Pakistan's reprocessing in the following sense. Theoretically, the learning curve of Pakistan's nuclear scientists increases quickly as blueprints and equipment (such as the cutting machine for reprocessing) reach Pakistan and are absorbed into its nuclear industrial infrastructure. But if Pakistan's intention had been to absorb the new technology quickly, and transfer it to a Pakistani facility that automatically became safeguardable under the agreement with France and the IAEA, Pakistan would have had to show its hand by renouncing its safeguards agreement. For those who take the uncharitable view that Pakistan would violate its safeguard agreement, it should be noted

---

*This section was written before France announced cancellation of the deal in August 1978. The foregoing point remains valid.

that to date there is no single instance in the world where a safeguards agreement has been broken, even when an opportunity existed.
India did not renounce its safeguards agreement on the Rajasthan
reactors after Canada broke its contractual obligations.

There are other self-inflicted constraints on Pakistan. Pakistan, unlike India, does not see a difference between a PNE and a
military test. On the contrary, it has taken numerous opportunities
to repeat that there is no such difference. It has also repeatedly
said that it will not conduct a test, peaceful or military. It will take
a strong provocation (the Kashmir dispute is now on the shelf) from
India or elsewhere for Pakistan to alter its existing verbal stance.
Pakistan's self-image is one of scrupulousness in regard to international commitments (unlike those perfidious Indians, Pakistanis
say), and it will require much external provocation to justify an
activity that would necessitate a change in this self-image. Of
course, anything is possible in an instance of great threat or high
uncertainty in the strategic and political environment, but one would
have to be completely pessimistic to assume Pakistani dishonesty
and bad faith now.

Finally, a mix of technological, domestic political, external
political, and resources-allocation factors have to be taken into
account in projecting optimistic and pessimistic scenarios for
Pakistan's nuclear future (without predicting what will occur). Even
assuming that Pakistan's scientific talent today is first-rate, its
nuclear industrial infrastructure is weak, as it still is in India even
though the latter has more experience with nuclear engineering and
theoretical problems. It is fair to assert that in Third World societies the rate of absorption of new technology is slower than governments plan for, and performance does not usually keep pace with
the published plans. Furthermore, as external threats decline, the
pressures to accelerate nuclear development also lessen, in an
increasingly safety-conscious nuclear environment. This trend is
strengthened if the domestic political environment is unstable. It
can hardly be otherwise, because a temporary regime cannot be
expected to make irrevocable commitments that are, in all probability, going to be reversed by the successors. On this basis, the
following advice might be useful to someone who wanted to avoid
nuclear proliferation in Pakistan: Ask the temporary Martial Law
Administration to increase the bomb-making capacity of Pakistan
at the expense of Pakistan's economic development; let this be known
to the Pakistani people; then through a destabilization plan get Bhutto
reelected and he will slow or reverse the nuclear commitment because of the pressure for resources that are needed for Pakistan's
economic development. This advice is not as simple-minded as it
sounds. It points to the centrality of economic development in

Pakistani politics today when it is going through an identity crisis.
It is looked down upon as a poor cousin by the Iranians and the
Saudis. The recent wave of Pak-Islamism (rather than Pan-
Islamism, which is no longer viable) has polarized Pakistani society
along north/southeast/west lines. More Islamism is no solution
for the pressing problem of economic and social reform in Pakistan.
Finally, as dependency on (and intrusiveness of) external sources
increases, and domestic factions with foreign links[45] emerge in
bureaucratic debates, the threat of uncontrolled nuclear proliferation also is likely to lessen. To an assessment of the last theme
this discussion now turns, by reviewing the Indian nuclear scene
and then hypothesizing general points about the South Asian nuclear
scene.

FOREIGN-LINKED DOMESTIC FACTIONS AND COMPETITIVE SUBNATIONAL ELITES

According to Dowty, foreign-linked factionalism is "the
presence within a state of a competing faction that seeks or accepts
aid from other states in order to seize or wield power by non-
legitimized means."[46]
The definition used here makes a change in Dowty's definition.
Since "non-legitimized means" is hard to define, and legitimization
criteria vary among societies, in the South Asian context whether
the factional activity is publicly defensible is a more telling attribute
of foreign-linked factionalism. The new definition reads: "the
presence within a state of a competing faction that seeks or accepts
from other states (or from groups in that state or in international
organizations) in order to seize and wield power by means that are
not publicly defensible."

Assumptions of the Model

The foreign-linked competitive subnational elite model is
based on a number of assumptions. First, the elite functions secretly. Public opinion and parliamentary opinion exist in the
society; elections are held from time to time. But the flow of public information within society is general and the public does not
have access to all the information available to the competing elites.
The press is nonspecialist and, because it depends heavily on official briefings, it cooperates with the competing factions to prevent
its sources of information from drying up. The threat of losing
sources of information is a big one because the society lacks job

mobility. Contacts by the press outside the country are hindered by travel restrictions, by official restrictions on the flow of information to the public, by discouragement of investigative reporting (partly because the art is not highly developed and partly because it is easier to collaborate with official sources and the rewards for such collaboration are high).

Secondly, the system is small and closed. This is achieved by keeping the bureaucracy's size small, by discouraging lateral entry into the bureaucracies or the social institutions (such as the communications media) that control and channel the communications flow within the society and between that society and the outside world. Socialization of the officers in the bureaucracies begins early in life (when they are in their twenties) and consequently incestuousness is easy to foster. In the name of an undefined national interest there is self-censorship in the press and in academic work.

Thirdly, political parties and parliamentarians, media managers, scholars, and other individuals are sometimes informed but not consulted about decision making. The reasoning underlying the decision is not conveyed because that would disclose the style of thinking, the pattern of thinking, and the assessment that underlie the decision. However, there is no moratorium on speeches; the system is one of secret decision making and unlimited, daily talk. The talk is mostly sloganeering. It is meant to signal the direction the government would like others to take, to signal what others ought to do. No indications are offered about perceptions of issues, the possibilities available, the choices made or not made.

Fourthly, the flow of information between the domestic faction and its foreign collaborator is greater than the flow of information among the competing subnational elites. Between the competing elites, communications occur through verbal and nonverbal "moves" so that desired outcomes can be achieved. The flow of directives from the competing elites and their domestic constituents is vast. This is mostly a one-way channel in the sense that orders or advice flows from the top to the bottom of the hierarchy whereas those on the bottom of the hierarchy offer reactions of grass-roots sentiment that may or may not affect subsequent orders or advice from the leadership to its domestic constituents.

This focus tells why, although certain decisions are made, decision making is not a phasal activity. When certain decisions are made there are competing decisions made. Consequently, the society may be confronted with two or more competing decision that may paralyze each other. In short, two or more competing decisions can exist but they do not necessarily function as building blocks for subsequent decision.

The point in studying foreign-linked competitive subnational elite behavior is not to prove that intraelite competition exists; that is already known. Rather, its existence is motivated by a concern with careerism in a developing society that lacks social mobility. Once a foreign-linked faction is in place in a developing society, its activity is routine and institutionalized. A visual representation of the process as it relates to Indian nuclear decision making is somewhat as follows:

FIGURE 8.2

The Decision-making Process: The First Cut

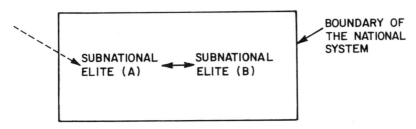

refers to the competition for power

refers to the external ties at the level of officials, scientists, and politicians; penetration and acquisition of influence is from outside and one-sided—the external agency has penetrated the subnational elite and feeds it the necessary intelligence and advice; the external agent is the controller of the moves of the foreign-linked domestic faction.

An example of the applicability of Figure 8.2 to India's nuclear decision making relates to the November 1967-February 1968 debate on the NPT in the Indian government. The dividing issues and the decisions are shown in Table 8.1.

Figure 8.3 indicates that officials, scientists, and politicians are useful targets of the external agency. In developing societies, many politicians are insular in their knowledge of international politics; their prime concern is to gain power and wealth. The more useful targets of externally induced penetration are the official and the scientist because the trained officials and scientists know the art of bureaucratic maneuvering; they have tenured jobs and politicians do not; they can reach the politician; they usually identify the range of choices available to their political master(s) and implicitly offer the desired choice. Given this, Figure 8.3 represents the process of decision making somewhat as follows:

FIGURE 8.3

The Decision-making Process: The Second Cut

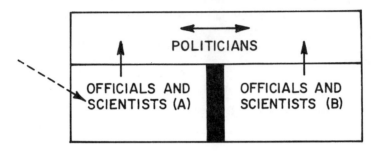

refers to external penetration of subnational elite.

refers to the shaping of the decision-making process by officials and scientists; mediation of differences between competing elites has to be done by politicians because officials or scientists belonging to competing subnational elites are politicized and the competing elites by themselves cannot negotiate a solution for their rivalries.

refers to the nonnegotiable barriers to decision making at the level of officials and scientists.

refers to the shift of decision-making responsibility and the responsibility of failure to the politicians, caused by the nonnegotiable barrier noted above. Because the politicians receive highly politicized advice that officials and scientists think their political masters would like to hear, the debate is elevated from the level of the officials and scientists to that of politicians. Decision making is now a consequence of making a decision that neutralizes the pressure of the opposing faction.

At least two examples of the applicability of Figure 8.3 to Indian nuclear decision making can be cited. Consider first the November 1967-February 1968 debate about India's final position on the NPT. During this time, there was a deep division among India's Ministry of External Affairs officials. One faction (foreign-linked) argued that India ought to sign the NPT because Americans were threatening to cut off aid and because of British pressure. The other faction (the nationalists) argued otherwise, saying that India should resist such blackmail, seek an independent stance, and avoid having its hands tied. At the official level the debate was inconclusive. However, one official linked closely with Prime Minister Gandhi was able to persuade her to decide against the NPT for a number of reasons.[47] A number of circumstances facilitated this decision. The faction opposed to the NPT had already carried their argument to ministers who were opposed to Gandhi. Her domestic position was weak. Public opinion supported the stand that she finally took on the NPT. It can be argued that she had no alternative to deciding the way she did. Still, the point can be made that the decision made had little to do with the merits of case and with the arguments as posed by the officials; the decision was based on what was good for the political fortunes of the decision maker (in this case Indira Gandhi).

TABLE 8.1

Issues and Decisions in Indian NPT Debate

Issues	Decisions
Whether or not India should sign the NPT	No signature "under present circumstances"
Whether India should have nuclear weapons, ever	No nuclear weapons
Whether or not India should have a crash PNE program	No crash PNE program
Whether India should have a slow research and development program with no irrevocable commitment to have a PNE	Yes
Whether India should have the quest for nuclear disarmament in the world	Yes (keep talking about nuclear disarmament without leading the debate); No (don't expect much by way of nuclear disarmament, lower the Indian disarmament profile)
Whether India should keep PNE option alive, theoretically	Yes

Source: Compiled by the author.

A second example of the process outlined in Figure 8.3 occurred during President Carter's visit to India (January 1-3, 1978).
The question of continuing U.S. fuel supply for the Tarapur reactor
under the 1963 agreement and the question of getting India to accept
full-scope safeguards arose again. There was a deep division in
the Ministry of External Affairs on the issues. One faction (foreign-
linked) made it known to the U.S. government before the visit that
India was "open to discussion" even though the Indian prime minister's position was that India could not accept full-scope safeguards
because these were discriminatory. Another faction in the ministry
took the view that India ought to be ready to close down the Tarapur
reactor if the United States failed to fulfill its contractual obligations. The decision finally made by the prime minister was to
reject the Carter demand. A concession to Carter might have resulted in an allegation of a sell-out by the Indira Gandhi Congress
Party and an increase in the strength of the foreign-linked domestic
faction, and might have allowed Carter to leave with the impression
that the new prime minister was soft. The decision not to accept
full-scope safeguards had little to do with the safeguards issue,
because for all practical purposes the main portions of Indian nuclear industry were already under safeguards. Indeed, the Desai
government had already requested, under the advice of the foreign-
linked faction, that safeguards on the Rajasthan reactors be upgraded to bring these into line with the safeguards requirements of
the Nuclear Suppliers Group of London.

In this particular instance, the actors were not only the competing factions within the ministry. Because the foreign-linked
faction had become extremely strong (for a number of reasons*),

---

*The reasons are strange but real. India's foreign minister,
being a Jan Sangh man, was known for his hard-line views (before
he joined the government) on a number of issues (including a preference to make nuclear weapons). After he joined the government he
decided to improve his image by being reasonable and soft. His
style of decision making was to be briefed by the principal secretary of the ministry, but he would not consult other officials in the
ministry, nor would he read the files. The foreign-linked faction
was represented by the Indian foreign secretary. Consequently,
the advice the prime minister received was filtered by the same
source that filtered the advice to the foreign minister. The Indian
press and the Indian intellectuals were kept in the dark. For
months the details of the agreements were not released to the public. The document in question was available in Vienna but not in

during September-December 1977 sources outside the Foreign Ministry intervened with the prime minister to neutralize the advice of the foreign-linked faction. These sources were unable, however, to intervene earlier (summer 1977). Then factional activity with regard to the upgrading of the safeguards on the Rajasthan reactors was not known to these sources; and secrecy of the foreign-linked faction carried the day.

Figure 8.3 can be refined further, as shown in Figure 8.4. An example of the applicability of Figure 8.4 to India's nuclear decision making is found in the period September-December 1977, when preparations were being made in India for the Carter visit. The foreign-linked faction was working through appealing to the ego of a senior minister. Figure 8.4 does not indicate the presence of the sources of advice outside the bureaucracy, because these sources have no institutional status. They reached the prime minister by secretly by-passing the institutional mechanisms. It is said that Carter was surprised by Desai's stance because the former had been led to believe by the Ministry of External Affairs that India was "open to discussion." It is worth speculating that the prime minister would have been open to discussion if the outside advice had not reached him, because all other channels of official communications would have advised a "sell-out" in the face of Carter's demands. At crucial junctures in the past, the other viewpoint in the ministry (that is, the one that did not represent the foreign-linked faction) had had its channels of communications to the prime minister blocked.

From Forging Foreign-linked Domestic
Factionalism to Creating Dependencies

In the Indian case, the strategy for creating dependencies has three interlocked elements. First, there is the offer of high technology under certain conditions written into a contract. Second, there is a unilateral decision to alter the contract's conditions after the contract has come into effect and after technology transfer has occurred. Thirdly, there is the cultivation of a foreign-linked domestic faction that is willing and able both to play the foreign

---

New Delhi, and requests for the document were turned down in New Delhi with the statement that "the document is public but a copy is not presently available." Such is the hold of the government on the flow of information in India.

game and to put forth the revised rules of the game to their political masters. The first condition is the basis for the third condition. It is the continuous offer of foreign imports that keeps the
bureaucratic base of the foreign-linked domestic faction alive.
Discontinue the foreign imports and one would also have to dissolve
or reduce the bureaucratic base of the foreign-linked domestic
faction.

FIGURE 8.4

The Decision-making Process: The Third Cut
(revised)

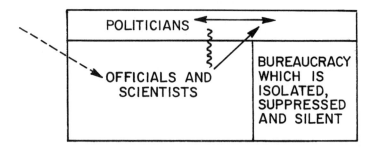

refers to external penetrativeness.

refers to the decision-making arena.

refers to "boring" the external viewpoint from within the
bureaucracy; playing on the inexperience, the ego of a
senior minister; this is a situation in which advice has
accepted by a senior minister and the minister is now
clearly playing into the hands of the foreign-linked faction.

Another minister has played into the hands of the foreign-
linked faction before, but he is also unpredictable and
can change because he is open to advice from outside
bureaucratic channels. Because this minister speaks the
language of high principles, because his self-image is
that of a moral man, he is difficult to reach. But if the
administrative strategy of an independent outside source
is sound, this minister can be approached.

Source: Compiled by the author.

The unilateral decision to alter the game rules has maximal and minimal positions. It is a reasonable assumption that the manipulator of the game does not expect acceptance of the maximal conditions. Acceptance of the minimal conditions is good enough for his purpose. A situation in which conditions are subject to change involves in this case articulation of a perceived threat. It is possible that the perceived threat may, as time passes, prove to be a false alarm. On this point a comparison between Canadian and U.S. nuclear supply policies is suggestive. Canadian policy is motivated by moral concerns. When Canadian thinking varied from that of India and Pakistan, the Canadian decision was to cut the bait and to let the fish swim. American policy on the other hand is not to cut the bait. Technology transfer is not canceled but it is postponed. Obligations are not repudiated but they are slowed in implementation. Joseph S. Nye, Jr., deputy to the under secretary for security assistance, science and technology in the State Department describes the current U.S. attitude as follows:

> Technology transfers cannot be delayed indefinitely, but
> they can be postponed until we have time to develop more
> proliferation resistant technology and more effective
> international institutions. In the interim, the question
> arises whether restraints on the transfer of sensitive
> technology are fully consistent with our undertakings in
> Article IV of the NPT. Clearly there is a degree of ten-
> sion, but we believe it is temporary and that restraints
> consistent with the fact that Article IV of the Treaty
> must be read in the light of Articles I and II, where
> states undertake to avoid steps which would lead to the
> spread of nuclear weapons.[48]

Clearly this formulation points to evolving change in the game rules. During World War II, the game rules involved collaboration in the military applications of atomic technology between the United States, the United Kingdom, and Canada. After the end of the war, the game rules changed and the United States decided to go it alone. Then President Eisenhower's famous "atoms for peace" announcement in 1953 made it easier to transfer technology and to encourage global spread of the U.S. light water reactors and associated technology. But once the world was dependent on the U.S. light water reactors and the supply of enriched uranium, then another alarm was sounded.

As Cyrus Manzoor points out, the NPT was presented to the world when the nuclear technological market was duopolisitic.[49]

According to Manzoor, in the mid-1960s a majority of the NPT sig-
natories were low on the proliferation potential curve. Manzoor's
point should be taken further. The premature alarm (the scenarios
of the sixth to the sixteenth nuclear powers publicized by Alastair
Buchan and others) had little basis in reality but it served a purpose: it became the basis of the NPT. Article IV of the NPT created
the vision of nuclear technology transfers and strengthened the constituency of peaceful users and of advocates of nuclear supply relations. Once the bait (Articles IV and VI) was thrown and taken, the
NPT became the vehicle and ostensible justification for the next
shift in the game rules.

The NPT game rules were intended to prevent and detect the
diversion from peaceful to military uses of nuclear energy. The
rules were not intended to prevent military uses of nuclear energy
because the military users of nuclear energy were by definition not
subject to international policing.

A post-NPT game rule change has occurred during the Carter
administration, and Joseph Nye outlines the shift as follows: "The
long run solution to these differences must be an international consensus on the nature and management of the nuclear fuel cycle."
This is to be done through the following means: making acceptance
of full-scope safeguards a U.S. national policy goal; requiring
restraints in transfer of sensitive technologies; creating fuel assurance for recipients that forego the full fuel cycle; and building a
consensus about the future structure and management of the full
fuel cycle.[50] The first condition increases the intrusiveness of
international and external agencies into national decision making.
It institutionalizes the foreign links of domestic factions by formaliz-
ing the inspection requirement for the entire nuclear industry. The
second and the third conditions deny the acquisition of a full fuel
cycle even by countries that have shown a low proliferation potential;
they raise the barriers against domestic technological innovation
and, through concerted NSG action, brake the learning curves of
Third World societies. Third World scientists are given the options
of demonstrating their failures in their indigenous scientific programs or staying in power and keeping their interests (as well as
their jobs) alive by cooperating with external agencies that can promote their interests. With regard to the fourth condition, the choice
of the term "consensus" is misleading. Consensus building in this
case lies in the hands of those who have the complete nuclear fuel
cycle and among those who defined the problem of nuclear proliferation in the 1960s. Note here that these four conditions say nothing
about Article VI (dealing with nuclear disarmament) of the NPT.
The new emphasis is on preventing rather than simply detecting the
diversion from peaceful to military use of nuclear energy.

The innovative element in the new thrust is to increase the external intrusiveness into domestic nuclear industry and to increase the dependency on external nuclear aid. Nye stated that Article IV should be read in terms of Articles I and II. This linkage is a part of the Carter strategy for altering the game rules. In fact, the four conditions noted by Nye rewrite the NPT because that international treaty does not restrict transfers of sensitive materials, equipment, and technology (as does the Carter policy) provided the transfers are safeguardable. The conclusion is irresistible that whatever the motives of the Carter administration, the effects of the new stance is to either generate a higher dependency of the recipient on the nuclear supplier, or to generate a paralysis in the recipient's nuclear industry. Neither of these effects impinges upon the freedom of action of the five nuclear weapon states—those who already have the full fuel cycle.

This perspective can be applied to the study of foreign-linked domestic factionalism in South Asian nuclear decision making. Pakistan is considered first. Pakistan did not sign the partial test ban treaty even though India did (1963). Pakistan's decision did not result in atmospheric testing. Similarly, Pakistan warned against the dangers of Indian nuclear proliferation in international forums, but this was not a building block for any other decision. Competing subnational elites produced two sets of opposite decisions. While the diplomatic elite produced the anti-India speeches, the economic and military modernization elite produced decisions to support economic and military modernization rather than atomic energy development.

India's nuclear behavior (as contrasted with the public posture) reveals the role of foreign-linked domestic factions and competing subnational elites in a telling fashion. The features of the factional and competitive activity are as follows. First, the United States and the United Kingdom stated, when the NPT was under negotiation, that they intended to cut off aid to India if the latter did not sign the NPT. This move was meant to induce India to accept the NPT regime. Canadian nuclear aid cutoff occurred in relation to the Indian test of 1974 and not because of India's refusal to sign the NPT. Secondly, whether or not aid cutoff was seriously intended as a threat is not the question. The foreign-linked domestic faction took the threat seriously and advocated that "India must accept the NPT because the United States is threatening to cut off aid and there are British pressures also." This was the majority view of the Indian Ministry of External Affairs. The "nationalist" faction argued that India could do without aid; India needed to resist foreign pressure; India should not be dictated to by others. But the "nationalist" view was a minority view. The foreign-linked domestic faction was oriented primarily to the United States and the United Kingdom. Soviet pressures were at best executed on an intergovernmental level, and there was no covert, subnational activity fostered by Moscow from 1967 until February 1968, when Gandhi decided against accepting the NPT "under present circumstances."[51] Subsequently, when nationalist opinion was overwhelmingly against the NPT, the ban against the treaty became permanent (verbally at least) but the foreign-linked competitive subnational activity continued.

The central point that emerges from a study of India's nuclear policy is that a foreign-linked domestic faction consisting of certain officials and certain atomic scientists has been able to increase India's dependency on external agencies since 1966, even though the declared national position is against the NPT and against the acceptance of full-scope safeguards on Indian nuclear industry. With the exception of the unsafeguarded CIRUS research reactor and two other facilities (a new research reactor and the Trombay reprocessing plant), the rest of operational Indian nuclear industry is now under international safeguards. The Rajasthan reactors (RAPP I and II) were originally under Canadian safeguards. Later these safeguards were transferred to the IAEA under a trilateral agreement. After Canada terminated its nuclear supply relationship with India in May 1976, India had the option of terminating its safeguards obligations with respect to RAPP I and II. Not only did India not renounce the "weak" Canada/India/IAEA safeguards on RAPP I and II, but through secret diplomacy India accepted an upgrading of safeguards as the price for receiving Soviet heavy water supply into these reactors.* The new safeguards agreement brings India in line with the safeguards requirements of the NSG of London, including the principle of pursuit and safeguards in perpetuity. Likewise, Indian rejection of the full-scope safeguards doctrine advanced

---

*The new safeguards agreement with the IAEA was initially negotiated by the Indira Gandhi government in September 1976 and was finalized by the Desai government in September 1977. During the September 1976–September 1977 negotiations, the deal was kept hidden from the Indian public. Even when information on the negotiations leaked, the Indian government tried hard to stifle a public debate on the subject, pretending all the while to be against the NPT and against international inspection. The contrast between the public speech making and the private behavior of the Indira Gandhi and the Morarji Desai governments is noteworthy.

by the Carter administration is a theoretical exercise. The acceptance of the Soviet heavy water safeguards, along with existing safeguards on Tarapur, leaves India's nuclear industry with a legal and operational status of having "almost full-scope safeguards." Practically, this means full-scope safeguards as far as the operational sectors of Indian nuclear industry are concerned. Therefore, even though the Indian rejection of the full-scope safeguards doctrine theoretically protects future Indian nuclear facilities (such as the Madras and Narora reactors) that are due to come into operation in the 1980s, it is an open question whether the protection is real. For instance, India is not self-sufficient in heavy water and is not likely to be self-sufficient until the late 1980s. There have been serious delays in its heavy water production facilities and the heavy water industry is accident-prone. So, if India fails to achieve self-sufficiency in heavy water production, and the new reactors are ready for commissioning, the use of imported heavy water (and both the USSR and the United States are willing to sell this commodity to India) will make these reactors safeguardable also.

Hypothesis

This review yields several hypotheses:

1. If and when conflicting foreign policy goals cannot be mediated, reconciled, or dissolved through normal or routine intergovernmental negotiations, or by threats, wars, legal and economic sanctions, or whatever other overt means are available in interstate reactions, then it makes sense for stronger societies to seek collaboration with covert subnational elites that can aid the cause of penetrating, neutralizing, or weakening of the competitive subnational or nationalist targets in the weaker state.
2. The foreign-linked subnational elite is motivated by a lust for power or financial gain.
3. Since it is foreign-linked and foreign-directed it is more organized than a competing subnational elite. The former has superior world-wide intelligence to back up its moves, compared with the intelligence resources of the latter.
4. If the foreign-linked subnational elite loses a particular factional dispute because the opposing subnational elite enjoys public opinion, parliamentary, and media support on a national issue, the setback to the foreign-linked subnational elite is temporary. The elite members are officials and scientists who enjoy tenure of jobs

and their activities are not subjected to public scrutiny. Consequently, such foreign-linked subnational elites can be suppressed temporarily but they cannot be eliminated from the political and social system.

5. The foreign-linked domestic faction does not encourage public scrutiny of the policies it shapes and exposure of archive materials is not encouraged even if all the moves are recorded. It is the strategy of this elite to speak the language of an undefined national interest but never to permit an in-depth public analysis of the so-called national interest.

6. According to Ward Morehouse, "in the interaction of science and politics in India, the political system has exercised the decisive influence on the scientific community rather than the other way around."[52] This chapter, however, shows that when linkage with a system external to the Indian political system exists, the foreign-linked scientist-turned-politician is not necessarily subservient to the civil administrator or the political master; and the scientist can, by having foreign-linked allies and allies in the civil bureaucracy, exercise a decisive influence on what can be done scientifically. That is, the scientist can veto something by asserting that it cannot be done even if the politician wants it done. But in a crisis in interstate negotiations, by expressing an inability to do something that only a scientist can do (for example, finding an adequate alternative fuel supply if the United States cancels its supply for Tarapur), the scientist can shape the policy and political choices of his political master if the latter does not have access to alternative sources of scientific advice from within the scientist's establishment. To influence political decision making decisively, the scientist and officials will escalate the conflict to the highest level and isolate the highest level of decision making from other sources of scientific and policy advice in a crisis.

Whether or not these hypotheses apply with complete reliability to the Indian and Pakistani nuclear cases is hard to tell until memoirs are written and the "leaks" are confirmed through archival material. Still, the foregoing hypotheses reveal interesting possibilities. These hypotheses can be seen to work in certain, but not in all, situations in the evolution of Indian and Pakistani nuclear decision making.

Figures shown on pages 213, 214, and 218 illustrate the Indian cases where the hypotheses are relevant. An obvious exception is the decision to explode the peaceful nuclear device by Prime Minister Indira Gandhi. One might ask about foreign-linked domestic players who tried to get India to accept the NPT during 1967-68 but failed and allowed the explosion of Indira Gandhi's peaceful bomb.

The situation requires the relaxation of one variable that exists in the hypotheses. The foreign-linked domestic faction has the best chance of success when: (1) the political leadership is divided and weak; (2) nationalist opinion on the subject is not articulate; (3) the prime minister's thinking is revocable; and (4) in the case of failure there is no risk to the careers of the foreign-linked elite personnel. In the illustration cited in Figure 8.3, the first, third, and fourth conditions were present. This accounts for the near-success of the ploy of the foreign-linked faction to get India into the NPT system. The second condition was modified by the existence of articulate nationalist opinion. It entered bureaucratic and cabinet-level discussions, and this accounts for the failure of the ploy of the foreign-linked domestic faction. In the decision to test India's PNE in May 1974 the political leadership was not divided; in fact, political czarism was in full play. Nationalist opinion favored the test, a point known to the prime minister through numerous public opinion polls. There was no political risk to the prime minister even though there was a scientific risk that the test might fail. The prime minister was resolved that there should be a test, and there was no public or cabinet debate about it. Finally, there was a risk to scientific careers if the prime minister's orders were not carried out and if the test was aborted through premature disclosure to intelligence services. This suggests that a foreign-linked domestic faction can be curbed or by-passed temporarily with respect to one phase of nuclear activity, leaving it free to assert itself in other phases.

In India's case, the thrust of the foreign-linked domestic faction in effect was first to get India into the NPT system. When that ploy failed, the foreign-linked domestic faction attempted to slow India's search for independence in nuclear technology and to keep India in a state of high dependency on an international organization (IAEA) and foreign nuclear suppliers (the United States, the USSR). In the latter strategy the faction succeeded. In Pakistan's case it is reasonable to infer that a similar pattern is at work, with one major difference. Pakistan never had its equivalent of India's Homi Bhabha, who was able to create some safeguard-free nuclear facilities (CIRUS and the reprocessing plant at Trombay).

CONCLUSIONS

Broadly speaking, South Asia's nuclear future can be examined in the context of two scenarios, an optimistic one and a pessimistic one. The emphasis has been on description and analysis of a process rather than on predicting a terminal condition for the late 1970s or the 1980s. A reason for emphasizing "process" is that the future of arms control and nuclear proliferation issues in the subcontinent rest on the evolution of Indo-Pakistan relations, on the role of foreign-linked domestic factions, and on how well nationalistic elites are able to find alternatives to foreign technological dependencies imposed from abroad.

There are two ways to study the overall foreign policy processes in South Asia. The optimistic approach takes the Simla agreement (1972), intended to normalize bilateral relations and to renounce the military option to solve the Kashmir question, as the starting point of analysis. Accordingly, the normalization process is seen as one of developing the habits of peaceful competition and limited cooperation on an intergovernment and intersocietal basis. The growth of trade and cultural ties between the two hitherto hostile societies will, according to this viewpoint, produce altered public opinions in the two countries. Furthermore, the flow of about $500 million a year from the Middle East into Pakistan's coffers helps Pakistan's search for foreign military imports and thereby strengthens its conventional military deterrent.

The premise in this perspective is that there is in fact a stable military balance between Pakistan's and India's military forces committed on the western front even though there is a military imbalance if Indian forces committed against the PRC are taken into account. The significance of this situation is, however, unclear. According to the Indian foreign minister, during his first visit to Pakistan in 1978, the "Kashmir issue was to be discussed after normalisation of relations but still there was much to be done in this regard."[53] But Pakistan's view is that: "a settlement of the Kashmir dispute is of fundamental importance since it would create a climate of mutual trust"; and "to expect a total rapprochement between India and Pakistan at this stage is totally unrealistic."[54] For Pakistan, "normalisation" may be intended to buy time until it is able to explode its own nuclear device. Finally, another premise is crucial in this viewpoint. During the 1964-74-78 period, there was no symmetry between PRC and Indian nuclear decision making, and there is only a connection between PRC nuclear weapons and India's nuclear option. If the PRC is content with a minimum deterrent (this may or may not be Teng Hsiao Ping's present and future intention) to deter the USSR, will not the slowing of PRC efforts to develop modern nuclear arms also further induce India not to move at a rapid pace? If India's nuclear policy is supposed to induce Pakistan to follow suit, will the low rate of proliferation in the Sino-Soviet and Sino-Indian pairs result also in a slowing of the Pakistani compulsion toward nuclear arms? No firm answers are available but proliferation and nonproliferation should be regarded as parallel and interlocked processes: while the first track favors a trend toward acquisition of nuclear options or nuclear weapons, the second track directs attention to a need to slow the process of acquisition. It can be argued that because bureaucracies do in fact seriously consider the political, economic, and military costs of nuclear decisions, a study of the possibility of acquiring nuclear weapons capability is itself an educational exercise within the bureaucracies.

Now the pessimistic scenario will be considered. The optimistic scenario in the India-Pakistan context seems relevant in a time frame of five to ten years, and the pessimistic one seems relevant thereafter. The line of argument is as follows: normalization has been, and is likely to remain, a retarded process. Intergovernmental ties can alter overnight and even trade links can be altered if political and strategic circumstances change. Investments in Indo-Pakistan joint projects could give institutional shape to normalization but still, the failure to solve the Kashmir dispute will mar the normalization process. While it makes sense to start the educational process by developing ties between the East and West Punjabs—and end the process by opening the Kashmir valley to tourism and trade—if this process were drawn out into the late 1980s, no Pakistani politician could afford to let the Kashmir issue slide from the public memory. While normalization is an on-going process that can diffuse military hostilities of the type experienced in 1965 and 1971, still the process has a plateau. That is, in Pakistani perceptions normalization makes sense in the context of a parallel development of Pakistan's military option and a nuclear option.

The pessimistic scenario is supported by Pakistan's presumed search for a viable and visible nuclear explosives capability. Even though the agreement with France has fallen through, if Pakistan is serious about reprocessing and about its nuclear option it will have to intensify its plan to have its own unsafeguarded reprocessing plant.

Evidence of Pakistani nuclear activity is therefore noteworthy. Shipments of Canadian nuclear supplies to Pakistan were held up after the Indian explosion, pending a review of Canada's policy. In 1976, Canada decided to terminate its supply relationship with Pakistan because of the French reprocessing deal. Canada intended to help by setting up a fuel rods fabrication capacity in Pakistan and providing heavy water supplies (about 4 tons at that time). At present Pakistan does not have its own heavy water production unit and foreign supplies are safeguarded. There are unconfirmed reports, however, that a West German company may establish a heavy water plant in Pakistan in conjunction with a fertilizer plant

in Multan. Pakistani scientists and technicians have been (and still
may be) in training (according to these reports) in Belgium, the
Federal Republic of Germany, and Canada. It appears likely that
they are gaining experience in separating plutonium from irradiated
nuclear fuel on a laboratory scale. A Belgian company may also
help Pakistan set up a laboratory for plutonium separation activity.
The embargo by Canada of nuclear supplies meant for Pakistan
(these are in some cases sitting on the docks in Montreal) has not
really slowed the Pakistani program because Pakistan already had
adequate reserve supplies. A suggestion that the Canadian reactor
in Marachi (KANUPP) cannot function without Canadian help is at
present premature.

It is unclear, however, whether Pakistan has decided to follow the plutonium route or the enriched uranium route in developing
its nuclear capability. Pakistan has secretly inquired from South
Africa about enriched uranium technical know-how. Luxembourg
also appears to be a possible source of supply of technical know-how.
Even though the plutonium route seems more likely in Pakistan's
case, it must not be forgotten that Pakistan's scientists have
trained quite rapidly in the last two decades. Access to enriched
uranium technology has an educational effect even if the decision is
not to follow the enriched uranium route because of its complexity.

The pessimistic scenario, therefore, refers primarily to the
flow of technological and scientific know-how from Canadian and
West European sources into Pakistan. The PRC is not considered
at present a source of dissemination of nuclear expertise even
though there is a Sino-Pakistan coordination board for nuclear
technology, consisting of two members representing each country
and the chairman of the Pakistan Atomic Energy Commission as
the chairman. The activities of this board are unknown but the
speculation is worth noting. It has been reported that in the last
three to four years that Pakistan opened the KANUPP reactor to
PRC inspection on a regular basis, and this has been reported to the
Canadian government. Could it be that Pakistan is making a long-
term political investment in the PRC through such an act, just as
the PRC did in Pakistan in the 1950s?

No conclusion can be offered because the foregoing discussion
refers to on-going processes. The foreign policy setting must be
clearly identified. Different scenarios appear to have different
implications for the rate and scope of nuclear proliferation in India
and Pakistan (if not Iran). If Indo-Pakistan normalization com-
bines with India-PRC normalization, it is conceivable that India
and Pakistan will both feel secure and be content with economic
uses of nuclear reactors that have a built-in defense use. This
study implies that it does not necessarily follow that Pakistan

must explode a nuclear device just because India did. Indeed, an
assumption is made here that the current Pakistani leadership is
astute; and it is one thing to make speeches for domestic and international audiences and quite another thing to make major resource
allocation decisions with major lead times and with major strategic,
economic, and political implications. Indeed, it is worth examining
the bureaucratic debates in Pakistan during the past. These debates do not point to an irrevocable trend toward Pakistani nuclear
arms. Still, it makes sense for Pakistan to follow Israel's and
South Africa's example in its nuclear diplomacy, rather than
India's, as it works its way through its domestic issues and toward
a search for a Pakistani identity in regional and international politics. On balance then, intraelite debates and creeping dependencies
rather than a nuclear chain best describe the India-Pakistan nuclear
behavior, particularly if the "optimistic" premises remain valid.
In this case, domestic and international politics account more for
nuclear activity than regional politics. In South Asia's case, the
definition of the region indicates an expanding scope. If nuclear
chains exist, the links are between China's nuclear weapons and
India's nuclear option on one hand, and between Indian and Pakistani
nuclear options on the other. But such symmetries are loose ones
and they reveal built-in domestic barriers against proliferation.

NOTES

1. William Epstein, The Last Chance (New York: Macmillan,
1976), p. 22.
2. Lewis Dunn and Herman Kahn, Trends in Nuclear Proliferation, report prepared for U.S. Arms Control and Disarmament Agency, Hudson Institute, HI-2336/3-RR, May 15, 1976. The
Dunn-Kahn chain begins with India and travels across regions and .
continents—into Brazil, Argentina, Taiwan, South Korea, and, of
course, Pakistan and Iran. The task of this chapter is limited to
India, Pakistan, and Iran.
3. New York Times, June 1, 1977.
4. The literature is vast. For examples see U.S., Congress,
House, Subcommittee on International Security and Scientific Affairs of the Committee on International Relations, Nuclear Proliferation: Future U.S. Foreign Policy Implications, 94th Cong.,
1st sess., October-November 1975; SIPRI, Nuclear Disarmament
or Nuclear War, monograph, 1975; and Stockholm International
Peace Research Institute, Preventing Nuclear-Weapon Proliferation, 1975. It is noteworthy that these themes are constantly and
prominently presented in U.S., Canadian, British, Swedish, and

Australian argumentation, but minimally so in West German, Japanese, or French views.

5. Walter C. Patterson, Nuclear Power (London: Pelican Books, 1976), p. 193.

6. For an assessment of India's debate and nuclear decision making see Ashok Kapur, India's Nuclear Option (New York: Praeger, 1976).

7. Confidential interviews, New Delhi, December–January 1978.

8. Dunn and Kahn, op. cit.

9. For background see "Atomic Energy and Space Research: A Profile for the Decade 1970-80," Department of Atomic Energy, Trombay, 1970; and annual reports of the Department of Space, Government of India.

10. Confidential interview, Moscow, November 1977.

11. M. Afaf, in Strategic Studies (Islamabad) 1, no. 2 (July–September 1977): 47-48; Sampooran Singh, India and the Nuclear Bomb (New Delhi: S. Chand, 1971).

12. For a general review of India's experience see A. N. Prasad and S. V. Kumar, "Indian Experience in Fuel Reprocessing," Bhabha Atomic Research Centre, Department of Atomic Energy, India, IAEA-CN-36/391(II.7), mimeo., undated.

13. SIPRI 1977 Yearbook, pp. 15-16.

14. Statesman, July 14, 1977.

15. See Kapur, op. cit., for a general discussion of strategic ambiguity.

16. Cited in William E. Epstein, "Why States Go—and Don't Go—Nuclear," in The Annals, 430 (March 1977): 19.

17. Confidential interview, New York, June 1977.

18. New York Times, January 4, 1977. Canada-Pakistan nuclear cooperation ended December 23, 1976. Also see Times (London), December 24, 1976.

19. New York Times, June 1 and 2, 1976. Apparently 95 percent of blueprints have been sent but not the crucial ones.

20. Michael Nacht, in Insecurity: The Spread of Weapons in the Indian and Pacific Oceans, ed. by R. J. O'Neill (Canberra: Australian National University Press, 1978), p. 16.

21. R. Tomar, "Myths and Mirages: Case of the Indian Nuclear Power Program," Department of International Relations, Australian National University, unpublished paper, May 16, 1978.

22. Facts on Nuclear Proliferation, A Handbook, prepared for the Committee on Government Operations, U.S. Senate, by the Congressional Research Service, Library of Congress, December 1975, p. 120, reveals India's plutonium production capacity as 200 kg. per year (1974 estimate). This estimate ignores delays

in commissioning reactors, shutdowns, and so on. According to one confidential estimate, India should have about 75-100 kg. of unsafeguarded plutonium after the 1974 test, and a part of this, if not the whole, is committed for the fast breeder program. The estimate of 460 kg. by 1980 also appears too high.

23. Z. A. Bhutto, The Myth of Independence (Karachi: Oxford University Press, 1969), pp. 152-56.

24. For general reports on atomic energy developments in Pakistan, see editorial, Pakistan Times, April 11, 1972; Pakistan Times, April 11, 1972 for a report on new projects; Pakistan Times, November 17, 1972 on the question of uranium prospecting and desalination project; a long article by Munir Ahmad Khan, chairman of PAEC in Pakistan Times, November 28, 1972 offering an overview of nuclear developments and prospects in Pakistan.

25. Pakistan Times, January 11, 1974, quoting the chairman, PAEC.

26. Pakistan Times, May 25, 1974.

27. The Age, May 28, 1974.

28. New York Times, May 8, 1974.

29. The Age, June 8, 1974.

30. New York Times, July 1, 1974.

31. Pakistan Times, September 30, 1974 and October 6, 1974.

32. Pakistan Times, December 31, 1974.

33. Pakistan Times, December 27, 1974.

34. Ibid.

35. Pakistan Times, June 15, 1975.

36. Pakistan Times, August 14, 1975.

37. Pakistan Times, editorial, February 27, 1976.

38. Pakistan Times, February 28, 1976.

39. Pakistan Times, March 2, 1976.

40. See Ashok Kapur, "India After Bangladesh," Bulletin of Atomic Scientists 28, no. 9 (November 1972): 28-30. In this case the lack of overconcern could be extended back to post-1971 developments.

41. Bhutto, op. cit.

42. Confidential interview, London, July-August, 1977.

43. See Kapur, India's Nuclear Option, op. cit., Chapter 9.

44. Confidential interview with a senior official, New York, June 1976. This official is fully familiar with the inner workings of Pakistan's atomic energy program.

45. For a general review see Alan Dowty, "Foreign-Linked Factionalism as a Historical Pattern," Journal of Conflict Resolution 15, no. 4 (December 1971): 429-42.

46. Ibid., p. 431.

47. See Kapur, India's Nuclear Option, op. cit., p. 196 for a general review of the debate.

48. Cited in Eighteenth Strategy for Peace Conference Report (October 13-16, 1977), The Stanley Foundation, Iowa, p. 65.

49. "Politics of Technology Transfer (with Special Reference to the Transfer of Nuclear Technology)," paper presented to Iran Conference on Transfer of Nuclear Technology, 1977, published in Annals of Nuclear Energy, Vol. 4 (Oxford, U.K.: Pergamon Press, 1977), pp. 225-33.

50. Nye, in Eighteenth Strategy for Peace Conference Report, op. cit., pp. 65-66.

51. Cited in George Quester, The Politics of Nuclear Proliferation (Baltimore: The Johns Hopkins University Press, 1973), p. 233.

52. "Professional Estates as Political Actors: The Case of the Indian Scientific Community," Philosophy and Social Action (New Delhi) 2, no. 4 (October-December 1976): 62.

53. Dawn, February 8, 1978.

54. Dawn, editorial, February 4, 1978.

9

SOUTH AFRICA'S NUCLEAR DIPLOMACY: APARTHEID WITH OR WITHOUT THE BOMB?

INTRODUCTION

Studying South Africa's nuclear intentions and behavior is difficult but conceptually exciting for a number of reasons:[1]

1. Until recently South Africa's nuclear behavior has not been subjected to a critical inquiry as have "unstable," "irresponsible," and proliferation-prone societies like India, Pakistan, Iran, South Korea, Taiwan, Brazil, and Argentina. In July 1970 the South African prime minister disclosed that his country possessed uranium enrichment technology that was "unique in concept" (this is discussed later). The real impact of South Africa's nuclear prowess, however, came with the "discovery" in August 1977 of South Africa's plan to have a nuclear weapons test.*[2]

"Nuclear chains"[3] are presumed to produce rapid proliferation between societies located in regions of conflict (India-Pakistan-Iran); South and North Korea; Brazil-Argentina; Israel-Egypt); but this concept does not presently seem relevant for studying the African scene. Even continent-crossing nuclear chains such as among India-Argentina-Libya[4] somehow never ended up with, or involved, South Africa.

3. Apartheid, rather than South African nuclear bombs, dominated the world headlines.

4. Even if it is true that Pretoria has secretly sold uranium to Israel and to Japan,[5] and that West Germany buys South African

---

*The likely fissile material for the proposed test was enriched uranium.

and Namibian uranium,[6] and that South Africa has cooperated technologically with Israel,* "there will still be important arguments
against South Africa so brazenly defying the world consensus on
proliferation"; and it has several times said that "it will not allow
its uranium sales to be used to increase the number of nuclear-
weapons states."

5. Pretoria might lose more by becoming the sixth nuclear
weapon power because its conventional superiority over its opponents
did not require a change in the rules of the game.

6. It makes sense for Pretoria to acquire nuclear weapons
capability now as insurance against intervention inspired by the
great powers or the UN, and to use its uranium deliveries to bargain technology transfers into South Africa. Overall, as George
Quester says,

> If Pretoria wishes neither to obtain nuclear weapons nor
> to help other 'nth' nations to obtain them, it might thus
> in time become appropriate to sign the NPT. Yet the
> Republic may achieve its ends more readily without com-
> mitting itself. South Africa can certainly observe the
> treaty without signing it. As an important supplier of
> critical materials rather than a receiver, it can afford
> to mold a policy of its own, demanding safeguards over
> most or all of its sales. For the interim, there are
> some clear bargaining arguments for such a non-
> committal position, whereby South Africa would co-
> operate with the NPT system but would not be bound
> to do so forever. On a yearly basis the threat of un-
> safeguarded uranium sales could thus be held in re-
> serve to deter overly stringent boycotts and embargoes
> in order to force the United States and Britain to ac-
> commodate South African interests where such accom-
> modation is crucial. In this light, it would be optimal

---

*According to Peter Janke:

On 31 March 1976 it was announced that defence spending was to rise by 40 per cent, which effectively doubled
the defence budget over the past two years. There was
no overall increase in government expenditure. Scientific know-how, including nuclear, will result from a
pact signed in April 1976 with Israel, which also has
unrivalled experience in low intensity warfare.[7]

for South Africa neither to surrender nor to exercise
the option of spreading nuclear weapons.
    Aside from this residual threat of selling
uranium to weapons producers, the Republic might
withhold an NPT signature simply to avoid unnecessary IAEA inspection. [8]

    These considerations point to a need and a posture of calcu-
lated ambiguity in South Africa's nuclear behavior. This is based
on the premise that there is no immediate threat to South Africa's
future that necessitates a nuclear weapon response. Yet there is
evidence that even before Soviet and American military satellites
observed the alleged South African preparation for a nuclear test
(1977), the Republic has been slowly but surely grooming its nuclear
presence. The underlying factors may be more complex than Western observers have noted in the public literature.
    South Africa's Atomic Energy Board (1949-   ) was established
to prospect uranium (1952-   ), of which it has the third (and by 1985
it is likely to have the second) largest deposits worldwide. The
United States and the United Kingdom were then the principal buyers
of South African uranium. In view of the loopholes in the UN embargo (August 1963),* defense and nuclear technology transfers from
Western sources have significantly aided the rapid growth of South
Africa's nuclear base. In 1963, a Federal Republic of Germany
banker approached Pretoria with an offer of Federal Republic of
Germany participation in nuclear research. A rocket research center was subsequently established, ostensibly with the financial support of the Federal Republic of Germany's defense ministry. In
August 1963, South Africa entered the missile field and in 1964 the
Rocket Research Institute was established. Tests took place during
1968-69; in 1971 and in 1973 a special rocket center was set up
(Propulsion Division of the National Institute for Defence Research)
to work on production aspects of missilry. Other developments have
given shape to South Africa's nuclear industry. SAFARI-1 (U.S.-
supplied; 90 percent enriched uranium fueled; 10 MWe; one atom

---

    *According to SIPRI (see Note 9) the loopholes are these: the
language of the UN resolution is vague and open to interpretation;
both Britain and France abstained on the resolution and declared
that they would not accept an embargo on arms meant for external
defense; items with civil-military uses are hard to embargo; and
control of resales were hard to implement. Compare SIPRI, Southern
Africa, pp. 124-26.

bomb per three to four years) started to operate in 1965 and the other research reactor started in 1967. [9] Since 1961, the United States has shipped about 220 pounds of uranium to South Africa. [10] France (Framatome) is supplying a 922 MWe reactor, which is expected to come into operation in 1983. Another one, also by Framatome, is due to start in 1984. [11]

During 1965-70, South African spokesmen denied that their program had possible military applications. [12] The civil use of nuclear energy for electricity production was pointed out, as was the export potential of uranium. South Africa has been involved in building the Cabora Bassa hydroelectric project on the Zambesi river in Mozambique and the Cuneno river projects in an area bordering Angola and Namibia (Southwest Africa). Despite the political developments in Mozambique, South Africa's participation in the Cabora Bassa project has continued, and 20 percent of the total hydroelectric power for South Africa could come out of this project. South Africa has extensive coal reserves, thus most power is likely to come from coal. Oil is not vital for South Africa and South African Coal, Oil and Gas Corporation (SASOL) is able to make oil from coal.* Most of the coal is located in the northern region. Nuclear energy development is going hand-in-hand with coal utilization. The nuclear power stations that are planned will be dispersed because of the distances involved in transporting coal; it is the transportation cost, not the mining cost, that accounts for a reliance on nuclear power stations. The first reactor will be in the Cape area; to date there is no decision about power stations beyond the Koeberg station. The export potential for uranium is obvious because South Africa seems not to insist on the stiff safeguards sought by Canada, the United States, and Australia. It is possible that the demand for uranium may not be as high as anticipated because nuclear power programs have slipped worldwide, and governments are deciding in favor of reprocessing. But, on the other hand, the demand for enriched uranium is growing because of the limited sources of supply and because buyers want to diversify their supply sources to avoid a dependence of their nuclear industry on political relations with the suppliers. Western Europeans, for instance, have found themselves shifting to Moscow as a secure source of supply, and it is possible that in the 1980s South Africa will enter the enriched uranium market.

---

*About 90 percent of oil comes from Iran and up to 1978 there was no real likelihood of an Iranian oil embargo against South Africa.

In speculations about the potential military uses of nuclear energy (leaving aside research reactors that could produce bomb materials in a desperate situation), the establishment of a pilot uranium enrichment plant in 1970 was a major milestone in South Africa's nuclear history. In October 1975 A. J. A. Roux, president of the South African Atomic Energy Board (SAAEB), thanked the United States, in particular, and several other Western nuclear nations for their help in training South African scientists, but it is not clear if American help, as distinct from West German help, contributed to the "unique-in-concept" South African enrichment process. This was not based on gaseous diffusion technology and seemed to be a modification of the German jet nozzle technology.[13] According to the announcement by the South African Prime Minister, Vorster, on July 20, 1970:

> The South African process, which is unique in its concept, is presently developed to the stage where it is estimated that under South African conditions, a large-scale plant can be competitive with existing plants in the West. What is more important is that the process still holds appreciable possibilities for further development, and research and development to achieve this are continuing.

Subsequently Dr. Roux reported that the government had firmly decided to construct, on a commercial* scale, a uranium enrichment plant that would start production in 1984, reaching full output in 1986. Its size and other details were to be decided in 1978.[14] Kratzer, a State Department official, noted that in 1973 the United States approved the sale of two computers to aid the operation of the uranium enrichment plant.[15] According to SIPRI, the West German firm STEAG was negotiating with the South African Enrichment Corporation (Dr. Roux is chairman), and in April 1974 STEAG and the South African authorities agreed to conduct a feasibility study of two uranium enrichment processes.[16] As of February 3, 1978, Pretoria had not decided on the size of the plant but it had already initiated discussions with the IAEA to explore the prospects and conditions for seeking, unilaterally, the application of agency safeguards.[17]

Speculation about the potential military uses of nuclear energy has been fostered to some extent by South African spokesmen them-

---

*As a "commercial" proposition the plant has slipped but the project continues in a modified form.

selves, in vivid contrast to Indian officials who maintained that the 1974 test was an implosion and not an explosion! Connie Mulder, a senior minister, asserted with telling ambiguity: "if we are attacked, no rules apply at all . . . if it comes to a question of our existence . . . we will use all means at our disposal, whatever they may be." And then he went on to describe the pilot uranium enrichment plant.[18] According to Jack Spence, "Dr. Roux did, however, claim that South Africa was by virtue of the new process in a position to manufacture nuclear weapons."[19] But by and large the official stance of Pretoria has been to stress the peaceful uses of nuclear energy. This discussion now turns to an assessment of the multiple uses of South Africa's nuclear strategy.

SOUTH AFRICA'S NUCLEAR DIPLOMACY: THE FRAMEWORK

The progressive growth of nuclear technology shows it to be a phasal activity—from establishment of the SAAEB in 1949 to the announcement of the development of a "unique-in-concept" enrichment technology in 1970, and thereafter. South Africa clearly has the uranium to mine and to export. One dimension of its nuclear policy is to engage in resources diplomacy, to make money and to influence Western buyers of much-needed uranium, particularly if these buyers face unpleasant cut-off threats or embargoes from North American and Australian sources. South Africa's success in emerging as a dependent ally of the Federal Republic of Germany in uranium supply is remarkable, and the exercise during January-July 1975 had an Australian angle. In Bonn, a coalition between the chancellor's office and the ministry of research and technology favored a commitment toward South Africa. The federal foreign office remained neutral on this issue, presumably because of its nonproliferation position. Australia's prime minister, Gough Whitlam, was anxious to establish a uranium supply connection with the Federal Republic of Germany and also to pave the way for a deal linking uranium and beef. But Canberra's conditions for uranium supply were much tougher than were Pretoria's and the latter won. Parenthetically, the chancellor's office and the research and technology ministry in Bonn were glad that the Australian official concerned placed very tough conditions; it made the task of rejecting the Australian uranium offer easier.[20]

Information on mining and selling of uranium, however, tells nothing about South Africa's nuclear intentions—whether these are in the direction of making nuclear weapons or of mounting an ambiguous nuclear option (of Israel's type). One line of argumentation is offered by Michael Nacht. He concludes that because: (1) South Africa has a uranium enrichment plant ironically called Valindaba (meaning "the talking is over"); (2) it has not signed the NPT; (3) its scientists have trained abroad; (4) it allegedly is working with Israel on nuclear weapons development; and (5) the political situation in South Africa is unstable and an all-white garrison state with a nuclear deterrent is possible, "South Africa must be considered a prime candidate for nuclear weapon possession within the next decade."[21]

A comparison of the analyses of George Quester (cited above) and Michael Nacht reveals two distinct lines of inquiry. Quester sees a nuclear policy and a stance of calculated ambiguity that serve as a viable basis at present for negotiating Pretoria's external relations with the Western world. Nacht, on the other hand, sees a gradual movement toward the unfolding of South Africa's nuclear option, if not nuclear weapons, in a decade. He is implying that there is a lack of sophistication in South African thinking, and he does not cast the nuclear factor in a wider net of economic, political, and military relations (as is explicit in Quester's analysis). Nuclear proliferation studies can become analytically richer if they try to examine the pressures and constraints for and against proliferation, and if the stress is on an assessment of the processes rather than on an instinctive or emotional reaction, which at times has distinct policy overtones.

Historically speaking, South Africa's prime concern is not only to have a viable state but to negotiate outcomes whereby its censure by the "world community" does not produce a total isolation, the status of a total outcast from the world. In its nuclear relations with the outside world it anticipated the trends and sought to act rather than to be left in a reactive situation. It is an interesting feature of South African nuclear diplomacy that it has never found itself in a one-sided situation where it is the recipient. Consequently it has been able to maintain and to develop a bargaining situation with external friends (and adversaries). It takes but it also offers, and it has managed to exempt itself from intrusive international rule making. A brief review of South African attitudes toward the NPT, the IAEA, and the United States brings out the implications of the foregoing points.

Even though South African nuclear diplomacy is calculatedly ambiguous with respect to the potential military overtones of its uranium enrichment plans, its theoretical positions are clear-cut (unlike those of Israel). But its positions are simultaneously supportive and threatening to Western, and particularly U.S., interests, as the following sketch of the details of its positions reveals. At the same time there is nothing irrevocable about Pretoria's nuclear diplomacy except a quest for a stronger network of bilateral and multilateral ties. The principal features of its positions may be noted.

First, South Africa has taken a stand against nuclear proliferation and against the NPT. South Africa claims that it will not
allow itself as a major uranium producer to contribute to the growth
of a nuclear weapon club (that is, it does not wish to add to the number of powers with nuclear bomb capability); and its own atomic energy program is devoted to peaceful purposes exclusively. Yet it
declined to accept the NPT. In 1968 it felt that the draft treaty did
not fully meet all the requirements by the U.N. General Assembly
(Resolution 2028) and it did not take into account the legitimate interests of those nonnuclear-weapon countries "which have a major
economic interest in the development of their own nuclear technology" (emphasis added). The discriminatory features of the NPT
were noted. It was pointed out that "there is no obligation of a really
compelling nature on the nuclear-weapon States to pursue negotiations, in accordance with article VI" of the NPT.
South Africa noted a number of other objections:

1. The definition of "nuclear weapon" or a "nuclear explosive
device" was unclear (although this was not a matter that concerned
South Africa).
2. The terms of Articles I and II could, given some interpretations, largely nullify the "inalienable right" referred to in Article
IV.
3. There was no guarantee that the benefits promised in Article V would in fact be made available without discrimination.
4. In particular, Article III was vague, its meaning was obscure, and it lacked clear definitions. What exactly was meant by
the agency's safeguard system? Did it refer to the system in effect
now or a system that would emerge in the future? It was pointed out
that at present IAEA safeguards did not cover mines and ore processing plants. Since South Africa's uranium is a by-product of its gold
mines, it was not prepared to place its mining industry under international inspection. Article III, paragraph 1, was held to go beyond
the present IAEA safeguards system. An international regime was
considered a serious intrusion into national sovereignty. Overall,
the IAEA safeguards system was viewed as a "delicate blend" of what
was "technically advisable and politically feasible," and this balance
seemed to be in danger. [22]

Second, South Africa's orientation is against the nuclear-weapon
states. South Africa participated in the Conference of Non-Nuclear
Weapon States (1968), which dealt with a number of themes: (1) there
was a need to discuss a nuclear disarmament treaty and not a nonproliferation one; (2) there was scepticism about the claim by the
NWS that the NPT was the first step toward effective nuclear dis-

armament; (3) if the treaty were a step toward nuclear disarmament, it could have a significant potential to promote international security; (4) South Africa did not belong to alliances and it needed to stand on its own feet; (5) the NPT was making demands on the NNWS by inviting the latter to trust completely the NWS with regard to military and economic security (the implication in the South African statement was that the actions of the NWS did not create confidence in their promises); (6) the treaty "assigned to the nuclear powers a built-in quasi monopoly" in certain fields of peaceful nuclear development, and South Africa's "almost unique position" as a uranium producer did not permit the development of such monopoly or a permanent restriction on the development of its potential (examples were given of how the spirit of Article IV of the NPT had already been violated by one cosponsor of the treaty with respect to South Africa—the United States was not named, though, at that time); (7) while the existing safeguards regime was tied to the principle of voluntary inspection, the NPT sought to alter it into an involuntary rule; (8) the problem of industrial spying was real, since the NNWS might find themselves in commercial competition with one or more of the NWS. [23]

Third, the South African position involves keeping the IAEA as a technical agency. South Africa perceived a nonpolitical role for the IAEA, leaving the political role to the UN where it "properly belonged." The IAEA ought not to be "weak" in permitting the introduction of political issues in the discharge of its responsibilities. It ought to encourage research by other member states rather than proliferate its own facilities. Clarity was needed with respect to plans to implement Article IV(2) of the NPT, concerning fullest possible exchange of nuclear technology, equipment, and materials for the peaceful uses of nuclear energy. [24]

Fourth, South Africa has taken a position on marketing its enriched uranium. The announcement by South Africa's prime minister on July 20, 1970 stated that "as a result of the increased demand for uranium in the enriched form, it is obvious that South Africa, as one of the largest uranium producing countries in the world, will consider in its own interest to market uranium in the enriched form."

This statement pointed out that a "new process" had been developed by South African scientists under the guidance of A. J. A. Roux and W. Grant. The statement pointed out that South African nuclear energy was meant entirely for peaceful purposes but it would not permit release of details through safeguards inspections. South Africa would consider joining the NPT as soon as the details about the safeguards system were known. South Africa was willing to consider collaboration with noncommunist countries to exploit the new process provided South African interests were protected.

Earlier it was noted that Pretoria has an anti-NWS position. U.S. writers, however, do not usually advertise the anti-U.S. orientation in Pretoria's nuclear diplomacy. A major speech by Roux in May 1973 (see appendix to this chapter) reveals three themes in South African diplomacy that are directed toward the United States. Pretoria's concern is with the implications of multilateral nuclear rule making that can hurt its commercial and political interests in the area of uranium exports and enrichment technology, and with respect to the potential military uses of its nuclear technology if national defense by all available means becomes necessary. Its strategic interest was, and still is, in guarding its interests against the United States by expressing its concerns about U.S. policies (this was before Carter became president); by building technological, economic, and political ties with European nuclear industry and other governments (Israel, for example) that are also threatened by U.S. policies; and by utilizing, or hoping to utilize, the above-mentioned ties to negotiate with the United States, to prevent the United States from renegotiating the rules of the game, and to see that the United States fulfills contractual obligations it has undertaken, as, for instance, to supply the fuel for the SAFARI-I reactor and the Koeberg power plant.

The nuclear links between South Africa and certain Western European societies are important because South Africa has not been intimately involved with post-NPT multilateral diplomacy, with the exception of its observer status in the Zangger Committee.* It participated in this committee. It accepts but did not sign the Trigger List (INFCIRC 209), publicized in 1974. It was not co-opted into the London Nuclear Suppliers Group (NSG), which took up matters that the Zangger Committee did not handle—that is, the question of securing restraints in the export of sensitive nuclear technology and equipment as distinct from safeguarding supplies in terms of Article III (2)(b) of the NPT. South Africa was kept out of the NSG primarily because of Soviet objections, but others also supported this move. South Africa was expelled from the board of governors of the IAEA in 1977 and was replaced by Egypt.[25] Membership on the board of governors goes to the most advanced nuclear nation in the region, and on this basis South Africa held the seat as a founding member of the IAEA. But the ouster of South Africa and its replacement by Egypt did not mean that the latter had become the most advanced nuclear nation in the world. The ouster was a political act by the

---

*In 1977, however, it joined INFCE and it participates constructively in this evaluation.

Third World majority in the IAEA, a rare instance where voting became politicized in the IAEA. In short, in multilateral and international forums South Africa lacks an effective voice. It was in this
context that Prime Minister Vorster of South Africa pointed out that

> countries like the USA have not honoured the commit-
> ments they have entered into bilaterally. So, for ex-
> ample, the USA has not honoured the undertaking to sup-
> ply fuel for the research reactor SAFARI I, which is
> under full International Atomic Energy Agency safeguards,
> in spite of the undertaking South Africa has given and
> honoured, that the burnt fuel elements will be returned
> to the USA for reprocessing. No delivery has yet been
> nade of fuel elements ordered from the USA two years
> ago, although the enriched uranium was paid for at the
> time that the order was placed. Up to now South Africa
> has not even received an indication whether an export
> permit for the elements will be issued.
>
> As you know, South Africa has decided to build a
> nuclear power station at Koeberg. South Africa has
> entered into a contract with the United States Energy
> Research and Development Agency for the supply of the
> necessary fuel for the initial period. What guarantee
> do we have that this contract will be honoured and that
> the fuel will be delivered in time?—is the question I
> am entitled to put tonight.
>
> We are still seriously considering accession to
> the Non-Proliferation Treaty and we would be prepared
> to discuss the matter with the US, who last week urged
> us to do so, but naturally the discriminatory actions,
> including those to which I have referred, will be raised
> and will have to be sorted out at the same time. [26]

Analytically, the three facets—expressing concern with U.S.
nuclear supply policy toward South Africa, building bridges with certain European nuclear industry and governments, and preventing the
United States from renegotiating the game rules—can be viewed as a
part of a process that treats either the second facet or the third facet,
or both, as the terminal conditions. In either case, Pretoria's
negotiating strategy is to escape the possibility of high technology
dependence on U.S. enriched uranium supplies for South Africa's
light water power program. Whether or not South Africa has been
completely successful in escaping the U.S. plan to induce technological and fuel dependence of certain proliferation-prone societies is
still an open question. It is noteworthy, however, that Pretoria

started to react to the implications of U.S. policy in the early 1970s, before Carter unfolded in April 1977 his plan to slow, if not delay indefinitely, the worldwide development of reprocessing and uranium enrichment capacities beyond the industrial societies in Europe and Japan.

South Africa spoke, as mentioned above, against the reliability of the NPT commitments of the NWS. But actually Pretoria's threat perception is refined, and differentiates among the NWS. The Soviet Union is perceived as a threat to the future of the Republic and to the Western world. The view is that it makes sense for the USSR to radicalize Black African regimes under Soviet guidance, and to control South Africa's vital economic resources. South Africans see an attempt to alter the global balance of power by the USSR. The premise is that whoever controls the joint resources of the USSR and South Africa can make use of denial of resources in their diplomatic dealings with the Western societies. According to an official document:

> Much has been said lately in the local and international press about South Africa's strategic significance as a supplier of minerals in the world. I would therefore, consider it appropriate to discuss our mineral resources against the background of the western world's needs and sources of supply.
>
> Recent developments in southern Africa, especially Angola and Mozambique, have led to much speculation about Soviet objectives in this part of the world which have a direct bearing on the future control of the region's mineral resources—particularly those in South Africa. There is no doubt that whoever controls South African mineral supplies and reserves, could well hold the West, indeed the world to ransom.
>
> Concentration of world production and reserves of gold, platinum, chrome and vanadium and, to a lesser extent, antimony, fluorspar, diamonds, and manganese, occur in South Africa and the Soviet Union.
>
> South Africa has become one of the five most important mineral producing countries in the world not only by virtue of its extensive mineral resource base, but also through consistent and realistic mineral policy and decision-making machinery.
>
> South Africa has consistently refused to participate in the establishment of producer cartels or to demand unreasonable conditions from potential investors and consumers of its mineral products. It has there-

fore remained one of the most important stabilising and moderating forces in world mineral supply. [27]

This assessment is shared by the London-based Institute for the Study of Conflict. It points out that

> the threat to the West lies ultimately not only in the Soviets influencing the interior countries but actually setting up pro-Soviet revolutionary regimes and exploiting their mineral wealth. When Mozambique closed its border with Rhodesia on 3 March there were goods to the value of R$ 45 million, including chrome, in the ports of Maputo and Beira, awaiting sale and shipment. All were taken and paid for promptly by the Soviet Union. Since that date Soviet use of Mozambique ports has increased by two-thirds whilst Western shipping has declined. Apart from high-grade Rhodesian chrome Soviet interest in African minerals is not for Russian consumption, for the Communist bloc is very largely self-sufficient in raw materials. More likely, the aim is to disrupt essential supplies to Western industrial states, which are heavily dependent upon imports. Indeed, recently Russia has actually exported chrome, a strategically important ore, to the US, although in its processed form it is not possible to tell whether the ore was originally Rhodesian or Russian.
>
> With clear indications that the Soviet Union is interested in either supplementing its own raw material production, denying or controlling Western access, or manipulating the world market in gold or diamonds, brief consideration should be given to what the West stands to lose. [28]

The fear of Soviet domination of South African resources is clear in South African thinking. It is unclear, however, whether the same threat is perceived from the PRC as from the USSR. In the past the fear has been expressed against communism. According to the South Africa 1974 Official Yearbook:

(1) Armed police are currently engaged in countering terrorists, trained and financed by the Soviets and Chinese, on the northern borders of Southwest Africa. They also assist Rhodesian forces to combat the violation of Rhodesian borders by these terrorists.

> (2) Internationally, the security of the RSA is affected
> mainly by the all-pervasive East-West conflict.[29]

The second part of this view no longer seems relevant for understanding the roots of South African diplomacy and military policy.
The evidence is vague, but it is probable that because Japan-PRC
economic relations are moving forward in light of the recent trade
pact, because the Sino-Japanese peace treaty was adopted in 1978,
and because the Japanese have the status of honorary whites in South
African thinking, the PRC's economic modernization, given this
background, may proceed in part on the basis of a division of labor:
Japanese technology, South African resources, Australian capital
(on deposit to the Bank of China branch in London), and U.S. tacit
concurrence.[30] This is not to suggest that a Pretoria-Peking-Tokyo
axis is in the making, but it is to suggest that Pretoria's anticommunism in the 1970s and the 1980s may be more differentiated than
the pre-Angola crisis thinking. For a brief period during the Angolan
war South Africa and the PRC were on the same side,[31] against the
USSR. It is conceivable that the PRC doctrine of uniting against a
common enemy could serve as a basis for cooperation between two
ideologically different societies. Today anticommunism has dis-
appeared in the South African rhetoric and the new focus is not anti-
Soviet but anti-Soviet imperialism. South Africans note that there
is a common call among some African countries about the implications of the USSR's expanding influence in Africa, and they worry
about the prospect that the West may desert Africa and thus reduce
African options vis-à-vis the superpowers. The concern here is not
that the West has deserted Africa and South Africa, but that it may
do so because of isolationist tendencies caused by bureaucratic inertia and an inconclusive policy debate on Africa in the Carter administration.

SOUTH AFRICA IN AFRICAN INTERNATIONAL
RELATIONS: IS THE NUCLEAR FACTOR IRRELEVANT?

In South African military thinking there is little public evidence
that Pretoria is interested in the military applications of nuclear
power. Nor is there a perceived fear of a nuclear threat against
South Africa from the existing nuclear-weapon states. In short,

---

This section relies mostly on confidential interviews: Ottawa,
July 1976; London, July-August 1977; Canberra, March 1978.

there is no evidence to indicate that South Africans fear the danger of a nuclear intervention by the great powers against the Republic. The focus instead is on possible conventional threats (low-level guerrilla operations escalating into revolutionary warfare involving conventional arms over a period of five to ten years. But there is no fear at present of an escalation into an operation of the Vietnam type. It is noted with satisfaction that the Soviet Union has never committed its own troops outside Europe, and that Cuban forces, even with Soviet support, do not have the military capacity, including the manpower, to sustain a Vietnam-like operation. Still, South Africa's military machine has been developed on the premise that sophisticated conventional arms are needed to guard against the revolutionary phase of military operations; these arms serve as a deterrent to make the price of victory high for a potential enemy. This appreciation refers to externally induced armed struggle rather than to spontaneous urban black uprisings like those in Sharpville (1960) and Soeweto (1977).

There are historical reasons for the existence of South Africa's naval capacity. In the past, South Africans saw a need to protect the Cape sea route; the Simontown agreement (1955) reflected that concern. It is pointed out that naval capacity of South Africa is not correctly balanced and that there are too many large naval units. It is argued that it may be better to have smaller ships like those deployed by Israel for protecting the coastline. Yet there is an argument for having bigger ships also, because the Cape sea is very rough and large ships are needed to cope with rough waters. Still, it is arguable that the present condition of the South African navy is a carry-over of the past. Protecting the Indian Ocean sea lanes has been a rationale or a rationalization that has had an effect on South African naval developments. The acquisition of submarines can be explained by the logic of deterrent; that is, raising the price for a potential aggressor. Moreover, if Angola emerged as a Soviet base (it is not suggested that it has), South African submarines could be used against Indian Ocean and South Atlantic targets.

South Africa's air force is primarily ground support and air defense based on interceptors. At present the threat is at a low level and consists of talk more than substance, but it is escalating all the time. Fortunately for South Africa, the Organisation for African Unity is not really an organization. In general, there is no real external threat to the Republic for the next ten years or so and then it will have to face up to a relatively serious threat. The short-term key is the future of Rhodesia. When it falls all efforts will be directed against South Africa by a coalition comprising Angola, East African states, and the Soviet Union. But the solution to the issues is not military; the problems are political, and South African politicians are trying to find a solution that will institutionalize South Africa's international relations in the African continent and also produce domestic reform. If there is a political solution the nuclear factor will become even less important in the long run than what it seems to be now.

The political solution is also economic. At present there is no serious threat of defection of Western capital from South Africa. The traditional sources of capital (the United States and the United Kingdom) have been diversified by introducing more European capital. Thus there is a shift in sources of capital but not a defection. In fact, there is a need for more capital because the blacks (excluding the Colored and the Indians) need much more economic development. Still, even now the real wealth of the blacks has increased by a factor of three in the past five years. Some of the Colored and the Indians have had a high standard of living; there is no real difference in the living standards between Whites and Indians, and the Colored are slightly behind. In other words, South Africa's future also entails an economic solution and if the economic well-being of the black community increases, much of the impetus for black radicalism in South Africa will disappear. This is the perception of South Africans, but whether or not it is sound is an open question that only the future can answer.

South African political thinking sees opportunities and challenges to the future of South Africa in the next decade. The central premises in current South African foreign relations are: (1) South Africa is the bulwark of Africa, and not merely of the West in Africa; (2) it will be accepted by the international community only if it is accepted by the African community; (3) it is important for South Africa to end the problem of the Rhodesian* issue; and (4) continued involvement in international relations for South Africa depends to a large extent on a greater involvement in African affairs. Internationally, as noted earlier, it makes sense for South Africa to build bridges with Japan and the PRC in a move to establish an international coalition against the prospect of a coalition of Soviet and radical African regimes directed against South Africa. The Pretoria-Tokyo-Peking connection is based on the PRC's policy premise that the "enemy of my enemy is my friend." This belief creates strange bedfellows but it is practical. In other words, the old argument that South Africa would have to sell its resources to the West is now a

_____

*Rhodesia is a net danger for Pretoria whereas Namibia represents a danger and an opportunity. Both have the potential to worsen substantially South Africa's position in the world.

wrong argument for South Africans, because their purpose now is to differentiate between radical and moderate regimes and to support the moderate regimes in Africa and internationally; and because of the globalized Sino-Soviet rivalry, the PRC is not radicalizing the African international environment. As far as nuclear, economic, and political relations are concerned, South Africa has Western Europe in the position it wants it in. There is a widely held view among South Africans that the arms race between the superpowers is largely irrelevant because new technology like the cruise missile and the neutron bomb deals with confrontation situations that are not likely to arise anyhow. In trying to win an arms race with the Soviet Union, the United States is working in the wrong direction, and American behavior in this area is based on a wrong assessment of the nature of Soviet priorities and the mode of Soviet behavior. The USSR is interested in establishing its presence temporarily but Moscow does not necessarily want a permanent presence, which is both impractical and unnecessary. The Russians have learned from Bonaparte and Hitler and from events in Vietnam the lesson about the dangers for a country of overextending its presence. What Moscow wants instead is to limit or to deny the availability of strategic resources to its enemies.* It is in the context of such a policy that radical regimes in Africa could form a cartel with the Soviet Union against South Africa. Even if the South African economy faces economic problems, East Asian states can help South Africa's economy by buying its goods. Japan is extremely aware of this and one motive for going ahead with the peace treaty with the PRC is that Japan wants to lock the PRC into an economic relationship. A possible combination now for the PRC is to import Japanese technology and South African resources in the context of a larger Japanese message to the PRC: "if you buy from me I will teach you."

Building an international coalition (among South Africa, Japan, the PRC, and certain Western European societies) is one line of action that is directed against Soviet behavior and against its alleged encouragement of radical regimes in Africa. Another line of action for South Africa is to build economic ties with African regimes and to utilize economic diplomacy to build a network of moderate regimes that are not militarily and economically hostile to South Africa. In this optimistic approach, South Africans stress the importance of their existing political and economic influence in Swaziland, Botswana, and Lesotho. They also argue that South Africa is heavily involved in

---

*Some analysts feel that there are limits to resource denial policy, but the idea cannot be dismissed.

Zambia, Mozambique, and Zaire. True, Kenneth Kaunda of Zambia accuses South Africa of racism, but the expectation is that this anger will remain at the verbal level. According to one study:

> South Africa supplies a wide range of development and technical aid to Southern African states, as well as to countries in other parts of the continent. The contacts are long standing. Before the independence era in Africa, South Africa had consular and trade relations with seven African countries, Angola, Egypt, Kenya, Mauritius, Mozambique, Rhodesia and Zaire. She had established relations with Botswana, Lesotho and Swaziland too, while private South African interests played a major role in the Zambian economic structure.[32]

Thus, South Africans argue, Pretoria could embarrass Kaunda by publicizing the economic details but that would only push him away and weaken his domestic position. The South African hope is that people like Kaunda may change their thinking after they see the benefits of cooperation. The target of South Africa's economic diplomacy is the elites in African societies who see the benefits of cooperation and development. At present the elite structure in African societies is weak and the composition of new elite structures is negotiable.*

---

*Tanzania may be considered a success story because it has not degenerated since independence as have many other African states. Tanzania has a radicalized population divided into small farming communities. It is a success, relatively speaking, because it has moved toward socialism in terms of socialist ideas in African politics. The establishment of its railways is an achievement and, overall, Tanzania serves as a model for African development. The picture elsewhere in Africa (except South Africa), however, is not promising. In Western perceptions Kenya is presently a model of development—judged by the popularity that the Kenyatta regime enjoys among Westerners. But Kenya has a corrupt elite and the gap between the rich and the poor is growing, whereas in Tanzania an attempt is being made to narrow it. Angola and Mozambique are also developmental models of a sort, in the sense that radical Marxist regimes have disrupted the economic life of the people and the political and the economic infrastructure has yet to emerge. Uganda is another case where the role of the personality of a single ruler is the dominant feature of political and economic life and it is probable

In this perspective the most crucial issue for South Africa is not black majority rule in Rhodesia but rather the type of regime that will develop in Rhodesia. If a stable regime emerges in Rhodesia then it is likely to induce moderation in Zambia, but if a militant regime emerges in Rhodesia then militancy in Zambia is also likely. A balance between economic and ideological consideration will have to be established if economic links among South Africa, Rhodesia, Zaire, Zambia, Angola, and Mozambique are to be fostered. At present the economic links are not negligible. South African ports are used by Zambia, Zaire, and Rhodesia. Zambian use of the Tanzam Railway is costly; a surcharge four times more than agreed to is being paid by Zambia.

At present there is no real short-term effect of Rhodesia on South Africa, nor is there a problem of the effect of a radical Mozambique on South Africa. Radical states have internal problems and they do not have time for external adventures. This applies to the present behavior of Angola and Mozambique. Furthermore, União Nacional Para a Independencia Total de Angola (UNITA), with tacit South African support, has a presence in Angola. At present UNITA controls territory in Angola that has cut off direct access for Zambia to the Atlantic and forced Zambia to use East London as a port. A Zambia-UNITA rapprochement might be effected through a bargain: Zambia would withdraw its support for the South West Africa People's Organization (SWAPO) and in return would be given access to the sea. The aim in this sort of trade-off is to by-pass the MPLA in Angola, isolate SWAPO, and undercut the role of Tanzania as the ideological base for SWAPO. South Africans argue that their main interest is to secure stability-oriented regimes in Africa, and that it is not their business to prescribe the ideological character of the regime in its domestic form. They see a "system" of African international relations where Gabon is pro-Rhodesia; Conga is pro-West, as is Cameroon; Tanzania is genuinely uncommitted in the sense that it takes what it can get but ideologically leans toward the East; Sudan is now moving to a pro-West position and what happens in Sudan also affects Kenya; developments in Kenya can determine the post-Amin elite structure because Uganda now is volatile and post-Amin Uganda may go pro-Western also. The situa-

---

that post-Amin Uganda will go into the Kenyan orbit after Kenyatta. It is, in this sort of fluid setting, that South Africans see themselves as a viable model of development whereby their technical and economic assistance can help evolve a community of development-oriented societies in Africa with more economics and less politics.

tion in Ethiopia, Somalia, and Eritrea is confused but it has little bearing on the situation in Southern Africa. South Africans stress that it is possible to conceive a belt of stable African states in a line running from north to south in Africa. Whether or not South African assessments are excessively optimistic, generally speaking the foregoing points to the existence of a strategy to induce the emergence of stability-oriented regimes whose internal and ideological character does not concern Pretoria as long as the regime is moderate in its external orientation. Therefore, if there is any merit in the South African policy of inducing the growth of moderate, stability-oriented African regimes, this can delay the onset of armed struggle against the white regime in South Africa (that is, if the latter fails to phase out gradually its policy of institutionalized separation, which finds no support in Black Africa and among the principal Western democracies). As Kissinger pointed out on April 27, 1976:

> No one—including the leaders of Black Africa—chal-
> lenges the right of white South Africans to live in their
> country. They are not colonialists; historically, they
> are an African people. But white South Africans must
> recognise as well that the world will continue to insist
> that the institutionalised separation of the races must
> end. [33]

Given the prospect of a delayed armed struggle in a five- to ten-year time frame, it is possible to argue that the decision to deploy nuclear weapons in an eventual South African garrison state* is also likely to be slowed down.

DOMESTIC POLITICS AND SLOW
SOUTH AFRICAN NUCLEARIZATION

Often a government's policies respond to parallel and, at times, contradictory perceptions and assumptions; in such circumstances, parallel and even contradictory postures and policies are necessary. This study finds such a parallelism in South Africa's nuclear behavior.

---

*This assumes that the white regime will not accept the gradual erosion of the policy of institutionalized separation in South Africa even though it is willing to see this happen in Namibia.

One hypothesis is that South Africa, like Israel, will continue to "play a game" and keep its enemies guessing. This hypothesis rests on the notion that South Africa has been told by its well-wishers in the West that nothing can be gained militarily if South Africa acquires nuclear weapons and that there is much to be lost instead. Accordingly, it ought to accept the NPT and thereby implement its frequent statements that the question of adherence to the NPT is under review. But according to this hypothesis, Pretoria will not sign the NPT because there. is little to be gained from this act and much to be lost—namely, the leverage that ambiguity brings to an "outlaw" state's strategic behavior.

The other hypothesis that strengthens the notion of "parallelism at present" is based on the idea that Pretoria at present does not really know whether it will need nuclear weapon status. That position would make sense primarily if Pretoria were to assume that South Africa will have to become a garrison state; that is, if the policy of establishing politically and economically viable black homelands failed to find favor with the South African blacks and if this failure were reflected in the rise of armed struggle within South Africa. Here the parallelism is between the uncertainty about the prospect of a constitutional and peaceful way of arranging the future of the whites in South Africa, and the need to have a nuclear option, which is ready for conversion into nuclear weapons should the need arise. In the latter instance, conceptually, Pretoria's behavior can in part be based on the psychology of an armed but insecure state in Mortan Kaplan's unit veto system.* In such a system small nuclear wars and threats are a part of the daily political life because the so-called international system is actually chaos.. As a refinement of current nuclear deterrence theory, the present practice of the superpowers is enlarged by the use of the nuclear threat to freeze domestic conflict also—something that current nuclear deterrence exercises are not concerned with. That is, the notion of freezing conflict exists in the behavior of the NWS and in the hypothetical South African situation of the future. But in the former case, the conflict is frozen with respect to the military and physical security of the threatened state and not necessarily with respect to the political authority struc-

---

*According to M. A. Kaplan: "There is only one condition under which such a system is possible, let alone likely. This condition is the possession by all actors of weapons of such a character that any actor is capable of destroying any other actor that attacks it even though it cannot prevent its own destruction."[34]

ture of the threatened state. In the latter case the scope of the strategy's ability to freeze conflict is widened.

The view that Pretoria's current nuclear postures and policies are parallel rests on the view that at present it makes no sense for Pretoria to decide to make nuclear weapons (even if it could) because that would further its semi-isolation in the African and the world community today. Yet, on the other hand, it cannot afford, politically and technologically, to commit itself against nuclear weapon development and deployment in a potential unit veto system unless it is certain that the future of the white regime in South Africa is secure or can be peacefully negotiated. The ambiguous nuclear option makes sense because it offers psychological assurance to the beleaguered whites. As the 1977 South Africa Official Yearbook points out:

> External: South Africa's foreign policy is based on its internal policy. Accordingly the country endeavours:
> - (i) through dialogue and assistance from a position of strength, to normalise relations, wherever possible, with all countries in Africa, particularly those in Southern Africa;
> - (ii) to achieve understanding by governments and citizens of other countries of South Africa's internal policies and the Western humanistic tradition upon which they are based; and
> - (iii) to emphasise the strategic importance of the country, the danger of Marxist infiltration and the extent of the threat of revolutionary takeover in Southern Africa in order to prevent, through Western diplomatic action, the build-up of Marxist influence and military power in neighbouring states.[35]

Whether or not the second and the third points are central, the approach set out by South Africa in the first point may be meaningful. At present it is assumed that South Africa's policy of "separate development" is not negotiable. Indeed, there is an elaborate public relations and a public education campaign mounted by senior South African ministers and officials to impress audiences in North America, Australia, and West Europe with the philosophical foundations and implications of the South African approach to plural democracy.[36] The exercise is heroic and makes interesting reading but it should not be necessarily regarded as the last word on the subject. The Official Yearbook (1977) notes that "foreign policy is based on its internal policy" and the notions of "dialogue" and "position of strength" are deemed to be central. In this context it is worth suggesting that an ambiguous nuclear option for South Africa contributes to the "position of strength" idea. Vorster's recent election victory and his tough speeches on nuclear matters (addressed both to the white public in the Republic and to the Georgian Washingtonians of the Carter administration) build the image of strength. In the optimistic* view, once the threat of the ultra-right sentiment in the Republic has been neutralized, and once the image of a peaceful transfer of power involving all parties in Southwest Africa (Namibia) has been established in the white psyche in South Africa, perhaps then the Vorster regime may be able to dismantle the institutional structure of apartheid and to reduce the incentive toward armed struggle in South Africa.

In this perspective, Pretoria's nuclear diplomacy appears to play the nuclear game of accepting international restraints on its nuclear industry, and yet it is not actually playing it. In this dualism—a sort of parallel between verbal behavior and action—the declaration about the use of nuclear energy for peaceful purposes is seriously intended for the present, as is the plan to acquire the means to shift to military purposes if and when the need arises in the future.[+]

In a sense, then, the ambiguity and parallelism in Pretoria's nuclear diplomacy and nuclear policy are a mirror of the ambiguity in South Africa's internal situation and its future, and of the prospects of success in inducing the growth of a moderate African

---

*This may well be an overoptimistic view if the premise is that the Vorster regime will play for time but will never dismantle apartheid.

[+]According to the statement by South Africa's minister of foreign affairs on August 30, 1978:

> The South African Prime Minister clearly stated and reaffirmed in Cape Town on 24 August 1977 the South African Government's support for the ideal that nuclear energy be used solely for peaceful purposes. This is and remains the Government's policy. The assurance given to the United States, French, British and German Governments regarding South Africa's intentions in the field of nuclear technology reflect firm Government policy.
> The Minister of Finance, Senator Horwood, categorically stated that the South African Government stood by its assurance.

international relations climate. South Africans admit that the former is more important than the latter; indeed, the former is the central determinant. [37] But they also point out that South Africa does not have some of the challenges facing other societies—the malaise of economic growth and distribution, and the internal human relations problems of a number of societies: the blacks and minority groups in the United States; religious wars in Ireland and Lebanon and in the Indian subcontinent in the past; communalism in South Asia today; cultural conflict in Canada and Quebec; ethnic conflict in Black Africa, which is currently subdued by the focus on white South Africa; ideological and subnational cleavages in the Arab world, which are currently subdued by the focus on Israel; and so on. True, say the South Africans, the white-black conflict in South Africa is more pronounced, but then there is no religious cleavage, and intertribal cleavages also exist that make possible the existence of coalitions between, for example, the whites and the Zulus in South Africa. Admittedly, there is a need to create an equitable society, but it is felt by some that it is possible to find an economic solution for a human problem, by narrowing the gap between the haves and the have-nots, by improving education, and so on. It is pointedly noted that in the case of SWAPO, for instance, in relation to Namibia, the argument is not about black development and black majority rule. Rather it is against sharing of power between SWAPO and other parties in Namibia. This has come about because of SWAPO's superior international relations, and not because SWAPO is willing to test its electoral strength in a free election along with other black constituents and whites in Namibia.

CONCEPTUALIZING SOUTH AFRICA'S
NUCLEAR OPTIONS

That South Africa has made rapid nuclear advances, more significant than India's (as South Africans claim), is undeniable. At present South Africa has no nuclear competitor in Africa. Zaire has had a research reactor in Kinshasa since 1959; Egypt near Cairo has had a research reactor in operation since 1961 (USSR-supplied; unsafeguarded); and Libya is building a research reactor with USSR help and will also import a power reactor from the same source. Libya has a cooperation agreement with Argentina. [38] President Nixon also offered power reactors under safeguards to Egypt and Israel after India exploded its peaceful device. Still, even if this points to the gradual nuclearization of the Afro-Arab-Jewish environment, the South African lead in nuclear technology, equipment, and materials is unlikely to be lost in the foreseeable future. Nor

is it likely that an African antiproliferation regime is likely to
emerge in the form of a NWFZ. The acceptance of the NPT has not
been followed by the acceptance of a NWFZ even though the idea has
existed in resolution form since 1963. [39] Failure to denuclearize
begs the question of whether nuclearization has already occurred.
Does capacity to explode a device mean nuclearization? Should the
existence of such a capacity now or in the future be viewed in the
context of the domestic political, external political, and strategic
environment, or is the evidence of capacity prima facie evidence of
phasal activity toward weapons production and deployment? This
study assumes that nuclearization is gradually taking place, in the
sense that nuclear technology is being injected into the Afro-Arab-
Jewish political, economic, and strategic environment. But the implications of this introduction are unclear. Nuclear power has some
obvious civilian uses (electricity production, agricultural, and medi-
cal uses) and also some obvious potential military uses—that is, developing bombs to freeze conflict externally. Given this view it is
necessary to conceptualize the South African case in light of the preceding discussion. What follows is an analysis and not a prediction.

South Africa, somewhat like Israel and post-1974 India, seems
to be following a strategy of stretching out its nuclear option.
Stretching out the option—threatening to make the bomb (as for instance in 1977), or moving quickly toward a bomb program—are two
separate options that bureaucracies and political leaders involved in
resources-allocation decisions usually consider consciously. According to William Epstein, the former director of the Disarmament
Affairs Division of the United Nations:

> Since the value of nuclear weapons in the context of
> Africa against either organized military forces or
> guerrillas is very dubious from the military point of
> view, and execrable in political and moral terms, it
> is conceivable that South Africa may opt for a nuclear
> policy similar to that attributed to Israel, namely, to
> acquire the capability of producing nuclear weapons
> very quickly but without actually "going nuclear" by
> exploding a nuclear device. It would help to increase
> the security of the entire continent and promote the
> cause of nuclear non-proliferation if South Africa
> should adopt such a middle position or "grey" area
> between a non-nuclear and nuclear status and remain
> a "latent" nuclear power. [40]

Epstein's view is somewhat overstated, but he is right in considering South Africa a "grey area." Even if South African nuclear

weapons make no sense at present in the context of the guerrilla and conventional warfare possibilities in southern Africa, still the NWS have not yet agreed to renounce nuclear weapons. The end-use of these weapons today as deterrents, compared to the use of the atom bomb against Japan, suggests that nuclear weapons are perhaps becoming less useful militarily but not entirely useless in freezing strategic conflict. Secondly, the curse that is said to attach to South African nuclear arms is diluted by the evidence of South African nuclear cooperation with West Germany, France, the United States, the United Kingdom, Israel, Japan, and possibly the PRC—societies that are respectable members of the Western alliance system. The curse, therefore, is more verbal than real. So until the end-uses of nuclear weapons are conclusively debated, gray nuclear activity will be hard to condemn. Indeed, it is arguable that, analytically, different types of gray (pre-weapon production and deployment but still proliferating) activity is now under way and that the South African nuclear option is different from the Israeli and Indian. The Israeli nuclear option functions in the context of a usually effective Israeli lobby in the United States. Even if Begin's recent moves have diluted or confused that lobby, South Africa has not for years had such an overt lobby and the isolation of the two societies is more acute in South Africa's case. The case of India's nuclear option is different from Israel's in the sense that there is no real electoral constituency in the United States to promote India's cause, and India lost its virginity by exploding a single bomb and then shifted gears, neither enlarging its nuclear option nor contracting it. All three cases have one common characteristic: their strategic behavior is ambiguous and hence troublesome for the arms controllers. In the 1980s the gray zones may become more complicated, as Brazil and Argentina become more vocal in their demands in nuclear and disarmament issues.

The diplomatic uses of South Africa's nuclear option merit attention. Nuclear weapons freeze the escalation of conflict—international and regional—without necessarily attending to the causes of conflict. Thus, these weapons aid in suppressing violence and its uncontrolled occurrence without necessarily resolving or preventing conflict. But a nuclear option seems to be a cheaper and an effective substitute for nuclear weapons in certain situations. The image of nuclear power introduces caution in the other side's thinking even if the other side is the stronger party. It is possible that a purpose of South Africa's growing nuclear presence is to buy time—to slow the emergence of radical regimes in Africa, to induce technology transfers into South Africa from advanced Western societies, and finally, to lock some of these societies into commercial relations so that the isolation of a racial regime is minimized. Minimizing isolation through the growth of nuclear ties should, therefore, be noted as a purpose of South Africa's nuclear option. Lastly, as mentioned earlier, South Africa's statements refer to the importance of negotiating from a position of strength. Insofar as a nuclear option contributes to the image of strength it has domestic and external uses: domestically it offers psychological assurance to the whites; externally the nuclear image shapes the negotiating setting. The following extract from an interview with Vorster on May 10, 1976 makes the point clearly.

> Q. Moscow has been exceedingly cautious in the mid-East since the October war, and many experts believe this stems from a healthy respect for the nuclear equation introduced by Israel. Don't you think Moscow's strategic thinkers—and game players in Africa—might be more cautious once they realize that you, too, have a nuclear capability?

> A. I am not aware that Israel has made any official pronouncements on the subject. We are only interested in the peaceful applications of nuclear power. But we can enrich uranium, and we have the capability. And we did not sign the nuclear non-proliferation treaty. [41]

Theoretically, one might also consider the potential military uses of South Africa's nuclear option. One obvious scenario is to establish a white garrison state armed with conventional and nuclear forces and to threaten the use of conventional and nuclear arms—first the former and then the latter—if Soviet-inspired, Cuban-assisted black Marxist regimes reject the current type of negotiations between blacks and whites in Rhodesia and Southwest Africa (Namibia). If autocratic single-party states emerge in Africa and those in power are not freely elected, and if such states insist on an armed struggle in South Africa, then a nuclear armed garrison state is a possibility in the 1980s. Such a state could conceivably direct its attention to short-range African targets, treating these as Soviet hostages, since it is not immediately likely that South Africa has plans or the capacity to develop an intercontinental capability. However, as mentioned above, Israel and South Africa signed a nuclear cooperation agreement in 1976. Given that a likely target of Israeli missiles could be the USSR, it is not inconceivable that the Israel-South Africa connection could take a military shape, just as at present the connection among South Africa, the Federal Republic of Germany, France, Israel, and the United States has taken a technological and political shape. This line of speculation, however, assumes the emergence of a unit veto system—a world of many competing and destructive nuclear powers, an anarchical system where medium-sized powers can veto the actions of the so-called superpowers.

No firm conclusions can be reached yet because the foregoing analysis refers to processes that are still unfolding. There is merit, however, in stressing the interplay among parallel and, at times, contradictory policy processes because contingency planners must respond to a variety of circumstances and assumptions, and intelligence underlying the policy processes is not always sound and explicit. South Africa's nuclear behavior responds to these pressures and constraints from within and outside the Republic. The fact that Vorster speaks for South Africa obscures the fact that there are hardliners and softliners in South Africa, as in other societies. The nuclear factor ought to be examined in a wider political, economic, and military setting. Taking an optimistic view, it appears that South Africa today seeks gradual internal reform and a network of externally moderate and development-oriented African societies. The philosophy of plural democracies expounded by South African spokesmen may be a self-serving exercise meant to justify racism. Still, South Africa has a point when it stresses the importance of ethnicity, development, and free elections involving all parties in societies. Its argument is directed against internationally reputable but still self-proclaimed exponents of black rule, ones who are unwilling to test their position in free elections open to all. In a recent interview the leader of SWAPO made this point clear.

> Nujoma reply:-
> Well, the question of black majority rule is out. We are not fighting even for majority rule. We are fighting to seize power in Namibia . . . for the benefit of the Namibian people. We are revolutionaries. We are not counter revolutionaries. You can talk to Kapuuo or Kerina and all those reactionaries about majority rule, but not in SWAPO. [42]

Vorster's reaction on February 28, 1978 to questions on the statement was short and sharp.

> He has let the cat out of the bag and he has now confirmed what we have always suspected and what we have accused SWAPO of and he has made it clear that he is not really interested in the welfare of the people but only in SWAPO's revolutionary doctrines for the sake of power over the territory and its peoples. Now that Nujoma has spoken, the western powers must obviously reply. [43]

The rejection of black majority rule by some African elites who do not wish to share power with other Africans suggests the difficulty of reaching an early settlement in Namibia and suggests further the danger of polarization among the blacks. Such latent or manifest polarization also offers opportunities for South Africa. For instance, the South African journalist David Woods predicted racial war in South Africa in five years and called for trade sanctions and diplomatic ostracism of South Africa.[44] But Chief Buthelezi told an audience of 15,000 in Soweto that sanctions against the blacks would mean "self-destruction" for the blacks.[45] At this level of political and economic interaction the nuclear factor seems not to be relevant. The issue is one of dismantling the mechanism for the institutionalized separation in the developmental processes of different peoples in southern Africa. Nor is the nuclear factor relevant if measures taken on the issue are intended to create a viable southern African economic community that involves Mozambique, Rhodesia, South Africa, and Namibia, along with other smaller economic and political units. Yet the issue is not simply one of breaking the institutional barriers outside South Africa, because the example of gradual internal change in South Africa is needed to induce moderation in Namibia, Rhodesia, and elsewhere.

Lastly, it should be noted that a policy or strategy of stretching out a nuclear option, while conceptually exciting, is problematic for the practitioner. A nuclear option contains a volatile mixture of contractual obligations (international safeguards), unilateral declarations ("we believe in peaceful uses only"), fluid domestic politics, fluid strategic environment, and fluid bilateral relations. Nuclear options are slippery and dangerous for the arms controllers, and it is only recently that arms control advocates have started to see the virtue of gray zones of nuclear proliferation. Promoting national security rather than arms control is the purpose of those who advocate the need for having nuclear options. In the South African case (as in some others), at present nuclear options seem useful primarily, but not exclusively, as tools of diplomacy. According to J. E. Spence, "the constraints against South Africa acquiring a nuclear weapon are probably weakening—particularly in view of the State's increasing isolation in the Western world."[46] This view turns mainly on how the "increasing isolation" is perceived by South African elites and whether they see the nuclear factor as contributing to or causing a reduction of that isolation. In the past, Western societies have not in practice permitted the total isolation of South Africa, even though an arms embargo has been in effect and there is considerable international opinion against apartheid. In nuclear supply relations, Washington has held up its enriched uranium shipments to South Africa, but it is possible that this action (which has taken place before) is not meant to single out South Africa. (India has suffered numerous delays in shipment also and the Canadians have in recent years been difficult with Euratom and Japan.) On the other hand, it is also possible that the price of a U.S. enriched uranium supply is Pretoria's entry into the NPT—about which the latter nation has made appropriate noise (the matter has been under review since 1968, says Pretoria). Experts, however, differ on whether Pretoria is sincere in its professed intention to review the NPT question if conditions are met. The conditions are hard to meet and, therefore, Pretoria's present position may be regarded as a polite refusal that appears to keep the dialogue going. Pretoria is not saying that it will make the bomb, but it is saying that if it gets isolated it may have to. There is a rather substantial difference between the two ideas. The latter formula places on Western societies the onus of not getting Pretoria's back to the wall. At the same time it places on South Africa's white minority the onus of keeping a gradual pace of internal reform as the price of securing the emergence of a moderate international and economic affairs constituency in faction-ridden and competitive elite structures in Black African societies. The problems mostly concern interactions between blacks and whites, but as far as the proliferation issue in South Africa is concerned it is hardly a clear-cut story. With respect to the planned 1977 test, South Africa's motive is still unclear. The test facilities were discovered by the Soviet Union and the United States in August 1977. Did Pretoria intend that preparations for the test would be discovered and understood as a threat although at that time there was no intention of carrying out the test? Or was the event discovered and stopped before it could be carried out as planned? If it is the former, it indicates that the nuclear game for the NNWS begins not with the demonstrated possession of the nuclear bomb but with the prebomb phase.

The preceding analysis offers an optimistic view of the setting of South African and African international relations in which Pretoria's nuclear options are taking shape. The optimism centers on the proposition that black Africans as well as Western Europeans and East Asians (Indians in South Africa and Japanese and Chinese outside) are willing collaborators—tacitly but not explicitly—of the white regime in South Africa. Yet pessimism is warranted, because internal strife in South Africa is unpredictable and it is likely to be fostered by blacks who reach the conclusion that they cannot stand the cultural oppression any longer from a racist regime. These people are willing to die for the cause. Internally induced civil strife, based on a real sense of black hopelessness, is a prospect that rulers may have to consider in the coming decade.

No firm conclusion can be offered about the context and the conclusion of South Africa nuclear diplomacy because optimism and pessimism are both indicated. There is optimism that calculated ambiguity is the name of the game of South African nuclear diplomacy for at least ten years; hence South African nuclear weapons are not likely. The premise of the optimistic view is that the whites in South Africa have made up their minds about the future of the non-whites but the nonwhites have yet to make up their minds about the future of the whites. According to this view, there are no real liberals in the South African cabinet today; there are minor gradations but no real differences. (Thus talk that Minister Connie Mulder is a secret pragmatist actually has a twist; he believes in flexible talk and tough policy!) On the other hand, it is still unclear whether the nonwhites have chosen the path of armed struggle or that of peaceful accommodation in Southern Africa. Another premise of the optimistic view is that within ten years massive but sporadic violence—that is, repeats of Soweto—are likely but that these do not necessarily mean a breakdown of the system.

In general, it can be said that with a reasonably predictable strategic context, South African nuclear diplomacy consists of stretching out its nuclear option and engaging in activities that buy time. It is not a foregone conclusion that the United States will be able to bring South Africa into the NPT. Moreover, even if it joins the treaty, that hardly cuts its options. Adherence to the treaty buys time because of the withdrawal clause; and adherence shapes the South African image and creates a better political climate for its diplomacy. The only real sacrifice for South Africa lies in the acceptance of irrevocable international safeguards requirements on the entire South African nuclear industry. Even with full-scope safeguards there is the doubt about the effectiveness of contemporary safeguards (as discussed in Chapter 5).

After ten years, the premises of the optimistic scenario become questionable. The starting point of the pessimistic thinking is that everyone (other than South African whites) agrees apartheid is morally wrong and that apartheid will not succeed in bringing peace in the region. On this point there is a consensus between Moscow and Washington, but at present their strategies in promoting change vary. For Moscow there is an opportunity to acquire a voice in southern African affairs if and when the time comes to settle the future of the region. To do this Moscow promotes unrest and armed struggle, and Angola is the model. For the United States there is a danger that further Soviet involvement will further weaken American influence in Africa and in the Third World. The latter prospect induces Washington to offer Pretoria a bargain: sign the NPT and the United States will deliver enriched uranium to South Africa; this will reduce Pretoria's isolation and strengthen the white regime. The problem with the bargain is that accepting it might present Pretoria with a no-win situation. South Africa might end up trading the utility of "calculated ambiguity" in its strategic policy over a ten-year period and its nuclear independence for the short-term security of American enriched uranium at a time when there are other potential suppliers of enriched uranium. And yet if there is going to be armed struggle in southern Africa, the United States is hardly able to help South Africa, particularly after the events of Vietnam, Angola, and Ethiopia.

The latter perspective suggests that in South African thinking the Pretoria-Washington connection has its uses and its limits. Pretoria wants Americans to appreciate better the strategic dimensions that could underline this connection (that is, the importance of raw materials and the role of the Cape for Western security) and to downplay the racial dimension. The 1977 nuclear scare had the advantage of altering the parameters of the Pretoria-Washington dialogue. But at the same time there are limits to this dialogue. In South African atomic energy circles there was surprise in the summer of 1978 when press stories circulated to the effect that there had been a deal made between American Ambassador G. Smith and Prime Minister Vorster, stating that South Africa would join the NPT in return for U.S. enriched uranium supplies. The surprise was understandable, because the United States does not seem to have much long-term leverage, President Carter needs South African cooperation to justify his clumsy antiproliferation diplomacy, and others may be able to offer South Africa the enriched uranium it needs. Secondly, from Pretoria's point of view, an essential purpose of the Pretoria-Washington engagement is to get Washington to appreciate that South African diplomacy is more subtle than it appears on the surface. In nuclear matters it has a lower and a different profile from Israel's: Israel allows stories about its ten to twelve nuclear bombs to circulate; South Africa discourages such speculation. South Africa has a lower profile at the United Nations than does Israel. Thirdly, South Africans see an identity of approach between themselves and the Black African states. Both stress the need to keep Africa free of great-power rivalries; hence both signal an anti-Soviet and anti-U.S. stance. In short, the growing cosmopolitanism in South African and Black African diplomacy points to a common approach even though racism is an irritant in white-black relations. Finally, as long as African institutions like the Organisation of African Unity remain deeply divided, South Africa takes comfort in the absence of a Black African consensus against Pretoria's rule.

Two types of circumstances could, however, alter the optimistic premises of the South African government. In denying the notion of sharing power between the whites and the blacks, Pretoria seeks to redress the sense of black alienation by dismantling petty apartheid and by improving the economic lot of the nonwhites in South Africa; that is, by giving them a stake in the economic system as a substitute for effective participation in the political system. Still, it is arguable that there is a terrible gap between what the whites are prepared to sacrifice toward these ends and what ought to be sacrificed to dampen confrontation.

Finally, a contrast should be noted between the commitments of the whites toward Rhodesia and toward Namibia. Even though the International Court of Justice declared that Pretoria's presence in Namibia is illegal, personal and historical ties between the whites in South Africa and Namibia are important as they are not with Rhodesia. The Afrikaneer connections between South Africa and Namibia require that there be no blood bath in Namibia so that there will be no backlash in South African white thinking. But if there is a blood bath and armed struggle emerges as the norm in southern African relations, then the possibility of an Afrikaneer laager* armed with nuclear weapons cannot be ruled out, however remote it may appear at present.

APPENDIX†

The USA, at that time the only established producer of enriched uranium in the free world, realised that many countries were not happy with a situation in which only one source of enriched uranium was available. On the other hand, as one of the most vociferous exponents of the Non-Proliferation Treaty, it would have to give a well-calculated push to counteract the erection of large-scale plants by other countries, thereby reducing the potential of countries to produce nuclear arms. It attempted to achieve this aim in 1970 by offering to make its uranium enrichment technology available to 10 selected countries of the free world. This offer was, however, subject to conditions which would clearly enable the USA to maintain its monopolistic position. It is interesting to note that South Africa was not one of the 10 countries selected. Several reasons can be advanced for this omission.

---

*Laager is the South African word for camp or encampment.
†Dr. A. J. A. Roux, "South Africa's Position in the World Nuclear Energy Picture," a paper presented at the Sectoral Industrial Congress of the Afrikaanse Handelsinstituut in the Carleton Hotel, Johannesburg, May 1, 1973.

The measure of success which the USA has achieved with its offer is not yet generally known. The future will have to bear witness to this. The fact that the offer was not acceptable to all the countries concerned can be concluded from the new conditions, at present being considered by the USA, according to which enriched uranium will be made available to builders of nuclear installations. In terms of these conditions, any organisation intending to erect a nuclear power station will have to order the enriched uranium required for operation of the station eight years before the time of commissioning if the USA is to provide the uranium, and will have to bind itself to purchase from the USA the enriched uranium necessary to operate the reactor for 10 years. The AEC proposals furthermore require the payment of some R2,8 million yearly for every 1,000 MW of power generating capacity, payable in three installments, the first being due at the time of signing the contract.

It would appear from the above that the USA has a mind to attempt to ensure that the additional enrichment capacity which will be necessary from the early eighties onwards to provide for the needs of the free world, will be provided either by plants which it will itself erect, or by plants over which it will at least have full control. Setting aside any political and international considerations, the USA is in a very strong position in view of the fact that it is at present the only established producer of enriched uranium and, as far as the gaseous diffusion process is concerned, has had many years of experience and possesses what is probably the most advanced technology. As will be indicated later, the process suffers from high capital cost and energy consumption. This means that it can only be reasonably economically applied in developed countries where a large amount of power can be made available at very low cost, e.g. the USA, Canada, South Africa, Australia and Sweden.

Meanwhile, France has not been inactive. She has been striving for years to gain the cooperation of other Western European countries in the construction of a large-scale gaseous diffusion plant in Western Europe—under her leadership and based on her technology. To begin with she made little progress in this regard. However, at the end of 1971, when it became evident that the offer of the USA to make its enrichment technology available to other countries had not met with general acceptance, France decided to share her enrichment technology with other countries. She succeeded in drawing together Britain, West Germany, Italy, Holland and Belgium in a cooperative group known as Eurodif. This group undertook a study of the economic prospects of a joint enrichment plant in Western Europe, based on the French gaseous diffusion technology. This study is still being pursued.

Furthermore, France concluded an agreement with Japan, in terms of which a cooperative study would be undertaken by the two countries to investigate the feasibility of erecting a joint gaseous diffusion plant in Australia.

. . . .

In these developments, even when seen only in broad outline, there are clear symptoms of a technological battle which could produce nothing but good if only it were not for the fact that there are, unfortunately, unmistakable signs of political overtones. When technological and economic considerations are affected by political factors, it is difficult to predict what the end result will be. Faced with the uncertainty of this situation, South Africa must, with its own new enrichment process, establish herself in the enrichment arena. This she is, in fact, already doing.

With the announcement of the Prime Minister on 20th July, 1970, that South Africa had developed a new process for uranium enrichment and had undertaken the erection of a pilot plant, our country was the fourth in the Western World, after the USA, England and France, to embark on such an undertaking. South Africa proceeded with this work with a view to clearing the way to finally being able to market her huge uranium sources in the most refined forms, as well as for the purpose of making a meaningful contribution to worldwide scientific and technological development. The motivation in all this was primarily to give back something of what South Africa has received from the rest of the world, and indeed continues to receive.

. . . .

However, the important question which arises is how viable is the South African process, looked at against the background, so often referred to, of the tremendous technological struggle which is going on, at least in the free world? From the nature of the case, the answer to this question is inherently bound up with the answer to another question, viz. how economically can the process be applied in practice?

The South African process has a separation factor between stages which is considerably higher than that of the gaseous diffusion process of the USA. This means that the South African process requires many less stages than the gaseous diffusion process for the same degree of enrichment. It is therefore obvious that unless the capital cost per stage of the South African process is very much more expensive than the gaseous diffusion process, the capital cost of a plant based on the South African process must be considerably lower than that of a gaseous diffusion plant of the same capacity. From experience with the cost of the pilot plant at present being built, and by comparison with the capital cost of a gaseous diffusion plant, which can be gleaned from estimates made by the United States Atomic Energy Commission,* it would appear that the capital cost of a large-scale plant based on the South African process will be less than 65% of that of a gaseous diffusion plant of the same capacity.

As far as running costs are concerned, energy consumption is by far the most important component for both the South African process and the gaseous diffusion process. It is a fact that the energy consumption for the South African process is at present somewhat higher than for the gaseous diffusion process. However, this does not detract from the fact that, even with the technology so far developed, the production costs of enriched uranium by means of the South African process in a plant erected in South Africa, will be lower than those for a gaseous diffusion plant of similar size erected in the USA with the help of American technology.

What must still be borne in mind is what the Prime Minister, in his announcement, mentioned about the great possibilities for development inherent in the South African process. In this connection it is worth noting that the energy consumption of the South African process has, over the past eight years, been almost halved every two years. No one would venture to claim that this rate of development can be maintained, but theoretical analyses, as well as the results of practical experimental programmes, indicate that the present energy consumption can still be reduced by 50%. In any event, it is certain that in the course of the next 18 months a reduction in energy consumption of approximately 25% will be achieved, which will make the production costs by way of the South African process some 30% lower than the USA process. Even if the first large-scale plant based on the South African process were to be burdened with the cost of the technological development work still necessary for the application of the process to a large-scale plant, while no such burden were allowed for in the case of a gaseous diffusion plant—a suggestion that is scarcely warranted—the South African process will still produce a product which will be approximately 20% less expensive than that produced by the gaseous diffusion process.

If all these things are taken into account, <u>it is clear that the economy of the South African process, even with the technology as it is at the present time, compares favourably with that of gaseous diffusion</u> even if the latter is seen in the light of the most favourable circumstances. This is so even without any consideration of new

---

*USAEC, April 1972:ORO-685; and USAEC, January 1972: ORO-684.

developments already in sight. The South African process has thus become a serious competitor in the technological struggle for the next large-scale plant in the free world, which will be necessary to meet the demands of the unsaturated market in the early eighties.

NOTES

1. Points 3-7 (except otherwise cited) draw on George Quester's excellent work, The Politics of Nuclear Proliferation (Baltimore: The Johns Hopkins University Press, 1973), pp. 204, 199-200, 202.

2. The initial alarm about the proposed test was sounded by Tass. See "Pretoria A-Bomb Threat," The Guardian, August 12, 1977 for the initial report. The Observer, August 14, 1977, in "South African Nuclear Warning After Theft," revealed the existence of a secret and long-standing nuclear relationship between South Africa and the Federal Republic of Germany. Pretoria's denial to Carter of the alleged South African preparation to conduct an under- ground test in the Kalahari desert is in The Guardian, August 24, 1977, as is the story about the French campaign against a South African test. An overview of the day-by-day maneuvers by the USSR, the United States, France, the United Kingdom, and the Fed- eral Republic of Germany is in The Guardian, August 29, 1977, in "Britain in East-West Moves on Pretoria A-Bomb." This story re- veals a vivid example of détente at work between the superpowers and among the principal nuclear suppliers in a nonproliferation is- sue. Even though Pretoria denied that it had plans to explode a nu- clear device, and it offered an assurance that it did not plan to do so in the future, the assurance was diluted by this statement of the finance minister: "I think it is time we told [President] Carter and a few other people that if we did at any time wish to do other things with our nuclear potential, we will jolly well do so according to our own decisions and our own judgment." See "South Africa Reserves Right to Decide Uses of A-Power," International Herald Tribune, August 31, 1977. For an assessment of Soviet and Western moves against Pretoria see "A South African Bomb?" editorial, Toronto Globe and Mail, September 2, 1977. For an explicit statement about Vorster's world views see his interview in The New York Times, September 17, 1977, and "Mr. Vorster Bares His Teeth" in The Guardian, November 3, 1977. The overall U.S. policy perspective was reflected in Ambassador Young's statement when he said, "I think by maintaining some kind of relationship we do have the possi- bility of influencing them [South Africa] to sign the nuclear non- proliferation treaty and accepting all of the safeguards that go with

the International Atomic Energy Agency." Furthermore, Young pointed out, "If you break the relationship altogether, there is no way to monitor and it is almost because you can't trust them that you have to stay close to them." The New York Times, October 31, 1977.

3. For instance, see Lewis Dunn and Herman Kahn, Trends in Nuclear Proliferation, report prepared for U.S. ACDA, Hudson Institute, H1-2336/3-RR, May 15, 1976.

4. According to a U.S. Congressional document, "the chain of transfer of nuclear technology is set from India . . . to Argentine . . . to Libya." U.S., Congress, Joint Committee on Atomic Energy, Development, Use and Control of Nuclear Energy for the Common Defense and Security and for Peaceful Purposes, 94th Cong., 1st sess., June 30, 1975, p. 7.

5. Quester, op. cit., p. 198.

6. SIPRI, Southern Africa: The Escalation of a Conflict (Stockholm: 1976), p. 128.

7. Peter Janke, "Southern Africa: New Horizons," Conflict Studies (London) 73 (July 1976): 16.

8. Quester, op. cit., p. 203.

9. SIPRI, op. cit., pp. 142-43, 148. This presumably relates to PELINDUNA-0/4, which went critical in November 1967. It was dismantled in 1970 and the heavy water and enriched uranium returned to the United States.

10. Myron Kratzer, Deputy Assistant Secretary of State for Scientific Affairs, Department of State, testimony before the Senate Foreign Relations Committee, cited in International Herald Tribune, May 30, 1976.

11. Frank Barnaby, "Africa and Nuclear Energy," Africa 69 (May 1977): 92.

12. Cited in J. E. Spence, "South Africa and the Nuclear Option," lecture to the Royal African Society, London, n.d., footnote 8.

13. For a brief discussion of South Africa's enrichment process see Ashok Kapur, India's Nuclear Option: Atomic Diplomacy and Decision-Making (New York: Praeger, 1976), p. 260.

14. A. J. A. Roux, "Uranium—Recent Developments and Future Outlook," paper presented at the Investment Conference of the Investment Analysts' Society of Southern Africa, Carlton Hotel, Johannesburg, February 25, 1976, mimeo.

15. Kratzer, op. cit.

16. SIPRI, op. cit., p. 149.

17. Speech by Vorster at a public meeting, August 24, 1977, reprinted in Republic of South Africa, House of Assembly, Debates, 1st sess., 6th Parliament, February 3, 1978, pp. 12-13.

18. Cited in International Herald Tribune, February 17, 1977.

19. Spence, op. cit., footnote 10.

20. Confidential interviews, Bonn, June 1977; Canberra, March 1978.

21. Michael Nacht, "Global Trends in Nuclear Proliferation," in Insecurity! The Spread of Weapons in the Indian and Pacific Oceans, ed. R. J. O'Neill (Australian National University Press, Canberra, A.C.T.: Norwalk, Conn., 1978).

22. R. Botha's statement, United Nations, General Assembly, 1st Committee, 22nd sess., New York, May 20, 1968, Provisional verbatim record, A/C.1/PV. 1571.

23. A. J. A. Roux's statement, Geneva, September 3, 1968, mimeo.

24. A. J. A. Roux's statement, Vienna, September 25, 1968, mimeo.

25. For South Africa's reaction to its expulsion from the IAEA's Board of Governors see SA Digest, June 24, 1977, p. 13.

26. Republic of South Africa, House of Assembly Debates, op. cit., pp. 13-14.

27. "SA's Strategic Significance as a Supplier of Minerals," South Africa Industrial and Business Intelligence, published by the South African Embassy, London, May 1977.

28. Janke, op. cit., p. 4.

29. South Africa 1974 Official Yearbook, 1st ed., p. 365.

30. Confidential interviews: Canberra, August 1975; London, July-August 1977; and Tokyo, November 1977.

31. Strategic Survey, 1976, International Institute for Strategic Studies, London, p. 50.

32. W. J. Breytenbach, South Africa Looks to Africa, Southern African Freedom Foundation, Pretoria, July 1977, p. 1.

33. Henry Kissinger, "The United States and Africa," Survival 18, no. 4 (July-August 1976) (London: International Institute for Strategic Studies): 173.

34. See his System and Process in International Politics (New York: John Wiley & Sons, 1957), p. 50.

35. South Africa 1977 Official Yearbook, p. 943 (emphasis added).

36. See for instance the address by the Secretary for Information, E. Rhoodie, to the Second South African Corporate Money Conference, Carlton Hotel, Johannesburg, February 18, 1977; and paper presented by C. P. Mulder, minister of information, to the International Conference on the Marketing of the International Image of South Africa, University of South Africa, October 18, 1977.

37. Confidential interviews.

38. Barnaby, op. cit., p. 92.

39. For a general discussion, see William Epstein, "A Nuclear-Weapon Free Zone in Africa?" The Stanley Foundation, Occasional Paper no. 14, 1977.

40. Ibid., p. 21 (emphasis added).

41. Survival, op. cit., p. 176.

42. Information Section, South African Embassy, Canberra, telex report provided to author March 1978.

43. Ibid.

44. The Age, Melbourne, March 10, 1978.

45. Notes on Foreign Investments in South Africa, back-grounder issued by Information Counsellor, South African Embassy, Canberra, March 1978.

46. J. E. Spence to Ashok Kapur, private communication.

10

NORTHEAST ASIA: GRADUAL MILITARIZATION AND NUCLEARIZATION OF THE REGION

INTRODUCTION

Predicting the future of nuclear proliferation and defense strategy in Northeast Asia is hazardous because a number of factors are involved in the process of gradual militarization and nuclearization of the region. This region (comprising Japan, North and South Korea, and Taiwan, with the impingement of the United States, the USSR, and the PRC) is a focal point of superpower gaming. This involves geopolitics and geostrategy of a number of states. The conflicts are muted and there are chances that muted conflicts can become aggravated in the future. The power politics of the region do not reveal a clear-cut terminal condition or even a discernible trend; overlapping and contradictory trends can be noted. The future of North and South Korea is unclear. Will North Korea succeed in sowing the seeds of internal dissension in South Korea by its policy of supporting all kinds of elements in the latter and thereby increasing suspicion and domestic suppression? What really is known about the quality of North Korean arms and the nature of military politics, and what are likely to be the implications of these elements on the post-Kim Il-Sung regime? If South Korea loses faith in the American commitment to its defense, will this pave the way for South Korean nuclear arms or nuclear options and will this drag Japan into a similar stance? Will Japan wipe its hands of Korea, arguing that the problem is one of domestic politics rather than one of military security against external aggression? If so, will the shrinking defense perimeter force Japan to rethink its neopacifism and to seek a sea-based deterrent? Or will Japan simply emerge as a "has-been" in the foreign policy and security sense; that is, a country that tried to shape its position in the quadrilateral (U.S., USSR,

PRC, and Japanese) setting and in the triangular (Japanese, USSR, PRC) process, but that failed to achieve an independent position because its leadership was old, unimaginative, and unwilling to take risks? Alternatively, could it be that at present Japan seems to be unwilling to accept the opportunities and obligations of political and military power politics but, as its economic resources diplomacy (for example, the fishery dispute* with the Soviet Union) comes under strain, will find itself constrained to strengthen its naval defense and deterrence capacity?

Predicting the future is complicated by the uncertainty of the future of Sino-Soviet relations and its implications for Asian and international security. The PRC at present projects a status quo image, and its central concerns are domestic, with a search to gain foreign allies to strengthen its modernization program and to develop its anti-Soviet constituency. But the PRC also faces several potential territorial disputes—with Taiwan, Japan, and Vietnam. Currently these disputes are shelved, not solved. In Sino-American normalization negotiations, the Taiwan issue is secondary in relation to a Sino-American search to coordinate an anti-Soviet stance. But the effort may not be entirely fruitful. Peking may recognize that it is neither a superpower nor an uncontested Third World leader, and there are diplomatic penalties for PRC interests in Western Europe and in the Third World if the Washington connection and the anti-Soviet theme is pressed too hard by Peking's emissaries. Similarly, in Washington politics, limits to the utility of the PRC connection become important as it becomes clear that PRC support for U.S. diplomacy does not necessarily strengthen the American hand in international forums. The PRC's rightist advocacy has helped strengthen its connection with the EEC but this connection is based on a concern with drawing the PRC into the world community and muting its isolationism, rather than on a concern with promoting

---

*The fishery issue should not be overemphasized. This issue has existed since 1957. Legally Japan has only residual rights to fish in Soviet waters. Only about 25 percent of Japanese fishing is in Soviet waters and Japan's 200-mile economic zone clashes with Soviet rights. Moreover, the issue has been constant in Soviet-Japanese relations and is thus manageable. In one sense it has nothing to do with military security. But in another sense it becomes linked with other issues, namely, the islands disputes and Japan's interest in keeping its economic and political options open toward the Soviet Union. Thus Japanese naval presence could help the negotiating setting in the future.

unlimited anti-Sovietism. So the Europeans are not taken in by the PRC theory that the USSR is making moves on the PRC front as a diversion, with a view to attacking Western Europe. A shift in the propaganda and declaratory positions is discernible, but the definition of strategic interests of the great powers remains ambiguous in some cases and constant in others.

Ambiguity and volatility remain the hallmarks of contemporary Asian international relations. On one hand the Sino-Soviet conflict is likely to continue, but on the other hand it is noteworthy that both sides are showing a willingness to consider a rapprochement. The PRC is modernizing its economy and its political institutions, and now recognizes that ideology is not a useful substitute for modernization. To modernize quickly the PRC needs leadership stability. Limited state-to-state normalization suits both Moscow and Peking because peace is needed for modernization. The dispute can be explained as a conflict between neighbors; but too much should not be made of the territorial aspect because the PRC needs to balance both the Soviets and the Americans, and Taiwan is not the real problem. Peking today cannot take Taiwan militarily, and what would Peking do if it took it? It would extend Peking's status as a Pacific power and arouse Japanese concerns about the need to strengthen Japan's naval presence. Taking Taiwan would cause the issue to be lost in PRC domestic politics. At the same time, Peking's voice cannot be ignored in strategic matters. Its missile force has the capacity to give Moscow pause, if not to deter Moscow.

Predicting the future is hard because past predictions offer little confidence in forecasting. In the 1950s and the 1960s the theme of Chinese expansionism and Peking-supported proxy wars was constant in the Western literature. Today, suggestions that there are proxies (for instance in Indochina) command little attention, as more is known about the constraints, motivations, and capacities of states who are able, irrespective of their size, to engage "great powers" through innovative diplomacy. So, by and large, the view of the PRC as an evil influence has died in American foreign relations because the PRC's principal concern is with modernization and its leadership for the moment appears to be stable. But if the leadership falters, Maoist ideology and revolutionary rhetoric may again erupt. The PRC today is not likely to upset Southeast and South Asian regimes because most large nations are looking for stability and normalization of relations so that urgent domestic economic and social problems may be solved. The PRC and India are not two great systems fighting each other—at least according to leaders in Peking and Delhi. Moreover, Asia is full of leaders and the emergence of a few centers of power seems unlikely at present. It is arguable that the Soviet Union will cash in on instability because Soviet involvement

makes matters awkward for its competitors. On this ground alone
the PRC is not interested in supporting instability abroad. Moreover, Chinese military forces cannot project influence abroad.
Finally, even though the old warlordism is still present in the PRC
in the form of regional military leaders, it does not necessarily imply that these lords are war-prone. Modernization gives them new
sources of power but it takes peace to modernize. If India can modernize, why not the PRC? the argument goes. India has demonstrated a capacity to absorb investments, modern technology, and
modern organizational skills from abroad, and it has been able to
improve on this basis. The PRC can and should do the same, according to this argument; to do so, however, one needs peace at
home and abroad.*

At present the Korean peninsula is stable, but what will happen
after the American ground troop withdrawal is unclear. Japan today
is neopacific, but will it stay that way, given that a defense constituency is emerging in Japan and is increasing the defense consciousness of the Japanese people? Is there a parallel between the
U.S. commitments to Australia and to Japan? It seems, to compe-
tent Australians, that there is no situation where the alliance with
the United States would be called upon to play a role in Australian
defense. If threats are to be inferred from existing capabilities, it
seems that the United States itself is the most capable of threatening
Australia and Japan; but this is an unrealistic notion in Pacific international relations today. The PRC lacks capacity to threaten Australia but it could threaten Japan. Even though Japanese thinkers
today stress the Soviet rather than the PRC threat in military terms,
the self-defense mechanism that is meant for the Soviet Union can
also be directed implicitly against the PRC. (The Soviets could in
due course threaten Australian targets but that would be an entirely
new matter because at present the range of the Soviet military machine
does not extend fully into the Southern Pacific.) So, if there are circumstances in which the alliance with the United States cannot help
Australian security, it is conceivable that such a perception might
also arise in due course in Japanese thinking—if the threats are real

---

*India serves as an example for the PRC in terms of the lat-
ter's modernization aspirations but not in terms of Maoist ideology.
Today the PRC wants to avoid foreign dependence in trade, technology transfer, investments, and economic cooperation. It is arguable
that India has been able to escape economic dependence, and that the
PRC should be able to do the same as it gains experience in international economic diplomacy.

but ambiguous, if threats deal with bilateral rather than multilateral issues, and if competitive economic issues require a military presence but the economic competition is not only between military adversaries. Today, the PRC's nuclear threat toward Japan is muted because it makes sense for Peking to woo Tokyo and it makes sense for the latter to seek the continental connection for trade and political reasons. Also, it is in Japan's interest to prevent the PRC from acquiring a political and military presence in Taiwan, for reasons noted earlier.

Today, Japan operates in a quadrilateral (U.S./USSR/PRC/Japanese) context, but it seeks to reduce its dependency on the United States by attempting to develop a triangular (Japanese/USSR/PRC) process in Northeast Asia. Does this mean that Japan will at some time be able to acquire the military capacity and the diplomatic intelligence to function as a balancer in the region? Alternatively, if Japan cannot act as a balancer, can it adopt an equidistant stance (that is, a detached posture vis-à-vis the great powers, based on enormous strength to permit detachment)? Yet a third alternative might be a situation where Japan can become actively involved with the great powers, as if (according to a Japanese source) "because we cannot trust them we must be friends, almost." The latter perspective suggests that there are growing pressures on Japanese economic and military security experts in the defense agency, Ministry of International Trade and Industry (MITI), finance ministry, and (to a lesser extent) the foreign ministry to revise the policy of being modest in attitude and profile in the high-risk arenas of military and political diplomacy.

Ambiguity and volatility also characterize the future of U.S.-Japanese relations. Some argue that Japan has set a new course in its foreign and defense policies after the Nixon shocks. Others maintain that Japan has survived the American military defeat in the Vietnam war, the shock of the sudden visit of President Nixon to the PRC, and the anxiety created by the announcement by President Carter that he would slowly withdraw U.S. troops from Korea. In the latter perspective the real tensions in the world today are seen as being in areas that concern the health of the domestic economy and of external trade relations, rather than in the strategic field. Thus the regional powers can afford to leave the management of military security to the superpowers. This perspective may not be a sound one if there is a connection among SALT III; keeping the military-industrial complex alive because it helps the economy, and provides for a stable arms race; and keeping the anti-Soviet debate alive, because of the fundamental (nonnegotiable) disharmony in U.S./USSR interests and policies. Before assessing the implications for regional nuclear options it is necessary to outline the security perceptions of the principal actor in the region—Japan.

JAPANESE SECURITY PERCEPTIONS

Japanese perceptions of the military environment reveal a mixture of confidence and concern, and the nuances of Japanese thinking have to be understood to grasp the roots of changes that may occur in Japanese security policy in the coming decade. To date, after the war Japanese security policy was based on the American umbrella, and the policies from Tokyo were intended to develop and strengthen the Pacific connections and to acquire a perspective based on insular defense contingencies. The contact with continental Asia was minimized in the strategic realm even though trade and economic relations with Southeast and South Asian states have been cultivated. Now the Japanese recognize the likelihood of an Asian continental impact on Japanese security in the future, and the perceptions run somewhat as follows.

The Soviet Union is one of the great military powers that is physically close to Japan. The increase in Soviet military capacity is remarkable. At present the global military balance is based primarily on the Soviet-American military balance, and to date Japanese security is protected by the collective security system of the United States. But this balance is now under some strain. There is a clear danger of advancing Soviet military superiority. The Soviet Union enjoys local naval superiority, although in certain circumstances the Soviet navy could be bottled up in the Far Eastern ports. But still the balance seems to change. While Soviet capacities are coming closer to those of the United States (and in some cases have exceeded U.S. capacities), even if the United States has superior military forces in terms of quantity and quality, the problems of American neo-isolationism and "political will" are entering the policy agenda.

At present, Europe is the first line of Soviet-American confrontation, and the Far East is the second line of military confrontation. Soviet deployments in the area east of the Baikal military district consists of about 23 (armored) divisions. It is important that the peacetime deployment reveals that the divisions are undermanned. Category I divisions are 70 percent manned, category II are 50 percent manned, and category III are 30 percent manned. Most divisions are in the second and the third category and most divisions are deployed along the Sino-Soviet border. The Soviet Pacific fleet is based in Vladivostok, and about one-third of the Soviet navy is in the Far East. Besides this, in the Kamchatka peninsula there is a submarine base (Petropabros) that bases D-class and Y-class submarines (the latter are similar to the American Polaris kind of submarine launched ballistic missile submarine). The Soviet Pacific fleet is modernized and the tempo of modernization is quick.

The destroyers and cruisers have surface-to-surface and surface-to-air missiles. Of the 120 submarines in the Pacific fleet, at least 40 are nuclear-powered. About 2,000 Soviet military aircraft are in the Far East region. Most of these are MIGs (19 and 21) but the defection of the MIG-25 pilot to Japan recently indicated that these are also deployed in the region. Japan's airspace is surrounded by Badger bombers.

The PRC military presence is mainly that of its army. Its air force is organized around MIGs (19 and 21), but the Chinese are developing an F-9 type of fighter. Still, the tanks and firing weapons of the PRC army are of Russian types, and military modernization is needed along with modernization in agriculture, industry, and science as outlined by the PRC government. The PRC navy at present is mostly for coastal defense, and it is far from becoming an ocean fleet. Still, Japan has to remember that two major powers surround it.

The Japanese stress that one area of prime concern for Japanese security lies in the Korean situation. At present, on the whole there is a balance on the peninsula even though there is a disparity in the forces of different services. The navy of South Korea is negligible, with a few ROK submarines and patrol boats. North Korea has three times as many aircraft as South Korea. Overall, however, the two military forces are in balance, although the American military presence is essential to insure that they continue to be so. At present the United States provides the Second Infantry Division and one wing of the Fifth Airforce to South Korea. But President Carter has announced a withdrawal plan for the land forces (about 6,000 by the end of 1978), with an offer to modernize South Korean forces further as a compensation to retain the military balance. The United States is considering increasing the capacity of the airforce by strengthening one wing of the Fifth Airforce. Moreover, the United States will provide the equipment of the Second Division after it withdraws from Korea, and there will be financial aid to modernize South Korean aircraft (fighters) and tanks. The aid question, however, is clouded by the influence-peddling scandal and congressional attitudes; so the question of compensation is still an open one.

For Japan the future of Taiwan is also important. Japan has developed its "Japan formula" to modify its presence in the region. It has established diplomatic ties with Peking and cut those with Taiwan, while it maintains an economic relationship with Taiwan. The "Japan formula" exists in a specific context—the United States is maintaining its military and economic ties with Taiwan, and Taiwan is not an urgent problem in Sino-American normalization talks. Overall, at present there is no obvious military problem in the Taiwan area and it is desirable for Japan that this area remain stable.

Overall, the picture is reassuring. In Europe the military balance is being kept by the bipolar NATO/Warsaw Pact and by the superpower confrontation. In Asia the military balance is tripolar and the United States, the USSR, and the PRC balance each other. The Sino-Soviet conflict continues, although there is also movement toward normalization in relations between these two. Until the PRC achieves its domestic policy of modernization, the situation is one of no war and no peace, and the conflict with the Soviet Union spurs modernization. The situation in the Korean peninsula is presently stable and a repetition of the conflict of the 1950s is not expected at present. Because Japan relies almost 90 percent on imports for necessary natural resources (particularly for its oil), it seeks stability in its immediate environment so that lines of communications remain open to carry Japanese supplies and exports. From this viewpoint, the growth of the Soviet Pacific fleet is felt to be a threat by the Japanese. At present Japan is reassured by the presence of the U.S. Seventh Fleet, the Fifth Airforce, and one division of the marines in the region. Still, it finds it necessary to build its self-defense capacity: to protect its lines of sea communications, it is planning to upgrade its antisubmarine warfare capability; and to protect the islands from air threat the enhancement of air defense capacity is also planned—the MIG-25 incident revealed major deficiencies in Japan's radar network. At present, the Japanese defense agency works under a fiscal constraint because the government's decision—based on an assessment of the economic prospects until the 1980s—is to keep the defense commitment to 1 percent of the GNP, whereas the defense agency would prefer a commitment of 1.5-2 percent of the GNP. So, assuming an upward revision in the defense expenditures, as defense consciousness grows in Japan (particularly among parliamentarians, the press, the political parties, and the people), the glaring gaps in Japanese defense forces are likely to be filled in due course. This refers to gaps in the context of the current regional situation and world situation as described earlier.

However, Japan's sense of security is based on the premise that there are no real doubts about the American commitment—about perceived American will—in securing stable military and international relations in Northeast Asia. But what if the United States also decided to follow the "Japan formula" in settling its normalization debate with China? In this case it would cut its diplomatic ties with Taiwan while retaining its economic links.* In this case the United

---

*This was written before the United States recognized the PRC in December 1978.

States would be forced to abolish its military commitment to Taiwan—
which is a key premise in the Japan formula for Japan. In recent
years, after the American military defeat in Vietnam and in view of
Carter's decision to withdraw ground forces from Korea, doubts
arose about the American commitment in Japanese thinking. Today,
however, the doubts are diminishing. But if the United States is
forced to abolish its military commitment to Taiwan the credibility
of the United States, in Japanese thinking, is likely to become intolerable, and several Asian countries could then conclude that the
American influence in the region has been weakened. A discussion
of this possibility does not mean that such an outcome is likely. At
present, the United States, the PRC, and Japan hope that an unstable
military situation will not arise in the area. The American strategy
(which Peking now accepts) of solving peacefully all issues in the
region buys time for all parties concerned. It is easy now for Peking
to live with this approach—that is, to downgrade the Taiwan question and to continue talking about Taiwan but not doing anything about
liberating it (particularly when it cannot, anyway, now). By giving
the modernization issue priority over the Taiwan question, in effect
Peking has signaled that, inasmuch as modernization will take 20-
30 years (if not more), the Taiwan issue can be delayed for a long
time or at least until the retirement in due course of the present
Taiwan administration, perhaps 10-12 years hence. Alternatively,
Taiwan may emerge as another Hong Kong, where the local administration actively cooperates with the PRC government and yet capi-
talism flourishes both to bring in dollars to the PRC and to offer a
political window to the West. Under these circumstances, no military action in the Taiwan region is forecast unless the above two
alternatives fail to mature over time. In short, the PRC's modernization priority is a consequence of real economic and social need,
and it is a consequence of the failure to liberate Taiwan by force.
If these are the real motives of PRC policy, the anti-Sovietism of
the PRC is a form of manipulation intended to goad the Chinese
people toward modernization and to divert attention from the failure
to liberate Taiwan by force.

CONCEPTUALIZING JAPAN'S STRATEGIC FUTURES

To speculate about the future of Japan's strategic environment
and its security policy, it is essential to identify the crucial assumptions and perspectives about the current situation and the implications
for the hypothetical futures. To project, one needs to identify the
starting points, and this is difficult because the exercise is speculative. The following is an attempt to bring optimistic and pessimistic

assumptions and implications under analytical control. The exercise is not predictive or prescriptive.

The first perspective argues that American diplomacy now has the support of Japanese and PRC diplomacy in challenging the Soviet Union globally and in Northeast Asia. This assessment requires no emphasis now on containing the PRC. Instead the emphasis is on containing the Soviet Union through various means. There is a military balance in Northeast Asia because the coalition of the United States, the PRC, and Japan is sufficient and necessary to keep the peace in the Korean peninsula and the Taiwan area. Limited upgrading of Japanese defense capabilities in maritime and air defense is needed to provide military support for Japanese diplomacy. Since the PRC is no longer held to be a nuclear threat (as it was in the mid-1960s), there is no need now for Japan to have PRC-oriented Japanese nuclear weapons. Furthermore, since the PRC and the United States share an interest in containing the Soviet Union in Northeast Asia, the protection of the American nuclear umbrella for the foreseeable future is assumed. Military modernization in Japan and in the PRC can, therefore, occur on the premise that there is no immediate danger of military hostilities in Northeast Asia and the "no war–no peace" situation provides time for military modernization. Thus the situation is not seen as one of finite crisis.

A second perspective starts with the view that after the American forces defeated and occupied Japan, U.S.-Japan relations were smooth for 20 years. Then came the post-1971 Nixon shocks. During 1973-76, the relationship became smooth again. At that time Japan reassessed its U.S. policy and concluded that the United States was not going to shift its primary focus in Asia from Tokyo to Peking. Instead, it would find a temporary solution to the Taiwan issue by shelving it through a formula providing for "peaceful change only"; this would permit Japan to enjoy the Japan formula (diplomatic recognition of the PRC and economic relations with Taiwan) for 10-20 years. Thus, after reassessment, Tokyo concluded that American strategic policy could be in harmony with both the PRC and Japan, and that a context also existed to harmonize Sino-Japanese relations. This implied a need to strengthen political and economic ties with the PRC, to continue economic ties with Taiwan, and to settle bilateral economic problems with the United States. Even if disharmony in bilateral U.S.-Japan economic relations seemed inevitable because of Japanese protectionism and American demands, there was a harmony of strategic interests among the United States, the PRC, and Japan. Then for the present (the time frame is undefined), Japanese security is protected by existing stability in the Northeast Asian environment and by the conjunction of the United States, the PRC, and Japan against the USSR. Even if the Soviet Union irritated the Japanese in fisheries matters and on the northern islands dispute, the Soviets could not really hurt the Japanese interests. The possibility of Soviet interference with Japanese fishing and shipping had a defense implication: Japan needed to foster defense consciousness among its political parties, communications media, and public, and to engage in gradual militarization should the American military presence fail to deter the Soviet interference. Since the U.S.-Japan security treaty did not call for American military support in Soviet-Japanese clashes on the high seas, gradual militarization of the Japanese defense force for operations beyond Japanese territory was called for. In view of the recent history of U.S. shocks to the Japanese psyche or, in general, the impact of bilateral relations on the Japanese, foreign relations merited attention as a potential source of insecurity for Japan. In short, this perspective varies from the first one in terms of the uncertainty about the American connection.

According to a third perspective, American-Japan relations face major problems but the correct approach attempts to manage problems, not to have a problem-free agenda. There is foremost a question of imbalance in U.S.-Japanese trade, and the problem lies in Japan's protectionist policy.* The controversy over Tokai Muro reprocessing plant (this is discussed later) has been settled temporarily, but the measures taken have only bought time and not produced a permanent settlement. In 1969, Japan declared that South Korea (and Taiwan) were special security interests for Japan (even though Korea was not consulted before this declaration (but Taiwan was) and it is significant that culturally and politically there is animosity between the two). President Carter's plan to withdraw ground forces from Korea seems manageable, provided the withdrawal is slow and in phases; provided North Korea does not succeed in eroding the fragile political and social fabric of South Korean society; and provided Peking restrains North Korea. But all these are major "ifs" that require considerable attentiveness to external

---

*This is the American view. However, the Japanese argue that, on the other side of the issue, the United States needs to curb its oil imports and strengthen the dollar. The reasons for Japanese protectionism are complicated. Because of excessive external dependence, Japan likes to hoard what it has and so it is natural to be protectionist. Secondly, the industrial nations have competitive economies and collisions are normal. Thirdly, there may be a general communication problem between the Japanese and the Americans because of language and cultural differences.

developments in regional affairs. Japanese attentiveness and intervention in South Korean domestic politics and economic growth, and
Chinese attentiveness and intervention in North Korean domestic
politics and (particularly) military policy are required. These policies imply a high level of tacit coordination between Peking and
Tokyo; they further imply the existence of coordination in Sino-
Japanese-American diplomacies in the Korean peninsula. This perspective suggests an optimism in managing the North Korean-South
Korean "dialogue"—with Peking, Tokyo, and Washington as the in-
termediaries. It also assumes a bilateral American-Japanese
agenda that contains manageable problems. For Japan, this perspective requires considerable diplomatic skill—in insuring that bilateral problems with the United States do not become unmanageable,
that Washington and Peking stay involved in South and North Korea
constructively in defense of stability, and that Japanese economic
assistance aids South Korean economic strength and social and political stability.

A fourth perspective begins by considering Japanese worries
about the Soviet naval build-up in the Pacific. Japan has a question
about American willingness and capability to keep the lines of communications open to Japan and Korea. This causes nervousness to
Japanese defense planners and in particular to the conservatives.
The leftists in Japan are willing to accept the Japan-U.S. security
treaty on a status quo basis; that is, Japan did not allow itself to be
dragged into the Vietnam war and this points to the limits of its
security commitment, according to the left. In this sense, Japan's
position on the security treaty is "thus far and no further." But as
new problems arise the security issue may divide the Japanese
further. Korea is one possible divisive issue. The socialists are
pro-North Korea and the Liberal Democratic Party is pro-South
Korea. The socialists would be aghast if North Korea took the
South, but still their political posture and loyalty favor the North.
So the Korean issue is a volatile one in Japanese domestic politics.
If Japanese economic and cultural diplomacy fails to keep South
Korea a viable entity, will there be a move in Japanese politics to
encourage Japan to come to South Korea's help by military means?
The issue has not yet been really posed in Japanese elite thinking
but it is one issue that could emerge in the future.

Soviet-Japanese relations are complex at present, according
to the fifth perspective. The Soviets have not had a good experience
in the Far East since 1905. When the Russians crossed the continent
but, rather than an area waiting to be colonized, they found a land
inhabited by two dynamic peoples—the Chinese and the Japanese. At
that time China was dormant and self-centered and the Japanese
were active but isolationist. It is arguable that under the surface

the Russians think the Japanese are militaristic and expect militarism to emerge overnight. Cultural antipathy between Soviets and the Japanese—and racial feelings—could form the basis of the responses of both. Neither seems to understand the other, let alone deal well with each other. The dispute over the northern islands[1] complicates the relationship and its prospects. The Japanese government has been under pressure to get back these islands but that pressure has been less intense than the pressure to get back Okinawa. Still, Japan cannot abandon its claim to the northern territories. It is likely that it will keep the claim alive to sensitize the Japanese public opinion about defense needs, just as the PRC is keeping its border dispute with the Soviet Union alive to induce public support for its modernization program. It is conceivable that the Sino-Soviet territorial problem will be settled before the Soviet-Japanese territorial issue is settled. In that case, low-level strain in Soviet-Japanese diplomatic and military relations over the territorial issue is predictable. It appears to be manageable, provided that Japanese maritime and air defense capabilities are upgraded and that these are seen as supplements to the American capabilities. This perspective assumes that Soviet forces will not invade Japan itself but will continue the harassment of Japanese fishing and the probing of Japanese defense mechanisms.

A sixth perspective states that, while President Nixon and Kissinger gained personal, domestic, and international mileage from the establishment of the PRC connection and the Shanghai communiqué, and Presidents Ford and Carter have reaffirmed their commitment to the communiqué, the commitment is not necessarily a step toward renouncing Taiwan and normalizing relations with Peking. It postpones the Taiwan issue but for President Carter in 1977 normalization with the PRC was a no-win issue. A repudiation of Taiwan would be seen as a sellout of an old ally. It would raise doubts about the U.S. military commitment in the Pacific. It would undermine the "Japan formula," which permits Japan to keep its presence in Taiwan and to keep out Peking's presence; the latter is insurance that Peking will not be able to threaten the Japanese and American lines of communications in the South China Sea. Carter's China policy also posed another dilemma: even if the United States benefits from the Sino-Soviet conflict, it would not be able to prevent a move toward gradual state-to-state normalization; it was unclear whether Peking was using Washington to help its modernization and its argument with Moscow, or whether Washington was using Peking against Moscow—to keep the two apart and keep them from causing problems to the United States. Carter's PRC diplomacy also contained a hidden danger. If Sino-Soviet normalization moved forward, the United States would be in a very awkward spot if it had in the meantime failed to normalize its relations with the PRC and to strengthen its détente with the

USSR. Only on the premise that the current character of Sino-
Soviet relations will not alter does the United States have a capacity
and an opportunity to act as a balancer of some kind. But even if
the premise is that Sino-Soviet relations will not change in the short
run is true (the time-frame is undefined), if the premise is probably
wrong in the long run (the time-frame is again undefined), there is
danger that Peking is using Washington to buy time, to obtain Western technology and capital, and to negotiate with the Soviet Union
from a position of strength or lesser weakness. The Sino-Soviet
relationship is not entirely one of conflict. For instance, the PRC
is receiving military replacements for MIG-17s but not for MIG-23s.
What is going from the Soviet Union to the PRC is not enough, given
that the structure of the PRC's military industry is primarily Soviet
and ad hoc imports of Western technology and individual weapon systems cannot alter the basic structure of PRC military industry. But
by making more visible its connection with the United States, Western Europe, and Japan, and by importing Western and Japanese technology, Peking can deny to Moscow the opportunity of obtaining improvement of relations with the PRC without making concessions.
Questions about the normalization process are not about the need for
normalization but about the pace and the terms for accommodation.
Sino-American connections could therefore persuade the PRC and
the Soviet Union to engage in a step-by-step improvement of their
relations rather than to produce a dramatic change or a change without making concessions. In return for providing the transfer of U.S.
and other Western technology and capital to the PRC, President
Carter would get to lead a coalition including the PRC, Japan, and
certain Western European nations against the USSR. But what if the
PRC betrayed the United States after the technology transfers had
taken place? It is conceivable that Peking could, at a later date,
claim (along with Moscow) that the détente with the United States was
exclusively a military and not an ideological action, and that the
united front among the PRC, Second World states (European nations
and Japan), and a member of the First World (the United States) was
a temporary expedient meant to gain time and technology for PRC
modernization. It is possible also that limits could become apparent
in the uses of the Sino-U.S. connection in world affairs. For instance,
in African diplomacy, PRC support for U.S. diplomacy against the
Soviet Union had aroused criticism from President Nyerere of Tanzania—a key recipient of PRC aid for the Tanzam project. The PRC
connection for the United States may not add to U.S. diplomacy in
Africa and the U.S. connection for the PRC may entail a diplomatic
price for PRC diplomacy in Africa and the Third World, where the
PRC portrays itself as a leader. Lastly, PRC and U.S. toughness
could induce Soviet toughness also. It is debatable whether this would

help the American strategic position. Toughness on both sides means that an intensification of arms races is needed; this requires choosing how to allocate scarce resources among American military, economic, and social needs.

According to the last perspective considered here, Tokyo's foreign policy and defense strategy is not naive and apolitical as is sometimes suggested by some Western observers.[2] Tokyo is one of the few capitals that has access to all policy-making mechanisms worldwide. The purpose of Japanese diplomacy is to maintain a delicate equilibrium with all great powers. For strategic and economic considerations it temporarily gave up a visible political role. Its immediate concerns are economic but a strategic role for Japan is gradually emerging and a long-term process—with an infinite time perspective—is underway. At present Japan has a 5 billion ruble import account with the Soviet Union, and this is likely to go up to 10 billion rubles by the 1980s. Southeast Asia provides 20 percent of Japan's raw material imports. Trade with the PRC is increasing. It is still, comparatively speaking, small, yet the rate of growth is significant. Canada, the United States, and Latin America are the other main suppliers. Currently Japan is trying to diversify its trade and import sources. (See Tables 10.1 and 10.2 for an overview of Japan's trade patterns.) At present Japan is almost totally dependent on the United States for uranium, fishery, and a trade relationship. It has a better bargaining capacity with the USSR than with the United States. The USSR needs Japanese investment in Siberia. Still, the delay in negotiating economic ties reveals that the logic of economic geography of that region is not inevitable and that politics intrudes into economics. But this is clearly an area of future development. At present, connections are emerging between the Japanese business community and the Soviet authorities. Japanese business interests (and MITI) want access to the Soviet authorities whereas Soviet industry wants access to Japanese technology and capital. But intergovernmental links are slow to mature because Japanese government policy and business perspectives vary, and in Japan the consensus-building process is meant to be slow but sure.*

At present, while Japan is trying to build its PRC connections, a number of triangular processes can be hypothesized. First, the

---

*It is also probable that the real discrepancy with regard to Siberian development is among Japanese politicians and in the foreign ministry. For example, MITI still wants to separate economics from politics, but the foreign ministry wants to use the islands issue for leverage.

TABLE 10.1

The Distribution of Japan's Export
(percentage)

	United States	EEC	Latin America	PRC
1971	31.2	7.0	6.0	2.4
1975	20.0	10.2	8.5	4.1

	USSR	Taiwan	Korea
1971	1.6	3.8	3.6
1975	2.1	3.3	4.0

Source: The figures are derived from Statistical Yearbook, Japan (Tokyo: Bureau of Statistics, Japan, 1973 and 1977).

TABLE 10.2

Japan's Trade with the USSR and the PRC
(millions of U.S. dollars)

Year	Export to		Import from	
	USSR	PRC	USSR	PRC
1970	341	569	481	256
1971	377	578	496	323
1972	504	609	594	491
1973	484	1,039	1,078	974
1974	1,096	1,984	1,418	1,305
1975	1,170	2,259	1,626	1,531
1976	--	1,787	--	1,463

Sources: Data from 1970 to 1975 are from Nippon: A Chart Survey of Japan (Tokyo: Kokusei-sha, 1972, 1976/77); data for 1976 are from China Trade Report (Hong Kong, January 1977).

northern territories dispute with the Soviet Union gives Japan a flexibility vis-à-vis the USSR, as does the development of the PRC connection. It is arguable that the purpose of developing these issues is to help strengthen Japan's negotiating position with the Soviet Union and the PRC in future deals of substance. It is also possible that the prospect of a Soviet-Japanese connection (which is clearly inherent in the ongoing trade and political contacts between the Japanese and the Soviets) offers flexibility to the Japanese in their negotiations with the Chinese. A third possibility is that the prospect of a slow evolution of Japanese relations with its two communist neighbors, simultaneously or in succession as a phasal activity, gives flexibility to the Japanese negotiating position toward the United States. The picture emerging now is one of a slow evolution and not one of rapid and systemic change in Northeast Asian international relations. It is a picture in which Japan gradually moves out of its political isolationism as it gains experience and confidence in international political diplomacy. Its modesty in attitude and profile, however, should not be confused with an apolitical stance.

Japan's connection with the PRC is more historical than current. The cultural identity is important but then there is also (probably residually now) antipathy about PRC nuclear arms. Today, the PRC's use of its arms is curbed by Peking's wish to appear as a respectable member of the international community; by deficiencies in PRC nuclear forces; by the PRC's need to be friendly with the United States and Japan; and by the PRC's strategy of maintaining peace to gain time for its modernization. But if PRC arms and modernization help Sino-Soviet accommodation—help improve the PRC terms for the bargain—this would erode a central basis of the current United States/Japan/PRC nexus in stabilizing Northeast Asian international relations. Such considerations indicate that the public posturing and the inner thinking of the PRC reveal a need for caution in moving toward expectations of détente in Sino-Japanese and Sino-American relations.

Too much should not be made of the Sino-Japanese peace and friendship treaty. The prolonged negotiations over this treaty indicate that rapid progress in bilateral relations should not be expected. For instance, much has been made of the antihegemony clause in the proposed treaty, but this is an artificial issue in intergovernmental negotiations. Whether the clause is in the preamble or in the text, according to one interpretation, its meaning lies in the Japanese interpretation that it is not directed against a third party. From another point of view, the Japanese willingness to sign the treaty now can be seen as a means to pressure the Soviet Union into accommodating Japanese interests in bilateral relations. A third interpretation is that Japanese willingness to enter into the treaty now is a signal that there are no immediate prospects of a Soviet-Japanese cordiality in political relations, in settling the territorial dispute, or in building trade ties now. Finally, the treaty debate in Japan can be viewed as the real purpose of intergovernmental negotiations. The real issues concern the future of the Taiwan lobby, of which Prime Minister Fukuda has been a prominent member or at least a strong sympathizer. Fukuda was under strong pressure from Ohira (the secretary-general of the Liberal Democratic Party (LDP) to strengthen the PRC connection by signing the peace treaty. The Taiwan lobby was, and is, a paid lobby, and is well entrenched in Japanese society. For internal political reasons—to divert attention from economic problems, to divert attention from the trade confrontation with the United States and Western Europe, to point to a Fukuda success—the movement toward a peace treaty made sense. Although strategically the treaty is peripheral in importance, it is significant in getting the Japanese public to rethink the commitment to Taiwan and to the Japan formula.

There are signs that Japanese foreign economic and security thinking is now in a flux. Three considerations dominate Tokyo's thinking at present. First, Japan faces no immediate security problem as long as it enjoys U.S. security protection and as long as the PRC is in its present mood. Secondly, Japan needs to sustain its fragile economy, and the notion of the Japanese economic superstate is plainly more an example of a futurologist's imagination than a picture of reality. Thirdly, Japan's sealanes are in tension-ridden areas, and it needs continental connections with Asia to diversify its supply sources and its markets. The Japanese style remains low-key but recently Japan has acquired a political role. Even though the Japanese government protests too much that it does not have a political role in Southeast Asia, it must remember that the average Japanese has an ego and would like to have a limited political role, particularly when that role is easily explained as a coordinated effort of Australia, India, and Japan to strengthen Southeast Asian regionalism and to encourage Hanoi to remain a moderate and westward-looking influence in Indochina's international relations.

There are also signs that Japanese decision makers and opinion makers are looking into the future. The nuclear issue is one such indicator. The ratification of the NPT was delayed because of the NPT debate in Japan. Then the safeguards agreement with the International Atomic Energy Agency was held up for a year and a half after the NPT was ratified in 1976. Japan's argument was simple: its laws had to be complied with before ratification could take place. Yet the inescapable fact was that Japanese safeguards negotiations were linked by the Japanese to the negotiations over the Tokai Muro reprocessing plant, and the safeguards agreement was ratified after the United States agreed to the Japanese position on the Tokai. This outcome was a victory for Japanese diplomacy. It restated the chief characteristics of the Japanese approach: it is modest in attitude and profile, and high on achievement. Tough Japanese nuclear negotiations indicate that Japan wants to keep its nuclear option intact and does not want to fall in line with Carter's antiproliferation policy. The evolution of Japanese nuclear negotiations—from the NPT to the Tokai and the safeguards issue—strengthens Japan's major reservations against the NPT.*

At present, Japan's central motive in the nuclear field is to acquire energy independence. One-fourth of its energy needs by A.D. 2000 will be nuclear-based, even though the estimates have been revised downward in recent years. (See Table 10.3 for an overview of Japan's energy position.) It plans to acquire fast breeder reactors, a reprocessing capacity, and commercial uranium enrichment capacity by the 1980s—or at least an experimental capacity in enrichment technology. Furthermore, as Japan shows signs of independent thinking and action on certain foreign and security policy issues, the cultural roots of Japanese-American relations and perceptions could become significant. The Japanese seem to have a love-hate[†] relationship with the Americans: there is hate for

---

*Japan's statement (February 3, 1970) emphasized the following points. The NPT was the first step toward nuclear disarmament, and adherence by all nuclear weapon states was to be desired. The treaty was discriminatory, and discrimination ought to disappear through nuclear disarmament. Because the NWS had special status they also had special responsibilities. Japan had a "deep interest" in insuring that the treaty should not restrict peaceful uses of nuclear energy. The NWS ought to take concrete nuclear disarmament measures and they ought not to use or threaten to use nuclear weapons against NNWS. For the full statement, see Donald C. Hellman, Japan and East Asia: The New International Order (London: Pall Mall Press, 1972), pp. 201-4.

[†]Alternative explanations for the love-hate dimension may be noted. It is possible that Japan accepts responsibility for World War II but hates the United States because of postwar development—that it was forced to join the U.S. camp in the cold war and not allowed to remain nonaligned. Hate may be caused by excessive dependence in economic, military, and political matters on the United States. Since the mid-1960s, love for the United States has declined; Switzerland, France, and West Germany are today more admired than the United States. But the United States is loved because it offers protection. See Figure 10.1.

TABLE 10.3

Comparison of Energy Supply-and-Demand Forecasts for Japan

	Fiscal Year 1975 (results)		Fiscal Year 1985								Fiscal Year 1990 (With Maximum Efforts)	
			MITI Forecast (August 1975)		NIRA (January 1977)		MITI Interim Forecasts					
							Under Current Policy		With Maximum Efforts			
	Actual Figures	%	Actual Figures	%	Actual Figures	%	Actual Figures	%	Actual Figures	%	Actual Figures	%
Economic growth (1975–85: annual rate)	3.0%		6.6%		6.2%		6.0%					
Demand												
Before energy conservation	390,000 MI		830,000 MI				740,000 MI		740,000 MI		916,000 MI	
Rate of energy conservation			9.4%				5.5%		10.8%		13.5%	
After energy conservation	390,000 MI		760,000 MI		680,000 MI		700,000 MI		660,000 MI		792,000 MI	
Supply Sources:												
Hydro–general	21,710 MW	5.8	28,300 MW	3.7	28,300 MW	4.1	19,500 MW	3.3	22,500 MW	3.9	26,500 MW	3.9
–pumped storage	3,150 MW	0.0	14,100 MW	0.5	2,000 MW	0.5	19,500 MW		18,500 MW		24,500 MW	
Geothermal	50 MW	0.0	2,100 MW	1.8			500 MW	0.1	1,000 MW	0.3	3,000 MW	0.7
Indigenous oil, natural gas	3,500 MI	0.9	14,000 MI	1.9	5,400 MI	0.8	8,000 MI	1.2	11,000 MI	1.7	14,000 MI	1.7
Indigenous coal	18,600 Kt	3.3	20,000 Kt	9.6	22,000 Kt	2.5	20,000 Kt	2.0	20,000 Kt	2.1	20,000 Kt	1.8
Nuclear	6,620 MW	1.7	49,000 MW	7.9	30,000 MW	6.6	26,000 MW	5.4	33,000 MW	7.4	60,000 MW	11.2
Liquefied natural gas	5,060 Kt	1.8	42,000 Kt	11.2	30,000 Kt	6.3	24,000 Kt	4.9	30,000 Kt	6.4	44,000 Kt	7.7
Imported coal	62,340 Kt	13.1	102,400 Kt	63.3	94,000 Kt	11.0	93,000 Kt	10.7	102,000 Kt	12.4	144,000 Kt	14.1
New energy	—	—	—		—		—		2,300 MI	0.4	13,000 MI	1.6
Subtotal (oil equivalent)	104,000 MI	26.6	485,000 MI		—		195,000 MI	27.8	228,000 MI	34.5	340,000 MI	42.9
Need of imported oil	288,600 MI (5,890 Kt)*	73.1			460,000 MI	68.3	505,000 MI (14,000 Kt)*	72.2	432,000 MI (20,000 Kt)*	65.5	452,000 MI (25,000 Kt)*	57.1
Total	390,000 MI	100.0	760,000 MI	100.0	680,000 MI	100.0	700,000 MI	100.0	660,000 MI	100.0	792,000 MI	100.0

*Amount that is liquefied propane gas.

Source: Japan Atomic Industrial Forum, Inc., "Nuclear Power Development in Japan" (Select Papers), undated, p. 5.

FIGURE 10.1

Nations Liked by the Japanese

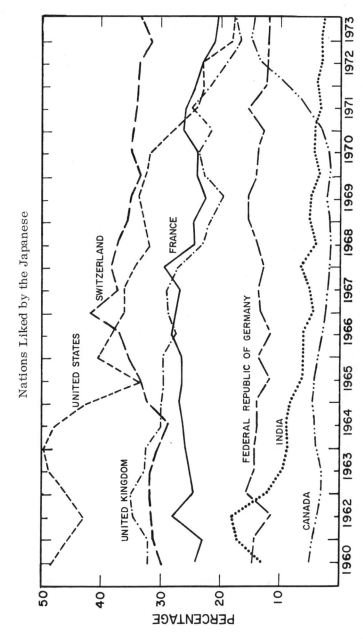

Source: Aki Wataube, "Japanese Public Opinion and Foreign Affairs: 1969-1973," in The Foreign Policy of Modern Japan, ed. Robert Scalapino (Berkeley: University of California Press, 1977), p. 126.

the defeat in World War II and for the subsequent occupation; but then there is also admiration for American culture. (See Figure 10.1.) The most serious issue for Japan now is that the United States is calling upon it to assume a greater defense burden and a role in cooperation with the United States in U.S. strategic policy. The defense issue is linked to the trade issue with the United States. On the latter, the American argument is that Japan is tight-fisted about allowing into Japan American imports except raw materials; and most Japanese concessions in trade matters are cosmetic or self-serving. For instance, permitting greater imports of uranium into Japan is hardly a concession, and the Americans and the Western Europeans want Japan to open its markets to finished products from outside. Unless Japan liberalizes its import policy, the United States will continue asking it to share the defense burden and increasing protectionism against Japanese exports to the United States. The linkage between trade and defense policy is telling, because it will take a 5 percent growth rate for the Japanese economy to grow; this requires that exports grow at double the rate of the growth of imports. To do this Japan has to enter into the market of high technology exports such as computers and precision-guided technology. Japan cannot export these now because of the Co-ordinating Committee for Export Controls to Communist Countries (COCOM) restrictions but it can, and is likely to, engage in such exports to the PRC either as a front for the United States or as its close follower. (This is not to suggest that Japan has subverted the COCOM list.) In the latter case, for example, the United States could make the first computer sale to the PRC (or to the Bank of China branch in Hong Kong) and then Japan could enter the market. Japanese computer technology is not as sophisticated as American IBM technology. But if Japan were able to enter the PRC market, it could improve its technology once volume sales were assured. At the same time, given the high dependence on foreign trade to sustain domestic economic growth, just as the supply prospects to the PRC appeal to the Japanese, the prospects of importing raw materials from Siberia are also appealing and the foundation for future deals is being laid through nongovernmental contacts. The pattern of such contacts is revealed by the atomic energy agreement signed in 1977 between a Japanese private atomic energy institution and the USSR. At present this agreement is devoid of content but it could become substantive in the future.*

---

*To elaborate: the bilateral arrangement is, in Japanese eyes, a nongovernmental one. It calls for cooperation and exchanges with respect to fast breeders and fusion and exchange of nuclear specialists

Overall, the last perspective mentioned above reveals that
the picture of Japanese negotiating behavior is multidimensional—
dealing with overlapping, even contradictory, contingencies in the
future. In the past Japan wanted "equidistance" with the Soviet
Union and the PRC. Today it realizes that it cannot be friends with
both, given the Sino-Soviet conflict and given its problems with the
USSR. A number of circumstances facilitate its moves toward the
PRC. It is an old stratagem that the "enemy of my enemy is my
friend." The PRC appears now to Japan to be the weaker of the two
and amenable to U.S. and Japanese ways of thinking in Northeast
Asian security matters. Thus the PRC seems to be the weaker and
more compatible of the communist states, and allying with it makes
sense. Given that disharmony of interests is the central factor in
Soviet-U.S. relations in the perspective of the Carter administration, and given that Tokyo is not willing to abandon its U.S. connection (now or ever), Japan seeks to be friendly to the PRC today and
chooses not to focus on its earlier concerns (expressed in the mid-
1960s) about the implications of a nuclear-armed PRC.

Today the PRC appears to have an outward-looking, moderni-
zation-oriented leadership, and it makes sense that Japan is strength-

---

between the two countries. There are also exchanges of two-thirds
of the research students from each country. An agenda item was to
consider Japanese supply of a nuclear reactor or reactors or components of reactors to the USSR. This was meant to be a private
arrangement. It was, however, taken off the agenda because of the
state of current relations and because of discussions about uranium
supply among Japan, Canada, and Australia. At present, there is
no specific link between reactor exports and uranium imports by
Japan. However, Japanese private industry seems to have an incentive to engage in nuclear exports to the Soviet Union and to explore
the possibility of Soviet natural uranium exports to Japan. The idea
is novel because the Soviet Union has an interest in exporting enriched uranium to Japan (as it already does to West European countries) but it does not presently have an interest in marketing natural
uranium. Still, this is a possibility that cannot be excluded from
future consideration. At present, political and cultural considerations on one hand, and commercial interests on the other hand do
not entirely coincide in Japanese thinking. It is excessive to describe this as tension between politicians and businessmen, but the
point can be made that politicians in Japan are generally cautious
people and are likely to debate all nuances of policy, while business
people are not required to be so cautious.

ening the PRC connection. But the practical effects of this move
are still unclear. A peace treaty is a symbolic gesture, since the
antihegemony clause has been beaten to death through Japanese-
style prolonged discussions in public about the third-party implication of the clause. Japan is not likely to gain much economically
from the peace treaty—that is, beyond its present economic relations with the PRC. The PRC can offer oil to Japan, but it has a
high sulphur and paraffin content, and the PRC needs to import new
technology to refine it. Moreover, the PRC's oil supplies are limited. In short, the PRC's economic needs from Japan are greater
than Japanese needs of the PRC.

At the same time, even if Japanese enthusiasm for equidistance from the USSR and the PRC is presently muted because of
problems and perceptions about the roots and implications of Soviet
foreign and economic diplomacy, the equidistance idea is not dead
or abandoned. Because expansion of Sino-Japanese trade has limited possibilities, Japan needs, for instance, to fish as much as possible in Soviet water. Japan is likely to think about making a comparable move toward the Soviet Union after it makes a move toward
the PRC. This suggests a new and interesting pattern of developing
equidistance; it suggests a diplomacy of activism—of attentiveness
to satisfying in part Chinese and in part Soviet concerns. Thus defined, equidistance does not mean a posture of indifference that is
based on enormous economic strength and a capacity to insulate
Japan from its communist neighbors. Rather it means a policy of
engaging the two communist states into functional issue areas (fisheries, atomic energy, maritime defense, continental prospecting,
keeping Korea stable, encouraging disarmament by all nuclear
weapon states, solving territorial problems, promoting regional
economic development, keeping sealanes open to all, and so on).
The Soviet Union wants a friendship treaty with Japan and this is not
as innocent as it sounds. It would effectively shelve the islands issue for the Soviet Union and it would amount to political suicide for
the Japanese government. But if this proposed treaty is seen as the
maximum aspired to rather than as what is expected, lesser avenues
of cooperation may have greater negotiating possibilities. Given
these factors, it is too early to talk about Japanese abandonment of
its equidistance stance and policy.

CHANGING PARAMETERS IN JAPANESE
DEFENSE THINKING

In 1969 Thomas Schelling suggested that Japan faced two
choices—to extend the status quo and thereby prove that it could be

"great" without "possessing commensurate military force," or to move toward an "autonomous military posture."[3] With the knowledge gained from the study of Japanese behavior during the 1970s, and bearing in mind the changes in the world and Asian scene, it appears that the choice before Japan today is neither to extend the status quo nor to seek an autonomous military posture. The following review of Japanese and other materials indicates that the debate is not about the utility of a Japanese military force but about its size and mission. Japanese thinking does not reject military power politics and the role of force in international relations. There is a debate between "idealism" and "reality,"[4] but the policies rest firmly on the latter while public relations rest on the former.

This is not to suggest that idealism is not taken seriously. Idealism is politically functional because the Japanese people are on the whole optimistic and do not like gloomy forecasts for Japan. But realism is intended to correct idealism, and a balance between the two is intended; the present assessment of the situation rests on realism.* Japan cannot simply extend the status quo because this has already changed, partly in Northeast Asia—as discussed previously. The following discussion reveals the circumstances underlying the transition away from the status quo of the past but it is not clear exactly where the transition is leading. In the 1950s and the 1960s Japan was clearly under the U.S. umbrella. Today it is less so but it is not in a position yet to mount an autonomous military posture. Nor is this necessary yet. It is therefore an open question whether the ambiguities in contemporary Asian international relations necessarily favor ambiguity in Japan's defense and nuclear policies. Gaston Sigur notes:

> The dangers of a US-Japan split, perhaps overstated
> by some in the early 1970s, seem to have receded as

---

*There are two "realist" schools. The Japanese foreign ministry "pessimistic realism" school of thought says that even though military security for Japan is impossible to achieve by military means, it is necessary to go as far as Japanese means permit. This contrasts with the view of the "optimistic realism" school. This school maintains that an internationalist peace and disarmament diplomacy is necessary, not because Japan is noble but because Japan cannot live without peace; its economy is too fragile; and internationalism is needed to cover Japanese weakness. The "pessimistic realism" school makes sense if the premise is that the Japanese/U.S. security ties protect only Japanese territory and not Japanese economic and political interests.

the energy problem has emerged and the US need to
strengthen its ties with its allies has become more
evident. The apparent lessening of tensions between
the United States and Japan, on the one hand, and the
People's Republic of China and the Soviet Union, on
the other, have tended to decrease the Japanese perception of the need for greater military strength.
Most importantly, the questioning of American determination and ability to carry out its guarantees to
Japan in case of need seems to have diminished somewhat, despite the failure of US policy in Indo-China.
As long as this kind of atmosphere prevails, it is likely that the policy of relegating defense to a relatively
low priority in the political and economic world of
Japan will continue. [5]

Evelyn Colbert notes further:

Important in bolstering Japanese confidence has been
the weakness—political, military, and economic—of
its near neighbors. Moreover, when the PRC seemed
most clearly hostile to Japan and most closely allied
with the Soviet Union, its own military power added
little to Moscow's, and the US deterrent was as effective against the one as against the other. As Chinese
Communist military power has grown, however, so
have Peking's differences with the USSR, while at the
same time the prospect of major military developments in Japan's vicinity has been reduced by the general climate of detente. [6]

These observations reveal that Japan's sense of security is
today primarily a consequence of external factors rather than of
Japanese military strength. Among these external factors is the
sense that the Sino-Soviet situation is one of neither war nor peace;
and a limited détente (no war and no peace) is very good for Japanese
security because existing Japanese forces do not have the capacity to
fight against external aggression. So the real defense for Japan lies
not merely in the security ties with the United States; it lies in the
premise and perception that a general nuclear or conventional conflict between the great powers is unlikely, and that in order to avoid
nuclear conflict the great powers also need to avoid conventional war
between themselves. In these circumstances the security treaty with
the United States is not expected to be used for Japan's defense even
though it obviously contributes to strengthening of the deterrent

against nuclear aggression in the region. In these circumstances
Japan can have security with light armaments. At present the Japanese people do not have a clear appreciation of defense problems,
and the consciousness of defense matters is limited but growing.
Because of external factors in the communist world, the question
about the reliability or lack thereof of the U.S.-Japanese security
treaty is not an urgent one today. It is unlikely at present that
American public opinion will become isolationist or turn in favor of
wanting to abandon Asia. If the American public mood favors isolationism and withdrawal from Asian commitments, this implies a
retreat to American seapower rather than a continuation, let alone
an upgrading, of existing treaty commitments. Still, the basis of
the security treaty lies in American international strategy and not
simply in bilateral relations with Japan. Another reason for the
American commitment to Japan may be to preclude a major Japanese
rearmament program. Rearmament does not necessarily mean militarism but it could become that if ultranationalist forces gained command in Japanese politics. There is only one hypothetical circumstance in which the security treaty could lose its value: if Japan
became militarily strong and at the same time its rearmament did
not harm the United States. This is an unlikely possibility in the
near future.

In the mid-1960s the PRC's nuclear explosion caused concern
about security in Japanese thinking. Today, a number of considerations have produced a relaxed view about the PRC. While Japanese
thinkers argue that limited reconciliation between the PRC and the
Soviet Union is probable, they also maintain that the military confrontation will continue for a long time. Because of the turmoil in
Maoist China, its modernization has been delayed by 10-20 years
compared with, for example, French modernization. In this century, PRC defense forces are directed primarily, if not exclusively,
toward the Soviet Union. The PRC is unlikely, even if it has the
transport facilities, to move its forces abroad. So no real threat
from the PRC to Japan seems likely in the near future. As for the
Soviet Union, while its air force can threaten Japanese targets in a
matter of minutes, its navy is vulnerable. The weak point of its
navy exists in the fact that its home port is in the Sea of Japan. Even
though it is popular to describe this as the Sea of Russia, the vulnerability is salient. Unless the Soviet Pacific fleet seeks home porting
outside the Sea of Japan this vulnerability is not likely to be altered.
Petropavlovsk in the Kamchatka peninsula may emerge as a home
port for the Soviet navy, but it freezes in the winter and logistic support for the port is difficult. Also, this port is vulnerable to a U.S.
blockade. At present it is unclear whether Soviet thinking involves
utilizing its naval presence to create a psychological fear in the

Japanese psyche or whether the Soviet intention is to have invulnerable forces. Given the ambiguities in the nature of the Soviet naval threat to Japanese sealanes, the Japanese reaction is to seek gradually to expand its naval presence southwest (about 1,000 miles) toward Taiwan, southeast toward Guam* (also about 1,000 miles), and around Japan (several hundred nautical miles). At present these are the rough lines of the Japanese sphere of naval influence; this is meant to be shared with the United States and it could eventually become an arena of confrontation. This area of sealane protection is likely to vary according to circumstances—that is, according to Japanese merchant shipping movement patterns and according to the activities of the Japanese submarines. At present the focus of Japanese thinking is against the Soviet naval presence, but it is conceivable that in the 1980s the PRC may be able to have about 40 ocean-going submarines. At present the PRC's navy is primarily a coastal defense mechanism, but the Pentagon is interested in assessing the long-term implications of the PRC submarine program. According to current estimates, it is directed at present against the Soviet naval presence in the Pacific and hence is defensive. But Japanese naval officers of the defense agency in Japan think that it could also be a potential threat to Japan in the 1980s. Even though high-level Japanese defense thinking discounts such notions, the speculation about possibilities for the future cannot be dismissed as fanciful. In any case, irrespective of whether the target is the Soviet Union or the PRC or both, there seems to be a consensus in Japanese thinking that even though the idea of providing convoy protection in the Pacific (let alone up to the Persian Gulf) is not practical at present, the Japanese navy ought to establish a limited antisubmarine capability that can provide surveillance, intelligence, and target identification. Right now Japan has only coast guard naval capacity and it cannot detect alien submarines in its region.

The preceding discussion casts doubt on Sigur's assessment that the "apparent lessening of tensions" has "decreased" the "Japanese perception of the need for greater military strength." Colbert's assessment of the PRC's military strength and "growing" Sino-Soviet differences is also doubtful. Since such assessments rest on the premise of détente, one needs to conceptualize the existence of a no war-no peace situation and its effect in generating an attentiveness to defense considerations in Japan. This is not to suggest militarism but it is to suggest gradual rearmament.

---

*A variation of this may be a development of a Japanese naval presence toward the Bonin islands (about 700 miles from Japan) instead of toward Guam, a major U.S. base.

F. C. Langdon offers a wider conceptual scheme to analyze Japan's future. He conceptualizes the range of Japanese choices as follows: (1) reliance on the United States or a neutralist defense policy with Gaullist overtones; (2) rearmament on a vast scale and acquisition of nuclear arms or the present policy of limited defense force plus an economic great-power status and a willingness to help poorer countries—that is, to seek influence through economic diplomacy and limited arms; (3) a corollary of the preceding point is to visualize the emergence of Japan as a third pillar of the world; the hypothesis is that it has "almost" realized that aim; (4) finally, Japan is seen as the major economic power but not as an armed superpower that seeks an arms race and domination over smaller countries. [7]

The present discussion casts a doubt on some such Western perceptions of Japanese choices. Schelling's choices—status quo (being great without having commensurate military force) or autonomous military force—are narrow. To assess the meaning of Schelling's ideas, it is necessary to examine "status quo" in two different ways: as Japan's policy of seeking influence primarily through non-military means; and as an assessment of changes in international, regional, and domestic politics. In the latter sense, the status quo has been broken but the new structure of international relations in Asia (or Asias) has yet to emerge in clear form. The strategic and domestic situation in the Korean peninsula is one of no war and no peace. The status quo in Korea is clearly changing but gradually. What, for instance, might South Korean capability be after the withdrawal of American ground forces? According to the Carter administration two premises are central in assessing Korea's future. The United States will make efforts to support modernization of South Korean armed forces; additionally, the United States will withdraw its ground forces slowly if there is no instability in the Korean peninsula. Given these premises, the South Korean forces can bear a North Korean military attack, provided they receive communications, logistics, and intelligence support from the United States. Therefore, if North Korea had a chance to attack South Korea, its line of action could be somewhat as follows. The North could encourage insurgency in the South; or it could try to weaken the political and social fabric and morale of South Korea and then attack the South— after the weakening of morale was established. In short, the point is that there needs to be social, political, and economic stability in South Korea rather than only a military balance, which both appreciate. It appears that the political status quo has already changed in the Korean peninsula and yet a new order has not been established. If the failure of domestic stability in South Korea leads to a war— preceded by insurgency and a loss of South Korean confidence in their

capacity to keep the peace—then even the United States cannot help
the South and will have to abandon it. Japan obviously is likely to
do everything to avert this situation through friendly diplomacy and
economic relations; the United States expects Japan to furnish this
kind of support. But if instability occurs, Japan's military assistance to South Korea can occur only in a very limited way. In this
instance, the decision to withdraw American ground forces alters
the status quo. It requires greater Japanese involvement in diplomacy in Korea. It implies a withdrawal of the American military
presence over time from the backyard of Japan, thereby altering a
contextual feature of Japanese security policy. But at the same
time it does not necessarily mean the emergence of an autonomous
Japanese military role and a force for that purpose. The existing
proccesses in the Korean case do not signal a connection between
altering the status quo and moving toward an autonomous military
capacity.

Likewise, in the case of Taiwan, if Peking has shelved its
claim to seeking an immediate solution to this issue with the United
States, if Japan has time on its side in pursuing the Japan formula,
if the prospect of war in the Taiwan region does not exist now or in
the foreseeable future, then the status quo has changed because of
the emergence of shared interests among the PRC, Japan, and the
United States against the Soviet Union. This identity may or may
not last in the coming decade, but it points to the absence of a clear-
cut link between an altered status quo and a tendency to acquire an
autonomous military force. Viewing status quo as an international
situation, from Japan's perspective the situation has changed remarkably with respect to the future of Korea, Taiwan, American
domestic politics, the PRC's domestic situation, Sino-Soviet relations, superpower détente, Soviet-Japanese relations, and so on.
Yet alterations in the international and regional status quo do not
necessarily imply a movement toward an autonomous Japanese defense force; but these alterations imply a change—an upgrading—
in the Japanese defense force structure, in its fiscal commitment,
in the growth in defense consciousness, and in a recognition of the
interface between economic resources diplomacy and defense and
deterrent capacity.

Some of Langdon's perceptions about Japanese choices seem
stark but some merit review with modification. If Japanese policy
makers respond to events and not merely to their own intentions,
the starting points of Japanese external behavior are different today
from what they were in the early 1970s. As some distance develops
in Japanese-U.S. relations because of trade problems and nuclear
issues, as Japan's economic superpower status comes under scrutiny
because of domestic economic problems and pressures from the

United States and the EEC, as Japan remains conscious of the need to retain and to enhance its international position, the choice is not simply to become Gaullist; it is not to acquire an autonomous military force; it is not to seek the position of the third pillar of the world economy; and it is not to become an armed superpower. Rather the line of action could be a mix of the following factors.

Because of the uncertainties in Japan's external environment, a central element of developing Japan's defense structure is to raise the defense consciousness of the Japanese people; that is, to begin a campaign of public education and re-education. This assumes that defense consciousness is high among Japanese elites but that the base of popular support for defense lacks full consciousness. Until there is a popular consensus, defense thinking will remain stymied by factional politics. In the government, defense consciousness has emerged through intergovernmental interactions, but a key step in Japan's case now is to improve the intranational dialogue on defense, as a prelude to defense decision making in the future. Among Japanese defense planners different strategies for raising defense consciousness are already under serious consideration. One view is that it is first necessary to raise the defense consciousness among Japanese political parties because they are mostly divided on defense issues. Once this has been achieved, then it is possible to raise the level of consciousness of the Japanese people. Another view seeks to utilize the influential press in Japan to enlighten the people. This view argues that the attitude of the influential press on defense matters is changing, and that once grassroots sentiment emerges, then members of the Diet (Japan's Parliament) will also begin to respond to the public mood.

If Japanese security policy is viewed simply as a response, a reaction to external developments, then it is reasonable to argue that the present strategic environment permits continued stability through a stance of light arms and continued alliance ties with the United States; here the key variable is the management of the Japan-U.S. security relationship. It is useful to hypothesize, however, that the real crisis (an infinite one) for Japan is partly internal and partly external. Its postwar policy of securing U.S. ties and a position of light armament is not based on morality and idealism. It does not represent a repudiation of the role of military force in foreign relations. The policy of seeking security through alliance ties and light arms is a policy of pragmatism and it is not based on a theoretical commitment to pacifism. Repeatedly, Japanese statements emphasize that the purpose of diplomacy is to promote the national interest "on the strength of our country's overall position."[8] In May 1969 Foreign Minister Kiichi Aichi approvingly revealed the advice he received from Albert Einstein. According to the latter:

There is a danger of inventions like the hydrogen bomb
being used for war. I want you as a politician to make
an effort to forestall war. That's the biggest contribution a politician can make to the human race. If there
should have to be a war, however, you should take up
arms, go to the forefront of the battle and die. What
Japan needs most at this time are men who love their
country with courage. Don't forget that such are the
really worthy Japanese. [9]

Aiichi made several other important observations. First, the
"ideal of the Japanese Constitution" entrusts entirely Japan's peace
and security to the good will of the international society. Disarmament, an end to nuclear testing, the development of UN forces, and
so on, are ideals worth pursuing to strengthen international society.
Secondly, "as the one and only major power" firmly determined not
to make nuclear weapons, it should become a permanent member of
the UN Security Council. Thirdly, one should give "equal consideration" to ideal and reality at all times, and on this basis Japan is not
able to entrust its security to the UN. Fourthly, "peace is maintained by the relationship of power"; "there is peace because there
is power," and international society has not reached the stage of
achieving peace without power. This reality underlines the deterrent
theory. Fifthly, General De Gaulle attached importance to the policy
of relaxing tensions but he also attached "great importance to national defense." Defense and diplomacy for relaxation of tensions
are "inseparable like the two wheels of a cart." Sixthly and finally,
if a national consensus on national security policy is achieved, if the
relationship between defense and peace diplomacy is clearly understood, then the argument moves to the level of deciding other defense questions, such as the extent of the defense build-up; whether
it is sufficient; from the viewpoint of national interests, which country should make up the deficiency in Japan's defense capacity; if the
United States is to be the ally, how the two nations should share the
defense burden. [10]

In October 1970, the Defence Agency published its first white
paper on defense. It laid the theoretical foundation for the evolution
of Japanese defense policy and a number of conceptual parameters
were revealed. First, it was the constitutional position that in the
"case of an armed attack from outside Japan, it [the Constitution]
does not prohibit the use of armed force in self defence in order to
repel such an evil." Self-defense was an "inherent right" for Japan.
Secondly, it was necessary to understand the relationship between
politics and military affairs and between diplomacy and military affairs, and these relations had to be "properly regulated." Thirdly,

the "first thing" to do to insure national security was to prevent foreign threats and aggression. Diplomacy to promote peace and to strengthen the UN, and disarmament and arms control were means to this end, as was the development of economic and social welfarism. Fourthly, a national consensus was needed if there was to be a viable defense effort. Fifthly, even with efforts to promote economic and social security of the Japanese people and to have international peace, such diplomacy was necessary but not sufficient. Hence advance defense planning was needed against "potential aggression" and "even rare emergencies" because "unpreparedness invites foreign aggression." Sixthly, for Japan it was necessary to have a policy of "autonomous defence" that corresponded "to the strengthening of its economic power and the rise in its international position." Seventhly,

> As long as we do not have nuclear weapons and other
> offensive armament, and as long as there are no major
> changes in the international situation, the Japan-United
> States security arrangements will be necessary for our
> protection . . . . such a system [of joint defense] is
> not incompatible with autonomous defence.

Eighthly,

> However, one point to which attention should be given
> in joint defence is that the nation must not harbor
> vague expectations toward its partner or fall into de-
> pendence on it, seeking to be saved by the partner.
> Such expectations and dependence will involve the
> danger of not only implanting a sense of irresponsibil-
> ity toward national defence among the people, but also
> of degenerating the national spirit.

And finally,

> With regard to nuclear weapons, we adopt the three
> point non-nuclear principle. Even though it would be
> possible to say that in legal and theoretical sense pos-
> session of small nuclear weapon, falling within the
> minimum requirement for capacity necessary for self-
> defence and not posing a threat of aggression to other
> countries, would be permissible, the government, as
> its policy, adopts the principle of not attempting at
> nuclear armament which might be possible under the
> Constitution. [11]

Several inferences can be drawn from these official perspectives. First, considering that the constitution (Article 9) was meant to demilitarize Japan, there are now no theoretical or constitutional barriers against rearmament under civilian control. Even the stance against nuclear arms is one of policy and preference, depending on external and domestic politics and depending on the assessment of Japanese national interests. Secondly, there is a stress on preventive diplomacy and a concern for relating defense planning even to "rare emergencies" that can happen unexpectedly. One implication of Japan's rejection of a policy of heavy armament and nuclear arms is that the current international and regional situation gives Japan, in terms of Japanese perceptions, a sense of security because of the complex interplay of factors and forces in Japan's environment. Another implication, however, is that if and when the environment changed, the present policy and its parameters could also change. Thirdly, the official perspectives reveal a constant attentiveness to the need to shape domestic support for official policies; hence the concern with national consensus. This makes sense because Japanese politics are fragmented and are vulnerable to external intrusiveness and influence in decision making. Japan cannot have much of an "autonomous defense" with a fragmented Japanese public. Fourthly, the concern with Japan's "international position" and economic power points to a need to assess the role of the Japanese self-image in its evolving defense policy. One approach is to argue that Japan's economic power has grown; therefore its international position has grown; and, therefore, both these developments require a greater defense investment—in the name of either joint defense or an autonomous defense. But there is another view: because the nature of the international system is not fixed and the environment for Japan is fluid, because economic diplomacy cannot necessarily be converted into political power and influence, because Japan's economic situation is now more complicated than it was before the oil crisis in 1973, the linkage of defense, economic power, and international position is complicated. Taking the concern with Japan's international position and the search for security arrangements that do not create dependency (both points are also highlighted in the 1977 Defence White Paper) as the independent variables, it may be hypothesized that, should the international and the regional situation deteriorate according to Japanese perceptions, and should such changes imply a threat to Japanese national interests, militarization and nuclearization of the Japanese environment through Japanese initiatives under civilian control and with popular encouragement could be the result. Seeking influence through economic power rather than military force is the preferred policy for Japan today. The Japanese approach is not unique because the Federal Republic of Germany has had a similar approach. The Federal Republic of Germany and the Japanese cases are not completely identical though, because the Federal Republic of Germany is in Europe and a part of NATO. U.S. strategy and interests in Europe are said to be more important to the United States than its strategy and interests in the Far East. This may explain the position of the Federal Republic of Germany as an economic power and a formal alliance partner in NATO, whereas Japan is an economic power that currently shares a joint defense relationship with the United States but nevertheless aspires to an autonomous defense status. The latter indicates that the integration of Japanese thinking and American thinking is not total. This may or may not be significant, because alliance partners often disagree among themselves while accepting the major alliance goals. Also, the quest for an autonomous defense could simply mean a public relations exercise to please nationalist Japanese opinion. Furthermore, a tightly fused defense relationship between Japan and the United States may currently be unnecessary also for external reasons—namely, the threat-perceptions about Northeast Asian security do not involve any imminence of war. Still, the range of choice is that Japan either goes the way of the Federal Republic of Germany and integrates itself into the imperfect but multilateral European economic and military community, where the multilateral forums dilute the U.S. impact; or Japan stays in a position of ambiguity (as it is now)—seeking the theory of autonomous defense while practicing joint defense in the context of continued weakness of the PRC and the Soviet Union in Asia; or Japan implements the theory of autonomous defense by moving not toward unarmed neutralism, not toward an anti-U.S. stance, not toward armed Gaullism, but toward a posture that innovatively and constructively establishes interactions with and distance from the great powers irrespective of ideology. This last course would, furthermore, stress continent-crossing, influence-seeking exchanges with major actors in Southeast Asia, South Asia, Middle East, Latin America, southern Africa, and so on, and would result in the adoption of a postneutral defense policy with post-Gaullist overtones, with an independent nuclear presence in a world that is not prone to disarm.

If neutralism is defined as the diplomacy of seeking peace and influence without reliance on military force, and if Gaullism is defined as the diplomacy of seeking influence through strategic arms and by repudiating formal membership in the Western alliance system, then Japanese behavior has elements of neutralism and Gaullism but neither concept describes completely the Japanese security situation at present and in the foreseeable future. For the "neutrals," like India, the meanings of neutralism or nonalignment have changed over time. In the 1950s it was nonalignment, or the diplomacy of peace without the full support of military force. After the 1962 crisis, peace diplomacy was buttressed with the existence of military force; this force was applied in the wars with Pakistan in 1965 and 1971, and, in 1971, military diplomacy was employed against the United States and the PRC. Later, nonalignment acquired another dimension: India exploded a nuclear device in 1974 and India's nuclear option also became a part of the Indian landscape. In this sense Indian neutralism or nonalignment after 1962 may be described as postneutralism.

The concept of post-Gaullism also describes the behavior of certain states in the world today. Gaullism was an attempt to create some political distance between Paris and Washington and thereby to build bridges between the Atlantic and the Urals. The exercise did not succeed because Moscow was interested in dealing directly with Washington. It rejected the existence of Paris as an independent deterrent. Paris was not accepted as an independent third force in international relations, just as Moscow has always remained suspicious of nonalignment as a third force. (Alternatively, Moscow has been willing to see nonalignment as an instrument to promote the cause of anti-imperialism and anticolonialism, but in a bipolar context.) While Gaullism revealed a tough French stance against the United States and a search for extensive negotiations with the Eastern bloc nations, post-Gaullism, as practiced by President Valery Giscard D'Estaing, gradually moved France toward the United States without discarding the French nuclear force. Indeed, in French thinking, the acquisition of nuclear arms was a symbol of the rule-making role of France in international security matters; and this was reinforced by the fact that all permanent members of the United Nations Security Council possessed nuclear weapons. Today, France has rejoined the international disarmament dialogue. It has made its point by insisting on a reform of the UN disarmament machinery as a condition for its participation. To an extent, therefore, French nuclear arms have been used to make the point that there is political mileage to be gained from the imagery surrounding possession of nuclear arms irrespective of the size and sophistication of the force. Still, it is useful to describe this as post-Gaullism. French entry into the international security debate, through its entry into the disarmament debate, was arranged by De Gaulle's successors. Paris paid the price of accepting the multilateral constraints of the rules of the Nuclear Suppliers Group at London in return for getting satisfaction for French interests in the disarmament field.*

---

*The price was the acceptance of the policy of not exporting sensitive reprocessing and enrichment technology whether or not effective safeguards are in place.

The foregoing analogies are not meant to suggest that Japan must go through the processes followed by India and France to shift from neutralism and Gaullism to postneutralism and post-Gaullism respectively. At first glance there seem to be no similarities among these countries. A closer look, however, reveals the applicability of the theme of postneutralism and post-Gaullism. It lies in the recognition that the great divide is not between these societies but between the United States on one hand and the Europeans, Japanese, and moderate Third World and moderate nonaligned nations on the other. The difference is substantial and turns on one point: whereas the United States learned nothing from the cold war, and is still preparing for another cold war, the others have learned the lesson that they need to develop cosmopolitan habits of cooperation. There is a need to prepare nations to practice the peace by developing interdependencies on issues that require the creation of opportunities for cooperation rather than a definition of strategic threats in narrow anti-Soviet or anticommunist terms.

The views of the future represented by this seemingly theoretical distinction differ substantially in terms of their practical implications. Preparing for another cold war implies that the primary stress is to be on political and strategic, rather than economic and commercial, relations. The former implies interactions among competitive subnational groups and requires projection of tough international positions and postures. The latter implies a stress on transnational activity, where the currency of exchange is common, ideology is of little or no importance, and governments seek to pursue interests and achieve consensus through extensive negotiations. Japan has sought to mold its international presence according to the second model. If the United States fails to settle its domestic debate on foreign policy, a number of considerations could strengthen the incentives toward a Japanese nuclear option if not nuclear weapons: if international peace diplomacy fails to move nations to disarm; if international economic cooperation diplomacy fails to win the argument to practice peace rather than prepare for another cold war; if American society remains fragmented on this issue and the trend is toward tough postures rather than toward extensive negotiations; and, finally, if the international consensus is against the use of nuclear weapons rather than against the development of ambiguous options to check ambiguous strategic situations.

Today Japan has to function in the context of fragmentation of the U.S. electorate, and there is a lack of consensus among members of U.S. elites about the future of America in world affairs. It is essential to note the basic shift that has already appeared in international relations. In traditional international relations and in the cold war, political and strategic perceptions shaped international interactions. The business, commercial, and financial institutions operated within the parameters laid out by the political and strategic elites. Today the political and strategic parameters are shaky; the political and strategic dialogue is limited to a select few academics and policy makers. When the political and strategic parameters were dominant, competitive subnationalism was muted and under control; this was more so in a bipolar system, when the enemy was clearly defined. Furthermore, nationalism and the state were the basic factors in international life, and multinationals were basically meant to be the servants of the nation-state.

Today, international economic cooperation implies the existence of an international elite network, where the priorities are primarily economic. The rules of the game stress a fair exchange of goods and value; the enemy is hard to define and a global civilization is emerging that is something like the cosmopolitanism of eighteenth-century Europe, even though the scale of global communications and of transactions today is unparalleled. Still, the rise of an international economic system signals the emergence of a world citizenry that is nonideological and optimistic. Here, the breakdown of bipolarity marks the rise of cosmopolitanism and the weakening of the central influence of the political and strategic elite. The breakdown of bipolarity also means that domestic conflict is no longer muted and subnational rivalry is more intense. Thus the competitive, subnational forces are challenging the cosmopolitan international economic forces who want to practice peace rather than to prepare for another cold war. In these terms the international system is fragmented into subnational forces and cosmopolitan forces. Wars are likely when the exchange-oriented cosmopolitan forces fail and competitive, subnational forces get the upper hand.

The failure of cosmopolitanism can mean two things. First, the communication gap exists not only between nations but also within a nation; secondly, the impact of interdependence is not fully understood. Interdependence refers to linkages between domestic and foreign policies, but furthermore, there are linkages among issues dealing with oil, balance of trade, arms sales, energy policy, human rights, and so on, and it is no longer possible to establish clear boundaries among such issues. [12]

The central lesson of postneutralism and post-Gaullism is that proud and powerful societies like France, India, and Japan cannot exempt themselves from the opportunities and obligations of engaging in international power politics even though the advocacy of cosmopolitanism favors peaceful exchanges rather than threat-prone activity. For France, the lesson was learned in the 1970s; for India the lesson was learned in the 1960s and 1970s (although Chapter 8 reveals that Indian nuclear decision making is fragmented). India's unwillingness

to reject the nuclear option and to disband its military machine reveals that it is an emerging power—as a regional influence in the
subcontinent and as a participant in the international nuclear and
disarmament debate. Unlike India, Japan took the road of international economic cosmopolitanism, but it now confronts the danger of
fragmentation (rather than isolationism) in U.S. foreign policy. Today there is no consensus between the United States on one hand and
Europe and Japan on the other hand. With respect to nuclear proliferation, the United States is still trying to prevent a nuclear war,
whereas its allies are trying to build channels of cooperation to promote the peaceful uses of nuclear energy. For Europe and Japan,
energy decisions must be made today because of the dependence of
these nations on foreign supplies. For the United States there is
plenty of time to decide. Without a clear consensus in the American
body politic on questions that affect others the issue is not American
isolationism. The issue is the U.S. failure to settle its domestic
dispute about its future role in world affairs. Isolationism can be
a deliberate stance based on enormous strength. But isolationism
can also be a consequence of domestic confusion and fragmentation—
where optimism and pessimism alternate. There is no one in America
today to integrate ideas and policies. Such a mood causes confusion in
the ranks of American allies. The points discussed above strike at
the heart of NATO and Western alliance relations. They indicate that
the Western alliance system is coming apart. It is in this context
that the following section assesses the future of Japan's nuclear
option.

JAPAN'S NUCLEAR OPTION

At present there is a case against the proposition that Japan
will acquire nuclear weapons. Japan lacks a domestic consensus on
the issue; nuclear weapons are costly, economically and politically;
they would not necessarily enhance Japanese security; Japan lacks
testing sites to develop an explosives capability; an explicit Japanese
nuclear weapons program would arouse an international and regional
reaction against Japanese militarism and would upset the existing
situation of no war and no peace in the region. Even if the constitutional position expressed by Article 9 is ignored, there are a number of important considerations against a nuclear weapons decision.
But, on the other hand, there is a case for an ambiguous nuclear option that stops at the pre-explosive stage. According to
Z. Brzezinski and George Ball, an isolationist America could result
in a nationalist and a militaristic Japan.[13] Chalmers Johnson argues
that Japan is not going nuclear but is going internationalist. There

is, however, a debate in the Japanese press about the implications of a nuclearizing PRC, and the delay in ratifying the NPT reveals serious reservations. But Japan does seem at present to have reached a conclusion against having <u>offensive</u> arms.[14] If Japanese internationalism is to be strengthened and maintained, the United States must "avoid acts and policies that deceive the rest of the world about its true strength and that create destabilising uncertainties about its willingness to fulfill its unavoidable commitments." But if the United States decides to go it alone or acts in strategic matters "in such a way that ambiguity rather than certainty is the norm, then it is futile to imagine that Japan, or any other comparably placed nation, is not going at least to attempt to bring order out of the resultant chaos through military deterrence."[15]

This view points to the theme of this chapter. Japan is likely to shape its nuclear option not simply because of evidence of an isolationist United States (as stressed by Brzezinski and Ball), but even if U.S. behavior fails to promote internationalism and cosmopolitanism in international life and if international security relations become ambiguous. The growing emphasis on military deterrence (including nuclear deterrence) is not a solution, but it is a position to fall back on, in which the old political and strategic policy parameters reassert themselves over the new ones that tried to secure internationalism and cosmopolitanism. There is ample evidence to indicate that international developments are affecting Japanese perceptions with respect to the future of internationalism. If the U.S. public and elite debate on the future of American foreign relations remains inconclusive—as seems to be the probability now—then the rise of the military and nuclear factor in Japanese external relations seems inevitable.

The Japanese case can be examined in terms of two hypotheses. First, nuclear proliferation is beyond control; the question is not to prevent possession of nuclear weapons but to prevent the <u>use</u> of nuclear weapons by limiting the use of these weapons against NNWS and by reducing the level of nuclear arms so that the arms race is toned down. This exercise can ideally lead to a situation where nuclear weapons in the future can acquire a status similar to that of gold and diamonds. Possession of such expensive items cannot be denied to those who want them. But at the same time, because of the risks of displaying these expensive things in an insecure environment, those who want them also have the responsibility to protect them. But because gold and diamonds do not harm others as does radioactive plutonium, the storage should be such as to ensure confidence among the entire community. So possession and storage are two separate issues and are not necessarily linked. This distinction could become meaningful in the Japanese debate if it became clear that Japanese peace and disarmament policy had failed to tone down the international arms race and that continued fragmentation (as distinct from isolationism) in U.S. behavior required the acquisition of a nuclear option and possibly nuclear weapons. Japanese defense discussions will not exclude the question of a domestic nuclear debate, but will keep the debate low-key and manageable until defense consciousness among the Japanese people is sufficiently high to permit the development of a consensus on external issues. In other words, let anyone who wants nuclear weapons have them, if they can, for the sake of the world, take precautions about safe storage.

The second hypothesis argues that the crucial matter is to prevent the possession of nuclear arms; that the development of an international consensus on this point is possible; that current international diplomacy (including Japanese diplomacy) on this approach is working but slowly; that proliferation can still be controlled; that India's 1974 test weakened the inhibitions among others because of its pace-setting capacity in the world; but that one need not be pessimistic about proliferation because it is not easy to make nuclear weapons, safeguards are there to catch diversions, and so on.

It makes sense to speak of Japan's nuclear option in terms of the first hypothesis. The status of Japan's nuclear industry has been discussed extensively elsewhere,[16] and it is also summarized in a subsequent section of this chapter.

The declaratory Japanese positions merit attention because they reveal attitudes and are sources of change in the future. The context is that Japanese security thinking has evolved in a phasal fashion in the postwar environment. Up until 1960, there was a total reliance on the United States. During 1960-65 the reliance became partial, and during 1965-68 it became selective. Thereafter, Japan adopted the notion of "autonomous defense," even though it has yet to implement this in terms of its equipment acquisition, budgetary commitment, and force structure policies. It is arguable that "de-Americanisation" (this is Makoto Momoi's term), which was signaled in the 1972 White Paper on Foreign Policy, was followed by a "re-Americanisation" in 1975. Thus it is not the intent here to argue that there are no zigzags in Japanese behavior. Rather, it is to argue that even with the changes there is a movement toward gradual militarization and nuclearization of the Japanese because of their perceptions of international and regional changes, and particularly of the future of U.S. foreign relations in world affairs.

There is enough ambiguity in Japanese statements to argue that its commitment at present against Japanese nuclear weapons and toward an international nonproliferation regime is highly conditional. A sampling of private and official views makes this clear. The following themes reveal the motivational and attitudinal factors

that could underlie a further evolution of Japanese security thinking
if the Japanese perceived a deterioration in the strategic environment, particularly with respect to U.S. capability and intent. The
spectrum of potential change can be identified in terms of the following themes.

Peace diplomacy and arms-build-up are considered first. According to Morinosuke Kajima (writing in 1969), former chairman of
the ruling Liberal Democratic Party's foreign relations research
committee and acting chairman of the foreign affairs committee in
the upper house of the Japanese Parliament:

> Japan's current state of disarmament and defenceless-
> ness does not necessarily spell a contribution to peace.
> Because peace calls for an arms reduction under one
> situation and a defence buildup under another . . . .
> if a nation, preoccupied with pacifism, neglects her
> armament, while her neighbour is looking for a chance
> for aggression, she is merely courting war—not peace.
>   On the other hand, she invites not peace but ag-
> gression, if her rearmament or arms expansion de-
> signed to secure peace leads to an arms race with her
> peaceful neighbour.
>   Every issue of peace must be treated individual-
> ly . . . . peace can be secured only by a superior
> military might—the combined capability of Japan, her
> allies, and protectors.[17]

On the effect of nuclearization of Japan's environment, Kajima
notes

> if the nuclear arms race continues unabated, and Asia
> becomes engaged in nuclear proliferation, the prob-
> lem of guaranteeing the safety of Japan will take on
> added complexities.[18]

Kajima also dealt with the NPT and the denuclearization of
the NWS.

> Since the nonnuclear-weapon state is permanently re-
> nouncing any intention to possess nuclear weapons for
> the sake of world peace and security, the nuclear-
> weapon state should in return, reduce its nuclear
> armaments.[19]

On the importance of peaceful uses of nuclear energy, including peaceful nuclear explosions, Kajima made a number of points.
It was a "matter of principle" to reserve the right to utilize nuclear
power for peaceful purposes. The NPT guaranteed equal opportunity to utilize the "benefits of nuclear explosion for peaceful purposes." The question of peaceful uses of nuclear explosion was
"closely related" to the peaceful uses of atomic energy. Even though
PNEs had not reached a practical stage, the problem of differentiat-
ing between military and peaceful purposes could be solved by international inspection. And "when" this becomes a practical question,
then nonnuclear-weapon states ought to have the "right of equal opportunity" without discrimination in the system of inspection.[20]

Each of the foregoing themes finds muted support in official
statements by Japan.[21] However, the Japanese style is to focus on
concrete issues and then to move to the broad ones. It is for this
reason that the focus of official statements is on the third and fourth
aspects rather than primarily on the first two—although statements
by previous governments, and Japanese behavior, indicate that the
first two aspects are givens in Japanese foreign and security policies.
The latter two aspects deal with immediate issues and the former
two refer to long-term possibilities. Since theoretical rights are
asserted in these aspects, implementation of the theoretical rights
could become real probabilities depending on Japanese threat perceptions; that is, if instead of viewing the current balance and the
underlying regional and international processes as stabilizing, the
Japanese were to conclude that U.S. foreign policy was moving
away from international cooperation and was paralyzed by the lack
of consensus about foreign policy and military and nuclear proliferation policies.

GROWING JAPANESE NUCLEAR NATIONALISM

Japan entered the NPT system formally in the mid-1970s,
after a prolonged domestic debate and with reservations about the
NPT.[22] The treaty was ratified after about six years of hesitation.
The safeguards agreement[23] with the IAEA was finalized after the
conclusion of the Tokai Muro negotiations with the United States,
which on a two-year basis permitted Japan to go ahead with its reprocessing work, pending the outcome of the results of the INFCE
(1977-79). So the approval by the Japanese Parliament (Diet) of the
safeguards agreement came in the context of embarrassing questions
from Diet members about Canadian, American, and Australian restrictions on uranium supply and about Carter's antiplutonium fuel
cycle drive. Japan Quarterly, an influential journal, for instance

argued that Japan was already a part of the NPT and accepted international safeguards. It was acceptable for the United States to suspend plans for commercial reprocessing but "it has no right to compel other nations to do likewise." In Japanese eyes Carter's nuclear policy raised a "number of doubts." "What value should Japan place on the role of the Nuclear Non-proliferation Treaty?" was one such question. Furthermore, because Carter's policy seemed to be a reaction to the Indian nuclear explosion in 1974, there was nevertheless a need to differentiate between parties and nonparties in the NPT system. The assessment concludes that "the new U.S. policy of curbing the peaceful use of nuclear energy might result in weakening the nonproliferation system."[24] In other words, the future of international and bilateral nuclear cooperation seemed to be in doubt in Japanese perceptions.

Japanese nuclear nationalism is fueled by a number of recent circumstances that affect Japanese perceptions and policies. According to the Japanese ten years have passed since the NPT was adopted by the world community. During this period many things have happened—particularly the oil crisis in 1973 and India's nuclear test in 1974. The NPT remains the fundamental framework for securing an international solution to the proliferation issue but the regime needs to be supplemented. Several measures have been taken in this regard. The London Nuclear Suppliers Group has established guidelines for exports of sensitive nuclear technology, equipment, and materials. Efforts are underway to strengthen the IAEA safeguards system. But there is a need to move toward nuclear disarmament (Article VI of the NPT), to implement Articles IV and V of the NPT, and generally to strengthen the NPT regime without interfering with the peaceful nuclear program of NPT parties. In short, there are problems with the NPT regime but officials have to be optimistic in finding solutions for these problems. Japanese sources reminded the United States about its reservations in accepting the NPT, particularly with regard to Article IV. Japanese sources also emphasize that their ratification of the NPT strengthened the regime and also facilitated the dialogue at the INFCE meetings, which took place without a U.S.-Japan controversy over Tokai Muro in the background. Consequently, if multilateral solutions are to be found, consensus building in multilateral and bilateral relations is desired by Japan.

Although the foregoing represents the general Japanese preference and approach to nuclear energy and proliferation questions, nevertheless concrete issues arise and these generate Japanese nuclear nationalism. Multilateralism is preferred to bilateralism in Japan's approach to these questions, because the former approach assists the Japanese negotiating position vis-à-vis the United States.

For instance, as early as 1959 Japan sought application of IAEA safeguards rather than bilateral ones. [25] In the 1958 U.S.-Japan agreement, the question of reprocessing was at the discretion of the U.S. Atomic Energy Commission. This agreement was re-negotiated. The 1968 agreement, as amended in 1973 (Article 8[c]), deals directly with the reprocessing issue, which became controversial in the Tokai Muro discussions because of Carter's insistence that reprocessing be delayed indefinitely. However, the Carter position conflicts with Article 8(c) of the 1973 agreement. In this agreement, when Japan wants to reprocess spent fuel of nuclear materials received from the United States, Japan requires only a "joint determination" with the United States to confirm that "effective safeguards" are in place according to Article 11 of the agreement. Joint determination, however, does not mean American "prior consent," which is what President Carter seeks—and this is what the 1958 agreement allowed. The difference is subtle but nevertheless fundamental. In the 1973 agreement, the sole criterion is a joint determination that safeguards are effective; it is not about the desirability or lack thereof of reprocessing. Prolonged and bitter discussions over Tokai Muro resulted in an interim agreement in 1977 to permit reprocessing of 99 tons of fuel during a two-year period—that is, pending the outcome of INFCE. So, in effect, today the United States accepts on a limited basis the Japanese interpretation of Article 8(c) of the 1973 agreement. This creates problems for Japan because of the fear that this "is a revival of similar provisions that were found in bilateral agreements until about ten years ago, at which time such provisions were deleted in the hope that the IAEA safeguards would take care of the matter." [26]

The Japanese dilemma is how to renegotiate with the United States when the 1973 agreement says one thing and Carter has a different policy preference. Japan's legal case in the U.S.-Japan 1973 agreement seems strong, but it is weakened by the Canada-Japan 1959 agreement. Article 3(d) of the latter says that nuclear materials shall not be reprocessed except as authorized in writing by the supplying party. This is a tough legal formula, and it gives a carte blanche to the Canadian and other suppliers. In the past this was not utilized, given Canada's willingness to be helpful to the Japanese. However, inasmuch as Canadian and American antiproliferation policies have evolved in recent years and have reinforced each other at the same time, even though the legal language varies from the Canada-Japan agreement to the U.S.-Japan agreement, there has been a tendency to shift interpretations and to let the outcomes be a consequence of bargaining strength and skill and of perceptions about the need to accommodate in bilateral relations. The Canadian argument has some merit because all Canadian agreements except with the United

and Euratom countries have prior-consent clauses.* But at the
same time the Canadian insistence on implementing prior consent
is diluted by the absence of any objective criteria about the circumstances in which such consent will be given or not given. This is a
problem common to U.S., Canadian, and Australian insistence on
prior consent for reprocessing of spent fuel. Furthermore, there
is the problem of "double labeling" or "double control": if all suppliers insist on prior consent—suppose Canadian natural uranium
sold to Japan is then sent to the United States for enrichment—Japan
objects to prior consent to begin with and to prior consent of all suppliers. The latter point is not academic, because Japan is currently diversifying its uranium supply sources and it would be unmanageable for Japan to have multiple centers of prior consent before it
could embark on a nuclear activity that is vital for Japan's economic
well-being. So there is a question about the future of prior consent
and on the meaning of the term "supplier." The question was discussed in the London group but all that is agreed is that a working
group has been established to deal internationally with the problem
of multiple controls. The question is important from another angle.
In case of violation of a contractual agreement, nuclear supply agreements require that the material be returned to the supplier. In the
case of Japan (and other nations), the question arises: returned to
whom? It may well be that Japan may be unable to do away with the
prior consent clause even if the problem of double labeling is settled.
Therefore Japan's quest is to secure flexibility in the implementation
of the clause and to secure definitions of criteria that identify the
circumstances under which such consent is given or withheld. If no
such internationally acceptable criteria are established by the nuclear suppliers, then the implication is that flexibility in implementation of criteria is a matter of bargaining between the supplier and
the recipient. In such a case, the supply relationship is likely to

---

*Recently the July 1959 Canada-Japan agreement was amended.
The principal features of the amended agreement are: (1) material
subject to the agreement may not be used for making nuclear weapons
or to further any other military use or to manufacture a nuclear device; (2) the verification is to be done by the IAEA; (3) Japan is not
to enrich uranium beyond 20 percent; (4) retransfers require Canadian "prior consent"; and finally, (5) reprocessed and plutonium and
highly enriched uranium "shall not be stored without the prior written consent of the supplying country." The question of double-labeling,
however, remains to be settled. See Canadian Department of External
Affairs, communique, January 26, 1978.

remain a hostage to the bilateral relationship—to perceptions about the relationship in the suppliers' thinking, to the negotiating skill of the recipient, to the quality of the domestic debate of the supplier, and, finally, to the availability of diverse supply sources that are not entirely subject to concerted action by the suppliers as seems to be the case at present.

Theoretical Japanese positions merit analysis because they reveal parameters of potential change in the future. The government of Japan has issued the following statement.

> No peaceful nuclear activities in non-nuclear-weapon States shall be prohibited or restricted, nor shall the transfer of information, nuclear materials, equipment, or other material relating to the peaceful use of nuclear energy be denied to non-nuclear-weapon States, merely on the grounds that such activities or transfer could be used also for the manufacture of nuclear weapons or other nuclear explosive devices.[27]

The statement went on to say that there was a "paper-thin" distinction between peaceful and military use of nuclear energy; that "utmost care" should be taken to protect peaceful uses that might be curbed in the name of prohibiting military use; and that utmost care should be taken to prevent military uses that could occur under the guise of peaceful use. The statement did not reveal how peaceful and military uses were defined and what sort of criteria might be used to establish the paper-thin distinction. But in not doing so it left open the question for the future and also established a distance from the NPT view that there was no difference between peaceful and military explosions. The Japanese argument seemed to imply that, even if there did not seem to be a clear distinction at present, if and when such a distinction arose the meaning of peaceful uses might possibly include peaceful explosive use. Private Japanese views suggest support for this interpretation. Thus, Y. Kawashima, a well-informed observer of the Japanese nuclear and political scene, points out that "whether development of nuclear explosive devices can be included in the term 'peaceful uses' is a candid question."[28] Another Japanese expert points out that the Japanese Atomic Energy Commission "should at least have complete knowledge of how plutonium can be changed into bombs." But after it has acquired the bomb-making capacity the Japanese AEC should renounce military use of nuclear energy.[29]

These remarks do not necessarily mean that Japan is engaged in a subterfuge to make nuclear bombs secretly. But they do suggest that Japan's renunciation of nuclear weapons and acceptance of the international NPT regime is clouded with many uncertainties. There are circumstances—international and regional political and strategic developments, the future of nuclear supply relations, the evolution of defense and nuclear consciousness within Japan, the concern with acquiring an independent nuclear fuel cycle, the Japanese mistrust of Carter's antiplutonium diplomacy, and so on—that require the Japanese to have an open mind about the need to balance the ideal of international nuclear cooperation with the reality of protecting Japanese interests through a heightened sense of nationalism.

A mix of three types of elements induces the Japanese to build their nuclear and political options. One element involves technical considerations and the other two are political ones. The technical element is that the purpose of INFCE is to get a better airing of views so that individual governments can demonstrate enlightened self-interest and may reduce their enthusiasm for plutonium, reprocessing, and enrichment. INFCE is meant to avoid the problems of having a cartel-like group decide international concerns without the participation of all concerned parties. The difference between the London Nuclear Suppliers Group and INFCE lies in a totally different approach. The former established guidelines and imposed them on third parties (recipients) without consulting them. The latter involves no imposition because no consensus is being sought and participation is open to all, irrespective of status vis-à-vis the NPT. Still, INFCE was a product of Carter's antiplutonium cycle position and the focus is heavily, in U.S. thinking, against reprocessing. The majority view of participants in INFCE is that no formal agreement on details is likely and there will be no outlawing of reprocessing. This should justify the Japanese position on reprocessing. But for Japan, INFCE is a diversion from the real concern with finding a technical solution to nuclear energy issues that go beyond reprocessing. Reprocessing is not the final solution for Japan. So far the solutions for nuclear waste storage are tentative ones; there is the need to find a solution for materials that come out of reprocessing. One approach may be to limit the scale of plants so that the amount of waste is not too much. Another problem is to find methods to improve IAEA safeguards technology because the system is not accurate enough to prevent or to detect nuclear proliferation. Here technical solutions are needed for technical issues. Thirdly, the development of peaceful uses of nuclear energy has problems to be solved—as for instance, the role of PNEs and the need to implement Article V of the NPT and to establish an international PNE service. The reliability of safety procedures concerning industrial applications of nuclear energy also requires attention, and there is an obvious need to educate the public about the issues and prospects concerning the growing uses of nuclear energy in the foreseeable future.

The search for technical and multilateral solutions, however, is complicated in Japanese thinking by the element of tough politics that has arisen in Carter's antiproliferation diplomacy. Carter's administration has engaged in tough, not extensive, nuclear negotiations and extensive negotiations have been seriously considered when opposing views have emerged from Europe, Japan, and certain Third World nations in equally tough fashion. The problem, according to confidential U.S. and overseas interviews, is that in formulating and implementing his nuclear nonproliferation policies, Carter has not listened either to his allies or to his adversaries within and outside the United States. Messages simply have not been getting to the presidential level. Carter's idea of a nuclear dialogue has not worked within the United States and abroad because Carter himself has not bothered to listen and his advisers have not dared to offer him advice that they feel (rightly or wrongly) he does not want to hear. Some Japanese and experts from several other nations agree that among Carter's advisers there is a "reasonable" group, consisting of Ambassador Gerald Smith and scholars-turned-officials like Joseph Nye and Lawrence Scheinmann (in the State Department), while the "unreasonable" group consists of radical antiproliferators like Jessica Tuchman (in the National Security Council), who enjoys the support of doctrinaire elements in the Senate (like Senators Ribicoff, Percy, and Glenn), in the House of Representatives (like Congressman Zabloski), and among scholars like Albert Wohstetter and Theodore Taylor. Among his advisers Admiral Rickover has been considered influential, but the fact is that the president and the admiral have rarely met, and the admiral has been content not to disturb the president provided the latter responds in kind. The Carter administration is deeply divided on the nuclear issues, and behind the tough posture lies a loose and a confused core of bureaucratic debate that has no consensus. With such confusion in the thinking of its prime ally, the Japanese seem to have no choice but to fend for themselves in the political and technical aspects of nuclear supply negotiations and nuclear energy planning, as well as their long-term debating about the future of international safeguards and their search for a reliable regime that does not prevent Japanese nuclear development.

The third element, which reinforces the concerns expressed in the first two elements, lies in the Japanese recognition that ideally there ought to be a "stress-free" world, involving East-West and North-South relations, and with that ideal there would not be proliferation problems. Such a quest has two different implications. One is that Japan will do nothing to hinder this quest, and even if the regional and international environment remains ambiguous and volatile, Japan will continue to avoid gloomy forecasts. The other, however, is that Japan will tire of its quest for multilateral solutions even for its bilateral problems and thereby revert to nationalism in the defense and nuclear area. The latter could become a method to respond to a fluid international system where at the very least the United States lacks a domestic consensus on its external policies.

The pattern of Japan's nuclear industry at present does not reveal a trend toward the acquisition of a nuclear weapons force complete with a command and control mechanism and a nuclear strategy. Ambiguities in the Asian and international environment do not warrant a premature decision to move toward weapons acquisition decisions, but such ambiguities cast doubt on the prospect of success in Japan's effort to find an international consensus that satisfies third-party and Japanese interests. In Japan's case, the quest for nuclear independence lies in the quest for an independent nuclear fuel cycle. The Ministry of International Trade and Industry (MITI) has drawn up a 20-year program to develop all aspects of the fuel cycle. Even if cost overruns and project implementation delays are probable— as is the case with nuclear industry worldwide—the projections call for growing emphasis on nuclear energy for domestic use, accompanied by a search for nuclear fuel independence. Table 10.4 offers an overview of Japan's nuclear program and Table 10.5 outlines the long-term nuclear fuel demand-and-supply estimates. At present Japan has contracted to develop a number of overseas uranium mines in Niger, Mauritania (with French collaboration), and in the Spokane region in the United States (with French collaboration). In this way, Japanese requirements are covered up to the second half of the 1980s, but for the 1990s problems are posed because of uncertain supply sources. It seems that for this period the Japanese uranium industry may not be able to expand single-handedly investment capacity. Japan may be forced to harmonize its interests with the existing and new uranium suppliers (including Australia and South Africa) and to proceed to the fast breeder route to eliminate or reduce dependence on uranium imports.

At present Japan's nuclear program is based on the following focal points, as outlined by an expert report. [30]

1. The most urgent problem to solve is the problem of finding sites for nuclear power plants to be constructed; this requires the understanding of the Japanese people, who are concerned about safety and environmental concerns.

2. The establishment of a nuclear fuel cycle is the key to the establishment of a Japanese nuclear power generation program. *

———————————

*This, incidentally, is also the key to Japanese nuclear independence should Japan ever decide to have a military program.

TABLE 10.4

Japanese Investment in Nuclear Fuel Cycle (cumulative)
(hundreds of million yen at 1975 prices)

	1976-85	1986-90	1991-95	Total	Scale of Facilities
Uranium mining	1,710	1,590	2,030	5,330	Development of mine
Exploration, development	(570)	(530)	(677)	(1,777)	capable of producing 7,000 St U_3O_3 per year, including fluorine production, by fiscal 1975
Conversion	100	140	180	420	
	(33)	(47)	(60)	(140)	
Enrichment					
Domestic plants	1,890	2,330	3,120	7,340	4,000 tons SWU per
	(630)	(777)	(1,040)	(2,447)	year by fiscal 1995
Fuel processing					
Fabrication	420	190	200	810	5,700 tons of uranium
	(140)	(63)	(67)	(270)	per year by fiscal 1995
Zircalloy tube	330	170	170	670	1,300 tons of cladded
	(110)	(57)	(57)	(233)	tube per year and 2,500 tons of zirconium per year, both by 1995
Reprocessing					
Light-water reactors	2,435	1,545	1,210	5,190	Two plants turning out
	(812)	(515)	(403)	(1,730)	5 tons per day
Breakdown:					
Reprocessing-related	1,955	1,005	710	3,670	
	(652)	(335)	(237)	(1,223)	
Pu-related	220	100	70	390	2,000 tons of mix oxide
	(73)	(33)	(23)	(130)	per year
Transport	260	440	430	1,130	11 ships, 88 casks, etc.
	(87)	(147)	(143)	(377)	
Fast breeder	—	20	430	450	
	—	(7)	(143)	(150)	
Waste					
Low level	1,220	940	1,270	3,430	
	(407)	(313)	(423)	(1,143)	
Breakdown:					
Conditioning	780	500	580	1,860	Reduction of volume pro-
	(260)	(167)	(193)	(620)	duced at nuclear power
Disposal	440	440	690	1,570	Reduction of volume and
	(147)	(147)	(230)	(523)	storage at site
High level	5	515	510	1,030	Solidification and stor-
	(2)	(172)	(170)	(343)	age facilities
Total investment	9,470	6,560	9,150	25,180	
	(3,157)	(2,187)	(3,050)	(8,393)	

Note: Figures in parentheses represent millions of dollars.
Source: Confidential source in Tokyo.

TABLE 10.5

Long-term Nuclear Fuel Demand-and-Supply Estimates for Japan

	1980	1985	1990	1995
Generating capacity (10,000 KW unit)	1,640	4,900	8,900	12,900
Natural uranium (short ton U_3O_8)				
Consumption				
Annual	6,700	16,100	24,700	33,400
Cumulative	30,200	92,800	199,000	348,500
Supply (annual)				
Through long-term contracts	8,900	11,800	14,500	21,700
Imports with development	1,100	2,100	4,100	7,100
Recycling	200	2,100	3,100	4,600
Total	10,200	16,000	21,700	33,400
Enriched uranium (tons SWU)				
Consumption				
Annual	2,000	5,100	8,800	12,200
Cumulative	12,000	32,000	60,400	114,600
Supply (annual)				
Purchase	2,300	5,600	6,700	6,500
International cooperative ventures	—	1,000	1,000	1,000
National product	50	500	1,000	4,000
Recycling	—	—	70	70
Total	2,350	7,100	8,770	11,570
Fabrication (tons U)				
Consumption				
Annual	510	1,590	2,790	3,800
Cumulative	3,360	10,200	22,000	39,100
Supply (annual)	730	2,150	3,350	4,550
Reprocessing (tons U)				
Consumption				
Annual	320	550	1,720	2,710
Cumulative	1,070	3,220	9,580	21,150
Supply (annual)				
From abroad	250	380	350	0
National	170	170	1,370	2,710
Radioactive waste (1,000 drums of 200 liters)				
Low level				
Annual	73	220	420	630
Cumulative	330	1,010	2,730	5,240
High level				
Annual	20	20	160	300
Cumulative	60	160	680	1,800

Source: Report of Nuclear Fuel Research Committee, advisory body to Agency of National Resources and Energy, MITI, Japan.

3. An independent nuclear fuel cycle requires acquisition of uranium resources and of reprocessing and enrichment capabilities.

4. The advanced thermal reactor and the fast breeder reactors are meant to succeed the present light-water reactor system in Japan.

5. Power generation by solar energy and geothermal power generation is still in the research-and-development stage at present, and there is no immediate alternative to atomic energy at present.

6. Transport and stockpile are easier for fissionable fuels than for fossil fuels; and anxiety about energy resources depletion can be dispelled with the fast breeder reactors.

7. The role of atomic energy as targeted is growing as follows, for instance: by 1985 it is 12.1 percent (of total energy sources) for the United States; 14.6 percent for the Federal Republic of Germany; 25 percent for France, and 9.6 percent for Japan.

The foregoing report reveals considerable sensitivity to the trends in the international environment: "the current circumstances surrounding Japan's efforts for the development and utilisation of atomic energy are very severe, while the international situation is also extremely fluid."

CONCLUSION

In his valuable study, John E. Endicott makes three points. A Japanese nuclear weapons decision will be postponed until the Japanese perceive a serious international threat that cannot be met through existing bilateral and multilateral mechanisms. Second, a PRC ICBM capacity in the future could negate U.S. strategic influence in Northeast Asia and thereby entail a Japanese security force that is independent of American decision making. Finally, as laser technology enters the strategic picture, defensive (such as laser ABMs, according to Endicott) weapons systems may become a viable alternative.[31] So the choice between a nonnuclear Japan and one armed with offensive nuclear weapons may be broadened.

From these observations and from the analysis outlined in this chapter, the general point to be made is that the Japanese commitment against nuclear arms is not irrevocable. Strategic circumstances may require a reassessment of the nuclear factor in Japanese external relations. At present the ambiguity and volatility in the strategic environment in Asia and in the world point to a need for Japan to be highly attentive to its external environment. Japanese nuclear and security consciousness is growing. The process is worth noting. The Japanese style is to focus on specific problems rather than to derive policies from a specific ideological or an attitudinal view of the world. Japan is encountering problems in finding multi-lateral solutions for its bilateral problems, and concerns arise about the lack of consensus in U.S. foreign policy (within elite groups and the public in the United States). The fragmentation in the U.S. decision-making process is likely to inject a concern for having Japanese solutions or alternatives for problems that previously were felt to require multilateral solutions. This is not to suggest that Japan will completely abandon internationalism. But it is to suggest that there is now a shifting emphasis in the balance of nationalism, bilateralism, and multilateralism in Japanese perceptions and diplo-macy. As long as multilateral and bilateral interactions check nationalist tendencies, the fears of a militarist Japan seem to be overdrawn if not completely inaccurate. The absence of a national consensus within Japan about security policies also inhibits rapid decision making. But as Japan becomes more involved in national consensus building—and a need for this is a constant theme in de-fense and nuclear discussions in Japan—the effect of the ambiguities in the international and regional environment on Japanese interests is likely to cause rethinking. Japan's external behavior has grown in scope. Today, Japan not only seeks a balance in its relations with the United States, the Soviet Union, the PRC, and certain parts of the Third World, but is gradually seeking points of contact beyond the relationship with the United States and Europe.

Broadening of these points of contact for Japanese diplomacy becomes an important source of change as the Indias, Brazils, and Irans begin to rethink their unilateral commitment against nuclear weapons, and as these countries begin to realize that it makes sense to limit dependence on the United States and to seek true nonalign-ment—stressing the norm of equal exchange rather than dependency on foreign sources of advice and materials. Today, although the superpowers try to minimize their importance, nuclear weapons are a permanent feature of the international landscape. But the super-powers do not effectively denuclearize themselves or repudiate the implication that possession of nuclear arms gives the right to man-age the world. The longer it takes to denuclearize, the greater are the chances that the nuclear debates will enter the bureaucratic agenda, particularly when nuclear energy is becoming a major ele-ment in the energy situations of many societies. As nuclear con-sciousness grows about the multifaceted implications of nuclear power, as societies recognize that multilateral diplomacies need to be balanced with bilateral and national consideration, these circum-stances are likely to affect Japanese perceptions. This chapter has not examined the possibility of a nuclear Taiwan or a nuclear South Korea and its likely effects on Japan. Rather, it is assumed that because the nuclear factor is usually assessed in terms of overall foreign policy and security considerations, governments in Asia and elsewhere will try consciously to ensure that there is a domestic nuclear debate (and thereby keep the option alive) and yet, at the same time, they will avoid costly (economically and politically) nuclear weapons decisions. If domestic nuclear debates and options become the international norm, pending the failure of the nuclear weapons states to denuclearize themselves (and this seems to be the case now), then Japan's nuclear option will play a part in Japanese thinking about its future in a world without consensus.

NOTES

1. For an overview of Soviet-Japanese relations and the Islands issue see Y. C. Kim, Japanese-Soviet Relations, The Washington Papers, vol. 2, The Center for Strategic and International Studies, Georgetown University (Beverly Hills, Calif.: Sage, 1974).

2. Japanese diplomacy has been described as passive or adaptive to other's initiative. See for instance, James H. Buck, The Modern System (Beverly Hills, Calif.: Sage, 1975), p. 225. Donald C. Hellmann thinks that Japan is not a skilled player and he takes a dim view "of Japan's capability for effective and responsible policy leadership." See Hellmann's foreword in his book Japan and East Asia (London: Pall Mall Press, 1972), pp. x-xi.

3. See T. C. Schelling and D. C. Hellmann's remarks in Conflict in World Politics, ed. Steven L. Spiegel and K. H. Waltz (Cambridge, Mass.: Winthrop, 1971), p. 367.

4. K. Aichi, The Search for National Security, Public Information Bureau, Ministry of Foreign Affairs, Japan, Japan Reference Series no. 4-49, p. 13.

5. Gaston J. Sigur, "Power, Politics, and Defence," in Buck, op. cit., pp. 194-95 (emphasis added).

6. E. Colbert, "National Security Perspectives: Japan and Asia," in Buck, op. cit., p. 216 (emphasis added).

7. F. C. Langdon, Japan's Foreign Policy (Vancouver: University of British Columbia Press, 1973), pp. xii, 2, 191, 197, Chapter 9, and p. 207.

8. Aichi, op. cit., p. 2.

9. Cited in ibid., p. 6.

10. The extracts are from different sections of Aichi's paper, op. cit.

11. These observations and quotations are drawn from White Papers of Japan, 1970-71 annual abstracts of official reports and statistics of the Japanese government, edited and published by the Japanese Institute of International Affairs. For statements that

reflect these views in the 1970s see Defence Bulletin: Defence of Japan—White Paper on Defence (summary) vol. 1, no. 3 (September 1977), Defence Agency, Tokyo, p. 10.

12. This paragraph has benefited greatly from a conversation with Dr. William Whitson of the Congressional Research Service. The responsibility for the views is solely mine.

13. Views of Ball and Brzezinski are cited in Buck, op. cit., p. 277. Also see Note 2 above. See Z. Brzezinski, The Fragile Blossom (New York: Harper and Row, 1972), particularly Chapters 4-6.

14. Chalmers Johnson, "The Japanese Problem," in China and Japan: A New Balance of Power, ed. D. C. Hellmann (Critical Choices for Americans vol. 12) (Lexington, Mass.: D. C. Heath, 1976), pp. 81-82.

15. Ibid., pp. 83-84.

16. For an excellent review see John E. Endicott, Japan's Nuclear Option (New York: Praeger, 1975). See T. Dixon Long, "Technology and Power: Japan Catches Up," in Japan: The Paradox of Progress, ed. Lewis Austin (New Haven: Yale University Press, 1976), Chapter 5.

17. M. Kajima, Modern Japan's Foreign Policy (Rutland, Vt.: Charles E. Tuttle, 1969), pp. 12-13.

18. Ibid., p. 112.

19. Ibid., p. 233.

20. Ibid., pp. 234-36, 238, 240-41.

21. With respect to the latter two themes see Information Bulletin, Public Information Bureau, Ministry of Foreign Affairs, Tokyo, vol. 21, no. 7 (April 1974), pp. 1-3; statement by Ambassador Nisiboro, plenary meeting of Review Conference of Parties to the NPT, May 7, 1975; statement by Japan delegation on Article IV at Second Committee of NPT Review Conference, May 14, 1975; and statement by Japan delegation on Article V at Second Committee of NPT Review Conference, May 15, 1975.

22. For the reservations see Y. Sato, "Japan's Response to Nuclear Developments: Beyond Nuclear Allergy," in Nuclear Proliferation and the Near-Nuclear Countries, ed. O. Marwah and A. Schultz (Cambridge, Mass.: Ballinger, 1975), pp. 246-47.

23. See Agreement between the Government of Japan and the International Atomic Energy Agency in Implementation of Articles III.I and 4 of the Treaty on the Non-proliferation of Nuclear Weapons, Vienna, March 4, 1977.

24. See "Carter's Nuclear Energy Policy and Japan's Position" (unsigned article), Japan Quarterly 24, no. 3 (July/September 1977): 273.

25. Y. Kawashima, "Safeguards for the Peaceful Nuclear Fuel Cycle," no publishing data, p. 309.

26. Ibid., p. 318.

27. Statement by Japan delegation on Article IV, May 14, 1975, op. cit. (emphasis added).

28. Kawashima, op. cit., p. 318.

29. Cited in Yanada Hiroyoshi, "From the Newspapers and Magazines," Japan Quarterly 24, no. 3 (July/September 1977): 356-50.

30. For these points see Japan Atomic Industrial Forum, Nuclear Power Development in Japan (Selected Papers), undated.

31. Endicott, op. cit., Chapter 6.

11

THE PROLIFERATION FACTOR
IN SOUTH AMERICA: THE
BRAZIL-ARGENTINE CASES

INTRODUCTION

Studying proliferation tendencies of two prominent South American states is conceptually useful because these cases reveal yet another variety of "proliferation." The Israeli route is to retain an undemonstrated nuclear option and yet not to discourage officially speculation about its existence. The South African route is also to retain an undemonstrated nuclear option but to discourage officially speculation about it. The Indian route is to demonstrate the option, to keep it partly hidden from international scrutiny and partly visible, but to deny its military use. Brazil and Argentina, like India, assert a theoretical right to acquire nuclear capabilities that make a nuclear option. These countries are important for the study of proliferation in two different ways. The NPT defines proliferation exclusively in terms of a nuclear explosion demonstration. President Carter, on the other hand, defines proliferation as the acquisition of plutonium reprocessing and uranium enrichment facilities. Under the new definition such sensitive facilities are strategic items. Brazil and Argentina meet the second test of a proliferation-prone society, and by the 1980s, if not earlier, Argentina and Brazil (in this order) will possess the capacity to make a bomb. To assess the significance of the nuclear factor in Argentine-Brazilian diplomacy, it is necessary first to examine the parameters, as expressed in the recent past, of the atomic-related activities of these states.

The parameters of the "proliferation" activity of these states rest on the following: the nature of the Argentine atomic energy program before the NPT came into effect; the positions of these states with respect to the Treaty of Tlateloco (1967), which creates a

nuclear weapon-free zone in Latin America—the first zone of its
kind in the world; the game rules of this treaty in relation to other
nonproliferation measures, particularly the NPT; the significance
of the West-German-Brazil nuclear agreement (1975), which transfers the full nuclear fuel cycle to Brazil; the quest for nuclear energy independence—self-reliance if not self-sufficiency—in the behavior of these states; the quest for nuclear disarmament and the
rise of an anti-vertical proliferation tendency in the verbal diplomacy
of these states; and finally, a suspicion about superpower behavior
that freezes existing distribution and organization of world power.
Even though regional rivalry between Argentina and Brazil cannot be
excluded as a motive for proliferation that is meant to guard against
the neighbor, the regional dimension should not be overstated, just
as the international dimension (anti-vertical proliferation, anti-U.S.,
and anti-Soviet attitudes) ought not to be understated.

This chapter indicates that gradual nuclearization of the South
American environment is the dominant tendency. Unless Brazil and
Argentina collapse because of internal disorder, the key premise is
that these societies are cohesive in their attitudes toward nuclear
energy and nuclear proliferation. Partly because of the impact of
these states' diplomacy on Third World thinking, and partly because
of a growing consciousness in the Third World of the implications of
superpower hegemony in proliferation and disarmament matters, the
prospect of the emergence of an anti-vertical proliferation chain
located in the Third World cannot be ruled out. Linkages among
certain Third World societies (namely, Brazil, Argentina, India,
and maybe South Africa) and between these societies and certain industrialized societies (namely, the Federal Republic of Germany,
France, and Japan) point to the emergence of diplomatic chains that
could limit the U.S.'s room for maneuvering in multilateral forums
for diplomacy relating to proliferation policies. The pattern of the
nuclear trade* reveals a devolution of the capacity for international
control that had hitherto been vested in the United States and the
Soviet Union. The superpowers are still important, but they are no
longer able to negotiate international outcomes that can ignore the
quest of an altered world order by many states in contemporary world

---

*The nuclear trade reveals North-South, East-West linkages
such as Canada/Argentina; the Federal Republic of Germany/Argentina;
the Federal Republic of Germany/Brazil; the Federal Republic of Ger-
many/India; the Federal Republic of Germany/South Africa; France/
South Africa, and so on. While the superpowers are still the leaders
in the international nuclear trade, their competitors are changing the
commercial and political parameters of the trade.

politics. This is particularly true with regard to post-NPT multilateral diplomacy. At the United Nations Special Session on Disarmament, held in New York during May–June 1978, Brazil in particular urged that the NPT ought not to be even mentioned in the final
declaration. Brazil did not succeed in eliminating the NPT from the
declaration. Still, its diplomacy signaled a growing suspicion among
many NNWS that the NWS, and particularly the superpowers, are
playing a double game in the disarmament field: they seek to keep
the unarmed nonnuclearized while avoiding sacrifices toward denuclearization of the overarmed. This suspicion first became evident in a multilateral setting at the time the NPT Review Conference
was held in 1975. Brazil's open attack on the NPT signals a massive
growth of that suspicion about the motives of the vertical proliferators.

The parameters and the implications of the South American
nuclear environment will now be considered.

ATOMIC ENERGY PROGRAMS OF
ARGENTINA AND BRAZIL

The details of the atomic energy programs of these states are
well recorded in the literature.[1] It is unnecessary to repeat these
except to note some of the major highlights.

The Argentine atomic program is older and more experienced
than Brazil's. Some of the Argentine atomic facilities are under international safeguards, but on the whole the program is geared to a
policy of autonomy in nuclear decision making. Argentina's program
is based on the natural uranium reactor cycle, whereas the Brazilian
program, by virtue of its cooperation with the United States and the
Federal Republic of Germany, is based on the light water reactor
enriched uranium cycle. The Brazilian nuclear industry at present
is entirely under international safeguards, but the Argentine nuclear
industry is not. The significance of this difference depends on an
assessment of the following considerations: (1) both states claim the
right to conduct peaceful nuclear explosions (PNEs) if they wish,
and the claim is asserted in terms of Article 18 of the Treaty of
Tlatelolco (1967); (2) both states do not accept the NPT and their rejection, like India's, is final; (3) if international safeguards are weak
instruments to prevent nuclear proliferation—and even if determination of diversion within a short detection time is problematic—
Brazilian acceptance of safeguards is by definition a false assurance.
This is not to suggest that Brazil has accepted safeguards now with
the intent to violate them in the 1980s. Instead two different points
can be made. First, safeguards can be legally renounced by a state

if its supreme interests (undefined by the NPT) are threatened. This is inherent in the time-honored international principle of law that permits alteration of legal obligations if circumstances change. Second, safeguards are irrelevant if, as Carter says, possession of reprocessing and enrichment facilities is the essential ingredient in the proliferation process. In the Brazilian context it is not irrelevant that segments of its space program, including missilry, are directed by its army and that this fact is advertised in the open literature.

Third-party assessment of the proliferation implications of the Argentine-Brazil atomic energy programs depends on two different schools of thought. [2] The first school maintains that safeguards do not inspire confidence and hence to control proliferation it is essential to curb the flow of sensitive equipment, materials, and technology to nonnuclear-weapon states. The second school expresses confidence in safeguards and asserts a need to implement Article IV of the NPT, which promised increased nuclear technology transfers relating to peaceful uses. In terms of the first school, Argentina, like India, is doubly suspect because it has escaped the imposition of full-scope safeguards on its nuclear industry. However, a brief look at the parameters of Argentine nuclear policy indicates that strategic ambiguity rather than a mad momentum toward bomb making to date is the essence of its strategic behavior.

During 1965-68, the period in which the NPT was negotiated by the superpowers, Argentina determined to establish its first nuclear power station. Its negotiating history, as outlined by a member of Argentina's National Atomic Energy Commission, Jorge A. Sabato, indicates that from the outset Argentine policy was to decide against the bomb and yet simultaneously to establish the parameters of autonomy in decision making. This was to be done by seeking self-reliance in fuel supply (including the manufacture of fuel elements) and by absorbing foreign technology into Argentina and maximizing local participation. As Sabato points out: "It is not 'imported technology versus native technology' which matters, but an autonomous capability to manage and control all the technology flowing through the economic system."[3] This view points to a distinction in Argentine thinking between "self-reliance" and "self-sufficiency." The latter implies the absence of a need to import foreign technology; the former implies a capacity to manage the imports in such a manner that technology transfer is not accompanied by a loss of control over the decision-making apparatus concerning the use of that technology. The significance of the Argentine program lies in the capacity to promote self-reliance when self-sufficiency cannot be achieved.

According to a press releast by the Argentine Embassy in Ottawa:

> Among its most important accomplishments we count the construction of the Atucha Plant, the first Nuclear Power Plant in Latin America. It is a plant working with natural uranium and heavy water built with German technology and that is in operation under full Argentinian responsibility since mid 74. In 1975 that plant produced more than 10% of all energy produced in the national territory, reaching a load factor of 85, 6%, one of the highest load factors during that period compared with all the other Nuclear Power Plants in the world.
>
>   At present a new Nuclear Powered Energy Plant— a Candu reactor of 600 MW—is being constructed by a consortium formed by AECL and an Italian firm. After some delays due to the re-negotiation of the contract signed on December 20, 1973, construction is under way in a normal working level that allows us to expect that the plant will be in operation at the end of 1980. [4]

Three points arise from a study of the Argentine case. First, this program grew in the context of chronic domestic social, economic, and political disorder. And yet a first-rate scientific establishment has been able to flourish and make decisions utilizing scientific and political criteria, as much as can be expected of bureaucratic organizations in industrial societies. This means that nuclear installations do not necessarily have to fall into irresponsible, unstable, and war-prone hands. Even though the point should not be overstated, because nuclear terrorism (a hypothetical contingency but still a live academic and policy issue) and subnational violence are real dimensions in proliferation studies, the Argentine case suggests a need to avoid hysteria on this point. Secondly, at present there is no external regime or rule that prohibits Argentina from making the bomb or nuclear weapons if it decides to do so. Thirdly and finally, the restraint against bomb making lies in the Argentine strategy of nuclear self-reliance without the bomb. Several considerations explain such self-restraint. For instance, an Argentine bomb would or could start a Brazil-Argentina nuclear arms race and thereby unnecessarily complicate Argentine security. The bomb would only prove the obvious, namely, that Argentina has bomb-making capability but it could not be translated into influence, given that Argentine societal and state institutions (for example, the state of the economy) are weak. It would be a mistake to permit international opposition to crystallize against Argentina and its development. Furthermore, an Argentine bomb would upset the balance between the strategy of "no bomb" and the strategy of nuclear self-reliance and autonomy in decision making. This dual strategy amounts to a policy of promoting the diplomacy that comes from the ambiguity of possessing an undemonstrated nuclear option. If policy is defined as the unstated portion of what is usually called strategy, and strategy is defined as the visible and stated part of what is usually called policy, then the seeming contradiction between nuclear self-reliance and decision-making autonomy, and denial of bomb-making intention is a necessary one. It is necessary to promote the policy of promoting the nuclear option; that is, to promote the nuclear diplomacy of a slightly visible nuclear option. In other words, a country (like Canada) may have a nuclear option but it may be dead as a diplomatic asset, whereas another country (Israel, India, South Africa, Argentina, Brazil, or Taiwan) may choose to make its nuclear option into a useful diplomatic asset. The latter approach seeks to shape the diplomatic process, and it is not time-bound. The use of a nuclear option as a diplomatic asset implies the denial of a rule-making capability to an external agency (the IAEA, the United States, or any nuclear supplier). It may be said that an attribute of power and influence is the capability and the right to make and to maintain the game rules (or to engage in system maintenance). Argentine behavior has the ability to deny power or deny influence. In this respect its behavior is comparable with India's, although the latter seems to enjoy greater visibility internationally because of its nuclear behavior and its involvement in a region of conflict. In short, the real significance of the Argentine nuclear program, apart from its obvious use as an energy resource, is that it is a useful diplomatic asset in a policy that seeks to guard against a freeze of international power relations.

Compared with Argentina, Brazil is a latecomer to the anti-superpower (particularly anti-United States) and nuclear diplomacy game. Until recently, in the eyes of many, Brazil could be regarded as an American agent in Latin America, as a subimperial power representing American norms. Today, the image of Brazil has changed, as it shows an increasing inclination to promote its national interests through a bolder international stance. Its evolving attitudes and aspirations now seek a global image and a potentially global scope of foreign policy operation.[5] For instance, the 1970 General Assembly resolution sponsored by Brazil sought to link development, security, and disarmament.[6] The effort to give conceptual or notional shape to Brazil's international concerns, which separate Brazil from the United States, has become prominent in the 1970s.

Its self-image encourages the development of a regional and international personality in international security policy-making forums.
The self-image is to project its international position in terms of its
hierarchical status in the international power structure, and Western thinkers sympathize with the Brazilian self-image. For instance,
Ray S. Cline ranks Brazil as the sixth world power.[7] At the very
least Brazil sees itself as a power comparable to Canada and India,
and as upwardly mobile from an "intermediate power" status to a
great power or international power status. An official document
expresses the Brazilian mood as follows.

> Brazilian diplomacy holds close to the basic national
> aims of development and security.
>
> [. . .]
>
> To countries with vast potentialities and international
> projection, like Brazil, this complexity in the inter-
> national scene is a challenge to demonstrate their
> presence, not their isolation. Contact, participation,
> free exchange of ideas will give countries greater op-
> portunities to answer national interest, whereas iso-
> lation dries up the capacity to act and be influential,
> both in the bilateral field and in that of multilateral
> action.[8]

Some of these aspirations are being translated into decisions,
and these reveal Brazil's regional and, at times, its international
presence. At present Brazil may well be a giant among Latin
American pygmies, but the future implications of its present foreign policy and security orientation should not be underestimated in
specific issue areas. If influence is the capacity to establish presence and to shape the outcomes in policy situations, Brazil's influence in specific issue areas merits attention. One example is the
shift in its policy on the law of the sea during 1966-70. In 1966 it
accepted a three-mile territorial sea; in 1970 it claimed a 200-mile
limit for its maritime sovereignty.[9] Its political diplomacy is gradually building bridges toward Black African and certain Third World
states by projecting the image of a harmonious multiracial society
in Brazil as a basis for harmonious interstate relationships. The
opening of diplomatic doors toward Moscow and Peking—even though
Brazil worries about Soviet naval presence in the South Atlantic—
suggests a globalization of Brazilian diplomacy. Latin America,
the United States, Europe, and Africa at present are the major targets of Brazilian diplomacy, but as its experienced foreign service
consolidates its gains, it can be expected to expand its scope of operation.

Its views of the world reveal a distinct antisuperpower, and particularly an anti-U.S. orientation. Consider the following samples of views of the world today and of existing power relations. They should be considered in the context of zigzags in Brazilian nuclear policies of the past, which now seem to consolidate in favor of a quest for an independent Brazilian nuclear fuel cycle. In 1946, Bernard Baruch, the U.S. delegate to the International Atomic Energy Agency, suggested that Brazil (along with some other countries) give up its thorium and uranium because of the "injustices of nature." The U.S. request was turned down, and in 1951 uranium export required permission of the highest Brazilian defense authorities. Still, Brazil secretly cooperated with the United States in shipping strategic raw materials to the United States for several years. In 1953, Brazil acquired enrichment equipment for uranium from the Federal Republic of Germany, but the transfer was blocked by the American Occupation authorities in Germany. (The equipment reached Brazil in 1956.) This incident revealed that the United States had no interest in Brazil's nuclear development. From 1954 onward, changes in Brazilian domestic politics led to a loss of interest in an independent Brazilian nuclear capacity. From 1955 to the late 1960s, Brazil's nuclear dependency on the United States was facilitated by bilateral ties; the dependency existed in terms of technology, materials, and equipment transfers. Still, independent Brazilian positions had started to emerge in the late 1960s. In signing the Treaty of Tlatelolco (1967) Brazil did not renounce its right to conduct a peaceful nuclear explosion. It refused to accept the NPT. In 1972 Brazil signed an agreement with the United States (this expires A.D. 2002) to supply enriched uranium for its Westinghouse plant. Still, in 1969, Brazil had started to build alternative nuclear supply options by arranging for joint consultation with the Federal Republic of Germany on gas centrifuge research. In short, even though the primary relationship in the nuclear and other fields was with the United States, Brazil had started to diversify its bilateral and multilateral diplomacy.[10] This was the context that paved the way for the first real blow for nuclear independence: during 1974-75 Brazil and the Federal Republic of Germany (with the initiative by Franz Joseph Strauss) announced a multibillion dollar nuclear deal, which involved German supplies of reactors, enrichment, and reprocessing capability and prospecting for uranium that in part is meant to feed German nuclear industry. The Federal Republic of Germany-Brazil deal was followed by the announcement of cooperation with France for the development of a fast breeder reactor.[11] There is speculation that France may also become involved in uranium prospecting in Brazil following its experience in Nigeria and Gabon. U.S. Senator Pastore's remark that the Federal Republic of Germany-Brazil nuclear deal created a nuclear peril in the American backyard revealed the distance Brazil had traveled on the road from nuclear cooperation with the United States in the 1950s to a quest for nuclear fuel cycle independence in the 1970s.

If proliferation is defined merely as a capacity to explode a nuclear device, Argentina is ahead of Brazil by many years. Also, if proliferation is defined as capacity to be free of international safeguards on the entire nuclear industry of a state (full-scope safeguards), Argentina is ahead of Brazil in this regard. But, on the other hand, if uranium enrichment and plutonium reprocessing plants are strategic items, and their acquisition itself constitutes proliferation, then the rapid nuclearization of Brazilian policy and industry, compared to the slower nuclearization of Argentina, gives Brazilian behavior the attributes of a crisis. The crisis exists in the minds of the antiproliferators because the Brazilian nuclearization was quick, unexpected, and seems to be beyond external control. The real significance of the Federal Republic of Germany-Brazil nuclear deal of 1975 is not that the nuclear fuel cycle is being transferred to a potential hard-core proliferation case. Rather it lies in the joint defection of two American allies in a vital international security issue. It is also significant that Brazil's theoretical positions are now being converted into action. In the 1960s its independence with respect to the NPT and the Treaty of Tlatelolco was verbal. In practice it accepted the constraints of nuclear and political cooperation with the United States. Its rejection of the NPT on the ground that it was discriminatory and its quest for PNEs in terms of the Tlatelolco Treaty (Article 18) were devoid of practical meaning. Furthermore, there was no real connection between its disarmament diplomacy and its nuclear policy. Its disarmament diplomacy appeared to be independent and the appearance was apparently sufficient to give Brazil the sense of participation and prestige in multilateral disarmament diplomacy. But on the other hand, its willingness to curb its nuclear aspirations during the 1950s and the 1960s made Brazilian behavior predictable. But in negotiating the Federal Republic of Germany-Brazil nuclear deal, the hitherto parallel dimensions of disarmament diplomacy and nuclear diplomacy have become linked. Consequently the parameters have changed, along with the future implications of Brazilian behavior.

The Federal Republic of Germany-Brazil nuclear deal has several features. Some of these reveal the existence of international constraints on Brazil whereas other features dilute the constraints. The safeguards provisions are the best that could be negotiated in light of the consensus of the London Nuclear Suppliers Group, which became public in 1978. It is reasonable to say that the safeguards provisions of the Federal Republic of Germany-Brazil deal in 1975 preceded the NSG guidelines of 1978 and are totally consistent with them. Articles III and II of the agreement forbid the use of nuclear technology, and other supplies for use in making nuclear weapons or nuclear explosive devices or for other military purposes. The safeguards will be in force for 20 years at the least. Should Brazil replicate German technology, the products are also safeguardable; in other words, the principle of pursuit of the NSG is in evidence in the bilateral deal. Legally, the duration of the agreement is 20 years, but the principle of pursuit in practice could extend the duration depending on the end uses of the imported German technology.

These features reveal the toughness of the safeguards regime on Brazil, and this makes sense for those who have confidence in safeguards. But on the other hand, there are provisions in the agreement that suggest that the safeguards are not foolproof. The agreement says explicitly that the safeguards regime refers to INFCIRC/66/Revision 2 document of the IAEA, and as discussed earlier, these are less than full-scope safeguards. The practical effect of the 66 regime may or may not be significant because, as noted in Chapter 5, the Federal Republic of Germany/Brazil/IAEA safeguards agreement has features of the 66 and the 153 system and one needs to examine the subsidiary arrangements to fully analyze the meaning of Brazilian acceptance of the 66 safeguards regime. Nevertheless, in formal and legal terms it is noteworthy that Brazilian acceptance of 66 safeguards leaves it with some room for maneuvering with the IAEA and its nuclear suppliers, and the principle is ratified that Brazil does not accept safeguards on its entire nuclear industry. Depending on the circumstances the notional and the factual situations may vary, but it is noteworthy that in the notional sense Brazil does not accept full-scope safeguards.

Secondly, the agreement allows safeguarded items to be substituted (Article VII). This means that if fissionable material under safeguards (say, 5 kilograms of enriched uranium or spent fuel) is removed from a safeguarded facility and is replaced by a different consignment of the fuel in question, this is acceptable to the IAEA. This offers room for movement of nuclear materials in and out of safeguarded facilities. Here again the distinction may be more theoretical than real but still the point has notional significance because of the absence of full-scope safeguards in Brazil. Having full-scope safeguards is analogous to sealing the cookie jar and then not worrying about counting the cookies or knowing the location of the cookies inside the jar. But in the absence of a seal on the whole jar, if some of the cookies are safeguarded and others are not, the movement of each has to be recorded just to ensure that the safeguarded ones are doing the job they promised to do. The problem of monitoring substitutable nuclear materials arises when an extensive flow of materials occurs between safeguarded and unsafeguarded facilities.

Finally, whereas faith in international safeguards on Brazil rests on a belief in safeguards technology and a conviction that no state to date has renounced safeguards and, except in matters of supreme interest, this is not likely to happen, there is still a pessimistic school of thought. This school argues that Brazil, like India and Argentina, claims the right to have its PNEs; and this is expressed publicly in Brazil's declaration on accepting the Treaty of Tlatelolco. On May 9, 1967 Brazil reaffirmed its interpretation of the sense of Article 18 of this treaty as follows.

> In the mind of the Brazilian Government, the said Article 18 allows Signatory States to undertake, by their own means or in association with third parties, nuclear explosions with peaceful purposes including those presupposing devices similar to the ones utilised in military weapons. [12]

Article 18(2) provides for international observation of the preparation and explosion of the device, but it is unclear if this entails a sharing of secret technical data concerning the trigger mechanism and critical mass. As a request for sharing of such data is likely to be hotly disputed by Third World states, the Brazilian commitment not to use German technology for military or explosive purposes leaves the question of future Brazilian intentions unanswered. Suppose Brazil, Argentina, and the OPANAL members collectively explode a peaceful nuclear device and no German technology, equipment, or materials are involved, and there are several witnesses to this exercise, what can the antiproliferators do? At the very least there is ambiguity concerning, if not conflict between, Brazil's PNE rights under the Treaty of Tlatelolco and the renunciation of military aims in the Federal Republic of Germany-Brazil deal. Accordingly, the international constraints are not as irrevocable as they may appear in the language of the Federal Republic of Germany-Brazil deal. Inasmuch as enriched uranium is at present being provided by URENCO (a Dutch, German, and British consortium), there is doubt about the possibility that plutonium derived from the uranium could be used to make Brazilian bombs. [13]

Brazil's evolving nuclear industry is becoming a central factor in the evolving linkage between its disarmament diplomacy and its nuclear diplomacy; and even though the Brazilian and Argentine nuclear programs differ from each other in their pace of change, the process of linking disarmament and nuclear diplomacy appears to be an identical one. In speculating about the future implications of the evolving linkage, it is well to regard Brazilian and Argentine views of superpower behavior as something more than rhetoric. If and when Brazil acquires the diplomatic and the material means to translate its attitudes into policies and outcomes, its current statements on disarmament, nuclear power, and international security policy can be viewed as operational indices or parameters of future Brazilian behavior. This study's purpose is not to predict the rate of change but to explore the process of change and its underlying reasoning.

BRAZILIAN AND ARGENTINE VIEWS
OF INTERNATIONAL SECURITY

Many industrializing societies have sophisticated foreign policy and security elites but still do not necessarily offer publicly a systematic set of ideas about power politics and dynamics of international change. Some states, like Japan, seek a combination of modesty in attitude and profile and high achievement, whereas other states, like India, follow the Japanese combination but reverse it— comparatively less achievement and higher profile, and perhaps false modesty. In particular, India is notorious for offering recycled views about morality in international politics and what ought to happen to lessen tensions. But on a specific matter like the nuclear option Indian officials become tongue-tied, and the gap between the oral briefing and the recycled speech is remarkable.

Brazilian speeches reveal an elementary conceptualization that U.S. audiences can readily understand. The speeches are interesting, because intentions seem to be quite explicit and the reasoning is explained along with the assessment. The following is a sample of views. It is not a comprehensive statement of Brazilian foreign policy or security policy. Its purpose is to enable the reader to see the nuances in Brazilian perceptions of the world and then to assess the implications of these nuances for nuclear policy making.

Nuclear Option and International Politics

In a lecture to the Canadian Institute of International Affairs in New York (June 9, 1972) the permanent representative of Brazil to the United Nations said:

By all standards, the decision not to go nuclear is a first political option made by those Intermediate States which are either members of military alliances or are

grouped under common ideological allegiances. Since
they trust they can count upon nuclear dissuasory protection, that is to say, with a defence against the inim-
ical Power, these Intermediate States have opted to
apply their limited resources to the development of the
prerequisites of national Power, to invest in the complex of social, economic and cultural elements that
lead to Power. Once this objective is attained, the
viability and, later, the maintenance of their first option will certainly depend on the over-all political
situation and on the state of affairs in the system of
inter-State relations. If we keep nourishing the concept of an international system where considerations
of naked force are paramount or, in other words, if
Power, and a fortiori its nuclear expression, continue
to be the ultimate ratio for the organisation of the inter-
State system, it will be but natural and logical that
every sovereign State with an already accumulated
potential to do so will be seeking to enter the Club of
the most privileged.

The alternative to this rather harsh scenario
would be, Ladies and Gentlemen, the reorganisation of
the international order along more rational and equitable lines, stripped of the tragic heritage of Power
politics, a legacy which is today disguised under the
veil of the partial acceptance of international legal
principles or under the deceitful assumption that a
state of peace can be brought about if Power remains
permanently divided amongst those who already possess it.[14]

Note here that the decision by an intermediate state not to go nuclear
is explained as a political act by a member of an alliance. It is not
an act that repudiates the protection of nuclear power; it is merely
an act that sees no immediate utility in national nuclear power.
Thus, taking the case of Canada, the repudiation is not of the protection of nuclear power to Canada from the United States; the rejection is only of Canadian nuclear weapons because there is no need
to leave the American nuclear fold. "The first political option" buys
time for domestic development but it is not a terminal condition. It
can remain the operative option, depending on the overall international situation. But once domestic development has been achieved,
the permanent division of international power among those who already enjoy that power is a major incentive, in the Brazilian viewpoint, for the development of the nuclear option. In this case the

first political option is merely a step toward unfreezing the existing distribution of international power.

Importance of Vertical Mobility and the Unfreezing of the Power Structure

Brazilian statements to international forums reveal a quest for an altered world order. The statements indicate that Brazilians perceive a need to alter the existing power structure; that is, a change is said to be desirable. At the same time there is a perception that the influence of Third World states is growing; this implies that a change is likely. One statement regards it a "central issue in today's international life" that there be a new international system that responds to the ethical, political, and legal values of the "community of States" and that will "transcend present considerations of Power."[15] It is unclear whether the quest is primarily against all power politics or against the "mere freezing of obsolete patterns of Realpolitik." Two notions are inherent in the Brazilian formulations. On one hand, the international system should guarantee "the interests of all States, irrespective of their relative Power"; these interests ought to be "duly respected." But on the other hand "at the very least," the system should permit "vertical mobility among them [the members of the system]."[16] The latter seems to be the operational element in Brazilian thinking because satisfying the interests of all members of the international system seems to be impractical; it is arguable that to transfer some resources to the poorest nations in the world is to show due respect to their interests. Creating vertical mobility among the top members of the international hierarchy is, however, a double-edged sword. On the one hand it permits the upward mobility of emerging powers. On the other hand it permits the downward mobility of the superpowers and the great powers. In either instance it offers a dynamic view of international life. Note, however, that the Brazilian admonition is not against power politics. It is instead against the attempt by the top members of the international hierarchy to freeze the membership of the club of powerful nations: to prevent new recruitment, to discard useless members, and, above all, to disallow the downward mobility of the top members even when their influence and power have deteriorated. The Brazilian admonition is not against a hierarchical structure of international power relations. Rather it is against a frozen hierarchical structure. In support of their quest for an altered distribution of power, Brazil points out that "no country, even the Superpowers, is immune to the effects of the policies of third States" ("medium and small Powers") in the international security debate.[17] Secondly,

The developing countries are now learning to work
together; their opinion is beginning to be felt and
it will weigh more and more in the years to come;
the major military, economic and technological
Powers are at the moment reckoning with this fact
for perhaps the first time. [18]

Thirdly,

disarmament negotiations have been experiencing a
growing bilateralization that limits all initiatives in
the matter to the two super-Powers, . . . as if the
developing nations did not have their own security
interests, which are qualitatively different from the
security interests of the great Powers or even of
the developed nations. [19]

It is noteworthy that Brazil speaks the language of security and
power rather than mere morality in international life.

Views of the NPT Regime

Brazil offers four reasons for not accepting the NPT. First,
Brazil accepts the idea of nonproliferation and the importance of
nondiscriminatory safeguards, but the NPT is a discriminatory document; it divides the world into two categories—those who can continue their independent nuclear technological development without
international constraints and those who cannot. Secondly, Brazil's
leaders cannot "curtail in any sense our possibilities for independent
technological advancement, which is a prerequisite for social and
economic development."[20] Thirdly, the nuclear-weapon states parties to the NPT are insincere because of their failure to fulfill their
promise of nuclear disarmament and to offer peaceful nuclear assistance to nonnuclear-weapon states. Fourthly and finally, the
nuclear-weapon states party to the NPT have failed to offer "un-
equivocal" security assurances to nonnuclear-weapon states.[21] In
particular the first two reasons make the Brazilian position on the
NPT nonnegotiable.

Nuclear Weapon Status Quo, Détente, and Arms Control

Brazil offers a number of thoughts that are subversive in
terms of existing superpower premises and approaches to interna-

tional relations. First, the Soviet-U.S. nuclear status quo helps the détente but it does not end the arms race. Secondly, "détente is not peace; it is not the institutionalised security we all seek." Thirdly, either "détente" is a hypocritical exercise—the unparalleled quest for massive destructive power accompanied by a profession "towards greater accommodation between rival nations"; or "détente" does not work because it "does not significantly extend itself to the strategical competition between the great"; or it is a failure because the nuclear-weapon states have the main responsibility for failing to "transfer apparent progress in the political sphere to the realm of disarmament." Fourthly, partial arms control measures are not acceptable to Brazil because they give a false impression of moving toward or solving the disarmament problem—whereas in reality there is no such movement, and furthermore, the measures codify the superpowers' arms race in terms of their own interests rather than the interests of the world community at large or the security interests of the medium and small powers.[22] The Brazilian remarks are directed primarily to the superpowers.

> The main responsibility for taking concrete steps towards disarmament lies with the nuclear weapon states; but the bilateralization or oligopoly of disarmament negotiations would amount to a futile attempt to ignore the realities of an increasingly interdependent and complex world scene, where bipolarity is gradually being replaced by multipolarity.[23]

This remark appeared in 1975, well before the Soviet-American détente ran into difficulties.

Link between Vertical and Horizontal Proliferation

Brazil is emphatic about the direct link between vertical and horizontal proliferation:

> horizontal proliferation is not a phenomenon of spontaneous growth, but a political and strategic subproduct of this vertical proliferation: as such it cannot be dealt with separately.

And further:

> horizontal proliferation, a problem of vast importance that cannot be overlooked, is nothing more than

a consequence of vertical proliferation: only through the creation of real conditions of security for non-nuclear States is it possible to neutralise their possible motivations for acquiring nuclear weapons. [24]

The Peaceful Nuclear Explosion Issue

Brazil takes a fundamentalist position on this issue. Even if it does not engage in PNEs, its PNE diplomacy is noteworthy. Several Western allies (for example, the Federal Republic of Germany and Australia) take the view that Article V of the NPT (establishing an international regime for PNEs) ought to be implemented, whereas the United States takes the view that the implementation should take place if PNEs are feasible, which in U.S. opinion they are clearly not now and are not likely to be. Brazil takes the view that even the implementation of Article V "would be tantamount to conferring the monopoly over this technology to the nuclear powers." This is clearly so, because under the NPT game rules only the five nuclear-weapon states could offer PNE services on behalf of an international PNE regime, and nonnuclear-weapon states would by definition be disallowed from doing so. Brazil also points out that IAEA studies reveal that PNEs can be significant in exploiting natural resources (whether or not they will be is another question) and the view that there is no technical difference between nuclear weapons and nuclear explosives "has not yet been the object of a technical consensus" in the CCD or elsewhere. Without the achievement of a technical consensus on this point in the CCD, the Brazilian attack is against the basic formula in the NPT that sees no difference between a nuclear weapon and a nuclear explosion. In other words, the very essence of the NPT is being questioned by Brazil. Finally, Brazil is deeply suspicious of the comprehensive test ban and peaceful nuclear explosion ban (or moratorium) negotiations that began actively among the United States, the United Kingdom, and the USSR during the summer of 1977.

> The sudden introduction of the question of the implications of peaceful nuclear explosion in the context of the comprehensive test ban is totally uncalled for as it places the conclusion of this important disarmament step once more as dependent upon the solution of a typically collateral measure. [25]

Note that Brazil's suspicion about a CTB/PNE ban or a moratorium emerged in 1975—that is, several years before superpower negotiations on the subject started actively.

Summary

Argentine views are explicitly and boldly presented but to avoid repetition with the preceding discussion they are presented here in summary form.

1. If the détente process leads to a continued increase in the military might of the great powers, what would happen if the world situation deteriorated? The question indicates that Argentine opinion is not taken in by the détente between the superpowers, but rather recognizes the implications of the military behavior of the superpowers vis-à-vis each other. It is interesting that the question was posed in 1975 when détente seemed to be strong.
2. Existing arms control agreements, according to Argentina, are not disarmament measures; nor do they freeze existing levels of arms. The underlying attitude of the superpowers seems to be one of "unfounded political paternalism."
3. The most urgent problem for the international community is to prevent the vertical proliferation of nuclear weapons. Those who engage in vertical proliferation cannot invoke the dangers of possible horizontal proliferation.
4. Argentina does not accept the NPT because it is discriminatory in character and does not have a balance of obligations and responsibilities between NWS and NNWS.
5. Existing arms control diplomacy of the superpowers is imbalanced. More time is spent on discussing PNEs than on prohibiting nuclear weapons tests, even though there is no consensus on the PNE question in the CCD.
6. A trend is emerging to bilateralize the negotiations, and the most important and urgent subjects are taken out of the negotiating organs (the CCD). Furthermore, the absence of the PRC and France affects the work of the CCD. [26]
7. Disarmament negotiations must be a collective effort, but at the same time the "States which possess the monopoly of nuclear arms" have a far greater responsibility.
8. Collateral disarmament (arms control) issues are a "subterfuge" that is designed to avoid adoption of concrete measures in the field of nuclear weapons.
9. Argentina is opposed to nuclear arms and these must be totally eliminated forever and as soon as possible.
10. The danger of horizontal proliferation is "intimately linked" with the "more serious and immediate" danger of uninterrupted vertical proliferation.
11. Nonproliferation (both vertical and horizontal) should be a universal aim, but the NPT is not the proper way to achieve this aim.

12. The NPT is objectionable because "for the first time in history" it legitimizes a division of the world into two categories of states: those who have a free hand in the nuclear field and those under restrictions. The NPT does not impose clear-cut obligations on the nuclear powers to disarm.

13. The NPT has led to a series of restrictive and discriminatory measures, which in some cases have disregarded contractual obligations between states.

14. The NPT freezes disparities:

To equate arbitrarily the use of nuclear energy for peaceful purposes with the presumed possibility of producing nuclear weapons and to impose as a consequence, unjustified limitations on the transfer of technology and nuclear material, is tantamount to an attempt to perpetuate the scientific and technological oligopoly established by a handful of industrialised States which is to direct detriment of the interests of the developing countries.

15. While Argentina is willing to support "fair and appropriate initiative" to prevent proliferation, and to cooperate with the IAEA in "laying down and observing the respective safeguards," it would like to stress with firmness that it will "exercise to the full our inalienable right to acquire, refine and apply advances in nuclear technology for the benefit and progress of the Argentine people."

16. Unlike the NPT, the Treaty of Tlatelolco recognizes no category of privileged states and is therefore acceptable to Argentina.

17. All concrete disarmament measures "presuppose the participation in the relevant negotiations of all militarily significant States whose consent is indispensable if they are to be put into effect." This particularly applies to nuclear disarmament measures.[27]

ASSESSMENT OF THE SOUTH AMERICAN
NUCLEAR OPTIONS

The foregoing views reveal that the proliferation question is viewed and assessed by Brazil and Argentina (and many other Third World nations) in the framework of the lack of progress in securing disarmament; the stress is on the special responsibility of the NWS, and particularly the superpowers, to achieve that goal. However, the foregoing views do not indicate whether in Third World thinking some NWS are more important than others in paving the way for nuclear disarmament. Some, for instance, argue that the United

States ought to take the first real step toward disarmament because of its technological and military superiority, and because Moscow cannot move unless Washington does—the premise being that Moscow reacts to, and follows, the U.S. lead in strategic policy making. Similarly, Peking cannot move toward disarmament unless Washington and Moscow make real sacrifices toward that goal. Under these premises the real capacity to set an example lies with Washington's decision makers. Thus the real pressure of South American disarmament diplomacy is on the United States more than on the Soviet Union and the PRC.

There are different ways to assess the significance of South American nuclear options. First, it can be assessed in terms of the regional rivalry between Brazil and Argentina, and the point can be broadened further as other Latin American states, such as Venezuela, start to worry about the implications of Brazilian hegemony. Secondly, Brazilian nuclear and disarmament diplomacy may be seen primarily as an international exercise. The two assessments are not necessarily mutually exclusive but it makes sense to conceptualize them separately.

The first type of assessment is found in a paper prepared for the International Institute for Strategic Studies in 1977.[28] This paper makes the following points. Brazil's reservations on the Treaty of Tlatelolco are an "opportunity to develop nuclear weapons." Nuclear options result in "hints, charges and innuendos" which "will in [themselves] aggravate tensions"; this makes it "more likely that one or the other eventually explodes a nuclear device." Explicit here is the notion of drift and escalation in regional conflict once nuclear options come into being. Argentina has "more obvious motivations" than Brazil to "go nuclear" and nuclear devices may be the "great equalizer" for Argentina, given that its domestic conditions have deteriorated whereas Brazilian domestic conditions have improved. For fear of coming second, Argentina may pre-empt by exploding a nuclear device before Brazil does. The paper recognizes that Brazil may be influenced "more by international than regional considerations," but while Brazil plays to an international audience it may provoke a strong Argentine reaction and this may result in a regional arms race. Finally, "even if no bombs explode" the results may be destabilizing.

The foregoing points contain a number of questionable premises. First, the opportunity to make a bomb or proliferate in some other fashion does not lie in the Tlatelolco Treaty, which permits (Article 18) PNEs under international observations. Treaties do not create opportunities, but national interests and perceptions of international life do. So the Tlatelolco Treaty should be seen as a manifestation rather than the cause. Secondly, the premise of drift and escalation

in the regional rivalry begs the question. Are we to assume that
actors in regional international relations (including members of
sophisticated foreign policy establishments such as those in Argentina and Brazil) are in practice a society of fools who do not know
better than to destroy the system in which they must exist? The
arms race model makes sense in the Soviet-U.S. context because
these are international powers with global arenas to play with, and
play in. With higher margins of safety there are higher margins to
make errors and not to be punished. Regional powers, on the other
hand, have fewer opportunities and less of a margin to escape penalties for making foreign policy and security mistakes. For regional
powers, the costs are high, both internationally and domestically,
as they clearly are not for self-contained societies like the USSR
and rich and powerful societies like the pre-Vietnam United States.
Among regional powers, pursuing arms races can be a dangerous
activity. Self-interest, past experience, and reasonable intelligence
are, therefore, likely to ensure a policy against uncontrolled arms
racing that leads to a breakdown of the system. In other words, it
is useful to note that even enemies, through constant interactions,
acquire some sense of the regional system in which they reside.
The "order" that exists between India and Pakistan and between
other regional pairs provides reassuring examples.

The institute's paper points to two different starting points of
the so-called regional arms race and proliferation scenario. One
starting point is that Argentina, for fear of being the second best,
pre-empts the game by exploding a device and using this as the great
equalizer. The other starting point is that Brazil plays to an international audience, its actions provoke reactions from Argentina, and
this results in a regional arms race and regional conflict. Both
starting points are inadequate because they treat the regional system
or subsystem as the framework for the development of nuclear options and nuclear arms races.

This intraregional perspective ignores the interface between a
regional power and a superpower. This interface is particularly
relevant with respect to two international security issues: negotiating
nuclear arms freezes and reduction, and secondly, preventing the
proliferation of nuclear options. The central theme that connects
these two issues is that neither NWS nor NNWS are willing to renounce their options (these vary between these two types of states);
that these powers are not willing to renounce their options because
of their unwillingness to ignore the opportunities and obligations of
pursuing their geo-political and geo-strategic interests; and finally,
that, for those who do not possess nuclear weapons, nuclear options
are useful diplomatic resources. Nuclear options cannot equalize
the power possessed by the NWS. But nuclear options can pressure

the NWS away from intervening and toward becoming more responsive to third-party interests.

With respect to international security policy making, nuclear options have the attribute of strategic denial of gain to the so-called superpowers. Most people are conditioned to think of international relations in hierarchical terms, with superpowers at the top and the poorest states at the bottom. In the conventional method of studying international politics, once great-power and superpower status has been acquired, it is codified in the international legal regime (the United Nations Charter, for instance). If new great powers or superpowers emerge, they make their presence felt through a process of upward mobility. And superpowers and great powers have the advantage that, because of their higher status, superior power, and international influence, the benefit of inertia as a policy instrument is on their side. With inertia they can achieve denial of gain to the lesser powers. In other words, superpower status plus international power plus inertia can assist in the maintenance of the gap between rights and obligations of superpowers and the lesser powers. These attributes can also delay the upward mobility of new aspirants like Brazil and India who do not always cooperate with the superpowers.

This perspective, however, ignores an opposite starting point of analysis, and this reveals the process for conducting the interface between a regional power and an international power. The premise here is not that intermediate or regional powers must always go upward to enter the big-power league. (They may, as Japan has done in international economic diplomacy.) Rather, the superpowers slide downward in certain issue areas. If superpowers remain superpowers, they can retain their rights and their distance vis-à-vis other powers in a hierarchical system. Their policies of intervention and inertia can help them promote their interests and also promote international system maintenance. But once the superpowers start sliding downward, and the gap between the effective influence of the superpowers and that of the regional powers begins to lessen in certain issue areas, then inertia no longer remains a viable strategy for the former superpowers.

Nuclear proliferation is one such issue area where American diplomatic inertia no longer works. It worked from the 1940s to the 1960s in international multilateral diplomacy but is ineffective as a policy today. This assessment explains excessive American antiproliferation activism in the 1970s. But the international reactions to Carter's antiproliferation "diplomacy" reveal that inertia is no longer possible as a policy for the United States and that the capacity to enforce U.S. prescriptions is lacking. The outcome, as of 1978, reveals that the diplomacy is clumsy because talk outweighs action;

that is, if action is defined as something that alters an existing condition to one's own satisfaction. The outcomes in the Japanese-U.S. renegotiations over Tokai Muro (1977) and the Federal Republic of Germany-Brazil agreement (1975) reveal that the level of talk in U.S. diplomacy today exceeds the capacity to act and to enforce.

It is, of course, premature to assert that the advantage of the strategy of inertia has shifted toward the nuclear-option or the threshold states and away from those who already possess nuclear weapons. As long as nuclear weapons have some military use—and today nuclear weapons are less militarily useful rather than entirely militarily useless—nuclear power will continue to enhance the status and power of those who possess it. But still it is plausible to make the following case: given the downward mobility of the superpowers on certain international security issues (for instance, in post-NPT diplomacy), and given the capacity of certain nuclear-option states to assert their presence in international security debates, viable and visible nuclear options are directed primarily toward international targets rather than against regional neighbors.

The failure of the superpowers to take meaningful steps toward a freeze on nuclear arms testing and toward eventual arms reduction and disarmament (a goal accepted by all NWS including the PRC at the United Nations Special Session on Disarmament in 1978), and the consequent rise of nuclear options in all the major regional and subregional centers imply that unless real sacrifices are made by the superpowers and other NWS, other powers are not likely to renounce their options either. If superpower nuclear weapons and lesser powers' nuclear options are tied to the compulsions of their respective regional and international environments, then options cannot be closed. Inertia in preserving the nuclear options rather than moving toward nuclear weapons is the game that enables the regional powers to avoid conflict with their neighbors, particularly when such conflict only dissipates the power and influence of almost equal neighbors.

Nuclear options are troublesome for the superpowers in another sense. Because of the failure to disarm, the nuclear options cannot be curbed (as Argentinians and Brazilians point out), and yet the growing consciousness about the failure to disarm is creating an international constituency against vertical proliferation rather than horizontal proliferation. This became clear in the debates and the final document of the UN Special Session on Disarmament.[29] States that previously appeared as apparent regional nuclear rivals are emerging internationally as partners in their quest for anti-vertical proliferation diplomacy. Examples of these partnerships in the disarmament field are India and Pakistan, and Argentina and Brazil. Furthermore, as hitherto regional rivals find an area for international cooperation, this can alter the habit of hostility into a habit of partial cooperation at the regional level also; that is, if there is a spill-over effect into different issue areas. Finally, and this may well emerge as a major consequence of nuclear-option proliferation in the 1980s, a global anti-vertical proliferation chain at the diplomatic level may be emerging. In the 1960s, during the NPT negotiations, Indian arguments were echoed by Brazilian, Argentine, West German, and Japanese diplomats. The diplomatic chain between these states was broken after India decided in 1967-68 against leading an anti-NPT lobby. Today that leadership has been taken by Brazil and Argentina, with the support of many Third World and non-aligned nations; the role of these nations in the United Nations and the role of the United Nations in the disarmament field is growing. Unless SALT II leads to SALT III—and even SALT II at present seems problematic—and unless the comprehensive test ban is the first step toward nuclear disarmament rather than a finite, nonuniversal exercise, the international setting encourages the growth of an anti-vertical proliferation diplomatic chain. As a verbal exercise, disarmament diplomacy cannot alter the parameters of superpower thinking, and UN diplomacy is a small cosmetic factor in superpower relations. But as horizontal nuclear-option proliferation becomes a consequence of vertical proliferation, and as the nuclear factor enters the bureaucratic debates of intermediate states in Latin America and elsewhere, the linkage between disarmament diplomacy and nuclear option policy of a number of regional influential states implies the beginning of a new trend in international politics of the 1980s.

NOTES

1. Particularly useful are: Jorge A. Sabato, "Atomic Energy in Argentina: A Case History," World Development 1, no. 8 (August 1973): 23-38; John R. Redick, "Nuclear Proliferation in Latin America," in The End of Hemispheric Isolation, ed. Roger W. Fontaine and J. D. Theberge (New York: Praeger, 1976); John R. Redick, "Regional Restraint: US Nuclear Policy and Latin America," Orbis 22, no. 1 (Spring 1978): 161-200; Stanley Foundation, "US Nuclear Policy and Latin America," Vantage Conference Report, Muscatine, Iowa, December 10-12, 1976; H. J. Rosenbaum, "Brazil's Nuclear Aspirations," and C. H. Waisman, "Incentives for Nuclear Proliferation: The Case of Argentina," in Nuclear Proliferation and the Near Nuclear Countries, ed. O. Marwah and A. Schulz (Cambridge, Mass.: Ballinger, 1975), Chapters 11 and 12; William Perry, "The Brazilian Nuclear Program in a Foreign Policy Context," paper presented at the International Studies Association,

Washington, D.C., February 22-25, 1978; Presidency of the [Brazil] Republic, II PBDCT: II Basic Plan for Scientific and Technological Development, 1976, particularly pp. 10, 14, 31-38; and Federative Republic of Brazil, The Brazilian Nuclear Program, 1977, official text.

2. B. Goldschmidt, "A Historical Survey of Nonproliferation Policies," International Security 2, no. 1 (Summer 1977): 69-87.

3. J. A. Sabato, "Atomic Energy in Argentina: A Case History," World Development 1, no. 8 (August 1973): 36.

4. Press Release, Argentine Embassy, Ottawa, July 5, 1976.

5. R. M. Schneider, Brazil: Foreign Policy of a Future World Power (Boulder, Colo.: Westview Press, 1976), p. 41.

6. Ibid., p. 35.

7. Ray S. Cline, World Power Assessment: A Calculus of Strategic Drift (Boulder, Colo.: Westview Press, 1975), p. 130.

8. Brazil, published by the Ministry of External Relations, Brazil, 1976, p. 11.

9. Schneider, op. cit., pp. 44-45.

10. This paragraph relies on ibid., pp. 47-50; and Rosenbaum, op. cit.

11. Rosenbaum, op. cit., p. 256. Note that the Federal Republic of Germany-Brazil agreement is under international safeguards known as INFCIRC/66/Rev. 2 and formally these are not full-scope safeguards. The Trilateral Agreement among the IAEA, the Federal Republic of Germany, and Brazil was signed on February 26, 1976.

12. Report on the Implementation of the Treaty of Tlatelolco and Some Comments and Views of OPANOL with respect to Article VII and Some Related Provisions of the Non-Proliferation Treaty, prepared by OPANOL, for Review Conference of the Parties to the Treaty on Non-Proliferation of Nuclear Weapons, Geneva, 1975, NPT/CONF/9, February 24, 1975, p. 20.

13. According to reports published August 2, 1978, August 4, 1978, and August 5, 1978 in the Guardian, even with the adoption of the safeguards there are still rumors of Brazilian plans to develop an atomic bomb.

14. Ambassador S. A. Frazao, "The Search for International Order: Power Relationships and the Emerging Changes in Today's World," lecture, June 9, 1972, mimeo., emphasis in original text, pp. 8-10 (hereafter cited as 1972 lecture).

15. Ibid., p. 13.

16. Ibid., p. 15.

17. Ibid., p. 29.

18. Statement by Ambassador Frazao, First Committee, UN General Assembly, October 30, 1974, official text of the Brazilian Mission to the UN, pp. 12-13.

19. Statement by Ambassador Sergio Correa Da Costa, First Committee, UN General Assembly, November 20, 1975, official text of the Brazilian Mission to the UN, pp. 2-3.

20. Frazao, 1972 lecture, p. 27.

21. Costa statement, op. cit., p. 7.

22. Frazao statement, op. cit., p. 4; and Costa statement, 1975, op. cit., pp. 3-5.

23. Costa statement, op. cit., p. 5.

24. Ibid., pp. 5-6.

25. Ibid., pp. 7-8.

26. Points 1 through 6 are derived from Argentine statement, October 30, 1975, First Committee, UN General Assembly, 2073rd meeting.

27. Points 7 through 17 are derived from the statement by the Argentine Minister of Foreign Affairs Vice-Admiral Oscar A. Montes, Tenth Special Session of the UN General Assembly Devoted to Disarmament, May 26, 1978, official text, mimeo.

28. G. F. Treverton, "Latin America in World Politics: The Next Decade," Adelphi Papers 137 (Summer 1977) (London: IISS): 39-43.

29. Resolution Adopted by the General Assembly, United Nations General Assembly, Tenth Special Session on Disarmament, A/RES/S-10/2 dated July 13, 1978.

12

RESEARCH AND
POLICY IMPLICATIONS

     Einstein generally urged us to reconsider our mode of think-
ing. This advice is particularly relevant for North American*
antiproliferation studies. Contemporary antiproliferation advocacy
suffers from laziness and busyness. It is easy to be hysterical
about proliferation because it is the currently fashionable thing to
do; because it is tough to produce empirical analyses of circumstances that hinder proliferation or favor it; and because hysteria
about proliferation serves American political and commercial
interests and it is easy to defend national interests in the name of
international security. A study of the proliferation processes and
of the effects on the negotiating behavior of North American states
opens up a debate about what proliferation is and whether existing
antiproliferation strategies serve the desired ends. For several
prominent North Americans, it is better to focus the debate on
antiproliferation policies because it is easier to prescribe solutions than to assess the causes and to rethink the definitions of the
problems. This book follows Hedley Bull's lead in stressing the
need to rethink the problem of proliferation. Such a debate is
needed on the question "what is proliferation?" before policy prescriptions are offered. The issues are not merely technological
and strategic; they are primarily, in the thinking of the threshold
states, geopolitical, with cultural overtones. The cultural roots
are hard to describe and to quantify but more research is needed
on this dimension in studying proliferation-inducing activity. The
implications are that if the cultural dimensions are effectively

---

*This refers to the United States and Canada.

analyzed there may be opportunities to mediate conflict among the NWS, the threshold states, and the NNWS.

This book shows that U.S. antiproliferation diplomacy is in disarray, even though the United States has tried to take a lead in this area for many years. There is no consensus within the United States, or between the United States and its allies, about the meaning of proliferation and about the desired alternatives. Even though the NPT was basically a cultural document, in terms of international diplomacy it had settled the question of proliferation: it defined the problem and offered a solution. However, President Carter has opened up the whole question and despite a global debate the thinking about the questions and the answers is unclear. Even on a purely technical subject such as nuclear safeguards, it is still unclear what should go into a safeguards agreement. The United States, under the influence of Albert Wohlstetter, has tried to force into the debate the idea of short detection time, whereas the NPT system (INFCIRC/153) does not depend on that idea. But even as the concept has been introduced, the underlying policy premises and implications are unclear and are likely to remain so unless governments are willing to examine their geopolitical and strategic interests in bilateral, regional, and international debates.

One ironic effect of President Carter's policy on reprocessing as outlined in April 1977 is that it is unnecessary now to make a bomb to proliferate. The reprocessing plant itself is a strategic item. According to this criterion there is a huge amount of proliferation, whereas in fact post-PRC proliferation reveals a low proliferation curve in the Third World. Worse still is the policy of denials—for instance, the denial of vital elements of French reprocessing technology (the cutting plant for the fuel rods) to Pakistan. This has the effect of arousing nuclear nationalism in Pakistan; this nationalism is directed toward France and the United States and not necessarily toward India. Carter's approach to reprocessing not only enhances the political status of those who possess reprocessing plants but it is also a no-win position. The general lesson to be drawn from Carter's policy is that Americans need to assess, first in their bureaucratic debates, the premises and implications of their attitudes and policies before these are made public. And Americans might learn something about proliferation if they took the time to listen to their friends and well-wishers abroad. The advice is to consult before policies are made public. Backtracking on ideas and policies, once these are publicized, is usually difficult and entails a loss of credibility.

The book has examined the post NPT multilateral diplomacy but it is not a defense of this level of diplomacy. On the contrary, the analysis reveals that post-NPT multilateral diplomacy has not really to date settled the central proliferation issues. Such diplomacy has its uses, but it cannot really debate the underlying foreign policy and security issues. The latest phase of this diplomacy, namely, the International Nuclear Fuel Cycle Evaluation, has suspended much of the proliferation debate. If the conclusion of the evaluation in 1980 takes us back to square one as far as questions and approaches are concerned, the two years of evaluation will have meant a loss of time.

For reasons of space the book has not stressed bilateral diplomacy. Given the limited results of multilateral diplomacy in settling the proliferation issues, a lesson for the United States is that more emphasis than before ought to be placed on bilateralized and private dialogue with the hard-core cases, in particular India, South Africa, Brazil, Argentina, and Israel. Several of these cases, if not all, will welcome such a private dialogue. Not that these states agree with U.S. antiproliferation policy of the type offered by Carter; on the contrary, they explicitly disagree, but there is a shared interest in cooperating in bilateral and international relations. Americans, therefore, need to consider making bargains with these societies by negotiating in terms of the interests of all sides. In other words, multilateral diplomacy at a level that is less than theology and absolutism has its uses as a forum for debates at the international level. But the real debates and questions are elsewhere. The foreign policy and the strategic communities will have to come to grips with the underlying factors, and this cannot be done in multilateral diplomacy.

Horizontal nuclear proliferation should be seen as a process that is increasingly becoming regionalized and may eventually become internationalized. It is useless to pretend that there is no link between vertical and horizontal proliferation. There is no direct link; for example, India, Brazil, Argentina, and South Africa will not make nuclear weapons just because the superpowers have nuclear arms. Still, there is a link in political terms: unless NWS, and particularly the superpowers and particularly the United States, are willing to take the lead in making sacrifices with respect to their nuclear arms, the threshold states will not sacrifice their nuclear options. This is one side of the process.

The first side of the process means that denial of nuclear options depends on superpower arms reductions leading to disarmament; the disarmament goal has been accepted by all nuclear weapon states including the PRC. The second side of the process is as follows. Whereas the failure of the superpowers to take steps toward nuclear disarmament and to fulfill their pledge in Article VI of the NPT has immunized the threshold states from renouncing their nuclear options, the failure of the superpowers to disarm has

also enabled the NNWS, including the threshold states, to put into
motion a strategy to establish an antivertical proliferation diplomatic chain. The UN Special Session on Disarmament in 1978
marks the beginning of this process, and the chain has the support
of prominent regional influentials and many Third World states.
In the past, it was easy to argue that the central balance depended
on the relationship between the superpowers; that Third World nations were weak; that even the PRC was useful as a poor third part
of the "triangle" and actually the real factors were bipolar. Some
still hold this view. It is, however, a misguided view. The Soviet
commitment to the present world order is limited, as Hedley Bull
points out.[1] Moscow has no real interest in seeing the emergence
of Third World or nonaligned nations as third voices in international
relations. Soviet thinking is still in terms of a bipolarized world;
the sense that the Soviet Union is one of two superpowers is an
essential part of Soviet political psychology. Third World leaders
are aware of the Soviet attitude, but still there are opportunities
for collaboration between Soviet and Third World leaders, even
though this happens on an opportunistic basis.

    Whatever the Soviet and Third World motivations, the impli-
cations for the United States are important. The Soviet Union is a
tough antiproliferator in practice, and because it has always been
so it does not face the problem of renegotiating nuclear supply contracts as does the United States. Furthermore, the United States
needs the prominent Third World nations for their economic resources, for their support of American goals in international economic diplomacy, and for their support of American goals in
international political and security diplomacy. Under the circumstances, it is not wise for the United States to isolate itself from
prominent leaders in the Third World in international security
relations. For instance, nuclear supply renegotiations are intimately tied to political relations, as the Canada–India nuclear
relations have shown.[2] Today, Third World leaders and analysts
are not interested in North American antiproliferation advocacy
that has religious overtones. But even if North Americans are not
able to secure agreement with respect to nuclear disarmament and
proliferation control, a debate (other than posturing) is possible
and ought to be encouraged.

    To date (fall 1978), Carter's antiproliferation diplomacy
seems a clumsy exercise if the rhetoric is compared to results.
As noted earlier, there is no consensus in domestic U.S. politics
about nuclear energy and nuclear proliferation. To an extent the
problem is beyond Carter: the relationship between the executive
branch and the Congress has led to confrontations and mutual suspicion. Carter has failed to direct the domestic debate on nuclear

energy and nuclear proliferation. To an extent, however, Carter
is the author of his problems on this subject, because he took a
public position before fully analyzing its international implications.
He has the dubious distinction of having annoyed the Japanese, West
Germans, Indians, Pakistanis, Brazilians, and South Africans,
and now he wants a present from INFCE to help save the face of his
proliferation diplomacy during the coming elections!

The book points to a major problem in American nuclear
decision making. This is a part of a larger problem in the Carter
administration—namely, the absence of a consensus in the foreign
policy debate and the absence of a policy synthesizer in the American
decision-making structure. This is compounded by the failure to
consult allies before decisions about proliferation policy are made
and publicized. The U.S. government needs to demonstrate a
capacity for extensive negotiations rather than tough talk. As the
U.S. government has learned in its renegotiations with India, it is
a mistake to start and end with the NPT as the exclusive basis for
policy making. U.S.-Japanese renegotiations also suggest the
necessity of securing intergovernmental agreement by recognizing
the interests and domestic political needs of all sides in a debate.
This experience indicates a need to bilateralize the proliferation
debate to explore the bases of agreement. In instances where
supply relations cannot be maintained, the quest should be to terminate the relationship gracefully and to establish simultaneously
other points of cooperation (rather than merely talking about possibilities). This is needed to satisfy public opinion; tangible cooperation that strengthens bilateral and international ties can mute the
effects of nuclear controversy.

One explanation for the clumsy American diplomacy is that
the United States has still not fully made up its mind about what
proliferation is and what should be done. It is fortunate that to date
the threshold states, for a variety of reasons, have also not made
up their mind about proliferating at a rapid pace or in taking a lead
in anti-American diplomacy. This is so because there is restraint
in the policies of potential proliferators, but restraint should not
be confused with weakness. This study suggests that the time has
arrived for Third World nations to make up their minds. The evidence comes from two directions. On the one hand, at the UN
Special Session on Disarmament in 1978, it became clear that in
the thinking of the Third World and NNWS (although there were
several exceptions), the time for talking about moving toward nuclear disarmament is over. Now the pressure is on the superpowers,
and particularly on the United States, to show results in the disarmament field. On the other hand, several Third World states are
taking steps to develop their nuclear options because they resent the

efforts to freeze the distribution of military and civilian nuclear power at the regional and the international levels. These states are in no mood to listen to endless talk. For them it is not a question of bargaining for aid, but it is a question of not permitting the North American states to alter their commitments unilaterally without consulting all concerned parties. The sense is strong that Canada and the United States are not the models of behavior to follow in the proliferation debate.

The central factor that fuels the demand for proliferation of nuclear options is the quest for a wider distribution of power, of which nuclear power is a facet. The trend is facilitated by the continuous decentralization of the international system and by the deterioration in the scope of consensus between the superpowers, between the United States and its allies, between the United States and important Third World nations, and even within U.S. elites. As Hedley Bull pointed out in 1976, the Third World is concerned more with change than with order. This is an important point. It suggests that the impact of American prescriptions on Third World thinking is likely to lessen even further as we enter the 1980s. Nuclear proliferation is one such element in the growing disorder. However, there is no need for excessive pessimism because a clear argument can be made to Third World leaders against uncontrolled disorder. This argument is not against disorder, but seeks to control disorder so that change is achieved without a breakdown of the system.

In his 1976 article, Hedley Bull argued that controlling proliferation is a "universal interest." The present study disagrees with this assessment, even though most NWS and NNWS, including the potential proliferators, speak the language of nuclear disarmament, antiproliferation and international security. The consensus against proliferation is mostly verbal, or at least currently so. Inasmuch as the proliferation argument is based on geopolitical and geostrategic disputes, these disputes have to he settled before proliferation is controlled. This may happen in the 1980s if normalization tendencies take shape, and even the prospect of Sino-Soviet accommodation cannot be ruled out once the PRC is able to upgrade its bargaining position. But then as the superpower détente slips and consensus formation in regional and international diplomacy becomes problematic, the result may be a gradual millitarization and nuclearization of the regional and international environment. If proliferation is seen as a process rather than a terminal condition, there seems to be a growing regional interest in nuclear-option development and an almost universal feeling against vertical proliferation in Third World thinking. It is noteworthy that the consensus (within the American foreign policy establishment, between

the superpowers, and between the United States and its allies) about
the central conditions of world order is diminishing; there is, conversely, a growing consensus that, as Bull points out, superpower
security does not necessarily precede international security. The
issue is not merely to get a "better" or an "even" distribution of
power. No one knows what these terms mean, and the current UN
jargon refers to "undiminished security." The mood in the UN
favors broadening the international security dialogue, breaking the
superpower stranglehold on the dialogue, and permitting a greater
consideration of the interests of the many rather than a select few.
A plea is made to prevent a freezing of the power relations and of
the authority structure that flows from the rights and special responsibilities of the superpowers. The anti-NPT and the antisuperpower approach argues against the discrimination inherent in the
maintenance of two categories of states, namely, those who have
nuclear weapons and those who do not. The argument is extended
against the implications of these categories.

One implication of antivertical proliferation and anti-NPT
diplomacy is that the membership of the nuclear club ought to be
widened to accommodate the major military powers of the world
rather than only the five permanent members of the UN Security
Council. This viewpoint suggests that the failure of the NWS to
disarm will result in nuclear weapons proliferation. This study
offers a less extreme position. It suggests that nuclear options
development and the projection of nuclear and disarmament diplomacy is the main direction taken by the potential proliferators, and
that these are dynamic dimensions of contemporary international
life. To succeed, this diplomacy ought to be able to eliminate the
discrimination in the rules of the game in the NPT regime. But if
discrimination is treated as a fact of life by the superpowers, then
it is possible that the conclusion will be reached in Third World
bureaucratic debates that it is up to each state to choose its destiny;
that any state that seeks nuclear weapons ought to be able to get these
weapons provided it moves toward that goal through self-help. However, before states jump to the latter conclusion, it is likely that
there will be a phase of active nuclear and disarmament diplomacy
accompanied by maintenance and development of nuclear options that
are not necessarily steps to nuclear weapon proliferation.

Such a strategy has research and policy implications. Usually
nuclear proliferation is controlled by compelling restraint by external means—namely, by raising the technological barriers against
further proliferation. The solution is from top to bottom—from
achievement of a superpower consensus to a broadening of that consensus among nuclear suppliers; and the approach is to enforce restraint on the part of the nuclear recipients from outside. This study

shifts the focus of analysis and indicates that there are limits to
what can be done through multilateral diplomacy and that the limits
have now been reached. Secondly, multilaterally induced technological restraints (international safeguards and nuclear supply
policy) are technically weak, and are weakening further because
many of the potential proliferators have already escaped international controls. Denials can at best slow but not stop their nuclear
development. The role of multilateral diplomacy is complicated
by political inhibitions among the nuclear suppliers, as is evident
from the failure of the London Nuclear Suppliers Group to make
acceptance of full-scope safeguards a primary condition for nuclear
supply. Thirdly, the study indicates that there is self-restraint in
the nuclear behavior of the potential proliferators because of their
perceptions of their strategic environment and their domestic and
external needs. The incentives and disincentives for proliferation
exist at this level of analysis. Finally, in the 1980s the quality of
self-restraint in Third World nuclear thinking is likely to weaken,
not because of irrationality and irresponsibility in elite behavior but
because, in their perceptions, their self-restraint is not matched
by self-restraint of the vertical proliferators, and is not likely to
be matched; indeed, third-party and Third World self-restraint may
be viewed by the NWS as weakness. If there is nothing to be gained
by self-restraint and much to be lost, the balance of the argument
is likely to turn on the utility of controlled disorder in the strategic
behavior of certain Third World states who actively seek to un-
freeze the power structure of the contemporary international system.

NOTES

    1. Hedley Bull, "Arms Control and World Order," Interna-
tional Security 1, no. 1 (Summer 1976): 3-16.
    2. Ashok Kapur, " The Canada-India Nuclear Negotiations:
Some Hypotheses and Lessons, " The World Today 34, no. 8 (August
1978): 311-20.

SELECTED BIBLIOGRAPHY

BOOKS AND MONOGRAPHS

Bhutto, Z. A. The Myth of Independence. Karachi: Oxford University Press, 1969.

Breytenbach, W. J. South Africa Looks to Africa. South African Freedom Foundation, Pretoria, July 1977.

Brzezinski, Z. The Fragile Blossom. New York: Harper & Row, 1972.

Buck, James H., ed. The Modern Japanese Military System. Beverly Hills, Calif.: Sage, 1975.

Bull, Hedley. The Anarchical Society. New York: Columbia University Press, 1977.

Cline, Ray S. World Power Assessment: A Calculus of Strategic Drift. Boulder, Colo.: Westview Press, 1975.

Coffey, J. I. Arms Control and European Security. New York: Praeger, 1977.

____, ed. "Nuclear Proliferation: Prospects, Problems and Proposals." In The Annals, vol. 430, March 1977.

Dunn, Lewis, and Herman Kahn. Trends in Nuclear Proliferation, 1975-1995. Croton-on-the-Hudson, N.Y.: Hudson Institute, 1-1-2336-RR/3, May 15, 1976.

Endicott, J. E. Japan's Nuclear Option. New York: Praeger, 1975.

Epstein, William. The Last Chance. London: Free Press, 1976.

____. "A Nuclear Weapon Free Zone in Africa?" The Stanley Foundation, Occasional Paper No. 14, 1977.

Ford Foundation and Mitre Corporation. Nuclear Power: Issues and Choices. Cambridge, Mass.: Ballinger, 1977.

Gelber, Lionel. Crisis in the West: American Leadership and the Global Balance. London: The Macmillan Press, 1975.

Gompert, David C., Michael Mandelbaum, Richard L. Garwin, and John H. Barton. Nuclear Weapons and World Politics (1980s Project/Council on Foreign Relations). New York: McGraw-Hill, 1977.

Hellmann, D. C. Japan and East Asia. London: Pall Mall, 1972.

____, ed. China and Japan: A New Balance of Power. Lexington, Mass.: D. C. Heath, 1976.

Janke, Peter. "Southern Africa: New Horizons." In Conflict Studies, London, 73, July 1976.

Japan Atomic Industrial Forum. Nuclear Development in Japan (selected papers), undated.

Kajima, M. Modern Japan's Foreign Policy. Rutland, Vt.: Charles E. Tuttle, 1969.

Kaplan, M. A. System and Process in International Politics. New York: John Wiley & Sons, 1957.

Kapur, Ashok. India's Nuclear Option: Atomic Diplomacy and Decision-Making. New York: Praeger, 1976.

Kim, Y. C. Japanese-Soviet Relations, The Washington Papers, vol. 2, The Center for Strategic and International Studies, Georgetown University. Beverly Hills, Calif.: Sage, 1974.

Langdon, F. C. Japan's Foreign Policy. Vancouver: University of British Columbia Press, 1973.

Marwah, O., and A. Schulz, eds. Nuclear Proliferation and the Near-Nuclear Countries. Cambridge, Mass.: Ballinger, 1975.

Myrdal, Alva. The Game of Disarmament. New York: Pantheon Books, 1976.

O'Neill, R. J. Insecurity: The Spread of Weapons in the Indian and Pacific Oceans. Canberra: ANU Press, 1978.

Patterson, Walter C. Nuclear Power. London: Pelican Books, 1976.

Quester, George H. The Politics of Nuclear Proliferation. Baltimore: The Johns Hopkins University Press, 1973.

Schneider, R. M. Brazil: Foreign Policy of a Future World Power. Boulder, Colo.: Westview Press, 1976.

Singh, Sampooran. India and the Nuclear Bomb. New Delhi: S. Chand, 1971.

Spiegel, S. L., and K. H. Waltz, eds. Conflict in World Politics. Cambridge, Mass.: Winthrop, 1971.

Stanley Foundation. Eighteenth Strategy for Peace Conference Report, October 13-16, 1977, Iowa.

Stockholm International Peace Research Institute (SIPRI). Nuclear Disarmament and Nuclear War, 1975.

____. Nuclear Proliferation Problems. London: MIT Press, 1974.

____. Preventing Nuclear-Weapon Proliferation, 1975.

____. Safeguards against Nuclear Proliferation, 1975.

____. Southern Africa: The Escalation of a Conflict, 1976.

____. Yearbook of World Armaments and Disarmaments, annual.

Treverton, A. F. "Latin America in World Politics: The Next Decade." Adelphi Papers 137 (Summer 1977), London: IISS.

ARTICLES

Barnaby, Frank. "Africa and Nuclear Energy." Africa, no. 69 (May 1977): 92-93.

Bull, Hedley. "Arms Control and World Order." International Security 1, no. 1 (Summer 1976): 3-16.

____. "Re-thinking Non-Proliferation." International Affairs 5, no. 2 (April 1975): 175-89.

Dowty, Alan. "Foreign-Linked Factionalism as a Historical Pattern." Journal of Conflict Resolution 15, no. 4 (December 1971): 429-42.

Goldschmidt, B. "A Historical Survey of Nonproliferation Policies." International Security 2, no. 1 (Summer 1977): 69-87.

Hiroyoshi, Yanada. "From the Newspapers and Magazines." Japan Quarterly 24, no. 3 (July-September 1977): 353-57.

Unsigned article, "Carter's Nuclear Policy and Japan's Position." Japan Quarterly 24, no. 3 (July-September 1977): 272-76.

Kapur, Ashok. "The Canada-India Nuclear Negotiations: Some Hypotheses and Lessons." The World To-day 34, no. 8 (August 1978): 311-20.

____. "India after Bangladesh." Bulletin of Atomic Scientists 28, no. 9 (November 1972): 28-.

____. "India's Nuclear Debate." Bulletin of Atomic Scientists, forthcoming.

____. "Peace and Power in India's Nuclear Policy." Asian Survey 10, no. 9 (September 1970): 779-88.

Kawashima, Y. "Safeguards for the Peaceful Nuclear Fuel Cycle," no publishing data.

Manzoor, C. "Politics of Technology Transfer (with Special Reference to the Transfer of Nuclear Technology)." Annals of Nuclear Energy 49, United Kingdom: Pergamon Press (1977): 225-33.

Morehouse, Ward. "Professional Estates as Political Actors: The Case of the Indian Scientific Community." Philosophy and Social Action (New Delhi) 2, no. 4 (October-December 1976).

Nye, J. S. "Non-Proliferation: A Long Term Strategy." Foreign Affairs 56, no. 3 (April 1978): 601-23.

Sabato, J. A. "Atomic Energy in Argentina: A Case History." World Development 1, no. 8 (August 1973): 23-38.

Zartman, I. W. "Negotiations: Theory and Reality." Journal of International Affairs 9, no. 1 (1975): 69-77.

____. "The Political Analysis of Negotiation: How Who Gets What and When." World Politics 26, no. 3 (April 1974): 385-99.

OFFICIAL SOURCES

Argentina

Argentine statement, First Committee, U.N. General Assembly,
    October 30, 1975.

Argentine Embassy, Ottawa, Press Release, July 5, 1976.

Argentine Foreign Minister statement, Tenth Special Session of
    U.N. General Assembly on Disarmament, May 26, 1978.

Brazil

Ambassador S. A. Frazao. "The Search for International Order:
    Power Relationships and the Emerging Changes in To-day's
    World." Lecture, June 9, 1972, to Canadian Institute of Inter-
    national Affairs, New York.

Brazil statement, First Committee, U.N. General Assembly,
    October 30, 1974.

____, First Committee, U.N. General Assembly, November 20,
    1975.

Ministry of External Relations. Brazil. Brazil, 1976.

Canada

Noble, J. J. "Canada's Continuing Search for Acceptable Nuclear.
    Safeguards." International Perspectives (July-August 1978):
    42-48.

France

French Embassy. "France's Position on Disarmament." New York,
    March 1978.

Address by Valery Giscard D'Estaing, before the Tenth Special
    Session of the U.N. General Assembly, New York, May 25, 1978.

India

Department of Atomic Energy, Government of India. "Atomic Energy and Space Research: A Profile for the Decade 1970-1980." Trombay (India), 1970.

Department of Space, Government of India, annual reports.

Prasad, A. N., and S. V. Kumar. "Indian Experience in Fuel Reprocessing." Bhabha Atomic Research Center, Department of Atomic Energy, India, IAEA-CN. 36/392 (II. 7), mimeo., undated.

Japan

Aichi, K. The Search for National Security. Public Information Bureau, Ministry of Foreign Affairs, Japan, Japan Reference Series no. 4-49, undated.

Japanese Institute of International Affairs. White Papers of Japan 1970-71, Tokyo.

Japan's statements to plenary meeting of Review Conference of Parties to the NPT, May 7, 1975; May 14, 1975; May 15, 1975.

Agreement between Japan and the IAEA on Implementation of Articles III. 1 and 4 of the NPT, Vienna, March 4, 1977.

Defence Bulletin: Defence of Japan—White Paper on Defence (summary) 1, no. 3 (September 1977), Defence Agency, Tokyo.

Pakistan

Pakistan Atomic Energy Commission, annual reports.

South Africa

R. Botha statement, U.N. General Assembly, 18th Committee, 22nd SRSS, New York, May 20, 1968, provisional verbatim record, A/C 1/PV 1571.

A. J. A. Roux statement, Geneva, September 3, 1968, mimeo.

____, Vienna, September 25, 1968, mimeo.

South Africa 1974 Official Yearbook, first edition, Pretoria.

South Africa 1977 Official Yearbook.

Roux, A. J. A. "Uranium—Recent Developments and Future Outlook." Paper presented at the Investment Conference of the Investment Analysts' Society of Southern Africa, Carlton Hotel,
Johannesburg, February 25, 1976, mimeo.

Address by the Secretary for Information, Dr. Eschel Rhoodie, to
the Second South African Corporate Money Conference, "What the
Government Is Doing to Provide a Stable Business Environment:
The Foreign Situation, Domestic Security, Race Relations, after
South West Africa and Rhodesia." Carlton Hotel, Johannesburg,
February 18, 1977.

Paper presented by Dr. C. P. Mulder, Minister of Information, to
the International Conference on the Marketing of the International
Image of South Africa, University of South Africa, October 18,
1977.

South African Embassy, South African Industrial and Business Intelligence, London, May 1977.

SA Digest, June 24, 1977.

Speech by Prime Minister J. Vorster at a public meeting, August
24, 1977, reprinted in Republic of South Africa, House of Assembly, Debates, first session, sixth Parliament, February 3, 1978,
pp. 12-13.

Notes on Foreign Investments in South Africa, backgrounder issued
by Information Counsellor, South African Embassy, Canberra,
March 1978.

United States

U.S. Congress, Joint Committee on Atomic Energy. Development,
Use and Control of Nuclear Energy for the Common Defense and
Security and for Peaceful Purposes. 94th Cong., 18th sess.,
June 30, 1975.

U.S. Congress, House, Subcommittee on International Security and Scientific Affairs of the Committee on International Relations. Nuclear Proliferation: Future U.S. Foreign Policy Implications. 94th Cong., 1st sess., October-November 1975.

Congressional Research Service, Library of Congress. Facts on Nuclear Proliferation, A Handbook (prepared for the Committee on Government Operations, U.S. Senate), December 1975.

U.S. Congress, Senate Government Operations Committee. Export Reorganization Act of 1976, Hearings, 94th Cong., 2d sess., January-March 1976.

Kissinger, Henry. "The United States and Africa" (speech). Survival. London: IISS 18, no. 4 (July-August 1976): 171-74.

Presidential Documents: Jimmy Carter 13, no. 18 (1977): 611-13.

Nye, J. S. "Balancing Non-Proliferation and Energy Security," speech at Uranium Institute, London, July 12, 1978, official text.

Soviet Union

Brezhnev, L. I. Report of the CPSU Central Committee and the Party's Immediate Objectives in Domestic and Foreign Policy. 25th Congress of the CPSU, February 24, 1976.

International Organizations

United Nations. The United Nations and Disarmament 1945-1970. New York, 1970.

Report on the Implementation of the Treaty of Tlatelolco and Some Comments and Views of OPANAL with Respect to Article VII and Other Related Provisions of the Non-Proliferation Treaty, Review Conference of the Parties to the Treaty on the Non-Proliferation of Nuclear Weapons, NPT/CONF/9, February 24, 1975, Geneva, 1975.

International Atomic Energy Agency. A Short History of Non-Proliferation. Vienna, February 1976.

Resolution adopted by the U.N. General Assembly, Tenth Special Session on Disarmament, A/RES/S-10/2, July 13, 1978.

Other Sources

Spence, J. E. "South Africa and the Nuclear Option," lecture to the Royal African Society, London, no date.

International Institute for Strategic Studies. Strategic Survey, 1976.

Tomar, R. "Myths and Mirages: Case of the Indian Nuclear Power Program." Department of International Relations, Australian National University, unpublished paper, May 16, 1978.

INDEX

Aichi, Kiichi, 303-04
Argentina: highlights of atomic
    programs, 332-34; views on
    international security, 347-48
arms control, 19, 20; arms re-
    duction and, 18; Brazil and,
    344-45; domestic bureau-
    cracy and, 21-22, 22-23;
    India's test (1974) and, 184;
    Partial Test Ban Treaty and,
    152; SAGSI and, 125-27;
    superpower agreements, 17-
    18, 39; the superpowers and,
    15; Third World and, 18-19;
    U.S. policy, 96; world com-
    munity and, 18 (see also
    Non-Proliferation Treaty
    [NPT]; SALT; SAGSI; Com-
    prehensive Nuclear Test Ban)
Asian international relations:
    ambiguity and volatility of,
    275; Japan and, 274, 275,
    276, 277; Taiwan issue and,
    275
Atoms for Peace Program, 58
Atucha Plant, 334 (see also
    Argentina)
Australia: INFCE and, 106

Ball, George, 311, 312
Baruch, Bernard, 337
Baruch Plan, 64, 94
Bhabha, Homi, 183, 196
Bhutto, Ali, 111, 171, 190, 191,
    197-99, 200, 201, 202, 203,
    204, 206, 207, 208
Bonn Summit, 123
Brazil, 98; against frozen hier-
    archical structure, 343;

anti-superpower orientation,
    337; globalization of Bra-
    zilian diplomacy, 336-37;
    NPT and, 344; quest for al-
    tered world order, 343;
    self-image of, 336; Treaty
    of Tlatelolco, 337; vertical
    mobility of states and, 343;
    views on arms control, 344-
    45; views on international
    security, 341-43, 344, 345;
    views on PNEs, 346
Brezhnev, Leonid, 153, 155,
    168
Brzezinski, Z., 311, 312
Buchan, Alastair, 220
Bull, Hedley, 1, 19, 356, 359,
    361, 362
Buthelezi, Chief, 261

CCD (see Conference of the
    Committee on Disarmament)
CTB (see Comprehensive Test
    Ban Agreement)
Carter, Jimmy, 5, 10, 11, 16,
    17, 32, 83, 84, 85, 86, 87,
    88, 91, 92, 95-96, 98, 104,
    105, 106, 115, 119, 161,
    209, 216, 242, 264, 281,
    283, 285, 286, 316, 317,
    321, 357, 358, 359, 360
China: dangers of Carter policy
    and, 285; foreign policy, 16;
    Japan and, 276; moderniza-
    tion and, 277, 281, 286, 299;
    nuclear image of, 52-53;
    PNEs and, 156-57; Soviet
    relations, 286; Taiwan and,
    281, 302; U.S. relations

ABOUT THE AUTHOR

ASHOK KAPUR is Assistant Professor in Political Science at the University of Waterloo, Ontario. He is the author of <u>India's Nuclear Option: Atomic Diplomacy & Decision-Making</u> (New York: Praeger, 1976) and has published in scholarly and professional journals on Indian Foreign Policy, Arms Control & Disarmament, and Asian International Relations. He holds a Ph.D. in Political Science from Carleton University, Ottawa.